PIONEERING ON SOCIAL
FRONTIERS

THE UNIVERSITY OF CHICAGO PRESS
CHICAGO, ILLINOIS

—

THE BAKER & TAYLOR COMPANY
NEW YORK

THE CAMBRIDGE UNIVERSITY PRESS
LONDON

THE MARUZEN-KABUSHIKI-KAISHA
TOKYO, OSAKA, KYOTO, FUKUOKA, SENDAI

THE COMMERCIAL PRESS, LIMITED
SHANGHAI

PIONEERING
ON
SOCIAL FRONTIERS

By

GRAHAM TAYLOR

1930

THE UNIVERSITY OF CHICAGO PRESS
CHICAGO · ILLINOIS

TO ALL MY COMRADES AND COLLEAGUES
WHOSE ADVENTUROUS FAITH AND LIVING
INFLUENCE INSPIRE THIS TRIBUTE OF
AFFECTIONATE APPRECIATION
AND
TO MY FAMILY
EACH ONE OF WHOM HAS CONTRIBUTED TO
AND SHARED IN LIFE'S WHOLE
ENDEAVOR

✸

FOREWORD

TO HAVE lived while the great changes of the past fifty years have been taking place, to have dwelt on frontiers of the social order where these changes have registered their most marked effects, and to have associated with those whose lives bore the waymarks of the trend of events has been the experience of a life lived over again in retrospect.

To share the impressions thus gleaned with those who have lived through only parts of this great transition, or whose observation and experience have been limited to some of the shore lines and eddies of the mighty current, may be the privilege of one whose working life spans the whole tidal movement as it swept through the main channels of these years.

Perhaps the distance between the whence and the whither, through which the flood tides of human life surge, may be reckoned more vividly from the extremes that met in the experiences to be narrated. Locally they were as far apart as was my eastern college town from my country parish in the valley of the Hudson; as was my New England city parish in Hartford from my field of action in Chicago and the Middle West.

In all these places my life has swung like a pendulum, almost every twenty-four hours, between the privileged few and the struggling many; between town and gown while at school and college; between landowning farmers and tenant farm hands, while for seven years working and fellowshiping with both; between the crowded tenements of the day laborers and the homes and offices of captains of commerce; between industrial wage-earners and their employers; between trade unions and manufacturers' associations; between academic circles and the masses of the people; between the native-born and the foreign-born populations; and in politics and religion, between conservatives and progressives, reactionaries and radicals.

Interest in this meeting of extremes may be added by the fact that in my experience they were waymarks of my out-leading from an individualistic educational and religious training to a more altruistic point of view for thought and action; from a somewhat self-conscious intellectual and spiritual development to a more social, civic, and community consciousness; from more or less of a class feeling to identification with the mass life in its democratic expression; from a sheltered childhood in the best home that parental love and ability could provide to manhood's struggles for a more neighborly community and a more homelike world, where each of all the children of men may share more of the fatherhood of God and the brotherhood of man.

That my moorings to the past held fast to the very conservative influences in which I was born, bred, and educated; that at first they only lengthened and never broke in adjusting the harbor anchorage to the rising tide; that in putting forth into the open bearings were always taken from what was left behind and also from what was far beyond and overhead—these facts throw into bolder relief the difference between what then was, what now is, and what is coming to be.

These frontiers and pioneerings are those of others also who often led the way and always inspired me to keep abreast of them in the adventures of social and civic faith here narrated. Yet the achievements attained seemed to be those of the *Zeit Geist* of the changing order.

CHICAGO COMMONS
    March, 1930

THE pivot of my life has been the *Spectator*, and so the *Spectator* must be the pivot of my book. The main influence on my life has been the *Spectator*, therefore I have made the *Spectator* the center from which in telling my story I have worked backward and forward.

The autobiographer who is going to succeed with his task must be genuinely and actively interested in his own life and therefore write about it willingly and with zest. He must start with the assumption that people want to hear about it from himself. To succeed with his task he must set down whatever he believes went to the making of his mind and soul, and of that highly composite product which constitutes a human being. By far the pleasantest literary experience is to dive into the depths of memory and let it lead you through the labyrinth of the past.

From *The Adventure of Living*, by John St. Loe Strachey, long-time editor of the *Spectator*.

CONTENTS

CONTENTS

PART V. THE EVOLVING SOCIAL CONSCIOUSNESS

INDEX

PART I
THE CIVIC FRONT AND REAR

CHAPTER I

CHICAGO—THE PIVOT OF THE STORY

IT WAS a great experience to begin my citizenship in Chicago during the period of the World's Fair of 1893. The currents of Chicago's mighty life were at the turn of the tide of the city's destiny. And they swept my own life along with them into a new era. Then the city's history and prophecy met. Achievements of the past were reflected on this retrospect. Visions of what Chicago could become hovered over it like a mirage in the desert. Pioneering spirits caught higher glimpses of civic ideals and new incentives to realize them from the Columbian Exposition, that scene of beauty which memory claims to be a joy forever.

In building its "White City," Chicago rose above itself, above all it had ever been and above what it could become, until it had time to grow into the gradual realization of this vision of its future. Higher standards of artistic architecture and landscape developments were inspired. The "Court of Honor," into which the swampy lake shore was transformed, did its part in suggesting the vast project of making over and leveling up the whole city to the higher ideals since striven for. Out of this vision grew the Plan for the Greater Chicago, sixteen years afterward.

Art, literature, and higher education laid private wealth and public resources under tribute as never before. Features of natural beauty, from the lake and river fronts to the park areas and outlying forest preserves, were gradually reclaimed. Museums of art, industry, and natural history attracted patrons and popular attention. Commercial buildings sank their foundations to bed rock and reared their structures skyward, combining beauty of design with increased utility. Building and zoning ordinances followed, to protect newer

3

residential areas from the invasions of trade and the over-crowding which had made family dwellings unattractive and insanitary. The public schools and the great libraries began to enlarge their buildings, facilities, and service.

The University of Chicago opened its doors to its first classes in October, 1892, while the city was preparing to welcome the world within the gates of its Columbian Exposition the following May. The dusty road running west from the nearby lake led to what became the Midway Plaisance, the great parked highway upon which the University campus fronts. The first four of its fifty or more buildings arose while those of the World's Fair were being erected. Ever since thousands of students have sung their "Alma Mater" song:

> The City White hath fled the earth,
>   But where the azure waters lie
> A nobler city hath its birth,
>   The City Gray that ne'er shall die.
> For decades and for centuries
>   Its battlemented towers shall rise
> Beneath the hope-filled western skies—
>   'Tis our dear Alma Mater.

And yet, until the White City's attractions had fled it located the Gray City. A correspondent of one of its professors addressed him as at "The University of Chicago near the Ferris Wheel."

At the call of the Chicago Theological Seminary I had come to pioneer the first department of instruction in any church institution to be wholly devoted to the social interpretation and application of religion. I began to teach the very same month in 1893 that Professor Albion W. Small entered upon his pioneering undertaking at the University of Chicago to lodge the first department of sociology to be admitted to the curriculum of any university.

The Seminary was then located on the West Side, near the center of Chicago's vast cosmopolitan industrial population. This old residential district had been settled and developed by families constituting the parishes of great churches. It had recently begun to be invaded by large industrial plants. Their men and women workers surged past my classroom windows, turning the single-family houses into tenement apartments. The quiet streets had become thoroughfares with a roaring traffic. They were lined with lodgings, restaurants, and places of cheap amusement, catering to a transient population. Chicago's rearage had caught up with what had been its advancing frontage.

Here then I found myself between two frontiers. The one in the front faced me with its advancing lines of academic research and its picket lines of social pioneers, who were followed by the supporting ranks of the more progressive citizens. And there was that frontier in the rear, across which lived and labored the vastly outnumbering multitude of wage-earning people and commercial middle men and their families who constituted the mass life to which religion was also to be interpreted and applied.

Voices called me both ways. Those in front were more familiar to me, as they were to my fellow teachers and most of my students, since they too were in the privileged minority to which we belonged. From the rear, where were the vast majority of fellow-men, came voices from the great inarticulate multitude—heirs of industrial, political, social, and racial disparities. Cries reverberated from nearby deserts of poverty, wastes of want, and the underworld habitations of cruelty.

Most of these voices were at first impersonal, belonging to no one in particular, but to classes and masses. From all these levels of less privileged life my happy home circle had shielded my eyes and a rigid schooling had shut out my thoughts. Even up to early manhood I had known only comparatively few who had silently suffered as victims of inherited or self-imposed misery, but now the voices of the great multitudes blended in one great undertone, which James Russell Lowell had interpreted to be "the cry of the human foundation."

It seemed to me that the advancing frontier could be seen more clearly from the rear than the more stationary horizon behind it could be penetrated from any position too far ahead. But this city wilderness might have seemed as "great and terrible" to me as was that which lay between Israel's exodus and the Promised Land, had it not been for what I brought with me from my home and parish experiences. They had deepened my liking for fellow-men, and had revealed family and neighborly relationships as common denominators, relating each divided fraction to the human unit to which it belonged.

While at Hartford I had read of the effort of the Rev. Samuel A. Barnett and his wife to reinforce their neighborly relations with the people surrounding their parish church in Whitechapel, East London, by expanding their own rectory home into the household of Toynbee Hall, the pioneer social settlement which they founded in 1884. I imagined that the Oxford University men who came there to live with them might be lifted to higher planes of social, civic, educational, and religious aspirations and service, by coming into neighborly relations with their fellow-citizens, in that dreary desert of London's most neglected life. This example also opened to my view larger possibilities of enlisting civic spirit and resources by crossing class lines to improve local conditions and industrial relationships. Therefore I made this one of the conditions of my acceptance of the Chicago professorship that I should have liberty to live and work with the masses of the people.

On coming to Chicago I was confirmed in this purpose by the impressions made upon me by the spirit and ideals exemplified by Jane Addams. Of course I was impressed with the city's vast area of two hundred square miles over which its streets sprawled and its buildings spread; with the tumultuous life of its heterogeneous population; with its terminals of a score or more of great railway systems; with the swift pace and mighty volume of its commerce and industries; and with the spirit in which some of its cultural and religious minorities were striving to keep pace with the will-power of the great majorities. But in the personality of Jane Addams, living on the corner of Polk and Halsted streets, I found a personification of spiritual and social ideals, dwelling in simple, natural, neighborly, human relations with her cosmopolitan neighbors, and exerting far-flung influences over the more privileged classes. And none has exemplified more than she the influence of an interpretative personality in mediating between class and mass, richer and poorer, the suburb and the city center, and, most of all, between the foreign born and those to the native manner born.

When I was a stranger she took me in, stranger though I was to her except in the fellowship of kindred faith. And I have never since gone out beyond the reach of her friendly counsel, or beyond the range of her varied experience and world-wide sympathies. To Hull House I frequently went to listen and to learn. To her example and counsel is largely due our family residence in a settlement household. Her brooding like a mother over the homes and homeless all about her demonstrated what the gentle strength and wisdom of our own home's motherhood might be and do within the settlement household and throughout the neighborhood. The consciousness of our own family's larger spiritual obligation was deepened so that it seemed to be a privileged opportunity to invest it where American democracy seemed likely to achieve its greatest triumph or suffer its severest defeat.

When after two years the Seminary failed to secure funds for building us a house in which to live and work, we solved its problem and ours by moving into a large rented house in the midst of a cosmopolitan industrial population that lay between the Seminary and the down-town commercial center. We felt that we were doing no more than what the families of tradesmen and commercial men had always done in serving the interests of their business; what the families of army, navy, and consular officers were everywhere doing in following the flag to their posts of duty; what missionaries' families had never failed to do in following the cross to any land or people. There we gathered successive groups of resident workers around our family circle to constitute a living link which might help relate more closely the classes so widely separated by the social cleavage. We also hoped to help inspire or constrain more representatives of the educated and religious classes to stand in the breach.

As yet our group was without a name. We were just a household. We knew what we were there for, but how to let others know this and what to call us perplexed us for a long while. We groped after some name which had at its root, if

not in its form, that good old English word "common." Underlying this word and its many equivalents is the idea of
sharing what each can be to all and what all can be to each,
what belongs to no one person, or class, but to everyone and
all the people. It is also the idea underlying the very conception of that community and communion in which society and
religion alike consist, and which constitutes the essence of the
social settlement motive and movement. The baptismal day
came when the name had to be forthcoming. It was demanded for the Seminary's announcement of the field work upon
which my classroom depended for the sources of its social
data. A business man of rare, quick wit appeared as I alight-
ed from an elevator on the upper floor of an office building to
meet the Seminary officials on this last day of grace. In desperation, this friend of ours was challenged for a name. He was
equal to this, as he had been in many another emergency. He
mused a moment over our preferences for something common,
murmuring "community," "commonwealth," "commons."
And as he stepped into the car going down Edward F. Cragin
said, "Call it Chicago Commons!"

It was done, and better than we knew at that moment.
The name built itself into the descriptive title of our work and
into the usage of the city. Its popular lineage, woven through
English history, was behind it. It told how the freemen of the
race organized in their early shires, municipalities, and guilds,
and later on combined to form one body representing the
whole people, known as the House of Commons. So the people thus represented, without primary distinction of class,
came to be known as "The Commons," the third estate as
distinguished from the Lords Spiritual and the Lords Tem-
poral. To this ideal of social democracy the name adds the
suggestion of those few patches of mother-earth still un-
claimed as private property, which like Boston Common at
least afford standing room equally for all, irrespective of
pecuniary circumstances or social status.

So we called our household and its homestead Chicago
Commons, in hope that it might be a common center where
representatives of the masses and the classes could meet and
mingle as fellow-men, to exchange their social values in some-

thing like a clearing house for the commonwealth. Here we hoped friendship, neighborship, and fellow-citizenship might form the personal bonds for that social unification which alone can save our American democracy from being cloven under any economic stress and strain. We dreamed that here the brotherhood of which we talk and sing might be more practically lived out and inwrought, as it must be if Christianity continues to be a living faith and its churches the people's fellowship.

In token of our confidence in the future support and development of this adventure of our faith, legal incorporation was secured, under the general statute of Illinois providing for corporations "not for profit." The articles incorporating the trustees of Chicago Commons Association vest in them the right to receive and hold in trust the property of the Association and to assume responsibility for the conduct of its work in accordance with its purpose, which was stated to be "To provide a center for a higher civic and social life, to initiate and maintain religious, educational and philanthropic enterprises, and to investigate and improve conditions in the industrial districts of Chicago."

Upon what I have seen, heard, and felt at Chicago Commons and forecast thence, my whole life proves to have been pivoted. Chicago Commons is part of me and I am part of it, although I am only a part of what many fellow resident workers, other comrades, and a host of neighbors have built into the foundations and superstructure of this civic and educational center. Yet it and I cannot be accounted for apart. Forth from this center, whence insight and outlook were taken, my story must proceed. Back to this source of incentive it must return, weaving like a shuttle every figure of its pattern upon the warp and woof of what was experienced here. For here extremes meet; diversities approach unity; the inner home life and the larger household circles intersphere; personal and neighborhood experiences blend; native and foreign-born tastes and temperaments, customs and traditions, react upon each other; differences in financial circumstances level up or down under the pressure of better or worse economic conditions and industrial relations; inherited and acquired standards modify or are modified by each other. Here personal judgment of what is considered "good" or "bad" differs with the prevalence of higher or lower commercial and political standards. And to us religion resolves itself into the actual or potential relationship between man and man, based upon the ideal of the relationship between God and man.

The motif of the theme to which this whole story is attuned, and which runs all through its impressions and interpretations of persons and events, motives and movements, finds expression in one of our Christmas greetings interpreting the spirit of Chicago Commons:

The Good Will to understand one another, to interpret misunderstood attitudes and situations, to reconcile and be reconciled to differences of taste and temperament, race and religion, heritage and aspirations, and through service and sacrifice to promote the unity of the spirit in the bond of peace.

CHAPTER II

ENGINEERING CHICAGO'S FOUNDATIONS

IF THE Columbian Exposition of 1893 furnished Chicago with the soil and atmosphere for the growth of civic ideals, its seed took root in the ashes of the two great fires of 1871 and 1874. They cleared not only the ground, but citizens' minds also, for new ideals by destroying what had been attained. The glory of the World Fair's "White City" began to illumine the darkest clouds which had ever overshadowed the city's past.

At the latest anniversary observance of the first and greater fire, one of its keenest observers thus vividly recalled the tragedies and comedies he witnessed under the lights and shadows of that unique experience:

Before it burned itself out it took more than 200 lives, made 100,000 out of 300,000 people homeless, burned over 2,000 acres and caused a loss of $200,000,000. Limestone walls melted by the heat seemed to be running down the sides of buildings like thin paste. A battery of church spires flamed high in the night. A huge bell was set to tolling at midnight by blazing embers. People rushed to and fro in a frenzy. A man was seen racing up and down the street with a window shade under his arm. A woman burned to death with her canary rather than let it perish alone. Some men battered in the heads of whiskey barrels, drinking the liquor as it gushed into the streets.

One of the oldest and most interesting survivors of the pioneering generation, Frank R. Chandler, described Chicago emerging from the gloom after the fire to march ahead with its slogan, "I Will." This marching motto, he says, might well have been suggested by a sign over the entrance of what he calls "the first office building—a one-story frame shanty of one room, built before the ashes of the burnt business district had fairly cooled." This sign read: "Everything Gone, Except Wife, Children and Energy." From these scenes he

dates "Chicago's entrance upon the period of her three *R*'s—
Resuscitation, Renaissance, Rebuilding."

Citizens pioneering the rebuilding of the city received a
noteworthy incentive from England to provide for its better
public equipment. It is estimated that between two and
three million books belonging to libraries privately owned by
individuals and various associations were consumed in the
great fire. Word came that within a month after the conflagration a London citizen, who was a member of the Anglo-
American Association, proposed "that England should present a free library to Chicago, to remain there as a mark of
sympathy now, and a token of brotherly kindness forever."
Under the enthusiastic leadership of Thomas Hughes, that
Association appealed to the people of England for the gift
of a new library to Chicago as a "mark of sympathy now and
a token of that sentiment of kinship which independently of
circumstances and irrespectively of every other consideration
must ever exist between the different branches of the English race." Authors, publishers, booksellers, and owners so
promptly and liberally responded that twelve thousand volumes, of rare value both for their intrinsic worth and as gifts
from their distinguished donors, were received within a year.
Meanwhile, the proposal to establish a free public library,
which had been discussed before the fire, was carried out by a
city ordinance in April, 1872. A large disused water tank was
the only safe temporary refuge available for the storage and
use of these books as they arrived from England, and of two
thousand more secured from Germany by citizens of Teutonic
descent. So that the Chicago Public Library was opened in
the tank with shelving for seventeen thousand volumes on
January 1, 1873.

To the skill of its pioneer engineers in laying beneath the
water-soaked soil firm foundations for the city's growth and
health, and to the will of its citizens in rearing the new city,
Chicago owes what it then began to be. So little above the
level of the lake was the site of the city that nothing could be
done to secure safe drainage, except to raise the grades of
many of its streets through whole areas of the city. This
these engineers did, in many places lifting the street level as

high as the roofs of the one-story cottage-built dwellings which for many years lined most of the streets. The wooden sidewalks were thus required to run higher and lower, with flights of steps leading up and down to the different levels.

In all this underground work, these pioneers built so well that some of their drainage system is still in use. Their successors reported, "We have not been able in fifty years to improve upon the high standard of workmanship established in the beginning." So thoroughly was the situation surveyed that many of the superseding methods were anticipated or suggested by the original plans for drainage. They even had some bearings upon sinking the foundations of the weightier and taller modern buildings down to rock bottom, in order to avoid risk of settling by building on "floating foundations" which always have been and still are in common use.

It required longer and more drastic experience to safeguard the health of the people than to protect their property. During successive cholera and smallpox epidemics from 1854 on the death-rate ran as high as one death to every twenty-one inhabitants. Since stricter sanitary measures and more vigilant health-department administration have functioned, not only has smallpox almost disappeared, but typhoid fever has been reduced to the lowest rate ever registered in so large a city. The length of life meanwhile has more than doubled since 1898.

These achievements of former generations are recalled here not only in justice to such unrequited service to posterity as should not fade from memory, but also because they are a parable, prophetic of achievements which have been, or are yet to be, undertaken both for the material and moral safety and progress of the city. In achieving the founding and rebuilding of the city these preceding generations heroically exemplified the distinctive characteristics of Chicago—to face its worst and to do its best. And this it has done over and over again, even more courageously in improving its social and political conditions than in overcoming its material obstacles and disasters.

The bed rock upon which these material foundations rest, and upon which the present and future superstructures of the

Greater Chicago are being built, is to be discovered in the Chicago spirit, the determination and aspiration of which could be neither quenched nor consumed. Chicago's heritage from the great fires thus became almost as valuable a civic asset as that of the World's Columbian Exposition. Indeed, the survivors, whose active citizenship spanned both great experiences, I found to be living links inseparably connecting these two great pivotal events. The incentive to rebuild a better city than the fire destroyed inspired many of these same citizens to create in the White City of the World's Fair an ideal which their successors might realize.

Although the "little fire" of 1874 is so called in comparison with the "great fire" of 1871, the second conflagration was great enough to arouse the rebuilders to see the necessity of laying over again the civic and social foundations of Chicago, which they discovered to be not only perilously unsafe but indecently rotten. It did not take them long, nor was it difficult to see that the fire and police protection, then most urgently needed, could be assured only by reckoning with the incompetence and corruption of the city government. The very month in which the second disaster occurred, and almost before the embers of their burnt buildings had cooled, a group of prominent citizens organized the Citizens' Association of Chicago to grapple with these problems of public safety. At their head was Franklin MacVeagh, who combined the culture of the East with the energy of the West, the business ability capable of building up a great commercial enterprise with the knowledge of finance and public affairs fitting him later to be the secretary of the treasury in the cabinet of President Taft.

For more than fifty years this Association has had such an important part in inspiring and realizing Chicago's civic renaissance that its first president's forecast of what was needed to be done and of what was needed to do it is an essential background of the history thereafter, and now, in the making. Absorbing as was the demand for immediate fire protection, Mr. MacVeagh claimed far further and deeper needs of the city to be the occasion for the existence and work of the Citizens' Association. In such words as follow he gave memorable expression to the rising civic consciousness, conscience, and ideals, which were as prophetic of future achievements as they were inspiring to those then taking their epoch-marking initiative:

The occasion for this Association may be stated thus: This city is governed, for the most part, by unfit and unworthy men, in an undignified, uncultured and demoralizing manner. Our system of government is bad and produces the rulers. This system must somehow be remedied.

We are organized to look carefully and thoroughly into the whole framework of our city and county system, to commend the best reforms we can arrive at, and then to summon the people of the city to their adoption. The city is always, but especially after an emergency like the fire or after an exhibition of unusual official immorality, full of good public impulses. Hitherto these have been allowed to waste themselves like the harmless flashing of powder because there was no organization that had the force to conserve and crystallize the best sentiment of the people. If ours is to be such an organization it will not only conserve but promote these best public impulses and this larger public thought. It will assure the citizen that if the public grievance he has is real, or if the public thought he has is worthy, there is here an organized body that can and will exert a large force to realize the purpose for which he, single-handed, is too weak.

Not only are the proper peace and comfort of our people and their homes at stake, not only is the financial credit of the city at stake, but even our honorable relationships with the rest of the world are this moment at open risk. The first fire the world accepted as a historic misfortune, the second challenged the world's criticism, a third would drop us into profound disgrace. Once the world showered us with charity, without one feeling but pity. We accepted it like proper men, without one thought but gratitude. Could this be repeated? If the world should be generous enough to help us in spite of its scorn, could we accept their help without humiliation? And so I say, not only would our commercial supremacy be gone, but our self-respect and our best relationship with the world.

Thus you will see that we are not an Association of a day only. Such reforms can only be formulated after long consideration, and realized only after long effort. We hope that the presence of the Association in this city, its thorough and able investigations, and its persistent unyielding attention to what it undertakes will have an inspiring influence upon many minds sufficient to arouse them to the better exercise of their citizens' rights. Thus indirectly we hope to improve the average city official life and character. Good citizens once aroused are more powerful than the bad.

As the oldest civic reform organization in America, the development of the Citizens' Association of Chicago is of unusual significance. It has strictly adhered to the lines of principle and policy upon which its founders laid down their purpose in bidding for the support of their fellow-citizens. Ever since it has kept faith with the public. Intelligently public-spirited citizens have never failed to respect the sincerity and accuracy of its investigations, or to volunteer financial support sufficient to maintain its continuous public service. The continuity and effectiveness of its service are due to the non-partisan, fair, and thorough way in which it has hewed to the line between public interests and those personal, corporate, and partisan "special interests," which are not readily distinguished by most citizens. For results, the Association depends upon the publicity given to its thoroughly authentic investigations and upon the good citizenship of Chicago and Illinois to act upon the information and recommendations offered. Citizens have thereby been prompted to protect the ballot, to prevent waste of public resources, to check graft in municipal contracts and state administration, to enforce the law against gambling, to prevent corruption and promote efficiency in the conduct of public affairs, to defeat bad legislation, and to support the enactment of better laws.

Characteristic of its broad and practical spirit is the fact that when other organizations arose to specialize effort in this widely diversified field the Citizens' Association always welcomed their co-operation and promptly turned its own special attention to some other public need waiting to be met. Thus in turn it tackled such evils as the preying of loan sharks upon city and county officials, race-track abuses, and the personal appropriation of the interest on public funds while on deposit by their treasurers. Still more important have been its constructive achievements in promoting legislation for civil service for state constitutional amendments, and for reorganizing the state government under a new administrative code.

Not the least, but indeed the most exemplary, characteristic of the Association is the steadfastness with which it has stayed on its job for over half a century, neither courting financial favors nor fearing partisan consequences.

CHAPTER III

PIONEERS OF HIGHER IDEALS

FIFTY years after the great fire a large assembly of citizens gathered at the City Club to commemorate the progress made since that epoch-marking event. Lorado Taft, the sculptor, spoke of Chicago's progress in art; Frederick Stock, conductor of Chicago's Symphony Orchestra, reviewed the city's musical development; and I sketched the half-century's advance in civic welfare.

Many and inspiring as were the achievements then appraised, larger loomed the men and women whose personalities spanned the two decades between the great fires and the World's Fair. Their ideals were high enough, and their persistence was courageous enough to overcome the great odds against which they achieved the glories of the Exposition and made possible the grandeur of the great plan for the Greater Chicago. It is of interest to note the significance of the fact that foremost among those thus inspired to set the higher standard for the cultural, aesthetic, civic, and social superstructures which we inherit not a few were sons and daughters of the pioneers who laid in the prairie the physical, commercial, industrial, and political foundations of the city that is coming to be.

Among these achieving idealists never to be forgotten by all who knew them, yet ever to be held up to those who have no memory of them, I mention a very few of the many to whom I am personally indebted for inspiration and for patient persistence in the pursuit of ideals which they exemplify. Acquaintanceship with them made one an heir of their great experiences and their greater achievements.

Foremost among those then living to whom Chicago's great transformation is due stood Charles Lawrence Hutchin-

son. His father was one of the pioneers who began to make
Chicago "the great central market," especially in grain.
While helping create the world-wide importance of the Board
of Trade, the successful speculations through which he acquired a large fortune led his fellow-speculators familiarly
to call him "Old Hutch." Like not a few citizens whose
fathers wrung from the earth, or from dealing in its products, the working capital of the city, the younger Hutchinson devoted what may have been an inherited ability for
promotion, to developing the cultural and aesthetic progress
of the city. Although by occupation a banker and prominent
in banking and other business circles, his absorbing interests
were the enjoyment and promotion of art. As the founder,
patron, and promoter of the Art Institute, now ra¹ying fourteen thousand subscribers, five thousand or mo' students in
its school, and by its democratic spirit and olicy winning
over a million visitors of all races and class s to its museum
and special exhibits, his name and examp' will ever live in
the annals of the City Beautiful. N other citizen was
thought of as director of the Fine Ar s Commission of the
Columbian Exposition. To none of i trustees does the University of Chicago owe more than o him.

Passionately fond of the beau s of nature, he shared with
many friends the charm of th rare planting on the grounds
surrounding his summer ho e at Lake Geneva, Wisconsin.
He also served many year s the commissioner of the South
Park System, which ow to his taste and administrative
ability much of its bea y. To his democratic spirit is mainly
due the development f its playgrounds and fieldhouses for
indoor recreation, e initiative for which was taken by
Henry G. Forema when president of that Commission. No
such recreation equipment as Chicago was then prompted
to extend thro ghout its borders has ever yet been claimed by
any other modern city. The fees Mr. Hutchinson received
for attending directors' meetings he devoted to his flower
fund, from which lovely blossoms came to cheer the sick in
hospitals and to brighten our social-settlement occasions.
The Chicago Plant, Fruit and Flower Guild has since enabled
the suburbs to share their garden growths with their walled-

in city neighbors, reminding them of flowery homelands across the seas. To him and several other citizens of like spirit and culture the city of Chicago owes much for linking together the commercial and cultural, the artistic and democratic, the urban and rural elements which are essential alike to the higher civic ideals and to the development of citizenship.

Although the first definite suggestion of planning the city-wide development of Chicago was made by Franklin Mac-Veagh and was inspired by the White City of the World's Fair, the Chicago Plan owes its initiative to Charles Dyer Norton, a young business man from another state, whose citizenship here began two years after the Columbian Exposition closed.

Within a year after he had taken up his residence here, Mr. Norton proposed to his fellow-members of the Merchants' Club that they should undertake a study for a plan which might inspire and guide their fellow-citizens in promoting the city's growth. The proposal was enthusiastically undertaken, not only by this group of younger citizens, but by the still more resourceful men of the Commercial Club, when the two organizations united. The study committee appointed in 1906 was continued with Mr. Norton as chairman. The results of its three years' work, in which eminent city planners and landscape architects from this country and abroad were called to assist, were published in the beautifully printed and illustrated folio volume issued by the Commercial Club.

The project thus brilliantly proposed was presented to the mayor and the City Council, and on November 4, 1909, the Chicago Plan Commission was constituted an official agency of the municipality by an ordinance confirming the mayor's appointment of commissioners, representing both the Council and citizenship, with advisory but no executive power. While this procedure was being taken Mr. Norton left the city to accept President Taft's appointment as assistant secretary of the treasury at Washington. When entering upon his banking career in New York City he was impressed with the possibilities of developing the river fronts and outlying districts of the metropolis, to serve the health and happiness of its East Side congested populations.

Appointed chairman of a committee of nine distinguished citizens to conduct a study of the region in which New Yorkers earn their livelihood and make their homes, he thus stated the aim of the vision which inspired him to undertake essentially the same project in both great cities: "To end wasteful local improvements, bring order out of disorder, replace congestion and waste with convenience and thrift, realize the potentialities of commerce and industry, and utilize the natural resources for beauty, comfort and pleasure."

In less than a year this seer of city planning died at the high tide of life, deeply lamented in both cities. Frederick A. Delano, another former leading citizen of Chicago and member of its Plan Commission, succeeded to the chairmanship of the New York committee. Its regional survey of the metropolitan area, including the counties contiguous to Greater New York, was supervised and published by the Russell Sage Foundation, under the leadership of its director, John M. Glenn. It is the most far-reaching city and regional planing project ever undertaken on so large a scale.

The rare personal qualities and great achievements of Daniel Hudson Burnham, as supervising architect under whom the composite designs for the World's Fair grounds and buildings were produced and executed, designated him as the first choice both of Chicago's study committee and of the Plan Commission to lead them in initiating the great project. To his creative idealism and practical promotion were chiefly due the co-operative spirit which developed the complicated plans that won the people at large to vote for the bond issue required to carry out the initial reconstruction. As among his professional colleagues he never assumed to be more than first among equals, so to all his fellow-citizens who knew him he was always one of themselves. No memorial which he left in architecture or landscape will so long be remembered as these words with which he sought to inspire his contemporaries to lay foundations broad enough to bear the greater superstructures which coming generations would build upon them:

Make no little plans; they have no magic to stir men's blood, and probably themselves will not be realized. Make big plans; aim high in hope and work, remembering that a noble, logical diagram once recorded will never die, but long after we are gone will be a living thing, asserting itself with ever growing insistency. Remember that our sons and grandsons are going to do things that would stagger us. Let your watchword be order and your beacon beauty.

No citizen worthier than Charles H. Wacker could have been found to follow Mr. Norton, and as chairman of the Plan Commission to carry on his initiative. In his mid-business career, when too few successful men will serve their city, he was one of the foremost of those who bore the burden of the Columbian Exposition, helping to carry it through to success by serving on its exacting Ways and Means Committee. At the retiring age, when still fewer men will sacrifice their leisure and pleasure or the opportunity to increase acquired wealth, he accepted the chairmanship of the Chicago Plan Commission.

"Personal friends," Mr. Wacker said, advised him "not to attach his wagon to a star," by engaging in work which, as they thought, was without any prospect of success. He did so, however, because he felt that "the good people of Chicago would not only aid us in our effort, but would insist that the improvements in the Chicago Plan be consummated." Critics had criticized the project as "visionary, a picture plan neither practical nor democratic, a dream." His rejoinder to them was made in these challenging questions: "Don't you know that all progressive men have at sometime or other been dubbed 'dreamers,' and that all monumental undertakings have been called 'dreams'? Have pessimists ever accomplished any great constructive work? Is it a sign of strength to doubt your own power, your own possibilities?"

In meeting his own challenge, he had not only to dream with his fellow-members of the Commercial Club and their artistic designers, Daniel H. Burnham and Edward H. Bennet, but he had to become an "exhorter," to plead and argue with all classes of his fellow-citizens in speech and print, by figures and pictures. In so doing he roused them by such incisive appeals as these:

We cannot afford to leave it to landowners and real estate speculators to decide for us how and in what direction the city is to grow.

Now is the time to consider and adopt such a plan. It is not particularly for the rich and aristocratic, who can get beauty, comfort and health in their city and country homes. It is primarily for the benefit of those who cannot afford to leave the city or get that which this plan proposes to give to every inhabitant of Chicago be he rich or poor.

When in ten, twenty or fifty years Chicago shall stand transformed in accordance with these plans, could it possess a greater moral asset for future generations than this example of lofty yet practical ideals, realized through the far-sighted wisdom, the unfaltering courage and the faith of its citizens which made such undertakings possible?

No one but he knew what exactions these vast undertakings laid upon him all these years in which he has volunteered his whole time in this service of his city. But we who have stood near him from the beginning as fellow-commissioners full well know what we and all his fellow-citizens owe to his inspiring devotion, to his imperturbable patience in waiting and working, to his cheery tact in overcoming opposition from those opposed to each other but never to him, and to his indomitable persistence and enthusiasm. For we have seen the transformation of ideals into action, of bond issues into achievements, of city ordinances into thoroughfares, of government decisions and railway agreements into water fronts, thus registering amazing progress in realizing dreams of beauty and utility. Again the power of a great purpose has also demonstrated its capacity to gather to itself the ways and means for its own accomplishment. And I have been impressed with the power of a great ideal to raise a man above himself and beyond the farthest reach of his own and others' estimate of his capacity.

Mr. Wacker looked so far ahead as to provide for the children of the schools a reader textbook on the plan. With tact and patience equal to his energy he won the very mixed membership of the Plan Commission to follow his leadership in promoting its ideals. Aldermen and other officials loyally supported his policies both in the Commission and in the City Council. Even those notorious for preferring bad measures to good ones upheld the Commission's policies without expectation of personal or partisan advantage. Forestalling sectional prejudices and misunderstanding, the people in all parts of the city were rallied to vote for bond issues, recommended by the Commission, by large majorities. No injunc-

tion or other obstructive effort impeded the wonderful progress of the great plan until, panic-stricken by the wastes of
the present city administration, taxpayers have defeated
indiscriminately all municipal bond issues by their referen-
dum votes since 1928.

The reclamation of the entire lake front and the building of
its parkways lying beyond inner lagoons have been achieved.
The vast projects of widening and extending inner and outer
thoroughfares, connecting hitherto-separated sections of the
city are being carried out. The straightening of the Chicago
River's channel and the projected re-location and consolidation of railway terminals promise to relieve the most serious
congestion of the city's street traffic. No suspicion of partiality or partisan interference or graft has cast a shadow on the
recommendations and promotions of this advisory commission. Chicago has never been more united than in its good
will to accept and carry out this its greatest project.

On retiring from his official leadership, after serving his
city in achieving so much of what was planned for its future,
this veteran citizen of seventy years, shortly before his recent
death had the grace and hope to greet "so splendid a body of
young men to membership in the Commission who will carry
on the work as we older men lay it down." Like the seer of
Chicago he was, Charles H. Wacker bade each and every
citizen to "look back upon the united effort and be inspired
for greater effort in the future." Anticipating the beginning
of the end which came two years after his retirement, he exclaimed, "We old war-horses may as we depart confidently
intrust to the shoulders of our young sons the burdens we
have borne."

Theodore Thomas was another pioneer whose lifelong
idealism and quiet, persistent enthusiasm, then winning a
following, inspired me on coming to Chicago. His worthy
successor, Frederick Stock, as director of the Chicago Symphony Orchestra, credits "the making of musical Chicago to
Thomas' summer-night concerts in New York City," which
I frequently enjoyed while a student in college. Chicago
certainly attested its rising standards of culture in inducing
him to leave New York to improve what he thought to be the

better opportunity offered here for building up a permanent orchestra and a sufficient clientèle of music lovers to support it. In contrast with the rented garden, which was the best provision that New York offered his summer-night concerts during fourteen years, stand Chicago's Orchestra Hall and its great Symphony Orchestra, which commemorate his pioneering achievements here and justify his faith in the West and his hope of this city's response to his leadership.

The congresses auxiliary to the World's Columbian Exposition gave evidence of leadership as capable of synthetic efforts as that which succeeded in establishing the symphony concerts. No differences were more difficult to synthesize than those confronting the purpose to hold a congress of religions. Preceding the spread of the study of comparative religion, the effort to bring together the representatives of the great ethnic faiths with representatives of the diverse Christian sects met with deep resentment and widespread criticism, because it seemed to yield the claim that Christianity is the only true religion. But there were those who were firm enough in their own faith to be broad enough to recognize the truth and values in other beliefs, and eager enough to welcome all the light from any quarter upon human destiny.

In the lead of these proponents and managers of the Congress of Religions was Charles Carroll Bonney, who bore the name of his forebear, Charles Carroll, the last survivor of the signers of the Declaration of Independence. A lawyer who had been a teacher, he was as much at home and as active in the world of letters as in the citizenship of his city and native land. More than tolerant, and yet not at all controversial, he rallied like-minded men and women to welcome distinguished representatives of the historic faiths of other lands. They were afforded the largest liberty for the exposition of their own beliefs and for the frank expression of the comparisons and contrasts they drew between the results of differing faiths upon the peoples and the centuries dominated by them. This congress of the world's faiths promoted the broader attitude and the more appreciative spirit of the progressive leaders in the foreign-missionary movements in which the churches of Christendom are enlisted. It also increased interest and tolerance in the study of comparative religion. It blazed the trail now leading to "The Christ of the Indian Road."

Most prominent among the women managers of the Exposition and its auxiliary congresses were Mrs. Potter Palmer and Mrs. Charles Henrotin. Each had attained social distinction both at home and abroad, which opened the way to enlist the interest and co-operation of leading people on both sides of the sea. Their presence graced the platforms of almost every assembly. Their intelligence and tact facilitated many committee meetings and helped solve many difficult problems. When presiding over a session of the Congress of Religions at which the status of women under the dominant faiths in India was discussed, Mrs. Palmer challenged the claims advanced by native religious leaders. Her insistence upon the higher status, larger liberty, and fairer equality with men enjoyed by women in Christendom finely exemplified her balance between courtesy and conviction, between deference toward the opinions of others and firmness in holding her own independent judgments, which were characteristics of her manner and personality.

Mrs. Palmer also served with distinction and efficiency in the section of the Congress devoted to philanthropy. When at the close of the wondrous Exposition year I expressed the strong desire of all of us enlisted in the city's social work that she would continue to serve with us in carrying the ideals of the Congress into action on our local fields, Mrs. Palmer significantly replied: "If I could help improve industrial conditions and relations I would be most interested to do what I could." She continued to give, and often opened her home and art gallery to conferences for the benefit of local causes. But later she withdrew from the active part in local and philanthropic movements which she bore so well when Chicago most needed the service of its influential citizens to establish higher ideals of civic progress and better standards of administrative efficiency.

Mrs. Henrotin carried those high ideals and standards of administrative efficiency for which she stood in the council chambers of the World's Fair into the management of numerous local agencies which she continued to serve almost to the end of her long life. They ranged from the General Federation of Women's Clubs to the little federation of working girls' clubs, organized by the social settlements of the city. Her husband's many years in the service of Belgium as its consul in Chicago extended the sphere of her acquaintanceship and influence abroad, where decorations and other honors were bestowed upon her by the sultan of Turkey, the French Republic, and the king of Belgium. Her gracious spirit, gentle manner, and versatile attainments attracted and held to her a multitude of friends in very different ranks, races, and faiths who alike valued her friendship as a personal privilege.

Preceding both of these leaders in social and civic service was one of their associates in the Exposition Congress, Mrs. Lucy M. Flower, then serving as chairman of the Department of Social and Moral Reform. Calling into co-operation the National Conference of Charities and Correction, she led the way in convening and conducting an International Congress of Charities, Correction, and Philanthropy, which proved to be one of the most successful of the whole series at the World's Fair. Moving beyond the range of philanthropic vision then quite rigidly restricted, she dared include among the topics for discussion "The Introduction of Sociology as a Special Topic of Investigation and Instruction in Institutions of Learning," for which I contributed the facts regarding social topics taught in theological seminaries. She dared indeed, because the terms "sociology" and "socialism" had been so ignorantly identified, even in the minds of the so-called intelligent classes, that the mention of either term risked the taboo of social, academic, and chauvinistic political circles.

Very few women were prominently enlisted in public work during the thirty years from 1873 to 1903, when Mrs. Flower was leading their way into it and its way into higher efficiency. But she herself demonstrated woman's high and versatile capacity for social service by deeds hereafter to be narrated.

CHAPTER IV

CHICAGO REACHING DOWN TO BUILD UP

DURING the great Exposition the city partially set its house in order, so as not to be ashamed of its outside appearance. Street paving and cleaning, especially in the vicinity of the White City, were extensively undertaken. The protection of public health and the safeguarding against fire were more vigilantly provided for. Stricter police regulation of the "wide-open town" policy of the city administration was temporarily conceded at the demand of the city's pride. The underworld was driven out of sight of those who did not seek it, yet could be found at most of its old haunts, and many new ones, except in the immediate vicinity of the Exposition.

The class antagonism in industry still smoldered, which had burst into the flames of the Haymarket Riot of May 4, 1886. The tragic trial and execution of the "anarchists," judged guilty of complicity "before the fact" of the bombing, had smothered but not extinguished the resentments. Widespread unemployment, after work on the World's Fair and its attendant enterprises ceased, left thousands of resident families destitute, and stranded hordes of homeless men who had neither means to buy food and shelter nor to seek their livelihood elsewhere.

No exhibit of the Exposition proved to be more vital and fundamental to the permanent progress of Chicago than that which exposed this perilous situation. Although in plain sight, it was realized by comparatively few until it was explored and laid bare by William T. Stead, the widely noted London journalist. He came to Chicago to visit the Exposition and report it in the *Pall Mall Gazette* of London of which he was the editor. So entranced was he with the architecture

27

of the White City that he was first and foremost to plead for the preservation of its most artistic structures. His initiative may have lasted long enough to give impulse to the movement to restore the great Fine Arts Building in Jackson Park. Twenty years afterward it resulted in a bond issue of $3,000,-000 voted for that purpose, subsequently providing a building equipment worthy of the great Industrial Museum founded by Julius Rosenwald.

Mr. Stead, however, became even more interested in the city itself than in the World's Fair. In an unpublished manuscript, he noted his impressions of Chicago and its destiny. "Equidistant between the Great Lakes system of the North and the immense waterway of the Mississippi and Missouri" Chicago was "bound to become the capital of the New World, with New York as its only rival." He expected it "to cover an immense tract of country, with space enough on the shores of Lake Michigan for a population of ten millions, when the transoceanic canal should be constructed, enabling steamers of all countries to discharge their cargoes at its wharfs." Recognizing this city to be "queen of the central and western states," it seemed to him that "if Chicago could mount the crest of the civic revival then rising in America, it might be the means of the regeneration of the whole country."

But "the contrast between the ideals of the White City, the increasing labor troubles and the hideous realities of the slums seemed to point to the need for a new movement of reform." So he plead "for the union of all honest men against rogues and boodlers." His impressions were received through first-hand contacts with the actual situation. Night and day for several weeks he explored it on the streets, in the cheap lodging-houses and saloons, the corridors of the City Hall, and at the police stations, to which places, and many more, homeless men thronged for shelter. Never shall I forget his tender touch and tone in conversing with some of these men in the lodging-houses, or his expression of silent pity as he looked upon their sleeping forms, which so thickly littered the damp, cold corridors and stairways of the old City Hall that we could scarcely pass through without stepping upon them.

His sympathy for the shelterless and hungry led him to offend some of his hosts at a social occasion of a large and influential denominational fellowship at which he was the principal after-dinner speaker. After graphically describing these scenes which we had witnessed the night before, he asked his hearers whether "as Christians they should not have had one course less at this dinner in order to give those other children of the Heavenly Father at least one course." Sitting next to him at the speakers' table as a fellow-guest, I noticed that he became sensitive at the askance attitude of a venerable and distinguished clergyman sitting opposite him. But I was hardly prepared for his whispered inquiry, "Who is that Son of Belial?" When I informed him that he was the pastor of one of the prominent churches of that denomination, my interlocutor responded: "The Lord will have to cast this demon out of him before that church can do the Lord's work."

Moved by the human instincts so completely possessing him, and encouraged by the response given by the trade unions more heartily than by any other group, he issued a city-wide call for a mass meeting to be held November 12, 1893, under trade-union auspices at Central Music Hall, then located at State and Randolph streets. Such a gathering Chicago had never seen before and is not likely to see again. The floor and galleries of the city's greatest forum were thronged by men and women of all grades, races, sects, and conditions. The churches were largely represented as special invitations had been mailed to every one of them.

On the stage there was such a grouping of people from the extremes of life as no one could have imagined to be possible. Side by side sat leading business men and labor leaders, representatives of the city government and of its exclusive clubs, preachers and saloonkeepers, gamblers and theological professors, matrons of distinguished families and notorious "madames" from houses of ill fame, judges of the courts and one of the men convicted in the Haymarket Riot trial who had recently been pardoned from the state prison by Governor Altgeld. Here, then, was the living exhibit which dramatically impressed upon all who saw or read of it the hard facts to which they had become ignorantly, blindly, or callously indifferent. It was just such a background as gave realistic emphasis to the stirring words spoken alike from the platform, the floor, and the galleries.

Mr. Stead surprised the applauding audience, in the silence which followed their greeting, by clasping his hands, looking upward, and with devout simplicity offering this prayer:

O Lord, Our Father, help us this afternoon to understand something of the love that is in the heart of our brother Jesus, and that whosoever does anything to relieve the sufferings and sorrow of the least of these his brothers does it unto him. We ask it for His sake and their sake. Amen.

As though his prayer had given him his theme, as it did the title of his book subsequently printed, his first words to his hearers were in the form of this challenging question: "If Christ came to Chicago today, what would he think of it?" Then for an hour or more he proceeded to answer his own question in what the daily papers reported to be "a singularly eloquent address." To me, when he was at white heat denouncing preventable evils, he seemed to rise to the stature of one of the Hebrew prophets. At his best he was the Christian apostle tenderly entreating us, by the sufferings of Christ, "to take home some of the sorrows of the men, women and children living in our midst and try to help them so as to understand something of the sorrow and agony of Christ—on the real cross which all are fashioning for him in whose hearts love is not."

Only by getting together all the forces which make for righteousness and for love could three such evils as he vividly described be remedied. Foremost among them was the industrial crisis, "due to the lack, the irregularity, the low pay and excessive hours of work." That "because a man is out of work he should be put to herd with criminals in finding no place to sleep except the stone floor of a police station," he thought to be "a disgrace to a civilized country." Second to this and still more disgraceful was not only the toleration but the police protection of the red-light vice district. Its victims, he thought, were to be accounted for chiefly by economic pressure, by children having fewer advantages than they should, and by the lack of places in which to meet friends in friendly intercourse. By lacking any such places, not only wretched men and forlorn women, but many young people as well, were driven or tempted into evil resorts. The toleration of a city government, which protects if it does not prompt evils that it might prevent or at least reduce, was the last and worst fault of a city capable of the "hopes born of the World's Fair." Such was his appeal for the united effort which it was the purpose of these mass meetings to prompt and organize. Some hissing but much more applause punctuated his arousing sentences.

Thomas Morgan, the veteran leader of the socialists, came next on the program to respond for labor. He began by a hearty tribute to Mr. Stead's plea for united effort; claimed that organized labor had long protested against evils which "never before had been told so forcefully as this afternoon"; and then declared that above all others Christ would condemn "the crime of silence—a silence which had been broken here almost for the first time in the history of our city." In closing Mr. Morgan startled the audience both to hiss and cheer by saying:

Now the veil has been torn aside and you members of the G.A.R., the Y.M.C.A., of your temperance societies, of your Sons of America and Daughters of America have been able to see the skeletons in your closet. [Prolonged applause.] Your laboring men may assemble peacefully on the Lake Front begging for work, and with the strong arm of the law are driven back into their tenement houses, that the visitors who come to see the White City might not see the misery of those who built the Garden City. Here and everywhere the puny voice of those who suffer is refused to be heard, is drowned out in some way or another, by this awful hopeless social condition.

Shall we hope from this day at least that those, who by their work have tried to bring the public mind to a realization of what should and is to be done, will be heard? After such statements as have been heard from Mr. Stead, will those with whom he now associates have some standing in the community? Will you again lapse into insecure security? Do you think the upheavals that have forced themselves on your attention from time to time are the last that will come around? Do you believe that under these social conditions here in this free country there are no anarchists, no bombs, no dynamite? Do you not believe some desperate man under the load which you allow to rest on him will get uneasy and will revolt?

Do not think that I, or these workingmen, wish to do harm. Give them a chance. If you well-to-do people do not listen, will not wake up, you do not know that in your midst, there may be, as at Barcelona, a desperate man who feeling himself all the injustice that is inflicted on his fellows, will kill, will destroy. This is no fancy picture. The reality exists from day to day everywhere. I say it only to shake you out of your false security. And, if the pleadings of editor Stead, in the name of Christ and for justice, cannot shake you out, may someone blow you out with dynamite.

At the mention of dynamite, great excitement prevailed. Cries of protests and threats against the speaker came from all parts of the hall, many rising to their feet, gesticulating violently. Their action aroused cheers from many others. I noticed some men moving toward the front to stand between the platform and the audience, as though to protect the speaker. The unfortunately repeated reference to dynamite came too close to the Haymarket Riot not to agitate citizens who had been shocked by the explosion of the death-dealing bomb which killed and wounded many policemen, and for inciting which alleged anarchists were sentenced to death and imprisonment for life.

Realizing the misunderstanding to which he had subjected himself, Morgan ended by exclaiming and explaining, as Mr. Stead rose to tell him his time was up and gently led him back to his seat:

I care not for your hisses. You know that the desire in the heart of any honest workingman is not for violence. I have lived in this town for thirty-four years and never committed a crime, never advised that anything should be done which any honest man should not do. I am satisfied that what I have said will be understood, will be justified and will be endorsed.

Called upon to take my part in the program before the tumult and the bedlam of voices had quieted down, I could not make myself heard. Hoping that an action might speak louder than words, I led Morgan to the front of the platform and shouted as loud as I could, "Who is afraid of little Tommy Morgan! He has been misunderstood." Back to the platform came the challenge, "We heard him," from the group who would hear no more, some of whom left the hall. But I persisted in claiming that he had said the right thing in the wrong way. Then American fair play and sense of humor got the better of the bitter enders, so that opportunity was given me to close my speech by affirming, "Christ's Christianity means a new chance for each man who will receive it. And those who will not give it will not get it."

The unanimity with which the extraordinarily mixed multitude acted at the close of the evening session of the mass meeting was the more remarkable because of the turbulent antagonisms with which it began in the afternoon. The action taken completely fulfilled the purpose of Mr. Stead in issuing the call for it. The meeting adjourned after adopting the following resolution with a roar of approval: "That it is the sense of this meeting that the formation of a civic confederation is feasible and practical and that a committee of twenty-one be selected as an organizing committee."

Although the immediate appeal of the facts and speeches of the meeting was for moral resentment against the shameless toleration of the city's open vice, yet bad city government was so clearly shown to be responsible for the protection and perpetuation of prostitution, gambling, and drink that political action preceded by several years any vigorous and effective attack on the underworld.

This appeal for political reform influenced both the selection of the committee and the acceptance of those selected. They were moved to serve by the notably broad and urgent call upon them to act for the city's sake. It read:

The object of this organization is the concentration in one potential, non-political, non-sectarian center of all the forces that are now laboring to advance our municipal, philanthropic and moral interests, and to accomplish all that is possible towards energizing and giving effect to the public conscience of Chicago. It is not expected to accomplish this in one day, but all great movements must have a beginning; and in consultation with leading citizens of all classes, who desire to see Chicago the best governed, the healthiest and cleanest city in this country, we are led to believe it opportune that such a movement should begin while our people are yet filled with the new ideas, new ambitions and inspirations drawn from the great Exposition and its valuable adjunct, the World's Congress.

The personnel of the committee was representative of all sections of the city and of all the various occupational callings of its citizens—bankers, merchants, manufacturers, trade unionists and more radical labor leaders, lawyers, ministers, teachers and social workers, women and men of distinction as well as from the rank and file of our democratic cosmopolitan citizenship. They were all chosen without reference to party or sect, yet included those of Catholic, Protestant, and Jewish affiliation, or of no religious connections.

When Mr. Stead returned to Chicago several weeks after his mass meetings adjourned, he found the Civic Federation well organized with its municipal, philanthropic, industrial, educational and social, moral-reform, and political-action departments starting their work along the lines to which his agitation had given initiative.

During this second visit Mr. Stead wrote and published his volume of nearly five hundred pages, bearing the title, which was the text of his Music Hall address, *If Christ Came to Chicago*. Having promised to print a stenographic report of this meeting, which he failed to secure, he published this book in lieu thereof. The idea and phrasing of this title "reached me," he explained, "like most of my religio-philosophical notions, through the poetry of James Russell Lowell." The text from the "Gospel according to Lowell," which he said suggested every page in this book, was in the couplet opening and the two verses closing Lowell's poem "The Parable."

> Said Christ our Lord "I will go and see
> How the men, my brothers, believe in me."
>
> Then Christ sought out an artisan,
> A low-browed, stunted haggard man;
> And a motherless girl, whose fingers thin,
> Pushed from her faintly want and sin.
>
> These set he in the midst of them,
> And as they drew back their garments-hem,
> For fear of defilement, "Lo here," said he,
> "The images ye have made of me."

As a journalistic report the volume is remarkable for the realistic way in which it makes the reader see what its author saw and hear what he heard. It is still more noteworthy in disclosing how quickly and accurately he, as a stranger, had discovered the actual facts of the menacing economic, political, and moral conditions then existing, incidentally describing the sources of his information with which he had been in first-hand contact. His written and spoken reproductions of scenes, situations, and persons that revealed the primary sources of his information were realistically true to life. In a few instances his snap judgments were unfair to some reputable citizens, or showed too high regard for others who proved untrustworthy.

While his descriptions were indeed vivid, yet they fell far short of the sordid demoralization they described. His language was not always chosen with a delicate sense of propriety and therefore shocked those especially who were as averse to plain speech as they were to facing the facts spoken of. This aversion toward having them told about their town, especially by any foreigner, prompted violent protests in the press against many of Mr. Stead's utterances. It also led certain citizens who resented any and every attempt "to knock the town," or perhaps still more the effect that this knocking might have upon their corporate interests, to check the wide circulation of his book. The huge piles of volumes that had been bulked in the windows, on the counters, and even on the floors of many stores suddenly disappeared. And it was rumored that certain interests had bought up the stock for destruction, in order to get the volume out of sight, although the chance to prove or disprove this suspicion was neither given nor taken by anyone.

Just why this resentment was more intense than any shown before or since against exposures of the city's defects and defaults is an interesting conundrum. That they were not slanderously wide of the mark as pictured by Mr. Stead was attested by Lincoln Steffens when, several years later, he came to write his true-to-fact volume on *The Shame of the Cities*. Of Chicago as he saw it, before Stead came, he wrote:

First in violence, deepest in dirt; loud, lawless, unlovely, ill-smelling, irreverent, new; an overgrown gawk of a village, the "tough," among cities, a spectacle for the nation. Criminally it was wide open, commercially it was brazen, and socially it was thoughtless and raw; it was a settlement of individuals and groups and interests with no common city-sense and no political conscience. Everybody was for himself, none was for Chicago.

Daring to say all this, he discovered that it was not much of a dare, for he added: "I give Chicago no quarter and Chicago asks for none. 'Good' they cheer when you find fault. We deserve it and it does us good." Later he affirmed, as had Stead, that a city which could "carry through a World's Fair triumph" and could "balance high buildings on rafts floating in mud" could do anything its citizens really wanted to do toward reforming an administration of public affairs so "preposterously and ridiculously" unworthy of their city.

But Mr. Steffens was a native son and Mr. Stead was a foreigner. Perhaps that is enough to account for the difference in the ways the same truth was received as told by both of them with equal frankness. Mr. Stead's single purpose to make the city ashamed of its unholy alliance between corrupt politics, grafting financial interests, and the vice lords of the underworld obscured Chicago's higher life and better achievements through the body of his book.

Yet many and apt were his historical and literary allusions to the contrasts and comparisons which he drew between our present plight and similar situations abroad from which civic pride and courage had delivered other cities. No more optimistic predictions of Chicago's future had been ventured by any of its own citizens than our foreign critic forecast in his vision of the city's progress at the opening of the twentieth century. While some of these predictions with which Mr. Stead closed his volume proved his glowing hopes for us to have carried him too far above his fears, yet as we read them, thirty-four years after he ventured to print them, they remarkably forecast many subsequent achievements. Among them he predicted the recovery and beautification of the lake shore; the opening of new thoroughfares and the improvement of old ones with subways facilitating transportation; the substitution of better for worse recreational equipment and attractions; the suffrage and full citizenship of women; and the federation of churches into a civic church, which was his cherished dream both for England and America.

This dream found another unique expression a few years later, when I was the guest of his brother, the Rev. Herbert F. Stead, and himself at their London homes. They had united for several years, as on this occasion, to celebrate American independence in the old motherland on the Fourth of July. Many assembled for this purpose at the Robert

Browning Hall Settlement in Walworth, so called because the poet was baptized in the old Congregational Church which had become the settlement-house, of which Mr. Herbert Stead was the founder and warden. The occasion was announced as "a demonstration of the desire for the unity of the English-speaking world." With rousing effect "songs of Republic and Empire" were sung by a large assembly in which workingmen and their families predominated. One of them who had been elected a borough mayor as a trade-union candidate greeted his hearers with a sturdy emphasis upon the sanctity of life, individual and national. "England," he declared, "is great that she may serve." And he added: "To deprive a nation of its life is murder." Another workman made an impassioned appeal for peace, declaring: "In the name of Mother Plymouth who sits by the sea, the time has come when war which has lost its prestige should be overthrown." "We want not empire but the unity of life. Dependence upon each other is greater than independence." The principal address was most significantly made by a retired army officer, General Evatt, C.B. His service in all parts of the Empire, he explained, had led him to link the Fourth of July to Empire Day;

for then English independence had been declared. The real empire had been made possible and permanent by the decentralization of the England of the Georges—the England of the rotten boroughs, of restricted suffrage, of corrupt practices and of colonial oppression. Because America fired the shot at Lexington, Canadian, Australian and New Zealand liberty and independent development were possible. On the American continent, as upon a vast screen, the figure had been projected of an England enlarged by the composite citizenship of the United States. Despite the infusion from every modern nation, America is the expansion of the English idea, which includes the stock of the Celt, the law of the Roman, the Saxon home and wifehood of woman, the Norseman's virility softening into Norman culture, the Huguenot heroism and England's constitutional government. Americans can scarcely conceive what America means to the world. By bestowing citizenship and independent manhood upon Ireland's serfs, exiled by a despotic landlordism from the home they loved, United States had served the whole race. In their secure future America had yet another and greater mission—to secure the free development of China's part in the world's progress.

It was here that Sir Martin Conway, the well-known traveler and mountain climber, facetiously averred:

July Fourth was well called Independence Day, because it was the day on which Great Britain maintained her independence. For had it not been for her separation from America, the imperial power would have passed from England and by this time would have been centered on the other side of the water.

T. W. Russell, one of the most prominent members of Parliament from Ireland, ventured to assert:

On Independence Day Ireland seemed to be almost the only country not governed by Irishmen. Not content with ruling America, the Irish actually have a Parliament of their own in Westminster, undoing the English conquest of Ireland by a bloodless revolution. With the soil emancipated from its landlords, Irishmen would stay at home, but those who had become American citizens would be the strongest bond between the empire and the republic.

William T. Stead, chairman of the meeting, racily kept the good humor flowing all through the program, but seriously said in summing up: "It was in a batter of blood that the Englishman got made. If the mixing of races by conquest made England great, the mixture of races by colonization will make America even greater." At his Anglo-American afternoon tea party on the lawn of his own house, fire-crackers kept the Fourth of July "glorious," and peanuts were served with tea, to round out democratic America's own way of celebrating.

On leaving this extraordinary occasion I was moved to apply to the Steads what was said of an American family: "There are three distinct species of the human race, men, women, and Beechers."

Hovering over all William T. Stead did and said and wrote in Chicago is the single motive by which he claimed to be moved, and by which it is only fair to judge the spirit of his whole endeavor:

To illustrate how a living faith in the Citizen Christ would lead directly to the civic and social regeneration of Chicago. For this new redemption for which the world waits is but the primitive essence of the oldest of all religions and has but one formula—Be a Christ.

Erratic though some of his traits and tendencies were, fail and fall though he sometimes did, yet he always fell forward, with his heart, if not his head, pointing in the right direction. No man of his generation more loyally strove to help steer the church and the ships of state toward their goal than William T. Stead. After he had gone down with the "Titanic" in mid-ocean, an eminent English journalist wrote:

His grave is where he might have chosen it, midway between England and America; his death was in accordance with his view of things. It attested the great realities that underlie the common movement of our life.

CHAPTER V

FEDERATED LEADERSHIP

THE scene shifts from Central Music Hall to Parlor O of the old Palmer House. As one of the larger group, nominated by the committee of twenty-one to act as the Federation's operating constituents, I found myself associated with fourscore fellow-citizens who were fairly representative of the citizenship. Outstanding among them were a few men and women with whose leadership I was then, and ever since have been, deeply impressed. Their experience in leading other groups with which they had been identified may not only have suggested them for membership and inclined them to enlist in the Federation, but may have also given some suggestion of its departmental work and of those best qualified to head it up. It is, however, with the rallying and achieving force of their personalities that the events with which they were identified are associated in my memory.

Foremost of those who took these first initiatives was Lyman Judson Gage. He had been chosen from among Chicago's leading citizens to initiate and organize the Columbian Exposition as the first president of its Board of Directors. From that eminence, and long previously from his advantageous position in banking and business circles, he devoted his quiet energy and winsome influence to lead his fellow-citizens in looking beyond the acquisition of wealth toward those qualities which would make the city great. In manner and judgment an ideal presiding officer, he held himself and the excited mass meetings over which he presided in self-control. In committee conferences and at crises demanding quick and aggressive action his deliberate, conciliatory attitude and diplomatic habit made him shrink from leading the attack on the fighting field, but did not disqualify him from recognizing and selecting fighters.

Mrs. Potter Palmer's interest in the Federation, which she served as one of its vice-presidents, is said to have dated back to her effort to have the World's Fair management grant "artisan diplomas" to recognize the skill of the craftsmen whose handiwork was a large part of the exhibit. As she succeeded in so doing only after the interest and co-operation of the trade unions had been enlisted, this experience may account for her inclination to promote the industrial department of the Federation. It may also have prompted her greeting to Thomas Morgan at one of the first committee meetings held after he was howled down while speaking at the mass meeting. I heard her say to him how pleased she was to meet him and how she had long hoped she might. Such genuinely respectful reciprocities, on equal terms, helped bridge the social chasm and give the right-of-way across to those on either side of the dangerous cleavage.

These early intermediary experiences led the Federation to call several national industrial conferences in Chicago to discuss from all sides right relations between workers and their employers, the trusts and public interests. The success of these conferences led its secretary, Ralph M. Easley, to resign in order to organize the National Civic Federation in New York City, entirely apart from the purpose, management, and procedure of the Chicago federation.

To meet the unemployment crisis an emergency call to one hundred charity and other organizations was issued December 9, 1893, to co-operate for the relief of poverty-stricken families and homeless men. The Relief and Aid Society joined with the lesser agencies of the city and the county government in constituting a co-operative committee which, on January 20, 1894, was organized as the Central Relief Association. When better times came on and the regular relief associations were adequate to meet the diminished demand, this emergency agency was disbanded.

When the Federation's Department of Philanthropy began to function again independently under the leadership of Mrs. Lucy L. Flower, she renewed its initiative by criticizing the wastefulness of the competitive administration of relief under the institutional management of restricted social cliques. Meanwhile, the more modern methods of the Charity Organization Society had demonstrated elsewhere the economy and efficiency of the more scientific case work, involving the co-operation of all existing agencies to secure the benefits of these modern methods of raising and disbursing relief funds, of registering and investigating applicants for relief, and of substituting employment for charity. Mrs. Flower led the Department in undertaking to build the experience of the Central Relief Association into the organization of a Bureau of Charities.

This brought her and others into conflict with the old-line Relief and Aid Society. Its four hundred contributors and their officials had assumed the monopoly of privately relieving the city's needy families, ever since the Society had effectively administered relief funds received from all parts of the land and the world after the great fire of 1871. This new claimant for adoption was rigidly excluded by the old-time possessors of the local fields for relief work. So far was this exclusion carried that when entering upon my sociological teaching in Chicago I was invited to meet the Relief and Aid Society directors, in a board meeting assembled, only to be admonished "to have nothing to do with the proposed Bureau of Charities" then being organized, "if I valued personal recognition and standing for my work in the city." Although acting to the contrary, I survived to see the new Bureau of Charities and the old Relief and Aid Society so peacefully joined together in the United Charities of Chicago through the successive leaderships of Ernest P. Bicknell and Sherman C. Kingsley that no man has risen to put them asunder, since the differences of their constituents are no longer discernible.

Among the achievements of far-reaching public significance due to Mrs. Flower's initiative was the deliverance of children from the improper care which they received at the county infirmary, by which new name the poor house at Dunning came to be called. There she found many normal children committed to the wards for the aged poor, and also in wards for the imbeciles and insane. The offer of privately supported

Catholic, Protestant, and Jewish institutions to care for them led to proper provision for both normal and subnormal dependent children at public expense.

The story of the way in which the County Commissioners were led to recognize their responsibilities under the law to care for foundlings illustrates the strategy to which private citizens had to resort to impress officials with the community's claim upon their service. Foundlings frequently had been left upon the threshold of the Home for the Friendless of which Mrs. Flower was one of the managers, as well as upon the doorsteps of private families. The police refused to take the children because "the city had no place for them and the county would not take them." Confronting the President and the executive committee of the County Commissioners with a foundling baby in the arms of a nurse, Mrs. Flower quietly remarked to these officials: "Believing it to be the duty of the County Board to care for such children, I have brought you a foundling left on our steps last night, and I now submit it to your care, since we are a private institution, not organized for the care of foundlings and cannot care for them." Motioning the nurse to put the baby on a chair in front of the President, she said, "Good afternoon, gentlemen," and turned to leave.

"You are not going to leave that child here, are you?" exclaimed the president.

"Certainly we are, that's just what we came for."

"Oh, wait!" he cried, "wait!" And while the little committee waited one of the officials was overheard to say "I guess they've got us."

Then she was asked, "What can we do with infants?"

And she replied, "It isn't my business to advise the County Board," and again started to leave.

After a private conference with his associates the President said, "I suppose you are right and we must take care of this child, but will you take this baby back to the Home and keep it until tomorrow if we agree to take it then?"

"We will do anything to accommodate you" was her comforting reply, and the next day they sent for the baby, having made a contract for the care of such cases.

Such discoveries of the plight of orphaned, dependent, and defective children led to the disclosures of the extent to which children were confined in the cells of police stations, the city prison, and the county jail, in close contact with vicious and criminal adults. Failing at first in the attempt to persuade the legislature to establish a state industrial school for delinquent boys, Mrs. Flower took the lead in raising a large fund to found the Glenwood Manual Training School, under private auspices with semi-public functions, for boys whose dependence imperils normal development. The care thus generously provided by Edward B. Butler and others led to the establishment of the state school, at St. Charles, Illinois.

As a member of the Chicago Board of Education Mrs. Flower had also worked back of all this, dealing with overt acts of delinquency. Truancy had to be dealt with as leading to, yet as less of a default than, delinquency. Therefore the Parental School for Truants was urged, and later adopted, as a part of the school discipline, forecasting the extension of this policy to include the employment of school nurses and the departments of child study and vocational guidance.

The recent establishment by the Chicago Board of Education of a special school for boys needing such special care as to put them out of adjustment with other grade schools succeeded in interesting them so well as to decrease the commitments of truants to the Parental School. It is hoped that learning by doing, thus exemplified, may be effective in reducing delinquency.

Latest, but perhaps the farthest reaching of all Mrs. Flower's achievements, was her leadership in securing the enactment by the legislature of Illinois, July 1, 1899, of a bill establishing the first juvenile-court law ever to be enacted anywhere. It was another triumph of women citizens over the tremendous odds of hope deferred by depressing delay, of public indifference, and of the hostility and jealousy of small politicians, some of whom knew that their fees in the old justice of the peace courts were at stake. To prepare for and conduct this campaign the Chicago Woman's Club was interested and enlisted, and the Every Day Club was organized by Mrs. Flower, aided by Mrs. Henrotin, Miss Addams and Miss Julia C. Lathrop of Hull House, and others. This small group of carefully selected women included representatives of professions, labor, and society. They functioned their own initiative by having other groups as guests, circuit-court judges, representative clergymen, teachers, and legislators among them. Catholic, Protestant, and Jewish institutions and their officials were counted in on the ground floor from the beginning of this effort, and were given full credit at the end for its achievement. One of the most venerated judges, Harvey B. Hurd, revised the first draft of the measure so as to insure its constitutionality. Its friends proved equal to the strenuous struggle to provide privately contributed funds to pay the salaries of probation officers and to rent quarters for a Detention Home, pending the persuasion of the legislature to provide appropriations for these features essential to the work of the court. They had been deliberately withheld when the bill was passed, in order to cripple, if not nullify, the operation of the act.

With the same devotion and alacrity with which she had responded to the call of every public responsibility and opportunity, Mrs. Flower withdrew from this service, which was dearer to her than her own life, to devote seven years to the tender and unremitting care of her husband during his illness. As happily for Chicago as for her, these highest qualities of citizenship which she exemplified were publicly recognized nine years after she had left the city by naming the first school devoted to preparing girls to enter the trades, the Lucy L. Flower Technical High School. Still more notably was the crowning service of her life recognized by the great gathering held at the City Club to commemorate the past achievements of the Juvenile Court and to forecast its future possibilities. In the quarter-century's retrospect no personality loomed larger, no one was more often or more appreciatively referred to, than Mrs. Flower, as the "mother of the Juvenile Court."

How much better these builders built than they could have known when building appeared at this conference. The surviving pioneers of the Juvenile Court movement, in their call for and conduct of the conference, claimed for it a future worthier of scientific guidance as its past achievements worthily called for commemoration.[1] This claim has been verified, and the expert guidance already enlisted assures a development which promises not only an increasingly scientific court procedure, but also a far better future for all character-building and correctional efforts.

So new is this kind of a court and so unlike others that perhaps it might better not have been called a court. Where it is intelligently conducted by wise and humane officials, it has a personnel and surroundings family-like in spirit, with a procedure as little like that of a tribunal as it could be made. In too many of the courts—probably a majority—there is as yet very inadequate understanding of what lies back of conduct disorders; so that children are summarily sent to institutions, or placed under poorly qualified and untrained probation officers. It will take more time and very persistent effort to bring the procedure in all juvenile courts up to the standard now set by some of them in larger cities. Nevertheless, in its essential spirit, changed point of view, and method, the juvenile court marks a great step forward.

As a regular function of the Chicago court, the psychiatric examination of the child was established to determine its normality and consequent degree of responsibility, as factors to be taken into account in the judicial and probationary dealing with it. Such a purpose should have designated this procedure at the initiative as that of "mental hygiene" and "child guidance," which terms have now come to designate the aims and methods of all such dealings with children. This scientific procedure soon stimulated modern psychiatric study of adult offenders coming before the criminal courts. It has since been applied to inmates of reformatories and penitentiaries. Early initiative and widespread advocacy were given this movement by Chief Justice Harry Olson of the Municipal Court of Chicago.

Noteworthy was the way in which the initial steps were taken to introduce this scientific procedure to Chicago's pio-

[1] *The Child, the Clinic and the Court* (a group of papers published by the *New Republic*, New York, 1925). Pp. 344.

neer Juvenile Court. Wherever and by whomsoever else the appeal for scientific inquiry may have been made, the practical demonstration needed to attach it to court procedure was undertaken in Chicago and spread thence. This demonstration originated with Mrs. William F. Dummer, another far-sighted, intrepid, public-spirited woman citizen of Chicago. Early in the nineties she was convinced that the connection between delinquency and such factors as the emotional instability, personal maladjustments, and mental defects of children could and should be scientifically studied. She, therefore, searched for an investigator both qualified and willing to devote his full time and best ability to the task. William Healy, then a young practicing physician, was found to be fitted for it by his scientific training and by his interest in, and aptitude for, the physiological and psychological research required. With freedom from financial care, privately provided by Mrs. Dummer, he began in 1909 his specialized studies of child life and his personal observations of such problem children as were referred to him for examination and advice by a parent, a teacher, or a judge. His aid soon came to be so indispensable to the Juvenile Court that he was offered deskroom in its building. After six years of this privately provided, semi-official service, the county of Cook in 1914 took over the Juvenile Psychopathic Institute with Dr. Healy as director, and made it a constituent part of the Juvenile Court.

Meanwhile, he had begun the collection of case material, which in quantity and quality had never before been available. Opportunity to use this data for publication came when he became the director of the Judge Baker Foundation, which was established at Boston for privately conducted research, as a memorial to Massachusetts' first juvenile-court judge. The pioneer volume, of a notable series issuing from this source, was entitled *The Individual Delinquent*, which was announced as "a textbook of diagnosis and prognosis for all concerned with understanding offenders." The briefer monographs which followed bore such titles as *Pathological Lying, Accusation and Swindling, Honesty, and Mental Conflicts and Misconducts*—indicating how far beyond the application of psychopathic technique Dr. Healy extended his methods and conclusions.

Long before he left his work in the Juvenile Court in Chicago he affirmed that "it would be much better, in my opinion, not to call this a psychopathic institute. Of the problems studied many are not at all psychopathic, nor do we commit ourselves to the idea that all problems of conduct belong to the realm of psychopathology." So original and scientifically sane have been Dr. Healy's contributions to the literature of these allied subjects that investigators and authors, educators, court officials, those enlisted in child welfare and other lines of social work, as well as many parents, have been inspired and influenced by what is recognized to be his epoch-making investigations and writings.

When in 1917 this department of the Juvenile Court at Chicago was taken over by the state of Illinois, it was called the Institute for Juvenile Research and was placed under the direction of Dr. Herman Adler, who left his professorship of psychiatry in the Harvard Medical School to become the state criminologist of Illinois.

The rapid and diversified extension of the scientific service here rendered indicates the country-wide progress which it is destined to make. Within the past decade its staff has grown from the director and two assistants to over eighty. Resident or visiting mental-health officers are attached to all the correctional institutions of the state. Permanently located and traveling clinics furnish full-unit staffs to welfare organizations and schools in Chicago and fourteen cities. Individual specialists are sent where special help is needed. Popular instruction is widely spread through institutes held at Better Baby conferences and at county fairs, where mental tests are given to six thousand children in the course of the summer. Technical training to equip recruits for professional service is offered university graduates and advanced students, who share the unique value of these clinics and the data they have accumulated. Research in the central problems of human behavior is provided by the Behavior Research Fund of $275,000, which was contributed by public-spirited citizens to be expended under Dr. Adler's direction within five years.

Two Behavior Research Fund monographs have been published by the University of Chicago Press, a technical study of *Brain Mechanisms and Intelligence*, by K. S. Lashley, and a survey of more than local significance, on *Delinquency Areas* by Clifford R. Shaw and assistants. To this extensive and intensive degree has the Illinois initiative already developed —and the end is far out of sight.

The reach into the future which the scientific study of the sources of behavior is making may be indicated by recent developments. During the past five years or more the Commonwealth Fund of New York carried out a program of study designed for the prevention of delinquency. It, however, was extended to cover a far broader range. With the co-operation of the National Committee for Mental Hygiene, demonstration child-guidance clinics were conducted in a number of cities, and consultant service was made available in several others. As a result, locally financed clinics were established in eleven cities. The program also laid emphasis on the work of visiting teachers and its value in the study and treatment of children who present problems of schooling and behavior. The National Committee of Visiting Teachers, specially organized for the purpose, conducted demonstrations of visiting teacher service in the public-school system of thirty communities, twenty-four of which organized this work on the basis of complete local support. This committee was also enabled to offer demonstrations of visiting-teacher service at a number of training schools for teachers. The New York School of Social Work was enabled to offer fellowships and practice work for those wishing to be trained as psychiatric social workers and as visiting teachers.

Following this five-year program the Commonwealth Fund established in New York City an Institute for Child Guidance. In addition to the study and treatment of children presenting behavior problems, and the conduct of research, the specific objective of the Institute is to provide training in practical child guidance work, and also in psychiatric social work for students from the New York and Smith College schools of social work, both of which are enabled to offer fellowships for this purpose. Fellowships are available for psychiatrists and graduate psychologists, awarded by the National Committee for Mental Hygiene.

As a part of the original program, a joint committee, including the executives of the co-operating organizations, was constituted by the Commonwealth Fund to promote the coordination of those various activities and to issue publications interpreting the methods and results of the program. It was gratifying to me to have my son, Graham Romeyn Taylor, selected to serve as the executive director of the committee and later as the director of the Commonwealth Fund's Division of Publication.

The profound significance of these far-reaching movements, emanating from the initiatives given the Juvenile Court and its institute in Chicago, is thus impressively estimated by Judge Charles W. Hoffman of the Juvenile Court at Cincinnati, in a recent article on "The Juvenile Court, the Community and Child Guidance Clinics":

In the enactment of the Juvenile Court codes for the first time the criminal procedure and punishment were abolished. Delinquency was defined as a status and not a crime. Under the old law, children were held to be responsible, wicked, deserving of punishment; they were sent to jails, reformatories, penitentiaries and in some instances they were hanged. It was finally realized that all this not only resulted in a tremendous sacrifice of childhood, but threatened the very foundations of social order. . . . . When it is comprehended in its fullness by the public, and the American Bar particularly, the way will be open for the conservation of the best potentialities of the childhood of our country.

CHAPTER VI

TRAIL-BREAKERS THROUGH POLITICAL JUNGLES

N O SOONER had progressive policies been initiated by the Civic Federation of Chicago to deal with the emergent problems of relieving the destitute and providing for child welfare than projects for coping with these and other menacing evils were found to be thwarted by public officials. In all its initial efforts the municipal committee ran head-on into politics. Its clean-up campaign could not be carried further than upon a few show streets in the centr shopping district. The public health could not be protec d from basement bakeries, unsafe milk, and inadequate est-house provisions to isolate contagious diseases. Mu n less could any hope be held out to secure better and cheaper gas or to rescue the lake front from the aggressive claims of private corporations upon the riparian rights to the extending shore line of made land.

The delay, evasion, and opposition encountered centered at the City Hall. To counteract the corruption and inefficiency in the City Council and its administrative departments was the problem facing the city. So, special subcommittees were appointed to secure better legislation from the state, including the civil-service law, a corrupt practices act, state control of party primaries, better revenue laws, and a new city charter—all of which proved to be for a long while well out of reach.

Meanwhile, the political-action committee reported election frauds and some arrests, convictions, and penalties it had helped secure. But it was timidly cautious not to interfere with the stand-pat loyalty demanded by "the organization" controlling both parties, to which their voters blindly yielded. Forming primary voters' leagues was the only suggestion then ventured. The first widely circulated appeal to agitate and act toward this end was addressed to the pastors of the city churches.

They were urged "to make the subject the theme of discourse and exhortation" on a Sunday when caucuses and primaries were close at hand.

Only a week after this appeal to piety to be patriotic had been heard from the few pulpits whose preachers heeded it all good citizens were shocked by an attack upon public rights which was as arousing to local civic patriotism as were the shots that "rang round the world" from Lexington, and those that were fired at Fort Sumter. This shot was aimed point blank at the rights of all the people in the public streets. It was fired from the City Hall by aldermen who conspired with those bribing them to do so. Forty-three of them voted franchises to new public-utility corporations—the Ogden Gas and the Cosmopolitan Electric companies. Although ostensibly aimed to compete with well-established lighting and transportation companies, these franchises were really intended to force them to buy off the pirates. To recoup the ransom levied upon them, the rates paid by the people for these necessities would inevitably be raised.

But there were patriots standing in the breach—eighteen of them. These loyal aldermen stood there the more bravely because hopelessly resisting the jeering gang, intent only upon jamming their corrupt measures through to enactment. In vain their three valiant spokesmen challenged the boodlers, charging them with high-handed violation of the city charter and the rules of the Council in withholding the names of the individuals constituting these unknown corporations, in granting them valuable privileges without compensation due the city, and in taking action without previous notice, investigation, or discussion.

These three spokesmen, John H. Hamline, James Robert Mann, and William Kent, deserve honorable mention, as the lonely leaders of those whom they rallied to stand with them and after them, against the traitorous spoilsmen of the commonwealth. Foremost among them was Hamline. For several years the stature of this educated, clear-sighted, courageous man stood out alone against the dark shadows cast by the cringing or overbearing parasitic figures surrounding him in the City Council. He had only fairly gotten his foothold in the practice of the law when he enlisted in this diverting and exacting civic service. In the council chamber he stood erect on two feet, looking every other man straight in the eye, single handed and alone, to represent and serve the great honest majority of his fellow-citizens. He stood there simply as the citizen he was, daring to be nothing less yet asking no credit for being anything more. Craving the fellowship of right-minded citizens in leading the forlorn hope against corruption within and apathy without the council chamber, he worked away with little help from these fellow-citizens and sometimes against their opposition. In time, however, he saw enough of them rally to enact the civil-service law, and still later, more of them unite in voters' leagues. Yet the organized work of these bodies neither discharged Mr. Hamline from personal service nor measured what he individually undertook to do. And he did what he undertook, not only because he had the right to be heard, but also because the state, as well as the city, had a right to hear from him as a citizen.

The most far-reaching service Mr. Hamline rendered, however, was by his example and personal influence to inspire a small group of capable young citizens to take active interest in public affairs. One such was James R. Mann, another young attorney, who worthily exemplified the spirit of his leader through two terms in the City Council. It was he who bore the brunt of attack and defense in challenging the gang's boldest raid. This Council experience and reputation led to his long and brilliant career as a member of Congress and speaker of the House of Representatives. It was his campaign for re-election that stirred William Kent to take part in the politics of his ward, although previously he had enlisted in the struggle for the reform of the civil service. When surprised by being urged to run for alderman, he won his seat in the City Council against the opposition of the machine leaders of his own party. They had been antagonized by his refusal to promise the patronage demanded by them for appointments to city jobs as rewards or retainers for party service. On taking his seat in the Council, Alderman Kent was warned by Mr. Mann "to attack all vicious measures but never to attack men, as it was poor policy in politics to make one's self personally disliked." But we shall see a little later how the fight grew too fierce for these amenities to be observed by the young champion after such a novitiate as now stirred his fighting spirit.

The Sunday following the grab of the gang in the City Council, Central Music Hall was again the scene of such an uprising as few other places of assembly have witnessed, except Boston's old Faneuil H. and Philadelphia's Independence Hall. This time the call came from within the body politic. But citizens could scarcely wait until the sixth day after the outrage in the council chamber denounce it. Not only adherents of the Federation respond to its call, but those allied with a hundred other organizations and thousands more besieged the doors, broke through the police lines after the hall was crowded, filled a neighboring armory for an overflow meeting, and still clamored for admission to both assemblies.

Lyman J. Gage was again presiding, with a dignified repose quite consistent with his self-poise and control of the situation, yet contrasting so strongly with the uproar of the multitude as more vividly to display the vehemence of the speakers and the excitement which responded to it. The one hundred and fifty vice-chairmen, of whom I was one, could claim no more distinction than to be announced from the chair as "representing every phase of the town's decency." Then the speaking began. The first thunder of applause answered a business man's ringing call "for men not partisans." It continued as he said, "Robbers belong to no party." The next speaker's claim that as a criminal lawyer he had "a right to speak in this case against the City Fathers" was greeted with cries, "That's right! Give it to them!" This prompted him to answer. "We have no offices, no patronage to offer, but only the power of intelligent public opinion." A more eminent attorney, John W. Ela, calmed his hearers enough to listen to his plea for civil service as fundamental to the political and administrative reform. From the platform where he preached Sundays to Central Church, Dr. Newell Dwight Hillis declared: "This city, which has been praised since the World's Fair in every foreign land, today is touched with infamy and its citizens are smarting under the sense of deep personal disgrace."

The more radical demand for the public ownership of public utilities by Henry D. Lloyd was significantly greeted with long applause. "At last," he said, "the people see the system that makes private property for private profit for a few out of that which belongs to the whole people and should be operated for the profit only of the whole body of people. Inherently vicious, rotten fruit, are these gigantic fortunes of gas trusts, street railways and other monopolies, which are discarded elsewhere in our own and foreign lands." In so saying he gave impetus to an agitation for municipal ownership that has been a political issue for which great majorities have voted in Chicago ever since. This declaration of his, and many another before and since spoken and printed, carried further because of his influential family connections, his wealth, and his social democratic loyalties. The climax of enthusiasm was elicited by Rev. P. S. Henson, a prominent local pastor noted for his witty and exuberant platform oratory. Reversing the story of Nebuchadnezzar's image with a head of gold and feet of clay, Chicago was likened to a giantess "with feet of gold and head of mud." This was greeted with roars of laughter and prolonged applause.

At last a man stood forth on this occasion whose pen was as incisive as his platform speech, whose legal ability and experience qualified him to apply sound judgment in distinctive public service then and ever since through his strenuous years. Sigmund Zeisler had already won distinction as chief assistant corporation counsel. He had volunteered valuable assistance in organizing and guiding the Civic Federation, and so was rarely equipped to fulfil the public responsibilities awaiting his further spirited response to civic duty. It was he who suggested and shaped the anti-trust clause amendment to the franchise ordinances whereby they could be declared null and void. And it was he who, a year later, drew the deadly parallel between Mayor John P. Hopkins' corrupt approval of the two boodle ordinances and his previous message vetoing them.

But neither did this inconsistency of the mayor nor the hissing disapproval of the galleries and the street throngs around the City Hall deter fifty-two of the seventy aldermen from voting the substitute electric-franchise ordinance. With still more brazen contempt for common honesty and public opinion, the privileges granted by this ordinance were publicly offered for sale two days after its passage.

It was Mr. Zeisler's full report on this whole procedure that furnished the Federation with the compelling argument for taking political action. A year before the action taken at the great meeting of protest was phrased in these general terms:

Resolved by citizens of all parties and classes in mass meeting assembled, That we denounce the City Council's grant to unknown parties the right to use practically all that remains of our public thoroughfare in reckless disregard of public rights. We honor the aldermen who conscientiously resisted by voice and vote the consummation of this iniquity. Every alderman who voted for these ordinances should be relegated to private life. We call upon the mayor to protect the city by vetoing these franchise ordinances. We recommend a legislative inquiry, also closest scrutiny of aldermanic candidates. For the preservation of municipal purity, prosperity and property, subordination to parties must give way to higher sentiments of civic patriotism.

A year later, convinced of the futility of generalizing appeals, the Federation decided to organize a non-partisan municipal league in preference to the proposal of some of its members to form a permanent municipal-reform party. This decision defined the policy of independent action within and across party lines, in adherence to which Chicago has acquired all the political and administrative gains since achieved. The object of the proposed league was stated to be:

To secure the nomination and election of aggressively honest and capable men for all city offices; to secure a just and equitable assessment of property appraised so that all property shall pay its fair proportion of taxes; to protect the rights of the people in the streets of Chicago and particularly to prevent the granting of additional transportation and lighting licenses to private corporations without provision for full compensation to the city, and upon condition that the same shall revert to the city in a reasonable time to the end that the city shall acquire and operate these utilities in addition to its water plant.

Although left free to act independently of the Federation, the league was tied up to a governing central committee of one hundred, including two from each ward and thirty selected at large. But before appointing it the organizers searched for a month to find a leader. When they found him he would serve only with an executive committee of nine and a secretary, all selected by himself. George E. Cole proved to be indeed a pioneer leader although he reported himself to be only "a second-class business man in the stationery business." Attention was called to him as a citizen who had been effectively active in working with a branch of the Federation in his ward. He told me that his civic conscience had been aroused into action by what he heard and saw at William T. Stead's Central Music Hall meeting. Then past fifty years of age and without any previous experience, he started to do what needed to be done nearest at hand in the politics of his own ward. He might have been remembered also for trying in vain to delay the Federation's previous indorsement of some candidates for public office, in order, as he said, that "the members might acquaint themselves with the qualifications of the nominee by investigations more thorough than that central body had ever contemplated." He is reported to have said to those who put up to him the leadership of the league: "There is no use sloshing around as has been done for years, but the only thing to do is to get a club, roll up your sleeves and wade in." This he did although he was little more than five feet high, but as someone said, "He knows he is no taller yet that he is tall enough."

When he concluded to "play the game," he first of all cleared his way by arranging the affairs of his printing and stationery business so that he could be absent for six weeks from his office. For the executive committee he chose a lawyer, a trade-union leader, a capitalist, a business man at the head of a great printing plant and another prominent in real estate. For his secretary and confidential investigator he chose a young attorney, Hoyt King. For advisers he relied upon Alderman Kent; Allen B. Pond, an architect; and Edwin Burritt Smith, an able lawyer whose legal caution kept courage the more aggressive for being within the limits of the

law. Thus on Lincoln's Birthday, February 12, 1896, the
Municipal Voters' League of Chicago was launched on its
course of direct action.

At the instance of the Rev. Jenkin Lloyd Jones, pastor of
All Souls Church and the intrepid spokesman for free speech
and social justice, Mr. Smith thus vividly reviewed the events
which led to the organization of this league:

> Three-fourths of the city council band themselves together to plunder
> the public and blackmail corporations. They sell every public right for
> which the purchaser can be found, and have organized a syndicate to hold
> the ordinance until a purchaser can be found. Spoilsmen's growing disre-
> gard for public opinion finally produced its effect. Private citizens slowly
> came to realize that even their personal interests were in danger, that there
> was a close relation between public and private interests, and that every
> man owes something in the nature of knightly service to the public. This
> led to the National Civil Service law. By 1894 the truth had taken deep
> root in Chicago. Private citizens had become aroused by the disgrace and
> danger of leaving the public interests of Chicago to a lot of common
> scoundrels. The Civil Service Law of 1895 prepared the way for the divorce
> of our municipal government from national politics—a separation which
> public opinion should at once decree and force. The aldermanic elections
> of 1895 were held in due time. The last appeal to the politicians had failed.
> A very few honest men were chosen to associate with a lot of the worst
> scoundrels ever gathered in one place outside the penitentiary. They bar-
> tered public franchises and blackmailed private interests. It was in the
> face of these conditions that a conference of citizens resulted in the organ-
> ization of the Municipal Voters' League.

More than to any man among its inner counselors the Civic
Federation owed to Edwin Burritt Smith the results of its
work that proved to be most effective. He made its political
initiative possible by making the Municipal Voters' League
practicable, as it could not have been if controlled either by
the Federation or by a delegated Central Committee of One
Hundred. No one aware of the risks incurred in leading such
an aggressive agency would have dared to undertake the responsibility without having a very few personally selected,
practically experienced colleagues, upon whose confidence,
judgment, and courage he could implicitly rely.

Not only was he legally well qualified to safeguard the
League's actions and publications from illegal extremes and
libelous publicity, but so rare was his power of analysis and

so clear was his literary style that his revision of the League's findings were as forcible to the average newspaper-reader as his articles on national affairs were appreciated by the readers of the *Atlantic Monthly*. Busily as he was engaged in his law office and in the courts, he always took time and spent all the strength required to participate in the committee meetings of the League and in public hearings at the City Hall and the state capitol. Freely and ably he responded to many calls to censor or write reports, deliver addresses, publish articles on the civil-service reform and anti-imperialism, as well as on municipal affairs. He also actively served as trustee and personal adviser of Chicago Commons and other agencies, social, charitable, and religious. No patriots ever offered wartime sacrifices in the defense of their country on any battlefield greater than Edwin Burritt Smith made at the altar of civic patriotism. Under the white heat of these civic emergencies through which he served his city he burnt out his devoted life at the prime of his maturity and before he could fully round out the distinction which his professional career promised.

Through the four most critical years of the League's campaigning George E. Cole stood foremost on the first line of action. He entered the first campaign, reporting to the citizens that after thorough investigation fifty-seven of the aldermen were found to be grafters—"a pack of gray wolves," they came to be called—and that several of the thirteen others were of doubtful character. The citizens surprised themselves and the League in registering their answer at the polls by electing twenty-two of the twenty-nine candidates indorsed by the League. Of the six aldermen re-elected two were indorsed, only two were opposed, and two had no fit opponents between whom and them any discrimination could be made.

In crediting the League's victory to Mr. Cole's leadership, the *Chicago Herald* graphically described him under the editorial title "Scalper Cole Happy" in these words of exuberant appreciation:

G. E. Cole, the political buzz-saw and threshing machine, did it. He refuses the credit. He gives the victory to the independent newspapers. A modest general who believes men with guns are equal sharers with the

commander in the glory of the battle. This man Cole is a rich find. He is as
hard as a billiard ball. He is about as big as Napoleon. There is not an
office he would accept on a silver platter or any other way. The independent
papers were at his side. A great wave of public sentiment was at his back.
He did everything other reformers had not done. He went home at sunset
last night with a string of neatly lifted scalps, extending from the Indiana
line to Evanston. This terror, the buzz-saw, did not get out a band to celebrate. He had his eye on another bad roost. He simply turned out the
light in the Municipal Voters' League sawmill and went home to talk it
over with his wife. It was the first practical hard-hitting reform movement
this town ever saw. The result is only the prophecy of the changes which
the same tactics may produce.

Through all these strenuous years Mr. Cole was as steady
in judgment as he was sturdy in stature, as open minded as he
was indomitably determined, as much in good fellowship
personally to those from whom he differed as in principle he
had the courage of conviction, as generous in giving credit to
others as he was willing to assume full responsibility for publishing the truth and the significance of the facts concerning
men and measures inimical to public welfare.

The next campaign was so much more complicated by
issues with party machines and with long-established utility
corporations as to be far more exacting upon the League
leaders than were its victorious struggles hitherto. But the
League stood the test. Of the twenty-seven outgoing aldermen who were reported to have bad records, twelve tried to
regain their seats, only three succeeded, nine being decisively
defeated. One-third of the Council lined up with the League.
While its leaders with patient courage also stood the test to
which the exhausting struggle subjected them, it wore some
of them out and bore most heavily upon their leader. While
the inroads upon his business moved George Cole only to tell
his corporation customers who withheld their orders to in-
timidate him that they "could go to hell" (though he assured
me he "tried to be a Christian"), the undermining of his
health he could not ignore. His resignation left to his survivors not only a heritage of reputation hard to maintain, but
also overlapping problems that inspired future policies.

Cole was far from being through with bearing public burdens, for he soon became one of the founders and president

of the Legislative Voters' League, in order to secure legislators more honest and capable of serving the whole state than a majority of them had proved to be in legislating for the city of Chicago. After fourscore years and ten he is still among the wisest counselors of the old Citizens' Association, which has taken over the executive functions of the Legislative Voters' League. Here again is exemplified the way in which Chicago's truest citizens stay on their jobs.

Meanwhile, the Executive Committee had been recruited, I with other advisers having been added to succeed retiring members and bring the membership up to nine. Alderman Kent accepted the presidency after his term in the Council expired and Allen B. Pond, a well-known architect, became secretary. During his successive terms the reports of the League bear the impress of Kent's militant Council career, which he carried on and still further out in the campaigns he led. And the language of these reports bear the imprint of his aldermanic vernacular, censored, however, by the more cautious but no less courageous attorney Smith.

This lingo he acquired in exchanging personal amenities with his fellow-aldermen. In debate personalities flew thick and fast, since they neither knew nor felt any other way of warfare. Although this was contrary to the council etiquette which he had been cautioned to observe as an intruding reformer, yet after the meetings he made friends of some of the enemies, especially those who were helpless to defend themselves against the shafts of his satire and wit, which, however stinging, were greeted by roars of laughter from those who enjoyed the fun even at each other's expense.

What Kent learned in discovering what was going on among the City Fathers, especially under their partnerships in the underworld, added to his influence with them both when in the Council and on the League. To this end he was assisted by a derelict, who was wise to the ways of the political underworld, known as "Doc Greene." His long-continued scouting service, devotedly true to his sincere friendship with Kent, received honorable mention in a unique tribute, inimitably Kentian in style, which the Chicago Literary Club appreciatively heard under the title "Me and Doc Greene."

One of Doc Greene's underworld intimates was Alderman Michael Kenna, of the First Ward, long and widely known as "Hinky Dink." He gained and retained continuously his seat in the Council by rounding up the floating voters and voting floaters whose votes held the balance of power and usually constitute the majority of the rooming- and lodging-house population scattered through the central business section of the city. Kent's knowledge of the underworld, and his fair fighting with its vice-lords and grafters, won the alderman's respect which grew into a friendship. Long after both had left the Council and had been parted by distance, he proudly confided to me his loyalty to his colleague, exclaiming, "There never has been a better alderman than Billy Kent."

After public attention had been fixed upon the bold way in which the city's rights and the people's property were bartered for private gain, and after some of the more notorious aldermanic franchise brokers lost their seats in their stock exchange at the City Hall, the surviving boodlers more and more took to cover. Ordinances that offered a margin of profits were more carefully drawn, and offers were sought at private sales. Therefore the League was obliged to seek the evidence upon which to base its reports along winding trails outside the council chambers. Some of these trails led to the offices of prominent business men, and their corporation attorneys, bankers, and newly acquired newspapers.

Neither Mr. Cole nor any of his successors, however, were burdened so much by encountering the enemy in the open field, nor their accomplices in these business offices, as by fellow-citizens who fired criticism, as from ambush. This they did in attempting to exculpate discredited officials and to exonerate grafting corporations. During the first campaign an open letter was published warning the League to have hands off these more than suspected gentry. Scarcely more to the direct charges against them was the voters' ratification due than to the League's outspoken challenge in reply to the forty-nine prominent citizens who signed this letter, among whom were some judges and clergymen. The town was stirred by the League's asking the public, over the heads of these apologetic citizens: "What can be the conditions in the city when men like you thus justify getting something for nothing?"

William Kent also took occasion to remind his fellow Yale alumni in like manner:

There are not two kinds of citizens, "good citizens and bad citizens." There are just "citizens" and enemies to the community. They will not be villains with dyed mustaches, nor will they all be dirty tramps that can be locked up in jail. You must learn to recognize them among the well-to-do of your acquaintances; some of them are men of influence and standing, men who are pious church members and good fathers. These enemies will be of your own house.

At Yale, Kent was an outstanding man among his fellow-students, as he continued to be among the alumni, noted for his originality, independence, and wit and also for his keen appreciation and cultivation of literary standards. This culture he maintained while acquiring the vernacular of his political associates, his use of which in ways all his own surprised those from whom he learned it. Although as heir and manager of a family heritage he associated with the propertied class on equal terms, he courted neither their favor nor that of the wage-earners in maintaining the rugged democracy of his manhood and citizenship.

Later as earlier, to conserve his always limited reserve strength he went into the open for his recreation, ranching and hunting in the Far West, finally removing to his California estates in the foothills of Mount Tamalpais. There he re-enlisted in national politics and was elected to represent his congressional district at Washington. In committees and on the floor of the House he made his mark in debate and upon progressive legislation, during a single term. While defeated in his campaign for election to the United States Senate, he spread and strengthened the progressive cause by his speeches throughout the state.

Urging in Congress, and in his campaigning, the protection of the public domain and its natural resources from predatory exploiters, he prompted an influentially signed protest to President Harding against the appointment of Albert B. Fall as secretary of the interior. Had it been heeded the Teapot Dome and other scandals which disgraced the nation might have been averted.

Exemplifying his patriotic propaganda for the dedication of distinctively rare and beautiful areas to the healthful recreational use of the people, Kent purchased the great grove of redwoods on the slope of Mount Tamalpais, across the bay from San Francisco, just as it was about to be cut into shingles and railway ties. Offering to donate it to the National Park Service, he urged its prompt acceptance to prevent the valley from being flooded as a commercial reservoir. The only condition of his offer was that the grove should be known as Muir Woods in honor of the great naturalist, John Muir. The correspondence that sealed its acceptance is characteristic alike of William Kent and President Roosevelt. The President wrote:

My DEAR MR. KENT,

I thank you most heartily for this singularly generous and public spirited action on your part. All Americans who prize the natural beauties of the country and wish to see them preserved and undamaged, and especially those who realize the literally unique value of the groves of giant trees, must feel that you have conferred a lasting benefit upon the whole country. I have a very great admiration for John Muir, but after all, my dear sir, this is your gift, and I should greatly like to name it the Kent Monument if you will permit it.

Mr. Kent replied:

My DEAR MR. PRESIDENT,

I thank you from the bottom of my heart for your message of appreciation and hope and believe that it will strengthen me to go on in an attempt to save more of the precious and vanishing glories of Nature for a people too slow of perception. Your kind suggestion of a change in name is not one that I can accept. So many millions of better people have died forgotten that to stencil one's own name on a benefaction seems to carry with it an implication of mundane immortality as being somewhat purchasable. I have five good husky boys that I am trying to bring up to a knowledge of democracy and to a realizing sense of the rights of the other fellow, doctrines which you, sir, taught to more vigor and effect than any other man in my time. If these boys cannot keep the name of Kent alive, I am willing it should be forgotten.

To this sentiment Theodore Roosevelt made this response:

By George! You are right. It is enough to do the deed and not to desire, as you say, to "stencil one's own name on the benefaction." Good for you and for the five boys who are to keep the name of Kent alive! I have four who I hope will do the same thing by the name of Roosevelt.

After Kent died in 1928 a tablet was placed on one of the trees by members of walking clubs, no one of whom contributed more than twenty-five cents. It reads:

WILLIAM KENT

Who Gave These Woods and Other
Natural Beauty Sites to Perpetuate
Them for People Who Love the Out-of-Doors
1864   TAMALPAIS CENTER CLUB   1928

His last public act was to deed to the state of California the virgin Redwood Forest tract of two hundred acres, known as the Steep Ravine, as his contribution toward a Mount Tamalpais State Park, adjoining Muir Woods. Previously he had given the state a tract of one hundred and thirty acres of redwoods, now known as Kent Grove, toward the acquisition of the finest growths of *Sempervirens sequoias*, through which the Redwood Highway runs. It is noteworthy that the earliest of these gifts was made when Kent was still under the stress and strain of political combat in Chicago. It was also when his friend and fellow-citizen, Stephen Tyng Mather, was entering upon his promotion of the National Park Service, to the distinguished administration of which he so generously gave not only his gifts but himself for twelve years.

In searching with my friend Kent through his files for relics of his fight with Chicago's "gray wolves," I found the following lines, which gave token of his scholarly and spiritual aspirations while under the dust and heat of those drastic struggles:

MAN'S PLACE

Infinite purpose Eternal,
Thou who hast placed me firm on the gravestone of ages,
Strong my foundation.
Take me, hand, brain, nerve and sinew,
Use me, crush me,
Grant that I leave to the future some mite of my doing.

Allen B. Pond, while by birth and acquirement qualified to enjoy and serve the fine arts, demonstrated what the scholar could be and do in practical politics by his proficiency not only on the Municipal Voters' League's Executive Committee, but also in serving very many other organizations promoting the social, cultural, and artistic progress of the city. This he did while under the professional exactions of the architectural firm of Pond & Pond, widely known for its distinctive designing of buildings for educational, social, and residential uses. He made his occupation subservient and tributary to his higher calling of citizenship, rendering distinctive service for city planning and on the city's Zoning Commission. No citizen of his generation served his city with more unselfish devotion, more unflinching courage, or to better purpose than he. Both the privileged circles in which he moved and the people's causes with which he identified himself have profited by what he brought from one to the other.

While the League kept out of mayoralty campaigns, in strictly adhering to its single purpose to secure the election of aggressively honest and capable aldermen, yet it became involved in the issues of such elections. This was the case when one of the reform aldermen, John Maynard Harlan, a Princeton University man, famous as a football player, was running as an independent candidate for mayor in protest against an attempt to secure legislative acts extending street railway and other franchises indefinitely and upon terms unjust to the city. From the stump in his city-wide whirlwind campaign he "threw the fat in the fire" in this bold way. Young attorney that he was, Harlan had the audacity to call the roll of eminent citizens who were directors of these corporations, naming them one by one, as though they were on the witness stand. After pretending to swear them in, he credited each one with eminence in business, social, and professional circles. Then he proceeded to ask them if they knew that their agents were "conspiring with public officials to commit grand larceny in burglarizing the city of Chicago." "You know it, now that we are telling you," he cried, and "can stop the robbery if you will."

This play to his crowd may have defeated him by aligning the more conventional majority against him. But he polled seventy thousand votes, taking enough from the Republican candidate to re-elect the younger Carter H. Harrison mayor, who in this term and in two succeeding ones kept the traders of the Council from betraying the city into the hands of legislative conspirators.

The third group of League officials were of the same fine, strong fiber. Charles R. Crane, who succeeded to its presidency, is another rare exemplar of the democracy of wealth to which Chicago owes much of its civic progress. His father, Richard T. Crane, was a real captain of industry. To his captaincy of the great Crane Company, manufacturers, he rose through every department of its works, which he founded, and through every stage of its development into its world-wide extension. Inheriting the democratic convictions of his father, with none of his rugged self-assertion, the son acquired a broader culture and social spirit. His family name and his connection with the Crane Company brought prestige to the personnel of the Municipal Voters' League, which then and since needed such personal service as he gave it far more than the financial contributions of its friends. Not only during his years of service on its Executive Committee and as its president, but at other times and in many ways he served the League and the city.

When the Police Department became notoriously corrupt and inefficient, he brought to his home town a detective police officer of New York City, Piper by name, who was given leave of absence to help Mr. Crane prove to the city administration and the citizens of Chicago the lack of discipline and honesty in the Police Department here. His report lacked none of the specific statements of fact that the accused officials might have demanded as proof. It cited days and hours, numbers of officers' caps and stars, places when and where they were and had no right to be, saloons and vice resorts patronized by them or regularly visited, presumably as collectors for "higher-ups." It turned the Department inside out and upside down—"Piperized" it was said then and since!

The breadth of his democratic spirit, and the extent and variety of his beneficence no one knows but himself, if indeed he has not forgotten most of it. It ranges from the University of Chicago and the Marine Biological Laboratory at Woods

Hole, Massachusetts, to the American College for Girls at Constantinople; from the Woman's Trade Union League and Chicago Commons to the earlier Russian revolutionists and later refugees; from close confidential relations with President Woodrow Wilson to special diplomatic services in Russia, Turkey, and as American Minister to China.

Outstanding most prominently among the officials of the League was Walter L. Fisher. While establishing his practice and reputation in the legal profession, he became secretary of the League when Crane was president and succeeded him in that office. His administration is to be credited with the more constructive policies upon which its work has proceeded ever since. To him also are due some of its more permanent achievements, not only in defeating unscrupulous opposition but in accomplishing abiding results. While at first the League waited to report upon candidates until their party nominations were announced, it was soon found necessary to influence the nominating procedure. Warnings and encouragements were issued before the primaries, advising voters in the several wards of what choices they might have at the polls. Candidates while seeking nomination appeared before the League to gain its support. In one campaign all the members of a party caucus came to the League's headquarters to secure for their good candidate its exoneration from the accusations of a slanderous opponent.

Although advantage was gained by thus pushing the line of attack closer to the sources of power, yet still more aggressive tactics were assumed for the strategy of the League. The abler members of the Council, who were elected by the influence of the League, for a long while were kept from effectively functioning by the discrimination against them in the appointments of committees and chairmen. Therefore the League persuaded those aldermen whom it had indorsed to hold a caucus for the nomination of the committees. For several years the slates thus nominated succeeded in securing better appointments with the help of successive mayors, who thus sought to promote the efficiency of their administration. This led the League to initiate state legislation for a nonpartisan aldermanic ballot. Since this enactment the office of alderman has been regarded more and more as independent of party significance and control, although partisan support continues to be given to candidates preferred by the organization. Hope is thus inspired for the recognition of the office of mayor as also non-partisan.

This later gain demonstrated, as had many earlier losses, the need of bringing the state legislature to protect and promote the city's vital interests. Again, however, it was in self-defense that its public-spirited citizens rallied at the state capitol. The League's struggle also shifted from the City Council to the state legislature, where its leaders unofficially stood aggressively with other fellow-citizens on the first line of defense. The issues pending were over traction and gas franchises. These and other special interests were found to be formidably intrenched with bipartisan support in both Houses.

Charles T. Yerkes was in command of the general situation. In the East and for several years in Chicago he had proved himself to be a past master in public-utility reorganization and in manipulating legislation of the "special-interest brand" for the benefit of such corporations. He had acquired control of the street-railway management in Chicago and needed the enactment of the pending bills he had introduced in order to carry out his far-reaching schemes. Following his personal slogan that "every man had his price," he found that neither a majority of the Chicago aldermen nor Mayor Harrison were in the market. So he transferred his brokerage to the state capitol.

The franchises, enabling acts for which he sought, were for such long terms as to be virtually perpetual. While the correspondents of all the other Chicago papers strangely reported these bills as more favorable to the city than to the traction interests, George C. Sikes in his dispatch to the *Chicago Daily News* laid bare the injustice which Chicago would suffer if these exploiting measures were enacted. The indignation aroused by this exposure of their intent and the corruption it involved precipitated a battle royal at the state capitol. The bosses of both political parties, including the Governor and a United States senator, gave Chicago's mayor and citizens an ultimatum to accept the pending bill. Chicago answered by introducing a substitute measure, drafted by Walter L. Fisher and sponsored by representative Mueller whose name it bore. In making good their threat, the bosses took no chance with either a discussion or a vote in railroading their bill to passage. The speaker gaveled it through. No sooner had he declared it adopted than he had to flee from the pursuit of the angry, overridden members of the House led by the Chicago delegation. They brushed aside several women who had been seated beside the speaker to protect him in the event of such an emergency and pursued him out of the chamber. When rid of him, they reconvened, appointed a temporary chairman, rescinded the passage of the bill, and severely censored the speaker. The next day he resumed the chair with apologies. The Mueller measure was passed and reluctantly signed by the Governor. It became the basis of subsequent traction ordinances also drafted by Mr. Fisher. Thus ended Mr. Yerkes' régime and residence in Chicago. Leaving as his memorials the partially wrecked traction interests and the Yerkes Astronomical Observatory, with which he provided the University of Chicago, he proceeded to London where he employed to better purpose his marked abilities in promoting the building of one of its great traction tubes.

By standing at the switch alone to save civic disaster, George C. Sikes was himself transferred to what became the main line of his own life's work. The Municipal Voters' League soon claimed his service as its secretary. The Bureau of Public Efficiency enlisted him as its special investigator, in which capacity he left his mark upon its fundamental studies. Los Angeles drafted him long enough to report to its taxpayers a plan for the consolidation of their city and county governments, and in New York City he investigated the management of its municipal docks. Chicago never had a citizen more sturdily, self-sacrificingly, ably, and bravely devoted to its interests.

Worthily following these heroic leaders of the early attacks upon such almost impregnable strongholds of political and financial exploiters came Charles Edward Merriam. Coming from his chair in the Political Science Department of the

University of Chicago to his seat in the City Council, his were the most constructive achievements that followed the destructive warfare of his attacking predecessors. Although still called, as they were, to fulfil the ancient commission of Israel's statesmen prophets, "to root out, pull down, destroy, and overthrow," he improved the opportunity thus made possible "to build and to plant." This he did in the Council chamber and its committee-rooms, and by his campaigning throughout the city while serving as alderman for six years, as well as through his classroom teaching and academic publication then and ever since. His official investigations of police and court procedure against crime, and of the municipal revenues of Chicago, and his many other constructive measures laid foundations and gave incentives to subsequent investigational and progressive achievements, in most of which he has actively participated. Both in accounting for bad conditions and in evaluating efforts for better ones Professor Merriam has never been more nor less than human, viewing both as cross-sections of one and the same community. From scenes of conflict and confusion, he never fails in speech or writing[1] to reflect glimpses that glow with prophetic hope and assurance for the greater city that Chicago is yet to be.

To strengthen the base of the Municipal Voters' League's operation at the city's center an all-year-round office was established, with a small experienced full-time staff adequate to furnish and file current information, watch the Council and committee proceedings at the City Hall, and keep in touch with situations in the wards. Initiative was also taken toward organizing the City Club of Chicago. The League's Executive Committee constituted the nucleus of the club's founders. Their purpose was to rally, inspire, and train a larger and more active co-operation with the League's purposes and methods, especially among younger men. The Club has amply justified the heavy exactions its founding and development have cost its leaders. So intelligently has it studied and understood many issues faced by the municipality that its criticisms and recommendations of public policies

[1] Charles Edward Merriam, *Chicago—a More Intimate View of Urban Politics.* Macmillan Co., 1929. Pp. 305.

have strongly influenced public opinion and have had to be reckoned with, when not heeded, by public officials. The erection of its centrally located building serves notice that the ideals and standards of citizenship for which the Club and the League stand have come to stay. Approximately twenty-five hundred members rally there. The still larger number of citizens, both women and men, who use the building, contribute to the influences spreading far and wide from this central source of power. They, with the equally large membership and clientèle of the Woman's City Club, which arose later, recruit leaders from the rank and file of an informed and inspired body of citizens. That the source of the League's strength lies out in the wards has all along been realized. Its sole reliance has been upon the informed interest of voters, with whom it communicated by special bulletins, as well as by pre-election reports. Respect for the fully recognized independence of the local voters kept the League from expecting branch organizations to be established. Racial loyalties also had to be reckoned with as superseding civic loyalty where immigrants of different races on attaining citizenship strove for supremacy. They were thus made the easy prey of unscrupulous partisan politicians, aided by self-seeking leaders of racial groups. Wards in which such conditions prevailed were too readily taken for granted as "hopeless."

The complexity of the situation faced by the more intelligent and independent voters in such wards, though difficult, proved not to be insurmountable. Their experience in one of the congested river wards on the West Side demonstrated this fact effectively during the early and later campaigns of the League. It was known as the Seventeenth Ward, now the Thirty-first, in which Chicago Commons was the center to which its neighbors of all classes, races, and sects rallied for their social and civic activities. At the time of the organization of the Voters' League Scandinavian citizens greatly predominated over the diminishing Irish and German population of the ward. But an Irish boss and his organization dominated politics. When the independent voters, organized in the Seventeenth Ward Civic Federation, waited upon this dictator they demanded only two things of him, that he nominate candidates for aldermen for whom citizens could vote without the loss of self-respect, and that the ballots be counted as they were cast. The boss merely replied that "the four hundred Italians holding city jobs under his patronage held the balance of power between the parties in the ward, and voted as he told them or lost their jobs." We were waved out of his office with his contemptuous parting challenge, "What can you do about it?" Our parting salute was "Wait and you will see." And he did see, as soon as we could arouse the majority of good citizens and help divide the Italian vote.

Before this was done the boss marshaled his four hundred retainers for party orators to address. Applause was elicited at proper intervals from an audience as yet unfamiliar with the English language, by handkerchief signals, given by the boss from the platform. An eminent judge, who after perspiringly addressing the crowd, congratulated the boss upon the enthusiasm of his constituency, heard only the drawling laconic rejoinder, accompanied by a sly wink, "Yes, for a bunch that could not understand a word you said." Not long after these tactics failed to deliver "the balance of power," the boss inquired of me, "How long do you expect to stay in the ward at Chicago Commons?" I replied, "We hold the ground lease for ninety-nine years." He exclaimed, "My God, I might as well begin to tell you things." This interview was soon followed by his application for membership in our federation of independent voters. It was promptly declined as was his contribution to the settlement work at Chicago Commons. His exit was at hand. And soon, like "the green bay tree" to which the psalmist likened the wicked as "spreading in great power," this bad boss and many another "passed away, and lo, he was not, yea I sought him but he could not be found."

Our first aldermanic victory in this ward soon turned to defeat. We indeed defeated the worst candidate, a boss of another party who was a keeper of dives and a beater of women, but we elected a man who proved to be so weak as to become the dupe of the gang supporting one of the boodle ordinances in the City Council. His fellow-citizens in the ward federation thereupon called him before them to account for his action, and appointed a committee to sit in the gallery of the council chamber to watch his vote until his term expired. At the next election politicians of the baser sort attempted to steal the seat to which our better candidate was elected, by shifting eighty of his votes to his opponent on the tally sheet of one voting precinct. Upon the discovery of this trick we caused the arrest of a judge and two clerks of this election precinct. One of them turned state's evidence and the other two were convicted and sentenced to a term in the penitentiary. Meanwhile, by mandamus proceedings, the recount of these ballots resulted in the seating of the candidate who had been counted out. This suppressed not only such corrupt practices in this ward, but also the violence with which the enemy sought to break up our independent campaign meetings by howling down our speakers or even attempting to drag them from the platform, and by blocking citizens' approach to the ballot boxes with ward heelers imported for the purpose from other parts of the city.

This incident is significant for these results. It secured a law-enforcing victory for the Municipal Voters' League in a campaign clouded by many defeats. It demonstrated what one of the most misgoverned wards in the city could do in setting an example to encourage the independent voters of other wards. And it demonstrated how little the defeated politicians are to be feared. For our unseated candidate, after yielding his seat in the council chamber to its rightful possessor, cordially greeted me with the sportsman-like remark, "Well, professor, I am down and out." To my cheery reminder, "You never were up and in," he as cheerily replied, "So it seems." The jig was up. So he proved himself to be a good loser without any intention of making a breach between himself and a personally friendly neighbor. After this for fifteen years this cosmopolitan ward of wage-workers distinguished itself for its representation in the City Council, by two aldermen, John F. Smulski and William E. Dever, who won wider distinction in subsequent public service.

The record of the Municipal Voters' League of Chicago is distinctively suggestive to the whole country for its long succession of able leaders and committeemen; for its steady, persistent, vigilant service, undaunted by defeat and unelated by victory; for conducting its last campaign in its thirty-fourth year as vigorously, if less spectacularly, than its first one; and for the small financial expenditure and the large measure of moral support with which it has given highest expression to the best citizenship of Chicago in achieving political gain.

It has been my rare privilege to share the great good fellowship of the men constituting the League's Executive Committee through all these thirty-three years. I served with its pioneer members and their successors through every campaign except the first, after which I was chosen to take the place vacated by the member selected from the ranks of organized labor.

For their civic patriotism, and the sacrifices they offered on its altar, many of these comrades deserved to be cited by the city to receive its recognition of the distinguished service they rendered their home town directly and their whole country by the example they set and the results they achieved. The qualities which Lincoln Steffens credited Walter L. Fisher as pre-eminently possessing have been notably shared by most of those filling the executive offices of the League. In part, at least, they deserve the tribute paid to him: "With the education, associations and idealism of the reformers who fail, he had cunning, courage, tact, and rarer still, faith in the people." And we may still claim what Steffens adds to his tribute, that "reform in Chicago has such a leader as corruption alone usually has."

Occasional reversions to lower standards of municipal administration such as Chicago suffered in the election of 1927, which superseded one of the best city administrations by the return of the very worst, are to be accounted for by very obvious facts. While the public-spirited citizenship has been growing in numbers, political intelligence, and organized efficiency, it has been outgrown by the increase of population from our own and other lands at the rate of seventy thousand or more incomers a year. This racially mixed multitude is admitted to the electorate far faster than ways and means are provided for training new voters for the good citizenship to which most of them aspire and could be led. Those that are so predisposed and equipped by no means make good the loss of so many citizens whose knowledge of the background and needs of the city fit them for leadership, but who transfer their legal residence to the rapidly growing suburbs. Serious indeed is this loss, with little hope of recovery until, or unless, either the city limits are vastly extended or the electorate is so changed as to include the regional citizenship.

Meanwhile, one of those overlooked emotional changes was reaching a climax that turned the tables upon the pride which heedlessly accounts for such an alignment of racial elements as had never taken place before. The superiority claimed for the heritage of the English-American stock seemed to the citizens of other inheritances to depreciate their cultures as well as their citizenship. This state of mind prompted the appeal of chauvinistic nationalism, ignorantly and blatantly proclaimed as the test of American patriotism. Response at the polls was less in loyalty to the deceptive slogan "America First" than an assertion by the newer immigrant citizens of their equality with the older citizenship. With these newer voters citizens of German and Irish descent united to express their anti-British feeling, "King George" having been made the symbol of the pride and power of a minority charged with depreciating the new majority. Its ranks were still further recruited by a large negro vote and by those who crossed party and sectarian lines to register their opposition.

By this fortuitous combination the city suffered in the return of William Hale Thompson, a former mayor, whose two previous administrations were discredited by inefficiency and corruption; the subserviency of a majority of aldermen which gave him almost autocratic power over a city which had promptly claimed to be council governed; the subordination of merit appointments by spoils patronage in the civil service; the attempted partisan raids upon the public schools and public library; and a rampant lawlessness under discredited law enforcement which imperiled life and property and gave Chicago the disrepute of being the world's crime center.

The reaction that was sure to come arrived on the primary and election days of the county and state in 1928. A tidal

wave of unparalleled volume and force unexpectedly defeated
the renomination of the state's attorney and the governor of
the state, and elected their opponents by still larger majorities,
repudiating also the mayor and his entire administration although but half through their term of four years. This three-
fold most powerful political machine that had ever been in
control of city, county, and state was thus overwhelmed by
a silent vote of the aroused citizenship. The blatant appeal
"America First" was only a bubble, which burst without a
single echo!

Although this protest vote was silent and unheralded, the
sources of its prompting and power had been neither inactive
nor obscure. The *Chicago Daily News* and the *Chicago Tribune* had continuously exposed administrative corruption and
had waged war openly and uncompromisingly against the
perversion of government. Other city newspapers echoed less
vigorously these attacks, only two of them under the Hearst
management offering any defense. The *Tribune* won a civil
suit against the mayor and other officials for the recovery of
$1,732,279 of public funds misappropriated for political pur-
poses. The rapid increase of taxation and the growing in-
security of property and life still further disturbed the electorate.

Legal and educational groups furnished specialists whose
thorough investigations in the interest of criminal justice disclosed not only the ineffectiveness of the laws and court procedure, but also the political interference with law enforcement, and collusion with powerful leaders of organized criminals competing for the profits of police-protected gambling,
vice, and liquor traffics. Despite the alliance of the law-enforcing officials with violators of the law, the voluntary protective and prosecuting agencies waged their war more aggressively upon both. The Chicago Crime Commission, organized by the Chicago Association of Commerce, secured
from the attorney-general of the state the appointment of a
special prosecutor. It was accepted by Frank J. Loesch, an
eminent member of the Chicago bar, who at the age of seven-
ty-six undertook the arduous task, serving as first assistant
state's attorney. When leading the investigation of a special

grand jury and vigorously prosecuting those guilty of violence and fraud at local elections, he was proudly cartooned as an exemplar of "The Spirit of 76." These aggressive movements received active support of the Bar Association and the Federation of Churches, as well as that of influential clubs.

The greater hardship risked by single citizens in standing out alone against political corruption than is hazarded by those more or less supported by an aroused public opinion was somewhat later exemplified by Clarence S. Funk. The heroism of his civic patriotism deserves far more recognition than it ever received. The risks he assumed and suffered were taken against all these odds. William Lorimer had been seated in the United States Senate unchallenged by the notoriety of the bribery which secured his election by the Illinois Legislature. Despite the confessions of bribed legislators, the failure of bribed juries to convict them, and against the opposition of nearly half the senators, Lorimer was deemed worthy to retain his seat by a majority of six. Meanwhile, Mr. Funk was put in possession of evidence more incontrovertible than the Senate claimed to have received. It was proof of the charge which Herman H. Kohlsaat dared publish in his newspaper, the *Record Herald*, that a bribery fund of one hundred thousand dollars had been contributed by special financial interests. Representing these contributors, Edward Hines, a prominent lumberman, asked Mr. Funk, as he confided to Mr. Kohlsaat, to secure ten thousand dollars from the International Harvester Company, whose general manager Funk was, toward reimbursing those who had raised the fund "to put Lorimer over." His offer to testify to this fact, which was approved by the Harvester president, Cyrus H. McCormick, reopened the case against Lorimer and resulted in his expulsion from the Senate by a vote of 55 to 28.

Meanwhile, to deter him from effacing this stain upon his country's honor, a conspiracy to defame Mr. Funk's character was framed by these public enemies. An alienation suit based upon perjured testimony by a man and his wife, whose names were long withheld, was filed in court. But Mr. Funk was not to be intimidated by any costs of self-defense. Nor was he deterred by the prolonged and expensive effort to detect and bring to justice the perjurers, whose confessions completely exonerated him from their infamous charges. And this exoneration was further attested by the expulsion of Edward Hines from membership in the Union League Club of Chicago, in whose building he had failed to compromise Clarence S. Funk's citizenship. But the costs at which he attested his loyalty were large expenditures to protect not only his character, but himself and his family from threatened violence, permanently impaired health, and life cut short at his untimely death in his sixty-fourth year. Inestimable is the heritage of his unassuming moral heroism which is left for his family, his country, and the Christian church to cherish and inherit. The Chicago Theological Seminary honored itself in honoring him by dedicating to his memory the "Clarence S. Funk Cloisters" in the buildings whose erection he supervised.

Chicago exemplifies what Professor Merriam states to be "one of the realities of American life, that municipal vision, intelligence, courage, organizing ability have been able to rear beautiful and stately designs of city structures in periods of ill-smelling fraud and corruption." For, all through these years of administrative retrogression, private citizens, individually and through their voluntary organizations, continued to register encouraging progress along many lines of social, cultural, and civic development, which promised later, if not earlier, recovery from political debauchery. Local improvement associations multiplied their members and increased their co-operation. Peace pacts between employers and employees increased their hold upon hitherto-contending constituencies. Interracial and international understanding rallied smaller and larger groups in societies cherishing the memories of old homelands, in councils of foreign relations, through the foreign-language and native journals, and in educational institutions. Our universities and professional schools came closer to the whole people in serving more practically than ever before the vital interests of the community, by their extension courses, their training for leadership, and by their fearlessly impartial investigations and disclosures of political, administrative, and industrial conditions.

The Chicago Plan Commission continued to be an outstanding demonstration of what could be projected and achieved by such co-operation of private citizens and public officials as commands confidence in the integrity and public spirit of the enterprise. It inspired the initiative of two other organizations with educational aims and investigation of methods, reaching still farther toward governmental reconstruction. The Chicago Regional Planning Association, representing federal, state, county, and city areas in the region centering at Chicago, united official and private citizens to study the trends of population and industry, in order to promote the orderly, co-operative development of intercommunication, transportation, sanitary and recreational facilities. Upon the initiative of the Chicago Forum Council the Institute of Local Politics was established by representatives of several civic organizations and clubs aggressively interested in public affairs, who were reinforced by specialists from three universities. Their findings, which disclosed the hopeless confusion of nearly one thousand overlapping government agencies, led them to found the Government Planning Association of Chicago and the Metropolitan Area to conduct researches and present representations to the public and its legislative bodies. The Municipal Voters' League meanwhile ventured to sound the aldermen as to their attitude toward the non-partisan election for mayor and the city-manager plan. Their replies, while varying as to these proposals, were surprisingly outspoken in expressing the desire to be freed from partisan interference in the discharge of their non-partisan aldermanic office.

Striking the balance between political setbacks and forward-facing movements among the people, retrograde tendencies are to be regarded as temporary and superficial eddies on the stream which is too deep and broad to be judged by the flotsam and jetsam, or even by the wreckage floating on the surface. It indicates not only the vicissitudes but also the direction of the courses we are taking over the great deep. What has gone overboard somewhat samples the better-and-worse goods in the cargo we are carrying. The losses and gains, the wreckage and salvage, intimate the risks and costs of the voyage. But the ports from which we humans started and toward which we steer, or even drift, measure the progress we have made. To those of us at least who have the geologist's time sense when on shore, and the courageous patience of Columbus when afloat beyond our charts, that progress is sufficient to justify us in steering toward the best that is yet to be.[1]

[1] See Lloyd Lewis and Henry Justin Smith, *Chicago—the History of Its Reputation* (Harcourt, Brace & Co., 1929), for a true description of what Chicago now is and how it came to be.

CHAPTER VII

THE UNDERWORLD AND BENEATH IT

DURING the years in which initiative was being taken toward the civic renaissance, barely outlined in the preceding pages, the moral issues with vicious evils were not ignored. While the Civic Federation and the Municipal Voters' League rightfully gave precedence to their attack on political corruption, they regarded as allies their fellow-citizens who, like Arthur Burrage Farwell, individually or in protective associations were fighting gambling, prostitution, and drink.

The exposure of the political and police protection of vice resorts by William T. Stead at his Central Music Hall mass meeting, and by the Municipal Voters' League campaign against the vice-lords in the City Council, extended the efforts of other local reform organizations beyond the protection of their own neighborhoods from the invasion of vicious resorts. Experience in such single combats against resort-owners, and for the rescue of their women victims, gradually demonstrated the necessity for a combined city-wide campaign to be directed against the attitude and policy of the city administration in tolerating and segregating commercialized vice, contrary to law.

Mr. Stead's allusion to his own experience in his single-handed effort and lone-voiced protest against the white-slave traffic in London warned us against unnecessarily involving any such personal costs as he had paid. Those who would know by what authority, and from what motive, he thus warned Chicago, should read in *The Life of William T. Stead*, by Frederick Whyte, the chapter bearing the title "The Maiden Tribute of Modern Babylon." Under this title Mr. Stead had in 1885 shocked all Britain, and much of the

English-speaking world, by his revelations in the *Pall Mall Gazette* of the sale of English girls into the slavery of vice, for the traffic not only in England, but also in Europe and South America. To prove it he bought a young girl and, with the co-operation of the Salvation Army, safeguarded her and himself from incrimination. On the criminal charge of abducting the child, but really because his exposé of the traffic scandalized the public and the press more than did the hideous facts exposed, he was arrested, tried, convicted, and sentenced to two months' imprisonment.

The virtue of his motive, however, in resorting to extreme measures was justified, both before his act and after he was adjudged guilty, by such eminent persons as Cardinal Manning, the Archbishop of Canterbury; Rev. Charles Spurgeon; William Booth, (general of the Salvation Army); Lord Shaftesbury; Mrs. Fawcett; and others whom he had taken into his confidence. But the clamor against the public exposure of such shamelessly flagrant vice and the personal vituperation against the man who dared to lay it bare were so tumultuous as to drown the voices raised in his defense. Nevertheless the subsequent passage of the Criminal Law Amendment Bill, which penalized the vice traffic so severely as to drive its traffickers out of the trade, was recognized to be so dependent upon this agitation to compel long-delayed action that the measure came to be called Stead's Act.

If more of us in Chicago had known these facts, not so many of us might have resented Mr. Stead's exposure of similar vices here, or misunderstood and maligned his motive in so doing. Here, as in England, he did justify many in thinking that he went too far and lacked delicacy in detailing too much. But some of us have learned that the chief end of man is not to gratify his own taste, and that it requires some of us to go a great deal too far to get the rest of us to go half far enough.

The odds against which individual, single-handed, protective efforts had to contend were exemplified by two experiences which we at Chicago Commons had in defending two young girls from capture by white-slavers. The mother of one of them appealed to us to find her fourteen-year-old daughter who had disappeared for a day and night from home and the neighborhood. We found her detained in a police station, near a commercial amusement park, as a witness against a man twice her age, who was caught by a policeman in the act of attacking her. When brought to trial this man's attorney claimed that the girl was the wife of the accused. The judge and jury were informed by us that the claim was based upon this extraordinary trick. While the child was committed by the court to a Protectorate to prevent her from being kidnapped before she could testify against the accused, he appeared with a justice of the peace and was allowed to interview the child. While unsuspectingly permitted to do so in the presence of a guard and separated from the men by a lattice screen, the justice pronounced them "Man and Wife!" Informed of this fact, and on the testimony of the police officer, the jury convicted the prisoner and sentenced him to seven years in prison. But the judge reduced the sentence to two years. The man was paroled in one year. The girl was obliged to marry him by her father to cover family disgrace. She was promptly hired out to other men by her captor. Her cohabitation with them was cited as an evidence of "infidelity" warranting divorce, which was promptly granted her aggrieved "husband!"

The other case was still more dramatic. Again a widowed neighboring mother asked our help in finding her fifteen-year-old daughter, who had disappeared while seeking employment, offered through an advertisement for "a prepossessing girl to wait upon an invalid old lady." We were informed that she was held against her will in the apartment of a procuress on a great West Side thoroughfare. Aided by the informant, an employee at the place who had pity for the child, two of our men residents at Chicago Commons gained admission to the apartment by strategy. While rescuing the girl from her captors they secured evidence implicating the man for whom the girl was "procured."

In securing a warrant for his arrest and that of the "old lady," I was suspicious of the two city detectives assigned to make the arrest because they admitted knowing the procuress for years without interfering with her traffic. So I hired the operators of the Pinkerton Detective Agency to watch the police detectives. But they had already given the tip to the man involved, who precipitantly fled from his business office to the northwest territory in Canada. He proved to be a prosperous, well-connected proprietor of a large and successful business enterprise, with an office in one of the best-known buildings on La Salle Street. The gray-headed woman of sixty or more years was shown to have been hired by him to manage the apartment he rented for her in order to trap girls for him.

During the trial I had to protect their intended victim from the ruffians lying in wait to spirit her away in order to rid the case of the prosecuting witness. I did so by taking the girl into the Chicago Commons household and by accompanying her to and from the courtroom daily. After the trial she went out of the state for two years to protect her from vengeance. There she married and became the good mother of a family.

While the jury was being selected the courtroom detective informed me that the clerk of another court was trying to "fix" the jury. Exposing him so that he disappeared from the scene, a trustworthy jury was obtained, despite the objection of defense attorneys to married or mature men. These lawyers, hitherto supposed to be reputable, stooped to introduce a compromising letter, alleged to have been written by the girl. It proved to be a forgery of her handwriting. Conviction was secured and the old procuress was sentenced to two years' imprisonment in the state penitentiary. I was sorry to have the case against the man, whose accomplice she was, stricken off the calendar because the prosecutor was convinced that "no jury of men would convict a man accused by a woman accomplice, who herself had been convicted and sent to prison." I could only force from the fugitive a written confession as a condition of his return to Chicago from his month's exile in Canada.

Experiences such as these prepared more and more of us to enlist in the organized movement to outlaw vice and rid the commonwealth of complicity with it. It was not until seven years after the awakening to this duty that Mr. Stead's ringing appeals to do it met with such response. To the credit

of the ministers of the Protestant churches, constituting
the Chicago federation of six hundred churches, they took
the initiative which proved successful against all probabilities
to the contrary. Impulse was given to their initiative by
Rev. Walter T. Sumner, then dean of the Episcopal Cathedral in Chicago, and since the Bishop of Oregon. The clergy-
house where he lived and the cathedral where he ministered
were within the district, on the Lower West Side of Chicago,
that was one of the three areas within which the police were
supposed to segregate and regulate vice resorts and their inmates. From personal observation of the evil effects of these
resorts, and from his experience in ministering to their inmates, he was prepared to state the problem to his brother-
ministers from his own experience. His frank and fearless
exposé of the shameful facts, and his fervent appeal to the
clergy and their churches to face these soul-destroying influences, won the unanimous adoption of his proposal:

That the mayor be asked to appoint a Commission of men and women
who command the respect and confidence of the public at large to investigate thoroughly the conditions as they exist and to enlist the support of
every civic, protective, philanthropic, social, commercial and religious
body in the city to carry out the plans suggested.

In offering this resolution Dean Sumner suggested as an
incentive for official and citizens' action that "if the present
administration does not subscribe to such a plan the political
parties should be pledged to make it an issue at the next election and that the press, the social settlements, the churches
and the public generally could be relied upon to back conclusions reached by such a commission."

To the surprise of those who knew him well, Mayor Busse
promptly appointed thirty citizens as members of the Chicago
Vice Commission, naming Dean Sumner, the youngest of
them all, as its chairman. I was the last to be appointed, and
in response to the urgent request of the Chief of Police.

The City Council confirmed their appointments and appropriated ten thousand dollars to cover the expenses of the
investigation. Toward the cost of publishing its report a contribution of five thousand dollars was received from John D.
Rockefeller, Jr., who had led the "Committee of Fourteen"

in making the first public report of such fact-finding surveys, which dealt with the situation then existing in New York City.

Outstanding representatives of Chicago's lawyers, physicians, women's organizations, teachers, social workers, the clergy, and the city's commercial and industrial interests accepted the mayor's appointments. Through more than a year of continuous and exacting service these thirty citizens, two of whom were women, faithfully fulfilled the purpose of the Commission, which was fearlessly carried out with the aid of a small staff of investigators.

The complicated factors of the problem, and the very forces requisite to any solution of it, required a broad survey of the sources and resources of the social evil, its secret and open operations, its relation to drink and narcotics, crime and the police, hygiene and housing, education and literature, legislation and administration. The difficulty and danger of acquiring accredited facts, the untrustworthy sources of information available, the guarded or politically protected resorts and their criminal, desperately revengeful keepers exacted great caution in selecting and checking up these investigators, and in verifying and finally publishing the information procured. Every statement thus required passed the scrutiny, challenge, and acceptance of not only the chairman and the committee, but before it was filed for publication it was read to and approved by the entire Commission.

The lack of authentic information regarding the relation between subnormality and sexual delinquency prevented the Vice Commission of Chicago from reporting more fully upon that feature of the situation which it investigated. While serving as chairman of this Committee on the sources supplying the victims of vice, however, I found very many inmates of the resorts I visited very far from normal. This was most noticeable in the lowest grade of these resorts, which admitted such inmates at first hand, or received them from the higher-grade places when they had physically and mentally depreciated. Many such had fallen when very young, some of them before they knew what it was to stand, and others after their ignorance and weakness had been taken advantage of, either by force or betrayal.

First among the causes given by most of the twenty-four hundred women and girls under the Committee's review, while most of them were in correctional institutions, was that their home conditions were unhappy or inadequate. Economic conditions came second, the lack of provision for healthful and innocent recreation came third, procuring for white slavery fourth, while the lack of all education in sex physiology and hygiene made every one of these sinister influences less repellent and more dangerous.

United States District Attorney Edwin W. Sims, serving the Vice Commission as its secretary and legal adviser, cited the case of an Italian girl which proved the existence of an international white-slave trade. This is the story she told him. When she was a young girl at play in the street of her home town, an American woman asked her, and also her mother, whether she would come to America with this pretended benefactress to be educated. Gaining consent, this woman gave the mother money, more than enough to pay for the girl's clothing outfit. On arrival at New York she was delivered to the keeper of a vice resort where she was forced to remain for some months and was then shipped to a Chicago resort. Attempting to escape, the keeper slashed her face with a razor, mutilating it so badly as to eliminate all traces of beauty. After two years she was rescued and sent back to Italy with her baby but a few months old. Almost unrecognizable in appearance, and bearing the shame of an unwed mother, neither family nor friends would receive her. So back to Chicago she found her way, where broken down by the abuse she had suffered and the single-handed struggle to earn a scant livelihood for herself and child, her reason gave way and at twenty-seven years of age she was committed to the state insane asylum. The federal authorities who had followed her case declared that they had "nothing but commendation for her."

In the commercially highest-grade resort, the Everleigh Club, which I visited during this investigation, I found the twenty or more inmates appearing so well in the early evening that it would have been difficult to distinguish them from high-school graduates or college students. They produced the pennants of several colleges, as though they used them to attract or amuse their patrons. The two middle-aged sisters who had long kept the place were intelligent and well mannered. They extenuated their nefarious trade by saying that it had to be, and that they, as well as others, might profit by conducting it as decently as it could be managed. When asked how they procured inmates, they replied that they always had a waiting list, but insisted upon each one of them answering for herself. Dean Sumner and I were permitted to interview them. The reasons they gave us were among those mentioned above, yet few of these inmates failed to claim that they were only there temporarily and would leave the life they were leading when they had earned a competence. Their "madame" somewhat boastfully bade us to persuade, if we could, any of them to leave forthwith. Before leaving the handsomely furnished clubhouse, bearing a name that ranked it as aristocratic, I inquired of the madame how she dared to deal so destructively with both the body and the very life of each inmate. Her hollow, hysterical laughter fittingly accompanied her flippant reply that she was writing what she would call *The Biography of a Lost Soul*.

Not until the mayor and the Police Department acted on the recommendation of the Vice Commission in closing segregated districts did this famous house of infamy lose the political pull which it had so long financially maintained and was compelled to close its doors, after which its proprietress left the city.

The official report of the Commission, entitled *The Social Evil in Chicago*, laid bare the facts of these shameless situations and held them up in the light of common day. The inference was unavoidable that if the citizens of Chicago and Illinois liked to tolerate this sort of thing, they were the sort of people who tolerated it according to their liking.

Its publication created a great sensation in the city and state. As the first public document of its kind it also made a deep impression upon the officials and citizens in many other cities. Over fifty of them promptly appointed vice commissions to investigate, report, and deal with their local situations. Either under some sinister influence, or because shocked by the unusually frank statement of fact, officials of the Post-Office Department at Washington prohibited the transmission of the Chicago report through the mail. But they were obliged to rescind their exclusion order by the claim of the Commission of the right to mail it as a public document. When the term of the Commission expired with the issuance of its report to the mayor and the City Council, its officers destroyed by fire all the data upon which its findings were based, in order to prevent any attempt to misuse them for political or blackmailing purposes.

The recommendations of the Commission were based upon the carefully authenticated, detailed, classified, and summarized facts disclosed by the city-wide investigation, compared with data gleaned from other cities in this country and abroad. The policies and procedure recommended were kept well within the range of commercialized vice and were addressed to federal, state, county, and city authorities and still more specifically to county officials, the corporation counsel, the Police Department, the Board of Education, the commissioner of health, park commissioners, parents, philanthropic and other organizations, and the press. All these recommendations were summed up in one sententious sentence—"Constant and persistent repression of prostitution the immediate method; absolute annihilation the ultimate ideal."

Federal action subsequently taken may have been more or less directly influenced by the facts and suggestions in the Chicago report. The safe conduct of immigrants from ports of entry to their destination came to be carefully guarded from the cruel exploitation of white-slavers whose bold operations were still further exposed by the Immigrants' Protective League of Chicago. The Mann Act, heavily penalizing the transportation across state lines of girls and women for immoral purposes, bears the name of the foremost Congressman from Chicago, Representative James Robert Mann. The State Department negotiated a "gentlemen's agreement" with the English, French, and other foreign governments providing for police and court co-operation for the prevention and punishment of the international white-slave traffic. The League of Nations subsequently secured the agreement of fifty or more nations to enforce this policy. Its investigation of the international traffic was suggested by Miss Grace Abbott, head of the Federal Children's Bureau, who unofficially represented the people of the United States at the League Conference Committee on this evil.

Local action on the Vice Commission's report was long deferred. For two years after its publication it was pigeonholed in the office of the next mayor, Carter H. Harrison, Jr., who continued the policy of toleration and segregation which he and his father had followed in previous terms in that office.

Meanwhile, the state's attorney of Cook County, John E. W. Wayman, was forced to act at the complaint of a woman that her real estate was depreciated in value by the toleration of vice resorts near her property, far away from the so-called segregated districts. Charged with responsibility for it before the grand jury, this official replied that since the city Police Department had failed to do its duty he would act. As I had supported his candidacy, in order to defeat a far worse candidate for the state's attorneyship, he regarded me as friendly and informed me when he would raid the most extensive red-light district, which was located on the South Side. That night, Dean Sumner and I were on a street many blocks of which for years had been lined with wide-open resorts on either side. About midnight police patrol wagons suddenly backed up to one of these resorts after another, so unexpectedly that they were found in full operation. In the glare of their lights the inmates were taken by wagonloads to the nearest police stations. None of the hundreds of dislodged women accepted the free lodgings offered them by "rescue" missionaries. Mobs of men surged into the vacated resorts, destroying or stealing much of their contents. Their doors were officially closed. Within twenty-four hours 135 warrants were served upon resort-keepers. While one and another of them were temporarily opened, either at the same or another location, by the connivance of the police, yet the district was dead and never came back to spectacularize the shame it had flaunted. No such red lights ever glared again so openly. Street solicitation ceased or was attempted under cover.

Most of these resorts were closed or kept on the run. When allowed to locate they were banished from most residential districts by the pressure of public opinion upon the authorities charged with enforcement of the law.

This scandalously spectacular raid, which marked the beginning of the end of the officially recognized red-light districts of Chicago, was previously approximated about as sensationally by an ill-advised and futile religious demonstration. Some of the churches were led into it by an English evangelist, whom they had engaged to conduct an interdenominational series of evangelistic meetings. Headed by the Salvation Army band and the evangelist on horseback, throngs of church people, mostly young folks and women, invaded this same district with the purpose of winning patrons and inmates from the resorts, against the toleration of which the demonstration was a protest. Police refused to let children enter the district, many of whom were led by their parents in the procession.

Evidently by common consent the resort-keepers closed their doors, darkened their windows, and some of them removed their inmates to other streets. So the crusaders passed unobserved by those they sought, through streets temporarily deserted by the crowds usually patronizing the resorts. No sooner had the procession disappeared and the voices of the singers died away than the question of their song, "Where is my Wandering Boy Tonight?" was rudely answered. Back over the route of march surged hundreds of men following the women inmates as they returned to their haunts singing ribald songs. The futility of this spectacular demonstration of this ill-advised religious zeal without knowledge stood out in humiliating contrast with the later reprehensibly sensational yet effective enforcement of the law. In justice to the better-advised churches and their clergy it should be said that many of them silently, and some of them publicly, protested against this demonstration as likely to do more harm to the innocent than good to the guilty.

A month after the Vice Commission rendered its report and disbanded, five prominent citizens of Chicago at the call of one of them, Clifford W. Barnes, organized the Committee of

Fifteen. It was incorporated "to aid the public authorities in the enforcement of all laws against pandering, and to take measures calculated to suppress the white-slave traffic." The initiative taken by these citizens both preceded and followed up that which secured the appointment of the Commission. Four years before that event they had secretly combined to back up a young assistant state's attorney whose successful prosecution they aided by furnishing means to secure evidence through further investigation. And when the political influence of the alarmed lords of the underworld succeeded in stopping the prosecution and ousting the prosecutor, he was employed by these five men to continue his work privately.

Mayor Carter H. Harrison, Jr., meanwhile, appointed a committee of aldermen, which might have been expected to bring in a report adverse to that of the Vice Commission. But it unexpectedly indorsed the findings and recommendations of the Commission. Still seeking support for the police regulation of vice in segregated districts, the mayor appointed another aldermanic committee to report the policies dealing with prostitution abroad. Although its observation was curtailed by the outbreak of the World War, its members saw enough to decide to agree with the conclusions of the Commission. Yielding at last to the increasing protest against official toleration of unlawful and disease-breeding resorts, to which the extension of suffrage to women may have added decisive emphasis, Mayor Harrison frankly conceded that he had been mistaken, claiming his correction to have been due to reading Raymond Fosdick's volume on *European Police Systems*, which proved the failure of segregating vice. Here follows his public declaration of his changed policy:

I have reached the conclusion finally that my ideas of the vice question have been wrong. I have no hesitancy in subscribing to the general indictment of the segregation plan. Its worst feature to me is the corrupting influence it exerts over the entire law enforcing arms of the government. Segregation means protected vice. Chicago is through with the segregated vice idea. There isn't anything that a conscientious person can say now in support of segregation. Repression means treating it just as any other crime is treated.

Mayor Harrison reached this conclusion only a little later than others of his fellow-citizens whose efforts had been direct-ed exclusively against the white-slave traffic, or for the rescue of its victims. Indeed, neither all the members of the Committee of Fifteen nor most of the members of the Vice Commission themselves, I among them, previous to their appointment had pronounced opinions against the so-called segregation and police regulations of vice resorts. They were not yet convinced that these measures were necessary to pro-tect the innocent and the community itself from worse aggres-sions of vice. Not until the investigations of the Chicago Vice Commission demonstrated the failure and futility of the segregation policy were well-informed, open-minded officials and citizens convinced of the contrary. The Chicago Vice Commission is therefore to be credited, perhaps most of all, for demonstrating the certainty with which a body of authen-ticated facts may be trusted to reverse public opinion and turn it from relying upon a refuge of lies. Once for all it con-clusively demonstrated that segregation had failed to segre-gate, regulation to regulate, and sanitation to sanitate.

By destroying this wholesale market for commercialized vice its traffickers were driven into fugitive retailing traffic and were kept moving. The way was thus opened also for far more effective legislation, making the illicit use of real estate for vicious purposes too hazardous for property-owners to risk it. The enactment of the Injunction and Abatement Law, secured from the Illinois Legislature by the Committee of Fifteen, proves to be the most effective weapon acquired against commercialized vice. It authorizes any judge, on the petition of any citizen, to issue an injunction against the owner of any property in which vice is harbored. In case the injunction is violated, the court can order the entire building closed and padlocked for a year, however small a part of it was proved to be illicitly used.

Warnings to the owners of property thus involved by publishing lists of their names in the daily papers brought scores of them to the Committee's office indignantly protest-ing against such publicity. Among them were officials of banks and other corporations, managers of large estates, and other prominent citizens owning real estate. Replying to their protests, the Committee claimed that it could not be expected to assume the responsibility and expense of keeping their property clean. Thereupon these and many other owners combined to do it themselves by strict supervision and detection of their tenants. Such a housecleaning as Chicago had never experienced followed. Ever since, the Committee of Fifteen has found few breaches of this law in such property, and when discovered prompt ejectment of guilty tenants follows notification to the owner, without publicity or court procedure in all but a few cases.

The establishment of many official and private agencies for law enforcement followed, notably the Morals Court for the trial of sex cases, and the Juvenile Court, with a woman judge, Mary M. Bartelme, assigned to the cases of girl delinquents. Later she was assigned to preside on this bench by her associate judges of the Circuit Court. Thus American cities have been led and enabled to efface at least their open shame in tolerating, and even affording, police protection to the very vices which their state laws prohibited and penalized as felonies.

Into this bottomless pit of Chicago's underworld I came not without personal experiences with many victims of vice and crime elsewhere. Through boyhood, however, I scarcely imagined that there were any who fell farther down below most of their fellows than the very few drunken men I saw on the streets, or the few others who got locked up in the county jail, for just what cause I knew not. But that there were enough such to people a world—an underworld—this side of the grave was not suggested to me even by the Bible. It did create the dreadful fear that on the other side of the grave far more had gone down to it in eternal misery than went up to immortal bliss. The one, if not the only reason why, according to what I had been taught, was because they failed to believe in the Christ, and therefore could not be saved.

Not until I came upon a story that impressed itself upon me by a picture did I imagine that there was an underworld on earth. It was old John Bunyan's story of "Vanity Fair."

In my father's beautifully illustrated copy of *Pilgrim's Progress*, a picture that never faded from my memory vividly depicted the great throng of visitors at that Fair as surrounded by those trying to sell them such mixed merchandise as I had never imagined. With "houses, lands, trades, places, honors, preferments, titles, countries, kingdoms," were listed "delights, pleasures, lusts of all sorts such as harlots, bawds, wives, husbands, children, masters, lives, blood, bodies, souls, silver, gold, pearls, precious stones and what not."

It was the picture, however, more than the print that revealed the reality of what the great Dreamer said was always to be seen, "and that for nothing" at this fair of ancient standing, namely, "jugglings, cheats, games, plays, fools, apes, knaves and rogues of every kind; also thefts, murders, adulteries, false swearers, and that of a blood red colour." Most of these terms might have meant little to me had it not been for the picture. There in the show windows behind the footlights were realistically pictured what the various nations had to sell. In English Row drink was playing havoc behind the sign "Entertainment for Man and Beast." The enticements of operatic song and costume were offered in Italian Row, and follies in the Spanish. The French ballet attracted to the bawdy-house in the rear, from the windows of which its inmates beckoned. Underneath a German beer- and gameroom the gamblers were shown to be robbing and killing one another.

Since the progress of the pilgrim was conditioned upon passing through this fair without purchasing any of its vanities, though at the cost of persecution, I took warning to see only the peril and nothing of the allurements of such scenes.

So the underworld on either side of the grave was at the end of the broad way leading to destruction, in the opposite direction in which the straight and narrow path led to the "Delectable Mountains" crowned by the "Celestial City."

The reality of what was thus prefigured in my imagination was only faintly reflected during student days. Yet there was enough danger threatened to drinking college mates to prompt me to lead in the successful effort to banish liquor from our fraternity banquets. One of the brothers who most

resented this action wrote me years afterward during his sea-
faring experience: "Your stand stood by me when in the
midst of temptations which, compared with those to which I
was then yielding, were as much greater as the ocean is to a
mill pond." The salacious stories told by fellow-students so
disgusted me that I refused to hear them in my dormitory-
room. But only the worst sources of sex knowledge were open
to me when what I needed and had a right to know should
have been taught me at home, at school, and at church.

On my country and city fields of pastoral labor I was
sternly confronted by these evils as I grappled with the problem of rescuing victims of drink and vice, both before the
law laid its hands upon them and while they were in correctional institutions. To the police court and station-house,
the criminal court, county jail, and state prison I was introduced by following thither men and women in whom I became interested through my mission and church work. They
were always persons, human beings to me, never merely cases.
Both their haunts and the public institutions whither I followed them were always human habitations, never mere dens
or slums, cells or places of punishment.

Therefore, before legal provision for probation was made,
police-court judges were persuaded to suspend the sentences
of first offenders whom we knew and commit them to our care
at the Fourth Church in Hartford. To co-operate with and
supplement the work of the Prisoners' Aid Society we regularly visited the jail and the Connecticut state prison at Wethers-
field. Monthly for about five years I visited the prison to
interview prisoners who were to be released the following
month. On one chapel occasion after I had addressed over
four hundred men, mostly between the ages of twenty and
forty years, the warden, a man of the old type who had few,
if any, scientific ideas or modern methods of dealing with
prisoners, grimly remarked: "Eighty per cent of these men
are here on account of conditions for which you and I, and all
the rest of us, are more responsible than they." This I found
to be true in the experience of very many of the hundreds of
these men who gave me their confidence, while in prison, after
their discharge, and some of them while on their way through

juvenile delinquency and adult misdemeanors to their criminal careers.

From that long panoramic procession of fellow-men I first learned, what subsequent study and experience still further taught me, of the sources to which wayward tendencies toward vice, misdemeanors, and crime are to be traced. The boyhood of fully half of these men had been in broken homes, broken by the death of father or mother or both, by the desertion or divorce of their parents, by the incapacity of one or both properly to rear their children, due to illness, intemperance, or inefficiency. In many cases the dependency in boyhood led to delinquency in youth and crime in manhood. The boy without a playground came to be the man earliest without a job. Unemployment among those able and willing to work pushed not a few of the weaker and less resourceful men either into robbery or accepted pauperism.

Convictions such as these thus forced upon me were clinched by many a tragic confession. Out from behind the bars came a middle-aged man to meet me in the prison office. The warden's presence lessened the chance of the more confidential interview usually obtained when I met a prisoner alone. It prompted this man's defiant attitude. When asked what he expected to do after his discharge, he replied: "I shall have to be what I have always been, a thief." Glancing at the warden's Grand Army button, the prisoner quickly added that he expected to begin at the next Grand Army encampment. When the indignant warden left me alone with the prisoner, I appealed to him to take the opportunity I would try to open to him to be a man among men in the working world. Hoping to touch his better nature, I ventured to ask whether he would like to have his mother hear what he had said about continuing to be a thief. His bitter rejoinder was, "Damn her! She taught me to be one. I know of no other way to make a living." So on his downward way he persisted in going—a way on which a large proportion of these young men had started for the lack of parental care, such as we are all dependent upon for making the most of self and doing the best by others.

Another man of better birth and breeding, although a re-

peater yet not incorrigible, met my inquiry almost as un-
promisingly. "No one cares where I go or what I do," he
snapped out. My assurance that I cared and was with him
because I did received no response except a quick, penetrating, inquiring glance, searching my sincerity. But when I
produced a letter from his sister, bidding me tell him that a
welcome awaited his return to her home, he swallowed hard,
and his eyelashes moistened a bit. Through these openings I
sounded his heart to find there the rootage of a new manhood
which needed only the recognition of the right to be, and the
assurance of the room to grow, in order to prove him worthy
of the fellowship of the church and the confidence of the
community, as well as of a foothold in the working world, all
of which he kept as long as he lived. Many such confirma-
tions of what a wiser prison warden said to me have been
registered all through my experience. As hundreds of Sing
Sing prisoners marched by us in the yard, he said: "Keep
these men's homes loyal to them while in prison if you would
save them when they come out." Pointing to a prisoner, he
added: "There is a man of whom we had high hopes as long
as his wife visited him, but who has become desperate and
incorrigible since she left him."

Very many, but by no means all, of these prisoners, as also
misdemeanants in police stations and county jails, gave evidence in their appearance and speech that they lacked ability
to resist adverse surroundings and wayward leadership.

Knowledge of the inmates of correctional institutions
emphasizes the classification of these institutions as well as
their inmates to be most essential to the fulfilment of the
state's custodial care and to justify vast expense. The distinction now permanently established in the law and the
court between the juvenile and the adult delinquent led the
way to further classification. None too early did we awake to
the necessity of so doing as a measure for the protection of
society. Until then, with little if any discrimination, younger
and older first offenders and hardened criminals were locked
in the same corridor, if not in the same cell, at all station-
houses and jails. They thus became schools of crime, as most
of the three thousand county jails are, especially on account

of idleness in such contaminating contacts. Judges and jailers had neither option nor space to do anything else. When asked whether he could not do something else with a youthful prisoner he was about to sentence, an old-time justice of the peace in Chicago struck the bench with vigor to emphasize what he said: "I'll give you one hundred dollars to tell me what else I can do."

The superintendent of the city prison was so intent to offset the evil effect upon the hundreds of boys while in the prison atmosphere and surroundings, even though not allowed to mingle with adult prisoners more than they had to, that he enlisted the help of the churches and the Board of Education in providing separately for their religious care and schooling. So much better did he know than we how much more evil boys could learn in a few hours of such close contacts than the Sunday school or church could get out of them in many years that he declared: "Two thousand boys had been sent nearer Hell for being in the city prison during the seven years of my superintendency, when the only guards I had to put in charge of them were adult prisoners."

The distinction between juvenile and adult delinquents, introduced by the Juvenile Court of Cook County at Chicago, led to the adoption of the probation system, which distinguishes between those who need only to have sentence suspended while put on their good behavior, under the oversight of a probation officer, and those who have to be confined for stricter discipline. Then came the indeterminate sentence and parole, again distinguishing between those cured enough of their distempers to be safe at large and those still incapable of self-control, needing longer if not lifelong detention. The psychopathic clinic not only enabled the Juvenile Court to determine the classification of its wards for treatment adapted to their condition, but it also opened the way for their custodians to deal with exceptional inmates incapable of responding to discipline adapted to the others, so as not to disturb the morale of the whole institution.

A recent personal inspection of sixteen outstanding correctional institutions in four states disclosed these modern methods to be well fulfilling their purpose in restoring delinquents to self-control and in protecting society both by returning them to good citizenship and by detaining the more dangerous ones for longer terms of disciplinary confinement than they had previously been definitely sentenced to serve.

At that far end of the criminal's trail the classification of institutions was found to be providing for the restoration to self-control or for permanent custody. Where this trail starts at the threshold of the home and school the scientific study of the sources of behavior promises such an understanding of the misunderstood child, such a readjustment of the maladjusted youth, such a guidance and drawing toward the better as will divert a problem child from his wayward life long before the overt act classifies him as a delinquent.

The hopeful significance of these and other progressive principles and methods which modern penological science is introducing to correctional procedure may be the better realized by what may happen where ignorance and political perversion control.

The following incident is cited as a warning of what happens at worst. Enlisted by a group of progressive citizens to lecture on civic affairs at the capital of a western state, I was made aware of the situation at the state prison located there which had culminated in a gruesome tragedy. One of these citizens, a former judge, detailed what had happened under the previous warden who had been appointed for political purposes. Informed by a former convict of an illicit traffic conducted by favored prisoners, this judge went with his informer to the gate of the prison wall at night. Answering the knock, the prisoner within the wall appeared, to exchange prison products for liquor and narcotics which the discharged convict delivered to him. The judge claimed that scenes of debauchery in the warden's apartment had occured which were witnessed by convicts who served his dissolute guests.

The tragedies which finally eventuated from this corrupt and corrupting administration were accounted for by two prisoners who were involved in them and with whom I was permitted to talk privately while visiting the prison. One of these men, a half-breed, was in the cell of the condemned awaiting execution for the murder of a guard. Charged with breaking a rule, which he denied, he was not only placed in a solitary cell, but water from a hose was turned upon him. Driven to desperation, he killed the guard who, he claimed, was responsible for this persecution.

The other prisoner was one of four who had recently escaped after killing a guard and the warden. Pursued for a week or more from farm to farm, they were overtaken by their pursuers while riding in a farm wagon, the owner of which they had compelled to drive them over the next stage of their flight. In the gun fire which ensued, the farmer and three of the fugitives were killed, this fourth prisoner surrendering and being taken alive. On the return trip to the prison the dead bodies were exhibited to gaping crowds at railway stations, and this fourth man was sentenced to imprisonment for life. He thus accounted for his part in the tragedy. Serving a sentence of fifteen years for robbery, he was suddenly tempted to join the others in the plot as they passed him on their way out of the shop. The impulse was strengthened by the disgusting food and other living conditions which had become intolerable. Confirmatory of some of them, I saw a large vat filled with garbage in a part of the cell house, from which swarms of flies were pestering prisoners in their cells. The record of this young prisoner prior to this first term of imprisonment was such as to lend credence to his claim that he was not a desperado and that with others he was better than some of the guards.

Stating these alleged conditions to be unworthy of tolerance by the people of that state, I was challenged by an elderly citizen among my auditors at the public lecture to say "why he should care for what happened to such fools or knaves while they were in prison." My reply was that he should care because of what might happen to him when they got out of prison, as most all of them would sooner or later. A member of the legislature then arose to protest against political opposition to his bill for the establishment of a reformatory where the younger prisoners might be removed from the contaminating influence which he knew to exist at the state prison. This reformatory was subsequently established.

Summoned the next morning by the governor of the state to answer for having made such charges publicly against the administration of the prison, I insisted that I had only repeated what many citizens knew to be the facts which were accounted for by the scandals of the former warden's administration. I had just finished saying so when a prominent citizen burst into the Governor's office and excitedly addressed His Excellency, bidding me to remain as I was about to retire. He told the Governor that all I had said the previous evening was true, adding that the present situation under the newly appointed, inexperienced warden was so perilous as to endanger the lives of his overseers in the shops in which he held the contracts for prison labor. While he threatened to throw up his contract unless the situation was immediately and thoroughly remedied, I was willingly permitted to retire by His Excellency without further categorical imperatives.

Not only by the slow pace of progress in public institutions yet to be won from their penal motives to correctional standards, but more still by the retrogression from better to worse administration, vigilant, courageous, and aggressive propaganda is demanded. The American Prison Association and the American Institute of Criminal Law and Criminology both see and guard the gains attested by penological science and practical experience. Back tracks are occasionally taken under the pressure of public alarm at outbreaks of spectacular crimes, which are erroneously thought to be preventable by inflicting such extreme penalties as will strike terror into the hearts of others, deterring them from repeating such offenses. But modern scientific methods that justify themselves wherever they have a fair chance to be honestly and intelligently operated are likely to be discarded after being discredited by political spoilsmen who covet patronage at any cost to public welfare. In Illinois they were charged by a grand jury with securing the parole of felons from the state prison for cash, having ousted the state's most experienced warden who stood in their way and who died broken-hearted under the discredit falsely done to his high reputation for long and efficient correctional service.

There are enough of us, if we would only inform ourselves and act, to replace officials who know so little and care less either for the public or the prisoner as to appoint wardens and guards who rely upon muscle more than mind. There is enough experience in the failure of the old vengeance and the success of the new intelligence to transform our penal institutions into educational, correctional agencies that would justify their existence and their cost by turning their inmates out better and not worse for being committed to their care.

The certainty and promptness of conviction and sentence can be shown to be more effective deterrents of crime than the severity of penalties. The death penalty itself is more and more discredited as a deterrent of murder by juries which refuse to inflict it; by court statistics which show fewer convictions where death is the only penalty prescribed by law; by legislatures which substitute life-imprisonment for it; and, not least, by enlightened prison wardens charged with the execution of those sentenced to die.[1]

[1] See *Man's Judgment of Death* and *Life and Death in Sing Sing*, by Lewis E. Lawes, warden of Sing Sing Prison; also his article in the *Survey*, October 15, 1927, "The Death Penalty at Sing Sing"; *Capital Punishment in the Twentieth Century*, by E. Roy Calvert (English, republished by Putnam's Sons, New York).

PART II
IN THE INDUSTRIAL ARENA

CHAPTER VIII

LIFE AND LIVELIHOOD

INDUSTRIAL conditions and relations as constituting a crisis in the life of an individual, a family, or the contemporary social order burst upon my consciousness and experience almost at once, soon after arriving in Chicago. Inbred prepossessions must have accounted for the failure of economic tragedies to make any impressions upon me in youth. Born and brought up in professional circles, and living from early youth to young manhood in a college town, town and gown characterized the only class distinctions I knew. The only class-conscious conflicts of which I was aware occurred when "townies" interfered, now and then, in a student fracas on the campus. Within the student fellowship, at school, college, and seminary, I personally knew no distinction between my poorer and richer, more or less cultivated, and influential mates. Although belonging to a college fraternity and a charter member of its local chapter, I sought broader fellowships than lodge or class afforded. I somewhat resentfully deplored the tendency in certain fraternity circles to stand aloof from comradeship with class and college mates.

This democratic spirit failed to function, however, across the line between gown and town which was strangely drawn in my consciousness. Strangely, I say, because there was neither wealth nor pride in our family circle to create an aloof spirit at home. And yet, somehow, but just why I never have been able to explain, townsfolk who did business in town, even more than those of them in business in New York, seemed to be in a class by themselves and not on an equality with the small minority living and working within academic and professional circles. Moreover, the social cleavage extended still more strangely between those earning their

wages by the labor of their hands and those earning their
salaries by brain work only. There must have been subtle
pressures in the atmosphere through which I grew up to
account for these obsessions possessing my youth. That they
were not outgrowths of my own nature became apparent as
soon as I got out of these narrower circles into the big world of
real life. Ever since, the class-conscious spirit has been abhorrent. Life has had no privilege so great, no mission so
high, as to live and work between the lines cruelly and disastrously separating fellow-men by race, class, and sectarian intolerance. To have shared however briefly and unconsciously this class spirit has enabled me to recognize it as clearly
on one side of the industrial cleavage as upon the other.

As I look back upon the cleavages I encountered among my
earlier neighbors, both in the country and city, I see that they
were due more to economic causes than to social caste. Landowning farmers had so little in common with their farm hands
and their tenants farming on shares and had so much to divide
them that it was difficult, and in many cases impossible, to
unite them even in church attendance and membership.
Even in my city work at Hartford I had seen little of poverty
or unemployment, except what seemed to be due to the individual faults or personal misfortune of those in whom I was
interested. I remember nothing that impressed me with the
crises that general industrial conditions bring upon the character of individual or family life and upon the order and peace
of the community. The human factors and effects so obviously brought to attention in the study of economics must have
been lacking in my college course. Aside from scant reference
to charity in church history, my training for the ministry imposed no obligation and impressed no opportunity upon
either the church or its clergy to be either interested or influential in the workaday world or in the ways in which men,
women, and children work for a living.

My information and contacts in Hartford were too individualistic to include insight into, or sympathy with, organized labor. At that time the trade unions were not strong
there, either among workers or in their influence upon public
opinion. My eyes began to open toward the reason for their

existence, however, when two men asked me questions with which they were face to face. One of them, a sturdy Scotch carpenter, asked, "How else can wage workers get fair wages and just compensation for injury except by the union's collective bargaining and organized defense?" Another expert mechanic working in a big machine shop, who was as independent an American as I have ever known, with a bitter sense of injustice asked me, "Why cannot employers be human, not to say Christian, enough to give notice of shutting down their shops so that a workman could know in advance of the last pay day when and for how long a time his wages would cease?" A third questioner brought the church into this new range of my vision. He was the manager of a large shop in a New England mill town. He came into my Seminary classroom to state the problem that weighed heavily upon his conscience and heart and to ask for more light upon it than he had as yet seen. He said, "I earn my living as manager of the mill and help support the principal church of the town, of which I try to be an active member. But I fail to get from the church the help I need in discharging the responsibility which I keenly feel for the welfare of the two thousand operatives employed in the mill, and I also fail to enlist these employees in co-operation with the church which would be as beneficial to it as to them. What can I do about it?"

The discovery of the vital relation between life and livelihood, character and occupation, came with my effort to help weak-willed men and women resist temptations connected with the ways in which they earned their living. Where the temptation to drink was involved I had to get many men to change their jobs in order to secure for them a new start and another chance to live a better life. So coarse was the conversation in the shops where some young women worked, and so great were the liberties which certain overseers tried to take with them, that to save their modesty, if not their characters, I had to suggest and sometimes help them to secure employment elsewhere.

Thus I found the way of making a living vitally related to the Christian "Way of Life." And thus I was led to the con-

viction that the evangelization of industrial and social conditions is necessary to the evangelization of the soul, still
more of the world. Gradually such conditions proved to be
as subversive to the Christian ideal of life among the richer
as among the poorer people I knew, in the so-called higher
circles of society as among what are either contemptuously
or pitifully termed the "lower classes." Therefore, for the
sake of religion's self-defense it more and more seemed necessary to seek to make livelihood tributary to, rather than
subversive of, the Christian life; to impress the inconsistency
of trying to live the religious life on the higher plane of Christian altruism, while either glad or sorry to labor on the lower
level of an industrial order, which is pagan when unrestrict-
edly competitive.

It required the hard facts and experiences awaiting me in
Chicago to confirm these slowly developing convictions into
positive teaching, and to prompt personal effort to exemplify
them in constructive action. The first shock came with the
sudden fall from the World's Fair piping times of peace and
plenty to the business depression and unemployment, dire
poverty and public emergency immediately following the
close of the Exposition.

What I saw and felt in seeking to see where and how the
hungry, shelterless, homeless men kept soul and body together was as transforming an experience as it is an efface-
able memory. I found them sleeping on the bare floors of
miserable lodging-houses and barrel-house saloons, in the
corridors of police-station cell rooms, on the stone floors and
stairways of the old City Hall, as well as wandering about the
streets begging for a dime, as the last chance to get under
shelter for the night. Then for the first time I imagined what
an inconceivable experience it must be not to have, or know
how to find, a place to sleep through the night already darken-
ing down upon one. The upturned faces and calloused hands
of the great majority of these sleeping men showed them to be
laborers, most of whom were in the prime of life.

To the homes of silently suffering families I found access
while receiving applicants for relief at the temporary emergency station set up on the lake front in Grant Park by the

Central Relief Association. In their tenement-house apartments all over the city my students and I found men, women and children, nursing mothers and infants at the breast, the aged and sick, in patient despair, illy fed, scantily clothed, dreading eviction after their "rent" was many months in arrears.

Then, and often, yes always since, the demoralizing degradation suffered by those willing and able to work yet forced to be idle and dependent has seemed to be intolerably unjust. Far beyond the resources of the small minority of the community sustaining local charities has the relief of the unemployed grown. Unjust, indeed, is it for the majority to burden these few with a load of responsibilities that can and should be borne only by the many. The sight of nearly a thousand men kept in idleness during a whole workless winter in the Cook County Poor House first raised the question whether relief employment at greater cost would not be a more economical public policy than thus to create a pauper class. These men lay so limp and spiritless on the floor of the old "Smokers' Alley" that they did not draw their sprawling legs and arms aside to let us friendly visitors pass over their almost interwoven bodies. A patient in the adjoining County Insane Asylum had more sanity than was to be found in the public policy dealing with these men, when she exclaimed, "If they will keep me here, why will they not give me something to do?"

The appeal of my honored colleague, Professor Charles R. Henderson, written during his last illness, was for his fellow-countrymen to consider recurring periods of unemployment as modern science and philanthropy regard the pests of the middle ages—evils to be scientifically anticipated and prevented rather than left for charity doles to relieve.

Within a year following this aftermath of the World's Fair came the strike at the Pullman car works. The insight it opened into the sphere of industrial relations between employing capital and employed labor was so sudden and startling that it has always seemed to have been brought to sight by the glare of a bursting bomb rather than by the dawning of a new experience.

For twelve or more years the town of Pullman had been growing up around the great car works. It had been designed and built by the Pullman Company as the social or civic feature of the great industrial enterprise initiated and developed by the genius of George M. Pullman. The town planning for its civic center, its broad streets lined with lawns and trees, its housing provisions at various rates of rent, its store, school, and church buildings, and its park, playground, and fountain enlisted the interest and enthusiasm of the founder as much as did the equipment of the shops with the most modern machinery and the best facilities for the Company's wonderful combination of skilled trades.

As one of the earliest efforts by American industrial corporations to include in its plant such ample provision for the comfort, health, and pleasure of its employees and their families, Pullman at once became far famed as a "model town." As was intended by Mr. Pullman and the directors of the Company, it attracted skilled mechanics, with self-respecting, aspiring families, a large majority of whom were of American birth and accustomed to the American standard of living. For more than a decade these standards and ideals had been steadily maintained, while the town population had grown to include nearly ten thousand men, women, and children. Its great manufacturing industry had prospered and developed most successfully. Its "parlor" and "sleeping" cars were in demand on all the great railways, and orders for coaches increased its profitable products. Among the exhibits of the Pullman Company at the Columbian Exposition was a little illustrated booklet entitled *The Story of Pullman*, which was issued for free distribution. The hopes of its president and directors were so high as to lead them to predict: "At an early date the beautiful town of Pullman will be as a bright and radiant little island in the midst of the great tumultuous sea of Chicago's population; a restful oasis in the wearying brick-and-mortar waste of an enormous city."

Only a year afterward came the industrial depression, causing a sudden and large reduction in orders, and consequently in the work of the shop. Then began the process of cutting the wages and also the hours of work. While the income of the workmen was thus being reduced from 22 to 25 per cent, the rents of the Company houses were exacted and deducted from the week's pay. A committee representing all departments and shops of the Company waited upon the management to urge the restoration of the former wage scale. This request was refused on the ground that business conditions made any increase from the reduced rate impossible. The disappointed workers were irritated the next day by the discharge of three members of their committee on the alleged ground of the lack of work for them. Although the Pullman shops had never recognized the trade unions, a small minority of their employees belonged to the unions of their respective trades. Some of these unions ordered their members employed there to strike. The Company promptly laid off all its remaining employees and temporarily closed down all its shops.

A month later the American Railway Union held its first annual convention in Chicago, having been organized a year previously "to include railway employees born of white parents in one great brotherhood." Some of the Pullman employees, hitherto unorganized, hastily joined this very general sort of a union. Against the advice of its officials, but as members of the order, they joined in what was a shop-crew strike. Then this Railway Union, to support these new members, resorted to the boycott of Pullman cars wherever found in use here and elsewhere. Such was the course of events as reported by the United States Strike Commission.[1]

In quick succession followed the interruption of travel and scenes of disorder throughout the country. Here in Chicago the sudden transformation of a great industrial plant and a great city's railway yards into a scene of war was profoundly impressive, as it opened to view both the sharp edges and the dark depth of the social cleavage. Ominously silent groups of men stood about. Company guards, hired from private-detective agencies, armed but without uniform, were stationed along property lines, at the shops, and where the Pullman cars were being switched. The city police patrolled both

[1] See also Graham Romeyn Taylor, *Satellite Cities*, chaps. ii and iii. Appleton, 1915.

sides of the line, or were held in reserve at their stations. Some conflicts between the strikers and the Company guards ensued, but without bloodshed or loss of life. Some destruction of property was claimed, the responsibility for all of which was charged by each side to the other. At last, by order of President Grover Cleveland, United States troops from Fort Sheridan took possession of the strike area. Silently strikers and citizens watched them marching, bivouacking, camping, standing on sentry duty, and stacking their arms ready for use.

Such scenes surely were serious enough to startle or stun the civic consciousness of any patriotic citizen. Protesting against this supersedure of the state's civil authority by the military power of the federal government, Governor John P. Altgeld claimed ability to control the situation if called upon to do so by the mayor of the city. So much of public opinion as found expression through the press approved the President's act as a prevention of more serious trouble. But the depth and intensity of class feeling could be realized only through personal contacts with excited or sullen men on either side, as they threatened reprisals for their losses, on the one hand, or resented blacklisting from further employment, on the other hand.

Whatever occasion had been given for the strike by the reduction of wages and other disagreements between the Company and the employees, a deeper cause for unrest at Pullman really accounted for the breach. Nearly ten years before Professor Richard T. Ely found it difficult to get any frank opinions on living and working conditions from the residents of Pullman whom he personally interviewed. They claimed to be afraid of "spotters" and the serious consequences which they might suffer if they spoke their minds, although "to beat the Company" was admitted to be considered legitimate under the circumstances. Thus early the "model town" was charged by Professor Ely with being "feudalistic," however benevolent, because of the Company's ownership of all the real estate property, including not only the houses but the stores, the schools, and the church, as well as the streets and all other facilities for public use.

Incidentally I learned from Mr. Pullman himself, during the World's Fair year, the extent to which this paternalistic ownership controlled the situation. Happening to meet him in the elevator of the downtown Pullman Building, I asked him what means the Company took to ally its employees and other residents of the town with its policies. His terse remark, to which he might have wished to add much had there been more time, fairly startled me when he replied: "A clause in every lease enables us on short notice to be rid of undesirable tenants."

After the strike was well over, Jane Addams summed up the motives which account both for the rise and the fall of this remarkable experiment. In her notable article she sympathetically compared Mr. Pullman's good intentions and the bitter disappointment he suffered from what seemed to him the ingratitude of the people for whose welfare he had ventured so much with the somewhat similar experience of Shakespeare's King Lear with his daughter Cordelia. With incisive ethical insight, for which she is perhaps most distinguished, she laid bare the subtle self-deception, to which she thought the whole tragedy was due, in these few words: "He cultivated the great and noble impulses of the benefactor until the power of attaining a simple human relationship with his employees was gone from him."

The pitiful disillusion came to an end through two other causes. Five years before the strike the annexation of Pullman to Chicago against the strenuous opposition of the Company had crippled its control of the town. And four years after the strike the Supreme Court of Illinois decided that the charter of the Pullman Company did not permit it to hold and occupy more real estate than its manufacturing purposes required. At the end of the period granted to dispose of these large improved holdings the Company's possessions were limited to its shops and office buildings, with a large tract of unoccupied land, which thereupon became available for purchase as the city grew over it.

The change from the paternalistic company control of the town to its democratic administration as a ward of the city of Chicago has been attended by some losses and certain gains to the resident community. In appearance the residence streets and their dwellings have lost the attractiveness which they had when they were uniformly well kept, cleaned, and bordered with grass, trees, and flowers. In school and recreational equipment the people have gained. In relationship between the Company and its employees there have been fewer matters to differ about, and on the whole more consideration has been shown by each to the other.

Politically the voters have been intelligently independent, electing the first socialist to the City Council, when both old party candidates were discovered to be unfit, and then, after seating two Republican aldermen, superseded them when they proved unworthy by two Democrats. With one exception any candidate for public office for a long while was disadvantaged by being closely connected with the Company in any way. The exception was in the case of John P. Hopkins, a man who was considered a valuable though independent higher employee. Upon being discharged after carrying the town for the Democrats against the Republican preference of the Company, he was elected mayor of Chicago, and, by the irony of fate, served in that capacity, not very creditably to himself or the city, at the time of the strike.

This first strike, of which I had been a close observer, impressed me so keenly that it led me into deep experiences and impelled me to take action along certain lines. It imposed upon me the obligation to understand, and make understood by others, the reasons and issues causing industrial antagonisms, and the feelings, fears, and hopes of fellow-men on either side which caused them honestly to differ. It disclosed the class spirit to be in possession of many on both sides. It was a trumpet call to refuse to be classified and to stand in between, in order to keep in such personal touch with some on both sides as might open opportunity to mediate before the lines of difference became rigidly set for conflict.

CHAPTER IX

BETWEEN CLASS-CONSCIOUS BELLIGERENTS

AN EVENT which threw me between the lines of conflict involved an experience which would have disillusioned any previously conceived obsession as to either party being always and all right. A great lockout was declared by the Building Contractors' Association against the Building Trades' Council during the erection of the Chicago Commons building. The deadlock between the two big organizations which controlled all building operations in the city indefinitely suspended all construction, which stopped short of roofing our building, while it was being damaged by the winter's storms. Moved by the losses to private property thus inflicted, and by the public peril of having no less than fifty thousand workmen locked out of their jobs, I sought opportunity to propose arbitration as the only way out of a disastrously long and bitter test of endurance. To this end I asked to be heard at a Sunday-afternoon meeting of the Building Trades' Council, which request was granted. Before doing so, however, I submitted to the editors of a morning and evening newspaper a written copy of the appeal I proposed to make orally, on condition that they would print it on the day following its delivery. After reading carefully what I had written, Victor F. Lawson promptly consented to publish it in the *Chicago Daily News*. So did Herman H. Kohlsaat, in the *Chicago Record Herald*, remarking that "if he could make such an address to the Building Trades' Council without getting his head broken, he would consider it a public service to do so." Thus assured of fair publicity, I appeared at the Sunday-afternoon meeting of the Council, and found myself to be the only person present outside of the organizations represented. A respectful hearing was given by about four hundred of their delegates to my appeal for submitting to the Chicago Real Estate Board's arbitration the differences at issue. In so doing I avoided entering into the merits of the controversy, except to state that it was aggravated by the alliance of certain of their leaders with certain crooked politicians at the City Hall in trading political influence for appointments to city jobs. This closing appeal to rid the unions of such suspicious double dealings caused excited charges during which one or two of the said leaders left the platform for the rear of the hall, apparently to be less conspicuous. The proposal to arbitrate was accepted and a committee appointed to request the Real Estate Board to take the initiative.

But the building contractors promptly and angrily refused to consider any such proposal, declaring that there was nothing to arbitrate and that they proposed to settle the affair themselves. Their resentment against any interference was taken so decisively before any effort could be made even to confer with them that further endeavor was deemed futile. As the lockout threatened to continue indefinitely and inflict serious damage on our unroofed Chicago Commons building, I made an attempt to have it inclosed merely for protection against the stormy weather. Our contractors agreed to do so on condition that the union men working on the job would work regardless of the demands at issue in the lockout. This concession was made by officials of the Carpenters' Union at my personal appeal, even though it involved working with non-union men. Our contractors, however, failed to get the consent of the Contractors' Association and regretfully refused my request. They also declined to allow us to supply the labor and assume the responsibility for meeting the contract requirements, while they continued to supply the material and oversee the job. My suggestion that we might conclude to inclose the building ourselves was met by threat of suit for breach of contract.

The friendliness on the part of both the contractors and workmen employed on our job was such as to secure from each other concessions enabling them to resume work on our building as soon as any construction was permitted to proceed. But there was an aftermath which evened up any odds to the credit of the union's consideration. When the building was completed invitations were sent to the workmen who had been employed upon it to a housewarming, and the unions to which they belonged were invited to meet a distinguished British trade-union leader—Ben Tillet—as the guest of honor. Without intimation to us, the Carpenters' Union notified its own and other unions' members that as the building was "scab-built" unionists should not attend its opening.

Immediately renting a neighboring hall in which to "receive" and hear the guest of honor, I asked to be heard at the next meeting of the Carpenters' Union. Upon being introduced to three hundred or more men in attendance as having a "grievance against the Union," I stated that in view of our open and friendly understanding previously attained the black-listing of the building in response to our invitation to celebrate its opening for the use of the great industrial population surrounding it was a breach of their honor, and moreover did discredit to the guest of honor. In response the chairman called upon the members to act upon the matter. Whereupon many called for "Duffy" to speak. With a rich Celtic brogue and with all the emphasis that could be given by stentorian tones and strong-arm gestures he defended the Union's social boycott of the building by making the roundly applauded declaration: "I would no more go near that building than I would enter one infected with leprosy, for the floor beams cry to the rafters 'scab-built,' 'scab-built!'" The chairman, announcing that the Union would take action after my withdrawal, in a sincerely, friendly tone and with a twinkle of humor in his eye assured me that "as a friend of theirs I might expect many a harder rap than this." The next morning's paper reported: "WHEREAS" I had been considered as a friend of labor, and had faced the Union with my grievance, and although I had been "found in bad non-union company," nevertheless, *"Therefore resolved*, That Chicago Commons' building be expurgated from all offense." Thereupon the telephone bell rang repeatedly with congratulations more facetious than complimentary. Nevertheless, we were no longer under the lepers' ban to warn all union-comers of our being "Unclean," "Unclean," since we had been officially given a bill of health certifying that we were ceremonially clean.

No touch of any such sense of humor came from the Contractors' Association, but the only aftermath of their action came long afterward in the reminiscent remark of one of the donors to the building fund that he had been followed to California with a suggestion from Chicago that he withdraw his contribution. Having formerly been a producer of building material, it is not a very far-fetched suspicion that this suggestion might have been prompted by this fact.

In no uncertain terms the logic of all these facts served notice of what anyone might expect who ventured to stand between the rigidly drawn lines of such belligerents, even though the venture was made in order to claim that the public had rights which both of them were bound to respect, and that the private citizen should not be left to suffer the worst injuries of the conflict as an unprotected, innocent bystander. It was a great and permanent advantage thus for a second time to be established in this position between the lines of class warfare so firmly as never to waver from the stand then taken for the supremacy of public welfare and the community-right and duty to protect its own peace. Incidentally, then and ever since it has appeared that the weapons of industrial warfare—strike or lockout, closed or open shop, unfair list or boycott, the vengeance upon the non-union "scab" or the "blacklisted" employee—can be and are employed for essentially the same ends, and are ever readily at hand for either, belligerent to use, however one side may more secretly or less violently use them than the other.

So far from having one's vision blurred, or one's judgment biased, or one's heart hardened, or one's courage daunted by such stern facts and lonesome experiences, they only emphasized more imperatively one's public duty, and more persuasively one's social opportunity, to understand actual situations, to interpret the personal interests and class attitudes of each side to the other, and, where opportunity was offered by both sides, to endeavor to mediate honest differences.

In order to understand divisive issues, much more to promote a better understanding among all concerned, I keenly recognized how necessary it was to come into personal touch not only with individual wage-earners and employers, but with the organized groups to which they belonged. Only thus can one know and feel the community of interests which hold them together and array them against each other. The way into close contacts on either side was not readily found, however. The establishment of family residence at Chicago Commons located us indeed between the lines of the industrial conflict. But at first it failed to open our way to the organized contestants on either side. Our neighborhood was very predominantly non-union, being composed very largely of recently arrived immigrants, so that my acquaintanceship there was with them. Some employers seemed to regard with suspicion anyone living among the laboring classes as exclusively identified with them.

The trade unions did not welcome visitors at their meetings. None of them was opened to the membership of anyone who did not carry the card of its trade. A Federal Union was irregularly organized to take outsiders into a nominal but not real connection with the labor movement. Employers' associations were also limited to tradesmen or manufacturers in single or allied trades. Had membership in either been opened to me I would not have joined because it would have aligned me with one side or the other, not leaving me free to stand between class lines for the interest of both and to serve the public welfare.

It remained only to await opportunity to form acquaintanceships with individual leaders or representatives on both sides. It was not readily acquired, however. Yet vital points of contact with the labor movement I soon found to be accessible. Visits to the headquarters of the best-organized and best-managed trade unions, often accompanied by a group of students, afforded insight into their aims and methods, chiefly through interviews with some of their ablest officials with whom I have long maintained more or less personal relationships. The Sunday-afternoon meetings of the Chicago Federation of Labor were open to visitors and acquainted me with some local leaders and their vigorous practice of free speech. Occasional attendance upon the annual conventions of the American Federation of Labor impressed me with the order of its procedure and the ability of its officials. Both compared very favorably with the members and spokesmen in state legislatures whom I had observed. Representative periodicals of the labor press supplemented the annual reports of trade unions and federations of labor and the publications of state and national departments of labor in enabling me to sense the actual situation facing the wage-earners. Trades' journals and reports of employers' associations, together with the proceedings and discussions of chambers of commerce and groups of economists, disclosed labor issues as equally vital to their interests. Wages, hours, jurisdictional disputes, the standard of living, collective bargaining, and ways of settling industrial disputes were the issues chiefly if not exclusively involved on both sides. The city federations of local trade unions go farther afield to discuss and pass judgment upon matters of current interest, but these judgments neither represent nor bind the unions whose delegates constitute the membership of these local central bodies.

The radical groups, both in their own organizations and in the free discussions in which they eagerly participate, are less concerned with these concrete situations and are almost exclusively interested in the advocacy of what they consider would be a better social order. But never have their representatives in the American Federation of Labor succeeded in securing more than a small minority of votes for any of their often-repeated resolutions and recommendations. These facts are cited here in proof of the claim that the trade unionism of the United States is the most conservative of all national labor movements in the world.

Nevertheless, these radical groups constituted no negligible part of the situation then and thereafter existing. Therefore, not only to some of their meetings did I resort for first-hand impressions of what they thought and how they felt, but conferred with many of them individually, as man to man with frank respect for each other's opinions, and offered free speech to them, as to all others attending certain public occasions at Chicago Commons. By such personal contacts and the insights they opened I learned what the adherents of violent measures thought of their own idealistic ends. And so at last I attained a better understanding of their motives than I could have gotten by standing aloof to denounce theories and measures which have never appealed to my reason, my faith, or my hope.

The socialists and anarchists were at the opposite and antagonistic poles of thought and action. As collectivists the socialists claimed more control for the body politic than any free, modern state had ever asserted, but not so much as the dictatorships in Russia and Italy have enforced. Their procedure was political and legislative. Their only weapon was the ballot. Their organization was that of a party. The anarchists held the individual to be so capable of self-control as to be amenable to voluntary association. Coercive law was therefore resented as an invasion of individual rights, and a device of a ruling minority to subject and exploit the wage-earning majority. Direct action and the resort to destructive violence were justified by some anarchistic spokesmen, while others claimed to represent a non-resistant attitude such as Leo Tolstoy advocated. They were organized loosely and secretively in small "sections." Their acts of violence proved to be taken, if not prompted, on individual impulse, as in the cases of the lone assassins of Presidents Garfield and McKinley.

The trade unionists, both in speech and action, demonstrated that they were men of the "concrete mind," as Jane Addams had described them to be, in contrast with radical theorists. They were found to be more dependable than the radical theorists were in efforts to realize social ideals and standards in legislative and administrative policies. Moreover, the radical groups fluctuate too much in both membership and location to count effectively in carrying on and out such movements. For this reason the Industrial Workers of the World, like the long-since-defunct Knights of Labor, failed to function further than to be more of a fellowship of unskilled, casual, or seasonal laborers, than a permanent organization effective either in defensive or aggressive influence.

The rise and spread of the I.W.W. are due to the long neglect of the unskilled and transient workers by the trades and labor assemblies and the state and American federations of labor. Against their ineligibility for membership in the union of any specialized trade, these laborers reacted in their rallying cry for "one big union." Although their organization is ostracized both by employers and the trade unions, yet it is the form given to the "shop union" wherever any company and their employees unite to organize all employed at any one plant. This they unite to do, not only to create a permanently organized and ever open way of communicating and co-operating with each other for the prevention and settlement of their differences, but more still to avoid or counteract the jurisdictional disputes between the unions of the trades which cost both management and men the loss of so much time and money. Denied the permanent foothold anywhere upon which alone home life and citizenship can be established, these wandering seasonal workers are merely tolerated, and sometimes are driven out when they have done their work. Where else, except in some I.W.W. hall or Hobo College, is human friendship offered or open to them? Whatever attraction or hold the I.W.W. has is due to its human touch upon men who feel no other.

Their national headquarters in Chicago attested to me the strength and the sacrifice with which these uprooted, scattered, ever moving, temporarily lodged, intermittently employed multitudes of men are capable of responding to whatever fellowship is offered them. The four-story building leased by them for several years sheltered the home office of these homeless men. There I found nearly a score of writers, corresponding or preparing copy for print in nearly as many different languages, the products of whose pens and press crowded the stock- and distributing-rooms occupying two floors with their polyglot periodicals and other publications. But with their burly president, William D. Haywood, I was not favorably impressed. His "strong-arm" policies contrasted very unfavorably both with his own kindliness toward these friendless men and with some sincere and intelligent members of this secretariat, which any church mission board would have been fortunate to duplicate.

Leaving some of them to suffer long prison terms for alleged sedition in conspiracy with him during the World War,

Haywood jumped his bail and fled to Russia to escape his sentence, thereby deserting both his comrades and the cause with the leadership of which they had entrusted him. He left it and his country, however, for the good of both, judging his career by its exemplification of the worst type of leadership from which the American labor movement has suffered most. Dying in Russia in 1928, the ashes of his cremated body were divided, one half ceremoniously interred by the soviet government at Moscow, and the other half by his American friends at Waldheim Cemetery, Chicago, near the graves of the Haymarket Riot "martyrs," on the latest commemoration of the day of their death. *Bill Haywood's Book* (1929) divulges and attests the futility of violence in thought and action as a motive or method in labor leadership.

Few and far between are any efforts made to understand and interpret these wandering seasonal workers and casual laborers by other than radical propagandists. Almost alone stands Professor Carleton Parker's disclosure of the psychological effects of the economic vicissitudes accounting both for their mental attitude and migratory habits. This discovery he made by camping with them on their trails, in order to acquire for himself and share with others an intelligent understanding of these misunderstood men. His interpretation of them is as scientific as it is human.[1] With his conclusions those who have known and dealt with these men best entirely agree:

> The casual migratory laborers are the finished product of an economic environment which seems cruelly indifferent in turning out human beings modeled after all the standards which society abhors. The history of the migratory workers shows that starting with the long hours and dreary winters of the farms they ran away from, or the sour-smelling bunk house in a coal village, through their character-debasing experience with the drifting "hire and fire" life in the industries, on to the vicious, social and economic life of the winter unemployed, their training predetermined but one outcome, and the environment produced its type. . . . . The cure lies in care-taking of its physical antecedents, and the stability of our Republic depends on the degree of courage and science with which we move to the task.

[1] Carleton H. Parker, *The Casual Laborer and Other Essays*. New York: Harcourt, Brace & Howe, 1920. Also Cornelia Stratton Parker, *An American Idyll*.

Certain incidental occasions led to a discovery that was as surprising as it was disappointing and discouraging. It was the disclosure of the intensity and intolerance of class-conscious feeling prevailing not only among those on both sides who were immediately involved in controversy, but as pronouncedly throughout one whole class as the other. Such a discovery came when our non-union neighbors around Chicago Commons became as class conscious, almost overnight, as were the striking teamsters. When the strike-breakers drove the police-protected coal carts down our avenue, men from the sidewalks, women from the tenement-house windows, and even the little children in the playground cried with one voice, "Down with the scabs," some of them hurling any missile at hand at the frightened drivers. Then we learned what most employers fail to discover, that the "solidarity of labor" extends beyond the membership of unions, and that on occasion the class-conscious spirit emerges from the whole working class—just as it does from the whole employing class.

Not more did this class feeling bristle up into the expressions of class conflict in radical labor circles than in representative groups of business men. From one such little group of excited employers I was drawn aside by one of them who broke his silence by remarking: "These fellows do not know that their labor troubles are only local expressions of a time-long, world-wide, two-sided struggle." At another dinner occasion, an old Catholic priest, who acted as chaplain and therefore was expected to say the last word before adjournment, playfully rebuked the toastmaster for his unwonted excitement. After being called from the chair to be informed of the progress of a strike at his factory, the chairman drew from his pocket a revolver, exclaiming as he laid it down upon the table in sight of all the guests, "This is what we have come to in Chicago." Thereupon, with Irish humor, this priest of a great industrial district parish closed the occasion by looking down sympathetically upon his far-smaller host to remark: "The trouble with you, sir, is that you are too little a man to be discussing such great subjects." As the company rose, color also rose to the very roots of the toastmaster's hair. In closer fellowships I have been glad to find that this class feeling, while a very real subconsciousness on both sides, only occasionally and for very brief periods rises to the intensity of a class-conflict spirit.

A great service was rendered me by Towner K. Webster, a broad-minded, large-hearted friend at the head of a manufacturing industry. Sympathizing with all efforts to promote a better understanding between capital and labor, and enlisting in them himself, he desired for me the wider acquaintanceship with business men which membership in the Union League Club would afford. He not only secured my election but generously paid my initiation fees, which at that time I was too overburdened with the financial responsibility for Chicago Commons to be able to afford. It proved to be one of the most considerate and valuable acts of friendship ever extended to me personally and professionally.

Thus I came naturally into personal contact with men in a great variety of callings, many of whom also had great influence in public affairs. Later, membership in the Chicago Association of Commerce opened outlook upon a still wider range of business interests represented by its six thousand members. The City Club, of which I was one of the founders, gave free expression to opinions of those especially interested and informed on politico-economic questions. The University Club also afforded a place and occasions for meeting professional and other men interested in academic fellowship and cultural interests.

Before I left Hartford, friends in manufacturing and mercantile enterprises of their own complained of the rapidly prevailing tendency to combine capital and operating plants for "large-scale production," with which it seemed impossible for independent smaller plants to compete. Two partners who had developed a satisfactorily successful bakery in New England on comparatively small capital let me see their situation as they saw and felt it. They told me that a stranger had called upon them at their factory office with the proposition that they should enter the "national" company in which enough of the bakery interests had combined to control the business. They replied that they were satisfied with their own plant and preferred to operate it independently. The propos-

al soon became a demand to enter the combination or to be
undersold in the market. After helplessly hesitating a few
days, these partners concluded to surrender to the demand,
hopeless of competing against as many millions of dollars as
they had hundreds of thousands. So thereafter they became
overseers in their own factory, operating their plant at the
orders from distant headquarters. This was the first insight
I caught as an eyewitness of the coercion within the ranks of
employing capital.

Other instances involving even whole communities multiplied. One of them closed up the one factory upon which almost all the people in a small New Jersey town depended for
their living. The other resulted in the abandonment of a large
industrial plant upon which a small city in New York State
likewise depended. There the big combine could afford to let
its recently acquired shops and machinery be scrapped and
charged up to the "profit-and-loss account," but employees
by the hundreds lost the savings of a lifetime which they had
invested in the purchase or building of their little homes,
which they could neither sell nor rent after the "works"
closed down and the "hands" were set adrift.

Despite the hardships involved, such combinations of capital seemed to be an economic advantage, and often a necessity, in order to increase profits by the decrease of the cost of
production, which not seldom reduced the price of the product
while improving its quality. Thus it dawned upon me that
competition is by no means invariably the "life of trade," but
when unrestricted becomes the deterioration of trade and
sometimes the economic death of the better traders. Therefore I came to the abiding conclusion that to legislate so far
against "trusts" as to compel those to compete to the interest
of whose profits, products, and prices it is to combine is detrimental alike to private and public interests.

Meanwhile, I could not avoid wondering whether the combination thus found to be profitable if not necessary on the
capitalistic and employing side of industry was any more
legitimate or less coercive than on the part of the wage-work-
ing employees whose only capital is their skill, their time, and
their strength. I wondered also whether the rougher coercion

suffered by non-union workers at the "strong-arm" of organized labor really hurt any more than the weight of the blow inflicted by a club of gold which drives independent capitalists either into the combination or out of business. Just why the same principle and virtually the same tactics are considered to be legitimate business enterprise on one side of the line and criminal conspiracy and outlawed radicalism on the other side I have never been able to discover. But the American sense of fair play has clearly shown in every industrial conflict which I have witnessed the rank injustice of claiming for one set of partners the right to organize, while denying the same right to their labor competitors. And equally unjust has it always seemed for those who claim the right, if not the necessity, to pool their brains and dollars for their own advantage to deny their employees the right and advantage of bargaining collectively in the competitive market where the skill and time of labor are sold and bought. To justify such discrimination must not one stultify one's self to hold it to be fair to conduct "business" collectively as the twentieth century requires, and yet to compel "labor" to bargain individually, as in the centuries preceding the factory system?

While convinced of the soundness of these principles, I have never had inclination or occasion to be obsessed by any illusion as to the angelic practice of them by representatives either of organized capital or of organized labor. Indeed, I have urged certain manufacturers who were being victimized by the unscrupulous exploitation of a "closed-shop" union, whose skill was necessary to their productive process, to organize as closely in an employers' association in order to meet organization with organization, so as not any longer to suffer the disadvantage in fighting singly and alone in the tug-of-war with a well-organized and disciplined union. When these manufacturers did organize, "Greek met Greek," resulting in an armistice on more equal terms, which led to a more peaceful, just, and friendly pact between those unnecessarily belligerent co-workers.

Our efforts at Chicago Commons to acquire and spread the ministry of understanding was far from being confined to the so-called laboring classes. Much less was it restricted to what might be considered the pathological aspects of the modern industrial order. We aimed quite as distinctly to serve those in business and professional circles who could be attracted to learn at first hand from the other half of the industrial world how they lived, labored, felt, and thought. For several years also the spring and autumn social economic conferences offered interpreters of eminence in our own and other lands, from whom rare insights and outlooks were attained by those who met and heard them.

Pursuing these purposes, I wrote and published in *The Commons*, our settlement monthly, a long series of articles on the rise, development, and significance of the labor movement, which I made the basis for a seminary lecture course introductory to others on the ethics of industry. As detailed in the next chapter, I accepted invitations to conciliate industrial differences and arbitrate strikes, but only when both employers and employees at odds with each other agreed to ask me to settle their differences. I also served on several industrial commissions appointed by the mayor of Chicago and the governor of Illinois.

It has been a most interesting and informing personal experience to swing between such extremes nearly every twenty-four hours through so many years. Starting the day with my teaching in the Seminary classroom within the university campus, stopping for luncheon conferences at one of the clubs or at the "Ways and Means" weekly conference of the Association of Commerce, returning to the cosmopolitan wage-earning neighborhood of Chicago Commons, spending the evenings with groups of workingmen or workingwomen assembled there, or attending elsewhere some larger or smaller public meeting, called to express and attract interest in some industrial, social, or civic situation, my daily life ranged over much of the whole gamut of human vicissitudes.

CHAPTER X

THE ANARCHIST TRAGEDY OF 1886

ATTEMPTS to suppress and to reassert the rights to free assembly and to free speech were so dramatically emphasized by the so-called anarchist tragedy of 1886 that it calls for separate comment as an event which attracted the attention of the world and challenged the concern of the American people. Although it occurred six years before I arrived in Chicago, the tragedy could be realized more vividly because the Haymarket where it occurred was only five blocks away from the old residence of Chicago Commons. A statue of a policeman stood there to commemorate not only the officers who had been killed by the explosion of the bomb, but quite as much to signalize the triumph of law over anarchy by the execution of the men convicted of inciting the act. Several years later the statue was removed as an obstruction to traffic and was re-erected in a public park a mile away.

The scenes enacted at Randolph and Desplaines streets and in the Criminal Court, as registered in the press and in the record of the trial, were re-enacted, not only before me but within me, through my personal contacts with many who had laid the tragedy to heart and with some who had witnessed it. The human-interest incidents and the personalities involved made a deep impression upon me and left their abiding mark upon public opinion and policies. I had heard Mrs. Lucy Parsons tell the story of the tragic part which she had borne through the whole course of these fateful events. She was the widow of Albert R. Parsons, editor of a radical paper, *The Alarm*, one of the four men who were executed. I first saw and heard her at Turner Hall, where radical labor gatherings were held. I had gone there with a small group of my students to witness the memorial meeting held to commemorate the "martyrs" who had died for anarchism.

On that eleventh day of November nine years before, they had died on the scaffold, and now nine years after—and every year since—not only here in Chicago, but at every great industrial center throughout the world, their "martyrdom" was celebrated. Over twelve hundred men, women, and many young people filled the hall. Silently they awaited the belated arrival of Johann Most, a notorious anarchist propagandist of New York City. The stage and the walls of the hall were festooned with red flags, intertwined with which were streamers bearing the sentiments expressed by the men from their prison and scaffold. Their favorite songs were sung by a chorus of young women dressed in white with black sashes. "Annie Laurie," which had been sung by Parsons in his cell just before he was executed plaintively followed "The Marseillaise." During an intermission, while I was being introduced to Mrs. Parsons on the floor of the house where she was seated, calls were made for her to speak. Her appearance on the platform was impressive. Tall, well built and poised, self-possessed and commanding attention by her serious manner and resonant voice, she began to speak thus: "I am the widow of Albert R. Parsons and the mother of his son. I charge the police and the court with murdering my husband. I live to bring up his son to take up the work which was stricken from his father's hand."

The police captain of the precinct then appeared upon the stage, touched her lightly, and bade her come with him. She followed, was taken to the police station, was charged with disorderly conduct, and was promptly released, as she had been whenever and wherever she had attempted to speak since the riot. This interruption was therefore no surprise to those assembled on this occasion, much less to her. One excited newcomer, however, started for the platform crying in stentorian tones, "Forwarts!" He was quickly followed by those who silenced and seated him. The chairman calmly announced in German: "The next speaker will be Herr Most." The meeting then proceeded in as orderly a manner as though there had been no interruption.

The appearance of Mrs. Parsons at one of our Chicago Commons free-floor meetings several years after the scene in which she figured at the memorial prompted the unanimous vote that she be heard on the following Tuesday. Taken by surprise and not a little embarrassed, I offered no objection to the proposal, which I knew would be regarded as a supreme test of the freedom of the floor. But I suggested to her that it might be an opportunity to disappoint her enemies by the calmness of her manner and the reasonableness of her speech, of which she was reputed to be incapable. Reminding her that she was not likely to be interrupted and silenced by arrest at such a privately conducted meeting, as she had been hitherto on public occasions, I expressed a hope that she could and would frankly and freely state the underlying motive which justified, to herself at least, her attitude toward the social order. The suspicioning look as of one who was hunted faded from her face as she replied: "You will not be disappointed in having spoken kindly to me." She seemed transformed, at least momentarily, from the creature at bay which she appeared to be when I saw her put under arrest. At the following meeting she happily disappointed my fears and realized my hopes. She produced and closely read a paper descriptive of her experience, from the time she came to Chicago from the Southwest to marry the radical editor. Sympathetic with the poor, indignant at the harsh treatment of the unemployed, especially the foreign born when attempting public demonstrations to call attention to their plight, she traced her gradually increasing convictions until she became convinced that nothing short of the end of the existing capitalistic industrial order would bring either justice or peace. She concluded with a very brief reference to the Haymarket meeting, stating that she had accompanied her husband when he had been sent for to speak, after it had been running some time. "And," she simply added, "my husband placed me near him while speaking from the truck in front of which the bomb exploded." Then, calmly as unexpectedly, and with a reserve that was as dramatic as it was surprising to me and everyone else in the crowded room, she took her seat. "Go on," cried some of the men. "I have finished," she replied.

"What happened afterward?" she was asked. "It is a matter of history," she answered. When finally asked, inconsiderately enough, to express her opinion of her husband's execution, evidently in hope of arousing her old-time bitter spirit, she silenced all further questions by decidedly remarking, "I am not here to defend his memory." But the implication of her stopping her story when and where she did spoke louder than any word could have done against the presumption that he could have expected any such catastrophe as occurred so soon after they had left the scene of it.

The day before that fateful May day, men on strike to enforce the eight-hour day had assembled in Chicago, as at many other city industrial centers. Here they met outside the gates of the McCormick Reaper Works. When the whistle blew at the close of the working day some of the employees who had not struck were roughly treated as they left the plant. The police protected them with clubs and gunfire. One striker was killed and several were wounded. That night and the next morning circulars were distributed calling a meeting of protest at the Haymarket, as the market wagon stand was called, at Randolph and Desplaines streets. One of these circulars was headed: "Working Men! To Arms!" It was taken as a threat of revenge. Police reserves were held at the station near the Haymarket to meet any emergency. But the crowd of about two thousand assembled there was found to be orderly by the mayor, Carter H. Harrison, Sr., who after hearing the speeches and moving about among the people advised the police officials to dismiss the reserves as there was no danger of disorder. But no sooner had the Mayor left than the police were marched to the truck from which the last speaker was closing his address. The captain ordered the small remnant of the crowd lingering there after most of the people had been scattered by rain to disperse. The speaker replied by asking: "Why, captain, as this is a peaceable meeting?" Then the dynamite bomb was thrown—for the first time as a missile it is said—by whom it was never discovered, then or since. Most of the police were blown off their feet, one was killed, six were mortally wounded, and fifty were more or less injured.

Then followed in rapid succession the police dragnet, rounding up all radical groups, with or without grounds of suspicion; the indictment, trial, and conviction of eight prisoners, on evidence proving the radical opinions of all of them, involving only one of them in making or handling bombs, but conclusively proving none of them to have either thrown the murderous bomb or to have known that it was to be hurled; the sentencing of seven men to death and one to imprisonment; Governor Oglesby's commutation of two death penalties to life-imprisonment; the suicide of the bomb-maker and the hanging of four; and the subsequent pardon of the three prisoners by Governor Altgeld, after they had served six years' imprisonment.[1]

Forty years after the tragedy occurred the anarchist case was critically reviewed by Sigmund Zeisler, in a paper read at the Chicago Literary Club, May 3, 1926, which was published in the *Illinois Law Review*.[2] He prefaced it with the statement that he was

the sole survivor of the thrilling drama—the presiding judge, the twelve jurors, all the counsel for the state and defense, except himself, all the police officials active in the case, the seven justices of the Illinois Supreme Court which reviewed and affirmed the judgment of the criminal court, the nine justices of the Supreme Court of the United States which declined to take jurisdiction, and the three pardoned prisoners, all having died.

Referring to Altgeld's intensive study of the record in the case and his conclusion that "the eight defendants had been convicted not because they had been proved guilty of murder, but because they were anarchists," Mr. Zeisler himself concludes that "this is today the judgment of the majority of thinking men and will tomorrow be the judgment of history."

The reporter for the *Chicago Daily News* who witnessed the execution again reported in its columns what he saw and heard four decades before. The first of the four men to speak from the scaffold said: "You may strangle this voice, but my silence will be more terrible than speech." Another exclaimed:

[1] See Waldo R. Browne, *Altgeld of Illinois* (New York: Huebsch, 1924), for a statement of many facts and a review of the situation in defense of Altgeld.

[2] "Reminiscences of the Anarchist Case," *Illinois Law Review*. Chicago: Northwestern University, November, 1926.

"This is the happiest moment of my life. *Hoch die Anarchie!*"
The next man echoed that exultant cry. The last of the four,
and the only American among the eight convicted men,
Albert R. Parsons, died pleading: "O men of America, let
the voice of the people be heard." The old reporter simply
added: "Then I understood why Eugene Field said he would
not take one hundred dollars to go to the execution." The
graves at Waldheim Cemetery continue to bloom with the
floral tributes of many who revere them as martyrs who gave
their lives in devotion to what they claim to be the higher
ideal of the social order.

Although while in the East I had shared the country-wide
indorsement of their conviction and penalty, ever since, at
closer range, that verdict of the jury of public opinion has
been challenged by these two questions: Was it just to condemn men for their opinions, however abhorrent, who were
indicted solely for murder? Might it not have been better
public policy at least to let the life-blood of these executed
men run in their own veins rather than to have let it inoculate
the blood running in the veins of so many others throughout
the land and all over the world with a virus for which they
were condemned? But neither by my own or others' question-
ing opinions have I been swerved in my abiding loyalty to law
as not only the indispensable basis and bond of any social
order, but also as the best friend of us each and all. Nor have
I ever failed to challenge by spoken and written word the lawlessness of lawbreakers both high and low, or to refute the
claim of idealists that mankind is inherently good enough to
do without law as far from the facts of experience.

The folly and futility of attempting to suppress anarchism
by the anarchistic use of the police power was illustrated after
the death of President McKinley, at the hands of the lone
fanatic assassin. Not only ignoring but also denying the
rights to all legal procedure, the police dragnet was spread
over the whole city. Without warrants or specific charges
men, women, and even their half-grown children were arrested wherever they happened to be found. Some of them were
taken from their homes at night, separated, held in solitary
custody without permission to communicate with an attorney,

much less with each other or with friends, simply on the suspicion of holding radical opinions or attending meetings
where they were discussed.

Among these thus unjustly treated were two men who had
been prominent in the economic discussions at Hull House and
Chicago Commons. Miss Addams, with Raymond Robins,
representing the Commons in my absence, waited upon
Mayor Carter H. Harrison, Jr., to protest against this impolitic policy of denying the justice of the law to the very
element in the population most needing to be assured of it.
Claiming as an extenuation of the action of the police the
need to protect all suspects from mob violence, the Mayor
gave his interviewers a permit to see the two prisoners and aid
them to secure legal counsel. This interposition soon led to
the discharge of all the suspects, not one of whom was held to
answer any charge whatever in court. The gratitude of those
in whose behalf we had interposed overcame any expression
of the resentment that they might well have felt against the
injustice which they had suffered.

There never were but very few men of this extreme type of
individualism in Chicago, or perhaps anywhere else in the
United States. Their idealistic estimate of mankind in general and in particular, as capable of voluntary association without any need of coercive law, is so far from the fact and so far
out of the reach of most men that anarchism as a basis for the
permanent social order appeals only to the imagination of
dreamers who brood apart and are incapable of organized action on any large or continuous scale.

CHAPTER XI

LABOR WARS AND PEACE PACTS

VARIED experiences in personally observing or participating in the settlement of strikes verify three abiding conclusions: first, as to the causes and occasions for honest differences and the motives and tactics on both sides which lead from controversy to conflict; second, as to what keeps the contestants apart or brings them together; and third, as to the rights of the public which both belligerents should be compelled to respect.

Factors which characterize many if not most industrial conflicts were extraordinarily emphasized in two critical situations five years apart, which dramatically exemplified worse and better consequences. There was a "walkout" of employees from several garment-making concerns, which spread throughout what was then a badly organized or disorganized industry. Alleged breaches of contract were the grievance announced by the strikers. Differing conditions of work existing in the shops of the associated and independent manufacturers had also caused unrest. When the deadlock had continued several weeks without prospect of being broken, the discredited Teamsters' Union suddenly and surprisingly declared a sympathetic strike. Immediately what had been considered a private affair between two parties became a critical situation disturbing the traffic and the peace of the whole city. The attempt to move goods of any kind resulted in frequent fights between the striking teamsters and the strike-breaking drivers, which grew to the proportions of a riot compelling extraordinary police force to restore order and clear the streets. The public and the press became exasperated at the continuance of these disturbances, and vented their ire upon Mayor Dunne for his alleged hesitancy and weakness

in enforcing the court injunction against strikers. His appointment of a Commission of Inquiry to inform him and the public
of underlying facts not yet divulged increased the impatience
of public sentiment. Without authority to compel testimony,
this Commission, upon which I served, urgently invited volunteer witnesses to furnish evidence of the wrongs on both
sides. The Chicago Federation of Labor refused to co-operate
unless every session of the Commission was open to the public, which was as impracticable as it would have been for a
grand jury to hold public sessions. In neither case could
possibly innocent parties be protected from the misuse of
merely presumptive evidence. Not only did the Team Owners' Association fail to respond, but personal appeals to individual merchants and representatives of great mercantile
establishments failed to elicit from them disclosures of the
wrongs they had suffered through the connivance of certain
agents of their own association and the Union in threatening
or calling off strikes for pay.

While the suspected agent of the owners disappeared from
the public view under the silence protecting him, the drunken
libertine whose leadership of the strike disgraced the Teamsters' Union and injured the reputation of organized labor in
failing to repudiate him flaunted his flagrant lawlessness and
indecency from day to day.

Although the Mayor's Commission was blocked from securing legal evidence of the long-continued conspiracy to
blackmail employers, and its functioning was made more impossible by what was virtually the conspiracy of silence upon
the part of the victims, I felt justified in assuming the risk of
publishing under my own name in the *Chicago Daily News*
such comments as follow:

The Teamsters' strike is more off than on. It never was alive, for it
never had a reason to be. It was made, not born. It was made to order.
The order for it never came from within the ranks of the Teamsters, but
was handed down. It was of, by and for their union officials and never
even seemed to be called in the interest of the men. It was "sympathetic"
only in form, never in fact. It was as remorselessly without sympathy for
the garment-workers, for the rank and file of the Teamsters and for the
union cause, as it was for the employers and the city innocently victimized
by it. Only the discipline of organization made it possible. Only the fear

of disorganization forced the rank and file to tolerate what they never initiated and could not justify. Mistaken loyalty to leaders lined men up behind them while they were under fire. The cause of trade unionism has been betrayed by those who sold men whom they could not buy.

But the treason has been by no means all on one side. To say so is not popular, but is just and necessary. Every one now knows that at least one organization of employers has been the backbone of the strike. It would have collapsed at the start, if indeed it would ever have been started, had not this employers' organization been the power behind the union leader's throne. Another organization of owners has for years kept in its employ the most notoriously corrupt agent that ever disgraced and disturbed the industrial relations of Chicago. He testified under oath that he was furnished with funds to fix labor leaders and control strikes to suit the interests of those who employed and paid him. It is still claimed in public that he was paid not to call strikes, but only to call them off, or prevent them from being called. If employers thus conspired to drive labor leaders to call strikes off, did they not put a premium upon calling strikes on? Was not blackmail the inevitable consequence of bribery? Are not those who paid the bribe accomplices with those who levied the blackmail?

If the legal investigation proves to be rigid in its impartial exposure and punishment of guilt, lawlessness will end with the strike. If this open sore of our city's life is not probed to the bottom, if only the easiest part of it to reach is cut off, and the hardest roots to cut out are left in, if only the already discredited are indicted, and the still accredited are allowed to cover their tracks, the moral effect of this disastrous struggle will be largely lost. The lawless elements on both sides will feel immune, the old trouble will break out again in the same disgusting spot, and the whole city will suffer again and again from what it ought to do away with now and forever.

This partial attempt to enforce law against one side only is precisely what happened, and failed. The Teamsters Union strike leader alone was indicted and failed to be convicted, as he could not have been expected to be when his team-owners' co-conspirator was left at large. The Union, however, was justly held guilty of violating its own constitution and agreement as well as the law of the land by the jury of public opinion, which unjustly failed to brand employers' connivance with corruption that aided and abetted the lawlessness.

Five years afterward another strike of the garment workers resulted in a far different aftermath. It fortunately occurred in one of the very best shops in the whole trade. Its partners, Hart, Schaffner & Marx, proved to be capable of independent and enlightened action, but only after struggling determinedly, though vainly, to adhere to policies which they thought to be necessary to protect themselves from unfair competition in a disorganized trade. Above this seeming necessity they were assisted to rise by the very active interest taken in the just and permanent settlement of the strike by a self-constituted committee of representative and influential citizens, which undertook to investigate the grievances at issue and publish their recommendations for the better adjustment of all interests concerned; by the City Club which rendered further service to both sides and the public by clearly setting forth in print the way in which two similar strikes were satisfactorily settled in Philadelphia and New York; and by the City Council of Chicago in unanimously passing the resolution offered by Professor Charles E. Merriam, then serving as the alderman of his ward, providing a committee to bring about a conference of the parties at issue, on the ground that "public interests demand a just and lasting settlement of the strike."

Pending the notable outcome of this conference for conciliation, efforts to provide the necessities of life for approximately one hundred thousand persons who had been dependent upon the earnings of the wage-earners then on strike prevented all but a few of them from being driven to acts of desperation. These efforts were heroically made for nearly two months, by other garment workers not involved in the strike, by the Chicago Federation of Labor and its allied unions, by the Woman's Trade Union League, and by private citizens who combined to furnish milk to the young children of the suffering families. To avoid hall rents, and street meetings likely to interfere with traffic, and to gather strikers near the shops where they had been employed, which might have precipitated violence, one of the great baseball grounds was secured for mass meetings. There on one bleak November day I saw hundreds of men, women, and children standing for many hours, listening to their spokesmen and conferring with one another. There these skilled workers who had made clothing which was keeping so many others warm were shivering in the cold. There some of the foremost women in the city were serving hot coffee and sandwiches to the hungry men and women, and milk to the many children in their mothers' arms or clinging to their skirts.

The notable agreement which did credit alike to the firm of Hart, Schaffner & Marx and the International Garment Workers' Union is too well known and widely adopted by the trade to need explanation now.[1] I can best serve the cause of justice and peace which it exemplifies by sharing with my readers the privilege I enjoyed of participating in two occasions which gave expression to the spirit that made this great achievement possible. It was a farewell dinner to Sidney Hillman, the young Russian Jewish clothing worker, whose success in mediating the settlement of this strike as the representative of his fellow-workers had led to his election as president of the Amalgamated Clothing Workers' Union. On either side of him at the speaker's table sat representatives of the firm and of their unionized employees, and also members of the Trade Board and Board of Arbitration which represent both in settling all the differences between them.

The hall was completely filled by shop chairmen and a very few invited guests. One of these chairmen, a grizzled old worker, pled with the guest of honor to stay with his shopmates here. "Don't leave us, Sidney," he cried, "you are our little father." A younger man arose to confess: "I was one of the few of your mates who so misjudged your plan and motive in settling our strike that I even threatened your life. But now I know that you were right when you answered our threats by declaring that we might take your life, but you would stand for the honor of the union in making and keeping this agreement." A representative of the firm, addressing the departing employee, said, "We have not always agreed with you, but we have never doubted the sincerity of your motives." Then Sidney Hillman rose to the occasion, in manner and speech indelibly impressed upon my memory. He began by saying, "I do not recognize any such person as you have been addressing as myself." And he ended by exclaiming, "It is the impersonation of democracy in industry, of constitutionalism in trade that we are greeting." The clergyman sitting next to me whispered, "This is the most religious occasion I ever attended."

[1] *Clothing Workers of Chicago, 1910–1922.* Chicago: Chicago Joint Board Amalgamated Clothing Workers of America, 1922.

Another dinner occasion, this time held at the Palmer House, was in dramatic contrast with the free lunch furnished the strikers when they met on the baseball grounds seventeen years before. Now six hundred or more of these clothing workers had come at their own expense, as had their employers and overseers, to commemorate the mutually satisfactory settlement of their differences by the chairman of their Trade Board, James Mullenbach, whom I am proud to number among my former Seminary students and fellow-residents at Chicago Commons. Again the very same leaders of the Clothing Workers' Union and of this employing firm faced each other, now as fellow-guests, vying with each other in praising the peace pact which had contributed to the prosperity and happiness of the firm and its thousands of employees alike. Again, those whose interposition in the almost forgotten strife had been resented as "intermeddling" were present, but as invited guests who had promoted peace. Again Sidney Hillman stood in between employers and employees, but now to be applauded by both for declaring that "conciliation without compromise for seventeen years had made a breach of the peace inconceivable." Significant in the industrial annals, not only of Chicago but of America, is the achievement thus commemorated of this working agreement between organized labor and organized industry. A trade formerly disastrously disrupted by strikes and lockouts was peacefully and prosperously reorganized, almost at every center of the industry, on the basis so justly and firmly established at the plant of Hart, Schaffner & Marx.

Experience in arbitrating several strikes of shops' crews in manufacturing and mercantile plants confirms wider observations and warrants the conclusion that industrial differences are settled far better by conciliatory conferences between the two parties directly at issue than by reference to third parties, however impartially judicial the latter may be. Although arbitration boards usually consist of three or more members, the chairman is almost always the only arbitrator, as the others are advocates of the two parties whom they are severally appointed to represent. Never accepting this chairmanship unless invited to do so by both parties to the controversy,

and always declining any compensation for what I considered
a duty of citizenship, I have scarcely ever been able to satisfy
either of them, as each wanted its own way, or no way at all.
As the arbitrator almost invariably finds rights and wrongs
on both sides, his effort to even up between them usually goes
too far to please one or not far enough to suit the other, and is
likely to be considered an intolerable compromise by both.
And yet in two instances at least where my decision was regarded with great dissatisfaction, time and distance seemed
to lend enchantment to the view. For I was referred to more
or less publicly as having "settled a strike in our factory to
the eminent satisfaction of all concerned."

On one of these occasions I was able to avert a strike by the
shop's crew which demanded increased pay for piecework on
the ground that a newly introduced machine could not turn
out as many pieces of the product as the one formerly used.
After standing behind each machine off and on for several
days, I decided that a slight increase per piece was due the
men. To my surprise and theirs all new machines disappeared within forty-eight hours from the factory floor and
were replaced by the old machines, which were brought up
from storage. Thus the suspicion was confirmed that the new
machine did not belong to the factory firm, but was being
tried out for its manufacturers at the expense of these factory
workers.

The other instance could scarcely have satisfied the shop's
crew against whose contention I decided that it received the
same wages paid for the same work in other factories throughout the country. The shop's chairman was a hot-headed
fighter who sustained the reputation of his Celtic blood for
belligerency. He vowed that my decision would not be accepted by the crew. I vowed that it should, and would be unless he could prove it to be based on erroneous information,
and if there was any authority in organized labor to force
union men to keep their agreement. Demanding conference
with the union to which these men belonged, I was confronted
by their strikers' chairman with their repeated refusal either
to accept my arbitration as they had originally agreed to do
or to prove my decision an error. The union proposed to defer

its decision, against my protest that it was unjust to hold up a whole factory by the refusal of this one crew to abide by the arbitration. I therefore appealed to the international union of the trade located in the East, with the result that the shop's crew was ordered back to work forthwith. In this and other experiences I found dealing with a thoroughly organized trade to be a far more certain and much less difficult way of settling industrial disputes than dealing with a shop's crew, whether composed of union or non-union workmen.

The question of "open" versus the "closed shop" has proved to be one of expediency rather than of principle, at least in some instances. On one occasion I was called upon to decide whether the employers in an old firm should be compelled to oblige every employee to be a member of the union or be discharged. Finding that less than 2 per cent of the employees were thus involved by their refusal to join the union, I won the agreement of the men to withdraw their demand affecting these few employees who had served the firm the longest. The employers also agreed to continue dealing with the union, thus reaffirming a policy that long afterward came to be known as that of the "preferential union shop."

The closed shop seems to be mutually advantageous in certain employments. For instance, the Chicago street-car motormen and conductors have received better conditions of work and the companies better service since their two-party joint agreements enabled them to avoid and settle differences between them. Before they were thus organized appeal was made to the City Council, on one occasion, to require the company to protect the motormen from the exposure to intense cold and high winds by providing vestibules, which ever since have been regarded as a necessity. And yet attempts were made, ostensibly by a group of employees, to "howl down" from the galleries the alderman advocating the protection of the men. When, however, the recently organized union proposed to announce its presence and power by striking, the president of their Amalgamated Union readily persuaded the men of the folly of so doing. On another later occasion when a great mass meeting in the union's hall decided by acclamation to order a city-wide strike, this same experienced veteran leader of their national union successfully withstood the hasty ill-considered decision. Although it had been taken despite his ruling that it was contrary to their agreement and to the union rule, he undauntedly threatened the expulsion of the Chicago locals from their national organization. Thus with cool judgment and persuasive speech he succeeded in securing the reconsideration and abandonment of a strike which would have been as disastrous to the union as it would have been both to the company and to the citizens.

The strikes hitherto instanced have been referred to, not to discuss the merits or demerits of the issues specifically involved, but to point the plea for a well-recognized, ever open, readily operated way of conciliating differences by those directly involved in them. If any evidence were lacking of the disadvantage to all concerned in not having such a commonly accepted way of peacefully preventing or settling industrial strife, the great steel strike of 1919 furnishes the fact. Rates of wages affording unskilled labor a minimum subsistence for the average family and semi-skilled labor less than the minimum of comfort; the long twelve-hour day, the twenty-four-hour shift from day to night work, and the seven-day week were recognized to be the occasion for the strike by all who impartially investigated it. Yet the real cause of the irritation, which accounts not only for this strike but for those that preceded it in the steel industry, is the fact that there was not then, and had not been, any open and mutually accepted way for conference between the steel corporation and its employees. The corporation had hitherto opposed standing shop committees, shop unions, industrial councils, or such joint trade agreements regulating wages, hours, and conditions of work as the trade unions insist upon for collective bargaining.

Perhaps more than any other industrial conflict in America this steel strike focused attention and discussion throughout the country upon the right of private citizens to investigate and make known to the public the causes and occasions accounting for such conflicts, and to elicit the interposition of an informed public opinion for the avoidance or settlement of such controversies. The "no-conference" attitude of the steel corporation, so-called by its employees and their supporters, characterized its attitude toward the public at this and every preceding emergency interrupting this basic industry of the whole land.

Several years before this strike and following the great up-heaval at Homestead, Pennsylvania, *The Survey* magazine, of which I was one of the editors, undertook to investigate and report labor conditions in the steel industry at Pittsburgh. This field of inquiry was selected as typical of industrial rela-tionships in most if not all plants engaged in large-scale pro-duction. After starting the inquiry, the offer of the Russell Sage Foundation to share the expense and direction of the investigation was accepted. It afforded increased financial and personal resources which enabled the staff of investiga-tors to extend the inquiry, and the Foundation to publish the result in ten volumes, under the general title of *The Pittsburgh Survey*. It was the initial attempt to collect at first hand such data. But the monumental work of Charles Booth, the great London shipper, reporting in seventeen volumes *Life and Labor in London* (1902), was the pioneer survey, though based on secondary sources available in public records and elsewhere.

Notwithstanding the guaranty of a fair and thorough in-vestigation given by the influential personnel of its manage-ment, which included the names of several eminent citizens in the commercial and civic life of other great cities, the steel corporation withheld co-operation. Nevertheless, results of the inquiry were repeatedly submitted to its officials in order to avoid any injustice and to check up all inaccuracies in the statement of facts. For instance, the list of workmen suffering injury and death from casualties was thus submitted to make sure that the names, ascertained through a house-to-house canvass, were those of the corporation's employees. The deaths due to preventable causes, largely under the control of the corporation and the city, were graphically displayed at the exhibition held at the Carnegie Institute to mark the close of the investigators' fact-finding. These deaths, occur-ring within the period under review, were indicated by figures of men, women, and children which stretched for hundreds of feet around the walls of a great inclosure.

The depth of the impression this single exhibit made upon citizens of Pittsburgh, as well as upon others who saw it, was best expressed by a prominent citizen of that city. At the final meeting, held in one of the largest of the city churches, to interpret the public spirit and aims and the thoroughgoing methods of the investigation, the former president of the Chamber of Commerce, speaking for himself, yet representing many who felt as he did, said that Pittsburgh could better afford to lose one of its steel mills every few years than to have lost this valuable laboring life from the city's population. And he added that he was ashamed of himself and his city to have awaited the discovery of this loss by strangers.

Andrew Carnegie subsequently offered to bear a large proportion of the expense which the city of Pittsburgh might incur in improving the housing and other living conditions where the steel-workers' families lived. Not until one of the well-known stockholders of the corporation requested its officials to make an inquiry of their own, on the ground that he objected to receive his income earned under conditions reported by the Survey, was there any indication of action by the company, and then only upon threat of mandamus proceedings in case it refused to comply with the stockholder's demand. While both the motive and methods of the survey were severely criticized by those resenting any inquiry by "outsiders," either of the living or working conditions in the steel plant or the city, yet the facts as published in the report of the Pittsburgh Survey by the Russell Sage Foundation have never been either disproved or discredited.

When, therefore, the strike of 1919 occurred the public was better informed and more inclined to assert the right of private citizens to inquire into the conditions and relations involved. To the credit of the churches, federated in their Inter-Church World Movement, they were the first to undertake an inquiry. Again, co-operation was withheld by the United States Steel Corporation. The unions, however, opened all their records, and offered all the help their headquarters could give to the Commission of Inquiry. Throughout its entire effort to ascertain the facts, and, more still, at the appearance of its findings, which unfortunately were widely published by the newspapers before its full report could be issued, all who were directly or indirectly related to this church investigation were not only challenged for "intermeddling" but were bitterly accused of extreme, and even seditious, radicalism.

As I was not connected with this investigation I could judge it independently. In reviewing this report for an eastern weekly paper I expressed regret that it was less judicial than it might have been, but attributed this partly to the non-communicative attitude of the Steel Corporation, which in this instance did more injustice to itself and the public than to its employees. Occasion was given me to assert and defend not only the right but the duty of the churches to understand and pass judgment on industrial conditions that affect personal and family life. The following editorial statement of a journal representing the National Manufacturers' Association furnished a sharp point with which to drive home this assertion both to the conscience of the churches and to the self-respect of their critics. Referring to Rev. Harry F. Ward, formerly pastor of a church near the Stock Yards in Chicago and later professor of Christian Ethics in Union Theological Seminary, New York, who through his preaching, teaching, and published writings had sought to apply Christian standards to social and industrial conditions, *Industry* said:

His amazing and almost incredible radicalism developed a condition in the Industrial Relations Department of the Inter-Church Movement which is appalling when considered from any angle. In other words he intimated that the teachings of Jesus Christ should be brought into the industrial field and that the cardinal principles set forth in the Sermon on the Mount should be injected by the churches into industrial relations.

Claiming the self-stultification of this naïvely false alarm to be more appalling than the fears of the wise editor, I printed this rejoinder:

Not only the right and freedom, but the obligation of the churches, in loyalty to their mission, to apply religion to living and working conditions cannot be questioned, at least within their fellowship. Not to do so would be disloyal to the divine commission of the Church, and would leave it without any real gospel applicable to an industrial age.

Despite whatever resentment may be expressed against alleged "meddling" in industrial affairs, and despite financial losses already suffered or threatened, the Church is sure in the long run to gain far more confidence and support than it may now lose by fearlessly taking an outspoken stand against industrial policies clearly inimical to public welfare, and against the tactics of industrial belligerents who violate the law either by violence or by over-riding constitutional rights and civil liberties.

Public sentiment has already given evidence of its appreciation of the courage and confidence shown by the Inter-Church Movement in undertaking this great adventure of faith in the right of the churches to know and make known living and working conditions, and to co-operate with all other loyal, patriotic agencies in making industrial conditions and relations consistent with Christian standards of human life and public welfare.

These ignorant alarmists had evidently just awakened to the movement within the churches that had been going on for a quarter of a century. Fully twenty years before a few of us who were in close-enough touch with the class struggle in industry to be concerned over its increasing intensity, and to deplore the aloof attitude of the churches toward it, petitioned the National Council of the Congregational Churches, to which we belonged, to appoint a committee to advise the churches what they could and should do regarding this situation. Promptly and heartily a committee on labor was appointed, which in accordance with our preference was called the Committee on Industry, in order to include all concerned in the industrial situation, thus avoiding the appearance of partiality for any one class. This Committee secured the similar action of the state associations of these churches. Their Industrial Committee in Illinois, consisting of a distinguished general in the United States Army (retired), two clergymen, a well-known university professor of economics, and the writer, presented recommendations which were unanimously adopted, without dissent even in discussion. As among the earliest declarations of the churches the action of the Illinois Association of Congregational Churches is worthy of record, stating as it does the attitude and action which the churches rightfully and dutifully should take:

Representing all parts of the commonwealth, and standing for its whole people, the General Congregational Association of Illinois recognizes the economic necessity, under existing trade and labor conditions, for the organization of employers and employees alike. The protective, peace-compelling, progressive and fraternal influence of these industrial organizations is recognized to be far greater and more continuous than their agency in promoting and intensifying the clash of personal interests and class strife. The struggle of these competitive forces is inevitable and would not be eliminated if both organizations disbanded, much less if only one were forced out of existence.

We, therefore, defend the right equally for each to organize for the protection and promotion of their respective interests and rights within the clearly defined limits of the common law.

We call upon trades unionists, individually and collectively, not only openly to repudiate but also actively to co-operate with the civil and police authorities in the detection, conviction and legal punishment of every one guilty of acts of violence in labor disputes.

We call upon employers, individually and collectively, to abjure and help suppress the scandalous abuse of legislation in securing special privileges at public expense, and the increasingly menacing attempts to pervert the common law and police power from their public function to private ends and unjust class advantage.

We would urgently reimpose upon the conscience and heart of our own, and all other churches and Christian people, their high and holy prerogatives of intercessorial prayer, mediatorial ministry and personal and collective sacrifice for the prevention of fratricidal strife, for the equitable adjustment of real differences between conscientious men and for the peace and progress of the entire community, through which service of interpretation and mediation, more than any other within our power to render, the kingdom of the Father is to be advanced among the men of this industrial age.

Several years later, in 1908, the representatives of thirty or more denominations, including more than eighteen million members, organized the Federal Council of these Protestant churches. It issued a declaration of principles applying mostly to industrial conditions and relations, which had previously been adopted by the General Conference of the Methodist Episcopal Church. This "social creed" of the churches at once became the basis for similar declarations by the several denominations and other religious associations, both Christian and Jewish, which appointed social-service commissions of their own.[1] During and immediately after the World War, almost all religious bodies in America and Great Britain adopted programs of principles for "industrial reconstruction." Notable among them for advanced positions firmly taken was the declaration of the National Catholic War Coun-

[1] See *The Social Work of the Churches* (ed. F. Ernest Johnson; Federal Council of the Churches of Christ, 105 E. 22d St., New York City). Pp. 238. James Myers, *Religion Lends a Hand*. Harper and Brothers.

cil on "social reconstruction"—a general review of the problem and survey of the remedies. These facts are cited to prove the groundlessness of the critics in charging the interchurch intervention in the steel strike to a few "near-Bolsheviki," who were also held responsible for the "social creed" of the churches, which was adopted and widely published twelve years before. They also show how rapidly and widely the social propaganda of the early pioneers of this movement was taken up and carried on throughout the religious fellowships of Christian and Jewish faiths.

Without presuming to claim that the marked improvements of labor conditions in the steel industry subsequent to the strike were due to any one dominating influence, yet the simple fact is that within five years after public issue was taken with the steel corporation's insistence upon the necessity for the twelve-hour day, the long shift between day and night work and the seven-day week in continuous production, these abuses have almost disappeared from the steel industry.

It is only fair to those in this industry who are to be credited with the better conditions which I have personally observed in their plants to state what I have seen, and how I dissent from the injustice of their critics who attribute these "welfare" achievements to unworthy motives. For instance, at the plant of one of the subsidiary companies in the United States Steel Corporation I saw how drainage and the elimination of mosquitoes had transformed swamp lands into a healthful, well-built village, housing many hundreds of employees and their families. So effective had been the sanitary and safety measures and precautions taken that the cases of malarial fever had been reduced from three thousand to fifty in a single year, and accidents involving serious injuries had been reduced nearly 47 per cent. At this plant educational facilities were provided far better than the county afforded in its district schools. Playground, bathing, and gymnasium equipment far exceeded that furnished either children or adults in the neighboring town. I found in continuous operation a Mutuality Committee, consisting entirely of workmen, to whom the reasons for the discharge of any fellow-worker were submitted. In case these reasons were challenged, the foreman who discharged the man was called upon by the superintendent to answer the Committee's objections. Although the final decision rested with the superintendent, or, on appeal from him, with the president of the company, yet the foreman and superintendent were expected to maintain the stability of the working force, and therefore were held accountable for unnessary discharges.

It is fair neither to the motives nor to the achievements of such investment of forethought, skill, and money for the safety, health, comfort, recreation, and general well-being of thousands of employees and their families that any reference to this welfare work should be made such as discredited the interchurch report on the steel strike: "The Corporation's executives, in order to meet the Corporation policy, are forced to grind the faces of the Hunkies, and to trust to welfare to salve the exacerbations." To discourage such obviously effective efforts to improve living conditions of employees by the implication of unworthy motives, or by disparagement contrary to facts, is as impolitic as it is unjust. Surely it is legitimate as well as a great gain for employers to claim it to be merely "good business" to provide facilities for the health, comfort, safety, and contentment of their employees. Many of them have claimed no other motive, and not a few have disclaimed any credit for philanthropy, much less for charity.

From a private interview with the man responsible for the better conditions in the steel plant just referred to, I am at liberty to quote only this reference to his motive. Pointing to the deposits essential to the production of steel lying close together and readily accessible, he said:

I have a reverence for these natural resources and for the industry creating products basic to the progress of modern civilization. Desiring to gather employees capable of sharing this respect for their work in this production, I try to provide living and working conditions that will attract and hold here such men and their families.

In contrast with what I saw and heard at this plant a year after the strike, which did not extend to this area, it is only fair to state what I saw and heard during a visit of observation at the Gary plant of the corporation. On the "picket line," as on the streets, strikers talked freely, unexcitedly, and to the same purport. They, and the frank and conservative local union official in charge of the strike situation there, insisted that the twelve-hour day and the long shift between day and night work were still required of most of the men, but the seven-day week of fewer. This was not denied by the local officials of the company, although others elsewhere had informed me that these conditions no loner existed at Gary. Contrary to their claim that the employees desired the higher pay earned by longer hours, the men themselves said that while some of them wanted to work overtime to increase their wages by "time and a half" pay, most of them preferred shorter hours at fair wages even though they earned less.

At the Steel Workers' Union headquarters a placard was conspicuously displayed containing the full text of the Constitution of the United States. At the military and police headquarters my informants all agreed that the "red" radicals numbered a very small proportion of the eighteen thousand employees and were either outside the unions entirely or not identified with their officials and headquarters. They had centered at the rooms of the German Socialists, where the German flag was the most conspicuous emblem. Their placards in pictures and print appealed to prejudice and passion for more or less radical action and were printed in English and other languages. Some of the illiterate or non-English-speaking workmen admitted being told that the steel mills were soon to be "taken over" by the workers and that when this was done they would get their share in the ownership. Resolutions were passed by two hundred delegates of the Iron and Steel Workers' Union denouncing all "reds" and all connection with the radicals, but the company insisted that the agitation for the strike was initiated by the radical influences and with threats of violence which were not promptly repudiated by the conservative union officials.

The colonel of the fifteen hundred United States soldiers sent to Gary on the requisition of the governor of the state and the mayor of the city was so straightforward and considerate in dealing with both neutral and striking citizens, union officials, and radical suspects that all except the latter had no complaint to make and much credit to express for his control of the situation. He had a saving sense of humor. His glee over running down a whiskey still was fairly infectious, as was his indignation and action against the man who imported a young girl into the town for immoral purposes. General Leonard Wood, then in command of the Military Department, while on a visit to Gary, saw several hundred former World War soldiers wearing their old uniform while leading a procession of the strikers. The next morning he held a private interview with some of their leaders and readily persuaded them not to complicate the situation by appearing again in uniform. Thus, reason better than force was tactfully and considerately relied upon to preserve law and order and to avert what might have been a tragic clash between comrades-in-arms.

In riding about the city with its mayor to see the situation from his point of view, I found him to be a man of equable temperament, firmly intending to be fair to the whole divided citizenship. He was outspoken in defending the right and justice of collective bargaining and in exonerating the responsible union officials from complicity with destructive radicalism. Referring to the fact that the Steel Corporation had preoccupied twelve unbroken miles of lake shore directly in front of the city, while its population was increasing to the eighty thousand then resident, he claimed to have been elected to secure access to the lake front as the one and only natural resource for healthful recreation and pleasure available. Since then, he said, the Steel Corporation had donated one hundred and sixteen of the two hundred and twenty acres of sand dunes on the lake shore recently acquired for park purposes. He considered it to be a harbinger of better times for Gary, when its citizens would settle down and pull together once more for the progress of the town and the happiness of its people. Had this belated consideration of the company for the natural desire of the city's population been shown earlier, perhaps so large a proportion of the inhabitants might not have taken satisfaction in open opposition to the corporation's policies, even though not involved in the issue of the strike. Several years before, when a social surveyor asked a high official of the corporation why this consideration for the city's need should not be shown, he replied: "You have the human point of view but ours is the business viewpoint." At last, however, these two views surveyed the one highway leading to both ends.[1]

However far short of "democracy in industry" shop unions and the sharing of profits or management with employees may fall, one and all of these measures promote better relations, more just conditions, and a more real community of interests in the industries which have adopted them. Another instance may be cited in support of this claim. Invited by the officials of the Industrial Council jointly managing the industrial relations of a great manufacturing plant to address the weekly conference of its foremen, I was accompanied to the meeting by a representative of the company and of the men. At the luncheon preceding the conference I found managers and men seated at the same table. Afterward for two hours of a working day, they discussed what they could do in the shops to help foreign-born employees to become good and intelligent American citizens. The freedom and equality with which high officials and foremen participated in this discussion were the more impressive because they were all employed at the steel works of this manufacturing industry, with which the recent strike had not interfered.

[1] See Graham Romeyn Taylor, *Satellite Cities* (Appleton, 1915), chaps. vi and vii.

CHAPTER XII

TODAY'S CHARITY THE JUSTICE OF TOMORROW

THE very modern claim that "the charity of today is the justice of tomorrow" both illuminates and inspires effort and hope for the future. Historically, it describes the slow but sure rise of the masses from subservient dependence upon the classes, whereby the recipient of gratuities becomes a freeman having his individual rights before the law to a foothold on the earth. It marks the steady transition from slavery to serfdom, from feudalism to the democratic state. It fairly dramatizes the contemporary movement in industry from the laissez faire policy, which separated master and man on either side of a new cleavage, to the already well-established principle and practice of depending upon public opinion and legislation to regulate industry and intervene in industrial disputes.

Interpreting charity as the forerunner of justice gives utterance to that passion for social justice which is achieving self-respect and a future for the individual and for the democratic body politic. In all this social progress charity mercifully reaches down, but justice looms high above. It is, and always has been, meritoriusly charitable to care for the sick and crippled, for the injured and the widows and orphans of breadwinners killed while at work. But the new justice is still more charitable in demanding of industry protection from death and disablement. Therefore, the laws of every modern state more or less effectively require protected machinery, sanitary shops, the elimination of industrial diseases, restriction of child labor and of the overwork of women. They provide for compensation for injury and death through employers' liability and insurance measures. No longer is it con-

sidered either charitable or just for the community to bear
or share the risks to health or life involved in any employment whose employers expect themselves to bear the risks of
fire, the costs of insurance, and the losses of depreciation
which the public should not assume. Therefore the state is
demanding a living wage from trades that would otherwise
prey like parasites upon the body politic.

Jewish and Christian faiths have exerted no greater influence upon public policy than to have the claim of every
human being to the necessities of life recognized and met in
every community where this religious influence prevails. The
English poor-law allied the state with the church in relieving
the dependent and in caring for the afflicted. It was a great
advance to have the state recognize the sanctity of the individual's right to live by providing the necessities of life
through public charity. But does not the right to life carry
the corollary of the right to work for a living, the right to
employment for earning the means of livelihood? However
charitable it ever was, or is now considered to be, to maintain
the unemployed or supplement the wages of the underpaid,
it more and more seems to be unjust to leave those unemployed through displacement in industry, or through no fault
of their own, to bear the crushing weight imposed by industrial depressions or developments. The provision of employment on public work to take up the slack in private industry
may be the best emergency measure. But at the best it can
only supplement efforts to regularize industry, so as to lessen
or prevent periods of unemployment. Hopeful initiatives are
being taken toward this end by some corporations employing
many in large-scale production, and also by some strong labor
unions in certain trades. Where employers and employees
co-operate, this difficult undertaking is found more feasible.
Insurance to tide employees over intervals of slack work thus
proves to be more practicable. Incentive toward such co-
operation has been given by Herbert Hoover, when secretary
of commerce, in urging ways and means of regularizing industry. As chief executive of the nation he is expected to give
far greater impetus to all efforts for the prevention of unemployment, in carrying out his proposal to accumulate public

funds for developing large-scale government work through long periods of time.

To whatever extent justice has relieved charity of these burdens which industry has imposed, and however commonly such protective legislation has been accepted as a matter of course, these great changes have been thrilling experiences in a life spanning so many of them. I have always been glad to be actively identified with the charitable relief agencies and the efforts of private philanthropy to prevent dependency and delinquency and restore those thus victimized to their foothold among their fellow-men.

It was with fresh inspiration, however, that I entered upon the new experiences opened to me by several appointments to serve on municipal and state commissions to investigate industrial conditions and recommend legislation or administrative measures for improving them. The experience in serving on two of these commissions under appointments by mayors of Chicago to deal with emergent unemployment emphasized the necessity of country-wide co-operation in meeting local problems. Temporary relief was elicited, but the only permanent result attained was through the influence exerted toward the establishment of the Illinois Free Employment Offices, upon the Advisory Committee of which I was privileged to serve with its efficient officials for several years. But in Chicago they were handicapped in dealing with thousands of unemployed men who drifted into the city from all parts of the land. The congestion of such a large unemployed population could only be prevented by a national employment service, such as a score of other governments effectively maintain, and the successful operation of which during the World War was practically abandoned by the United States government, at the demand of private employment agencies, backed by employers' associations which feared the dominating influence of organized labor over the public service.

I was glad to be still more directly enlisted in securing justice in industry by Governor Charles Deneen's appointment to state commissions. One of them was the Illinois Industrial Commission, charged by the legislature to investigate conditions and recommend legislation for the protection of the health, safety, and comfort of employees in many industries of the commonwealth. The bill it presented, which was enacted by the legislature and has been enforced by the state labor commissioner, has prevented many perils to health, limb, and life to which unprotected dangerous machinery and unsanitary shop conditions had exposed the workers in many industries.

The final meeting of the Commission was marked by a notable event. The three members representing labor presented a tastefully printed souvenir to their associates, expressing in fine phrase the appreciation deeply felt for the harmonious spirit which had made possible the public service rendered by the Commission. The Commission's bill was claimed to be the "New Labor Code," because it was deemed to be the "basis" of just and reasonable working conditions. While joining their colleagues in asking its enactment into law, these workmen declared "their fundamental thought to be that the employer will make its legal enforcement unnecessary, and the employee—safer, healthier and more contented— will contribute his not unimportant share to the common good." Then, after paying respect to the governor and the legislators of the State Assembly, these representative officials of organized labor thus expressed their appreciation of their fellow-commissioners who represented the employers of the state:

It is peculiarly gratifying to meet with men who though holding differing opinions and points of view have not allowed them to interfere with the impartial investigation of conditions surrounding labor or the consideration of remedial legislation. It emphasizes the value of conference and discussion to the end that we may find common ground upon which both sides can stand without the sacrifice either of principle or self-respect.

We are grateful to those unselfish representatives of the great third interest—the public—who for weeks and months gave their time and effort that justice might be done the worker. Under less favorable circumstances the duty imposed on this section of the commission would have been to hold the balance of power as mediators toward harmony. Owing to a truly remarkable spirit of mutual confidence, the division lines were at once practically abolished. In the presence of such men the evil spirits of sharp practice, undue influence or mutual distrust would have fled abashed.

No more notable or decisive token of the intersphering of charity and justice has been registered in America than by the change of the name and scope of the National Conference of Charities and Correction in becoming the National Conference of Social Work. Since then justice has met charity more and more on equal terms on this broadly national platform.

CHAPTER XIII

HEROES OF THE CHERRY MINE
DISASTER

SATURDAY, November 13, 1909, is a date never to be forgotten for the insight it gave me as to both the depths and the heights of common humanity. With my colleagues on the Illinois Mining Investigation Commission, I was summoned to Cherry, where the greatest disaster ever suffered in the coal mines of America had occurred that afternoon. In the brightest lights of its life such a mining village is not cheery to an outsider. Some people live a long time "at the mines." Fewer come expecting not to stay long. Those who stay do not expect to live there always. The "company" itself shares with the people the uncertainty as to how long the work will last. So here everybody and everything had the appearance of being temporary. The buildings looked somewhat like the tents or shacks which at first sheltered the pioneers, their saloons, and even their churches. They are put up to be taken down. The railroad station and the company's office, the humblest cottage and the church, the sparsely paved and mostly unpaved streets, and whatever "local improvements" had been attempted—all showed the investment of as little as possible at the little village of Cherry. Only the school building seemed built to stay.

Such uncertainty and transientness deprive family life of most of the conditions that make it thrive. Conveniences and comforts, as well as what are considered necessities elsewhere, are provided neither at private nor at public expense. Things are crude not only at the start, but they stay crude and raw and barren longer in mining towns than almost anywhere else. So at best life is not as bright and well conditioned "up" on top of the ground in the sunlight and fresh air as elsewhere on the green earth. Down in the dark, and sometimes damp, mines, conditions of labor to say the least are not favorable to the best temper, sense of security, or personal development. Nevertheless men of as sturdy manhood and nobility of spirit work underground as can be found under the open sky, as I was soon to see. But no one need wonder that the miners' migratory life, their little share of daylight and sunshine depress, unbalance, and by turns excite and sometimes demoralize many. No one need wonder that saloons, bad houses, and low shows thrive in those mining camps, at least where there is no other provision for recreation or social interchange, to relieve the dull routine of toil, always in the dark and seldom beyond the reach of danger. Such was the background of life upon which the appalling shadow of death fell in Cherry.

Standing out and towering above all else the huge "tipple" strikes the eye of the arriving stranger. It contains the machinery for hoisting the coal from the main shaft which it covers, and it connects the mine car tracks with the trestle from which the coal is loaded upon the railway cars. Three hundred feet away is the airshaft with its great fan forcing a strong draft of fresh air through the shafts and the passageways down to the second and third levels, three hundred and six hundred feet below the surface. Clustered closely about this grim center of the little town were its two hundred little houses, a few small stores and saloons, a barber shop, two churches, and a school. These roofs sheltered about two thousand persons, whose family groups were chiefly Italian, Slav, Lithuanian, and Austrian, with fewer of Scotch, English, French, Belgian, and Greek racial stocks.

The alarm of fire spread through the camp at the appearance of smoke and when the first cage full of escaping miners came up. The whole village quickly crowded around the mouth of the hoisting shaft. Soon a rope line, guarded by deputy sheriffs, kept the crowd at a safe distance. Mine inspectors and company foremen called for volunteers to go down to warn and rescue the men underground. Village merchants as well as miners responded. At their demand the hoisting engineer promised to obey only their orders. At their command from the cage he lowered them. At their signal he began to lift, but received another to lower, after which none came. Excited men from the surface called upon him to hoist. Although replying that he could not break his promise to the rescuers, he was threatened and finally driven from his post. When others raised the cage every man of the ten in it was found burned to death. A day or two after I stood to say what I could, across the coffins of four of them, to the grief-stricken families and neighbors gathered in the little church. I could think of no words more fitting to comfort the living or to pay tribute to the dead than "Greater love hath no man than this that a man lay down his life for his friends."

After a hose had quenched the flames at the foot of the shaft the way seemed clearing to begin the work of recovery. Deputy sheriffs began to tell the agitated people to be calm, as they would be given the first chance to see their men living or dead. To clear the hoisting shaft from smoke and let the men up more readily, the fan was reversed, but only to make the escape shaft under it a roaring furnace of flame. Then came the order to seal both shafts. Workmen quickly covered the mouth of each with heavy planks. Railroad rails were placed across them, and over all cartloads of sand were dumped to smother the flames below. It seemed like burying alive the last lingering hope for loved ones. Wives then knew for the first time that they were widows, children that they were fatherless. There these little broken family circles sat from early morning until late evening those chill November days. Their dumb silence of grief was broken only by the undertone of sighs from the women and by the prattle of their little children. In the darkness of that dreadful night they turned with cries and tears from this last stroke of cruel fate. Group by group they slowly went to their desolate homes. Through the night and early in the dawn, singly or in groups of two or three, they wandered back. The daylight found them silently gathering again and wistfully looking at the sealed sepulcher of their unburied dead.

Meanwhile, the mine rescue crews from their stations at the University of Illinois and at Pittsburgh, Pennsylvania, had been rushed to the scene. Soon after their arrival the state mine inspectors accompanied by the mining commissioners met them to decide when it would be safe for them to descend the shaft. Although the rescue men thought it too soon to make the attempt, they yielded to the judgment of the others, and the first of them to hazard his life hesitated no longer than to adjust his oxygen helmet. Having preceded the rescuer to the mouth of the airshaft which had burnt itself out, I mingled with the miners from Cherry and adjacent villages. One of these men excitedly swore that "practical miners" would soon put these "book miners" out of their way and go down to rescue the men below, among whom was his brother. I ventured to remind him of what happened to the first rescue party. Then all were hushed as the brave "book miner" from the State University was lowered down the airshaft. His horn signaled that he had safely reached the lower level. Then all was silent. Men shouted down the pit to get some response. Faintly the little horn gave the signal to lift. Blackened with smoke and drenched with perspiration, he was wrapped in blankets and taken to our headquarters in the Pullman car. There he urged that another descent be attempted down the main shaft, toward the base of which the fire was again approaching. Another rescuer bravely made the attempt, calling upon Chicago firemen to bring the hose down with him. The fire laddie, whom I knew, hesitated a moment to murmur, "I have never been in a mine before, but here goes." And down he went with equal courage. Some months afterward he stopped me on the street in Chicago to ask whether there was any chance for him to be accepted for mine-rescue service, saying, "It was great at Cherry!"

But again the best these brave men could do failed to reach either the dead or the living. All odds seemed to be against them. The water stalled in the hose. The main shaft had to be sealed again and the work of recovery and rescue suspended. Meanwhile, the living were not forgotten. It was a thrilling sight to see civilization itself come to the rescue. The state inspectors reinforced the company officials. The deputy sheriffs were followed by a guard of state militia to clear the way for the rescuers. The mine manager and the executive officials of the company from Chicago did all that heartstricken men could do to discharge their grave responsibilities. Representatives of the American Red Cross, with their visiting nurses and charity workers, came promptly from Chicago. Representatives of the Congregational Home Missionary Society of Illinois were the first from any church agency outside the village to appear on the scene. The parish priest of the local Catholic church was already on his rounds from house to house. So were members of the little Congregational church of the village. Sisters of charity were on the way, and the Bishop of the Diocese soon followed.

The village barber had already closed his shop to open a free-lunch counter in the basement of the Congregational church, which was supplied with food and service by village neighbors. They had found some widowed mothers so grief stricken that they failed to feed their children. In the Knights of Pythias Hall representatives of the public and private agencies who were on the ground met to reckon the resources available to meet the dire and immediate needs of the stricken community. The president of the United Mine Workers of Illinois was the first to speak, pledging the prompt payment of the death benefit of one hundred and fifty dollars to the heirs of every dead miner, and an additional five thousand dollars from the treasury of the Union. "Take the money," said this Scotchman, "but for God's sake send women to visit the widows." The secretary of the National United Mine Workers turned over its check for another five thousand dollars. Money and personal helpers thus were promptly at hand to meet the immediate needs of the stricken community. Preparations to care for the dead then followed. A farmer donated land suitably located for a cemetery, and the mine company offered to bear all the funeral expenses. To take the village children away from the scene of sorrow and its still more gruesome experience yet to be suffered a playground was improvised by social workers from Chicago. A director of play was promptly provided to organize and lead the games, which soon restored to the children intervals of happy play, unburdening their parents from their care while bearing the burden of grief, which childhood is mercifully unable to share.

When thermometers, lowered to the bottom of the shaft,

proved that the heat had subsided sufficiently to attempt the recovery of the dead, hardy young miners, pronounced sound and strong after medical examination, lighted their cap-lamps and bravely went to their ghastly task to recover what was left of their fallen comrades. The cages which lowered the living soon began to lift the dead. Load after load, day after day, the victims of suffocation and flame arrived on the surface until two hundred and seventy-four bodies of men and "trapper" boys were laid side by side. The long line of the dead was inspected by the pitifully longer procession of the living. Indescribable were the recognitions and the still more woeful alternations of fear and hope when identification was difficult. One by one each body was borne away, follow-ing the woman who claimed her "man," or the mother who found her "boy." To some little homes two or more lifeless forms followed the lonely woman and her younger children, while a very few of the lonelier "single" dead had no kith or kin to claim them.

Not all who had been checked off that morning as having gone to the bottom were accounted for by the list of the dead. Some were "missing." For eight days no sight or sound of them had been seen or heard. Dead or alive, they must be far from the bottom of either shaft, behind the pockets filled by deadly gas. Who they were and what befell them while thus buried alive one of them can best tell. For the privilege of knowing the most heroic of all who survived the struggle for life and to save others from death, I went to the little home of George Eddy, the night boss of the mine. There I found him with his wife—both British born—and their little child.

This is the story he told me. He had arisen from his morn-ing sleep and finished his noonday meal when he saw smoke in the direction of the main shaft. Shielding his wife from alarm, he merely remarked that he was going over to the "tipple." When he reached the cage a miner stepped off re-porting that a fire had started below, and George Eddy stepped on the car going down to warn the men. Meeting the "face-boss," Walter Waite, at the bottom of the shaft, the two went in opposite directions to get the men out of the passageways and recesses, running east and west for over half

a mile in either direction. After warning as many as they
could, they stood at the bottom of the hoisting shaft, to help
the miners who were nearly overcome by the smoke to board
the cage, carrying some of them in their arms. Although these
two men could have stepped on it with every man they
helped to do so, they dashed back through the smoke for one
more effort to save other men. Just as they were about to run
to the cage to save their own lives, they heard voices and saw
lights farther back in the mine. There they found nineteen
men at work who had not been reached by the alarm. One of
them rushed toward the shaft and was seen to fall dead in a
pocket of white damp a short distance away. Eddy and
Waite, more experienced than these eighteen other miners,
warned them to go farther back, where they walled themselves in by building a "stoppage" to prevent the spreading
of the gas. Persuading the men to put out their lights, so as
to save more air for breathing, they settled down to their
vigil between life and death.

"Did you ever sit down in the dark and wait to die?"
Eddy asked me, as he interrupted his story. "It's awful lonesome," he added, without waiting for me to reply. And then
he went on with his tale of how these twenty men fared during
those eight days while they waited in the dark to die—or to be
rescued. After waiting—how long none of them knew—hope
faded. One of them threatened to kill himself, but was prevented and was encouraged "to live or die all together." Another elderly man complained that his share of water was
taken by someone. A stronger voice asserted that the men
who had the best chance to live longest had a right to a larger
share of the food and drink left. "We will share and share
alike," cried Waite. Wondering what was done to protect the
weaker from this stronger man, I ventured to inquire. But
Eddy only replied, "We are not telling on one another what
happened when we were all up against it down there." But
he continued to tell the better things that happened. When
at last he and Waite had their own hope fade almost out, one
of them suggested that it was time to pray. So the "Catholic
boys" were advised to do it their way and the others did like-

wise. None of them being accustomed "to lead in prayer," one of them started singing:

> Abide with me; fast falls the eventide;
> The darkness deepens; Lord, with me abide!
> When other helpers fail, and comforts flee,
> Help of the helpless, O abide with me.

"Somehow," Eddy continued, "singing the song gave us new hope." Waite broke a hole in the stoppage and exclaimed: "Fresh air!" When it was decided that one of them should venture to crawl through the stoppage and explore the way to the shaft, someone else went because Eddy had to confess, "I am all in." Not far from the stoppage had the other man gone when the rescue party met him and took all the imprisoned men to the fresh air and sunlight, where all survived except the one feeblest among them, who had pled for the protection of his water. While telling in simplest phrase of native dialect this story, the crooning of the baby in the cradle caused its mother to say with a sigh: "Child, you are the only one that can laugh since the mine caught fire." And then, as though to twit her man, lest he should grow proud in telling his story, she asked me what I thought of a man who left his family and risked his life "to save other women's husbands." Quickly George's rejoinder came: "Think how much the wives of other men think of me for doing so." So sunshine chased the shadows!

When ten years after I heard that George Eddy had died, I published in the *Chicago Daily News* a tribute to his courageous manliness, following the recital of his heroic deeds with these words:

This man, George Eddy, who with his "buddy," Walter Waite, risked all to save so many, now goes to his last rest in peace. No taps sound the signal that this hero of peace "gave the last full measure of devotion," but, as old John Bunyan said of his hero, Great Heart: "All the trumpets sounded on the other side" when George Eddy was welcomed there.

That my appreciation of his heroic deeds and my reverence for the nobility of his manhood were not too high, I cite what was published by another man far more capable than I of judging the qualities of men as tested under such stress and strain as he himself has shared with his fellow-miners.

I quote from what J. E. Williams wrote of "The Cherry Disaster as Seen through the Eyes of a Practical Miner":

The name of George Eddy deserves to go down in history as one of its bravest heroes. He stayed down there to the last, helping others on the cage, when by a single step he might have got on himself and been hoisted out of danger.

The supreme value of a catastrophe like this is in showing how plentiful is the raw material out of which heroes are made. Given a sufficiently commanding motive, the men who will lay down their lives are more numerous than they who will run away. Against the one man who failed by running away from his post as cager at the lower level, when panic stricken and leaving the men below to perish, there were scores who stood nobly to their tasks and risked or lost their lives for their fellows.

At the coroner's inquest, which as one of the Investigation Commission I attended and at which I had authority to question the witnesses, the experiences of survivors who escaped before the mine was sealed brought to light other deeds of rare heroism deserving honor both for the living and the dead such as is given the "unknown soldier" who fell in the World War. Indescribable were the scenes through which these few survivors barely escaped who took the last chance to save their own lives after working as long as they dared to save the lives of others.

The faults and failures to which the verdict of the jury attributed responsibility for the disaster were pitifully preventable. A car loaded with baled hay for the mules stabled on the upper level 300 feet below the surface was run under a torchlight from which burning oil was dripping. Two boys, one under the legal working age, who testified that he had never been instructed as to his duties, were in charge of the car. Two men "thought there was no danger" from the slow-burning hay. One of them, the cager who was responsible for the car, wheeled it about from one point to another where water was available and, panic-stricken when the timbers caught fire, fled from his post at the shaft without releasing the automatic stop. This prevented the cage from descending to the lower level, leaving the men there with no way to escape their fate. Another man who testified that he "could have put the fire out with his coat" passed by thinking that the cager did not need his help. Who of the officials was responsible for the dripping torch the office clerk of the mine swore he "did not know." No warning against perjury, or any persuasion, elicited from him any other answer, so noncommittal he felt his duty to the company required him to be. The verdict of the coroner's jury held the company responsible for carelessness in handling the hay and for violating the laws of the state in relation to means of escape, but with the full knowledge and consent of the mine inspectors for the district.

High upon the honor roll of Illinois and the nation the name of John E. Williams belongs for effecting the just settlement of the mine company's liabilities without litigation, as well as for helping to devise and execute the wise administration of the liberal charitable relief fund. Together they provided the largest compensation for the death of breadwinners ever received in Illinois by their dependents. He had been a miner in earlier life, and for many years had been a frequent contributor to a local paper at Streator, Illinois, and was the manager of the town's theater. With consideration as great as his sense of justice was strong, he insisted that the mine company was legally liable, but not morally culpable, because it had provided as good working conditions as other mine operators in the state, and even better than the average. Had it increased its cost of production by taking greater precautions, he held that this company would have been disadvantaged in competing with other operators. Through his thorough understanding of the rights and claims both of the operators and miners, and by his fair interpretation of each to the other and his persuasive plea for a just settlement, the St. Paul Company granted $1,800 to every family whose breadwinner had been killed. This was a far cry from what I had heard in the state capitol in Connecticut twenty-five years before, when the lieutenant-governor of the state, appealing for a more just employers' liability law, stated that hitherto their payments to the dependents of their employees killed while at work had not averaged more than $50.

The hope with which Mr. Williams proposed the settlement was realized, chiefly through his own exemplification of the spirit for which he then pled when he wrote long before negotiations were begun:

The work of rescue and service to the dead brought out heroes in plenty. May we not hope that the service of the living may give rise to another and finer type of heroism, the heroism of patience, forbearance, generosity, magnanimity, self-surrender? War is always hell, whether on the battle-field or in the court of law. May it not be the office of this appalling tragedy to lift men above the spirit of combat to a plane of truth and justice that will be prophetic of the new social order, where differences will be settled by human will and wisdom and not by brute force? If this could be the outcome, these hundreds of dead would not have perished entirely in vain.

Irrespective of what the company might do and without waiting to hear, the generous heart of the American people promptly and liberally responded to the mute appeal of human sorrow and suffering. Mayors of cities, citizens' relief committees, labor unions, business firms, local churches, newspapers, the Illinois Coal Operators' Association, the United Mine Workers of America, the Red Cross, and many individuals fairly vied with one another in the promptitude with which to express their sympathy by their gifts. The state legislature supplemented these charitable funds by appropriating $100,000. The Cherry Relief Commission intrusted its executive officer, James Mullenbach, with the administration or guidance of practically all these funds. Thus it was possible to pay allotments in lump sums to widows without children or those whose children were over fourteen years of age, as well as to the widows living abroad who had not yet joined their husbands, and to those who promptly left America for their old homes across the sea. Pensions were provided for families with young children, sufficient to maintain them until the eldest child reached the working age of fourteen. Fifty of these Cherry families thus received "compensation" aggregating $90,000 and $87,240 from the contributed relief funds, totaling $177,240. In contrast with this provision fifty families, which one by one had lost their breadwinners through industrial accidents in ten leading cities and were left dependent upon charity, were reported to have shared relief funds aggregating only $8,749.

The legislation prompted by this disaster more than fulfilled the hope of our Commission that it would result in national as well as in state enactments. In accordance with the recommendations of the Mining Investigation Commission, the Illinois legislature enacted measures for protecting miners from fire, for the increase of resources and facilities for the rescue of lives endangered in mine disasters, and for promoting the technical efficiency of all persons working in and about the mines in order to prevent accidents and conserve the coal resources of the state. This legislation was promptly followed by a liability act of the modern type providing optional acceptance of stated compensation for designated injuries or death, in lieu of suit for damages. The "fellow-servant" clause in former laws exempting employers from liability for accidents due to the "contributory negligence" of fellow-employees was eliminated by the passage of the new act, which thus did away with the legal cause of long-standing injustice.

Prompted by the Cherry Mine disaster, Senator Cullom of Illinois secured congressional action providing for a country-wide investigation of mining accidents which resulted in the establishment of the Federal Bureau of Mines. Its first director was Dr. J. A. Holmes, chief of the Technological branch of the United States Geological Survey, whose expert service on the Mining Investigation Commission contributed so much of its efficiency and influence. Thus at last national attention and action were secured for the protection of 600,000 coal-miners, working at 6,000 mines, producing annually about 500,000,000 tons of coal. Their death-rate from accident at this time was four per thousand miners in the United States and two and a half per thousand in Illinois, compared with only one in a thousand of those working in or about the mines of England, Belgium, France, Austria, and Germany, whose governments support a comprehensive educational system for all classes of such employees.

CHAPTER XIV

SOME LEADERS IN BRITAIN'S INDUSTRIAL CRISES

THE glimpses I caught of a few British labor leaders and captains of industry stand out in comparison and contrast with those I was meeting in America. These impressions may be all the more interesting for having been taken when the new unionism was supplanting the more independent leadership of the old trade unions. The first leader of this passing type whom I chanced to meet was John Burns, who had fairly won his fame in leading the great strike of 1889 which righted the wrongs so long suffered by the dock laborers. He represented the great wage-earning constituency of Battersea in Parliament and was also a member of the London County Council. I found him living with his family in frugal comfort in his little two-story house. His library, which lined the walls of one of its first-floor rooms, impressed me with the careful selection of authoritative books on economics, political science, civics, and social philosophy published in England and America.

Brusque yet kindly, egotistically opinionated yet socially minded, his aggressive self-assertiveness more than compensated for his short stature, but was in keeping with his burly appearance. Somewhat confidentially in manner, though no less emphatically, he remarked early in our interview: "I have reason to think that King Edward would like to meet me, but John Burns knows his job; he ain't seeing kings." I remember, however, that when the King did send for him to offer an appointment in the cabinet that the honorable John donned his court costume and waited upon His Majesty. I also remember that this was the beginning of the end of his representing labor in Parliament and in the Trade Union

174

Congress. Later when visiting Chicago, "incog," as he said, he was asked by Miss Addams, who had invited a few of us to meet him, what he thought of Chicago. "Your mayor is an ass," he bluntly replied. "But," she interposed, "he is so sincere." His rejoinder was, "All asses are sincere." To her further question as to what he thought Chicago most needed his characteristic reply was, "A hundred John Burns's." This remark magnified Chicago in stating that it needed so many of him! But his manifest devotion to public service offset his all too obvious self-esteem. To these amusing memories I may add another which perhaps reflects upon myself. Telegraphing to my wife that I would not meet her as early as I had expected, because I was "spending the day with Burns," when I returned I found on her table my telegram reading, "Will not return for lunch. Spending the day with Bums." It was all the more amusing because she expressed no surprise and seemed to take it as a matter of course, which needed no comment.

The new unionism was then at hand with its very different types of far abler leaders. It was already in evidence at the session of the Trade Union Congress held at Leicester, which I had the privilege of attending. The delegates resembled their brethren in the American Federation of Labor, with certain obvious differences, most of all, by their farther-reaching policies. They gave the appearance of a steady, sturdy, intelligent body of men who had assembled to attend strictly to their business interests. Punctuality, parliamentary order, short discussions, and brief speeches, mostly conversational in tone and temper, with sometimes an impatient pressure for the vote before the subject had been thoroughly thrashed out, but always with an acceptance of the final decision— these features characterized the proceedings. The diversity of racial differences and dialects in American labor gatherings was conspicuous by its absence. There were not so many good speakers as our men produce, and there was far less impassioned oratory.

Their personal qualities may be appreciated the more by others, as it was by me, in knowing something of their affiliations. I found Arthur Henderson, long prominent in Parliament, and later foreign secretary in the Labour party cabinet, to have been a Wesleyan lay preacher, leading the brotherhood movement in that church; Philip Snowden, who became the distinguished chancellor of the exchequer, had been chairman of the Primitive Methodist Conference; the steelworkers' representative, a leader in temperance and mission efforts; the bookbinders' delegate, prominent among Roman Catholic workmen; the typographical union's spokesman, a Baptist local preacher; and Will Crookes, from South London, a leader of the "Pleasant Sunday Afternoon" at the Robert Browning Settlement, who also ran his own "open-air college" at the dock gates Sunday mornings.

Decisions of the Congress on points of public policy were reached after far more thorough deliberation than its sessions allow. Delegates came up from their local conferences, at which subjects referred to the Congress for final deliverance were repeatedly discussed. Indicative of previously reached conclusions was the debate on the question whether the parliamentary representatives of labor should be chosen only from the ranks of those working at their trades. The narrower and broader positions taken by the unions were thus brought to a test of their strength by a vote representing 506,000 favoring the larger liberty of selection against 235,000 insisting upon a more restricted choice.

Directly opposite to this conclusion to which the British Congress has ever since adhered was Samuel Gompers' boast that the American Federation of Labor did not need to go out of its ranks of wage-earners working at their trades to find leadership. The broader policy of the British labor movement, and the broader intelligence of its prominent leaders, have proved to be very advantageous in welcoming from outside the ranks of wage-workers such men as Philip Snowden, who won country-wide recognition as a financier; Keir Hardy, leader of the Independent Labour party, who led the way of labor representatives into Parliament; George Lansbury, editor of the *Labour Herald* in London, who while serving in Parliament was a member of the Royal Commission on poor-laws and signed the famous *Minority Report*.

Prominent among these foremost leaders was Sidney Webb,

who when appointed secretary for the colonies in the Labour party cabinet was created a peer, to represent labor in the House of Lords. Through Miss Addams' introduction, I was so fortunate as to meet him in his statistical laboratory where I found him busily at work. No such private collection of sources and other data on British industrial history and current conditions exists anywhere as this one which, in skilfully and readily accessible arrangement, combined the treasures gathered and so effectively used by the genius of Mr. and Mrs. Webb. I was so unfortunate as to miss meeting Mrs. Webb, who has shared equally with him in their joint productions and has also achieved distinction for the publication of her own investigations, issued before and since her marriage. Her recently published volume, *My Apprenticeship*, acquaints its readers with her earlier years, when she was Beatrice Potter, and portrays how freely and responsively the daughter of a father and mother of high station in commercial and literary circles was drawn into industrial research. To the joint achievements of Mr. and Mrs. Webb the British labor movement and the whole English-speaking world owe such a historical background and such current guidance as organized labor in no other country can claim. It was my privilege also casually to meet several of Mr. Webb's fellow-members of the Fabian Society, to whose individual and joint investigations and interpretations their own and other lands are indebted for a better understanding of current conditions and for more effective equipment to improve them.

Recognized under this broader policy as eligible to leadership, J. Ramsay MacDonald was then chairman of the Labour Parliamentary Committee. When, reinforced by many Liberals, the British Labour party inaugurated the first labor administration in the long history of the British Parliament, he was its only choice as prime minister. And this choice was reaffirmed at the second triumph of the party in 1928. That the caliber of such a leader had to be reckoned with in a great emergency was demonstrated when in 1911 the country-wide strike of the railway and other transport unions precipitated a great emergency. It was just after he had made possible the peaceful settlement of this strike that I was privileged to

renew the good fellowship which he had established with
some of us settlement workers in Chicago by participating in
our social economic conference held at Chicago Commons
and Hull House in 1897. Invited to meet him at his little
family apartment in Lincoln's Inn Fields, I found him gray
and grim with the struggle and sorrow through which he was
passing, although in the prime of life. The shadow of death
had been hovering over his home during the fatal illness of his
wife all the while he had been spokesman for labor in Parliament and in conference with the ministers of the crown
through this industrial upheaval. Simple, grave, and manly
under his struggle for the life of the mother of his five children,
as he was in the struggle for those who had intrusted him with
their leadership, he told me the story of the strike as im-
personally as though he had been a spectator instead of the
one who had held the key to the grave situation. His brief
tale of it began with the government's negative answer to the
strikers' question: "Do you intend to urge the railway managers to meet the union leaders?" Within two days the strike
spread rapidly in response to hundreds of telegrams calling
transport workers out from their work. The dockers at all
great ports threatened a sympathetic strike. Coal-miners
began to quit work. The food supply might soon be cut off.
Lloyd George, to whom with two cabinet colleagues of the
Liberal party had been committed the conciliation of the
strike, called MacDonald into conference, as chairman of
Labour's Parliamentary Representation Committee. Firmly
he adhered to the insistence that the government should constrain the managers to meet the men. Although at one point
while the government hesitated he threatened to move a vote
of censure in Parliament for the government's dilatory conduct of negotiations, yet all the while he and his fellow-members held the hundreds of thousands who were in industrial
revolt loyal to the efforts being made to secure peace with
honor. Meanwhile, Lloyd George, having put the mobilized
military and police forces under the strictest orders to avoid
provocation either by the display or the use of force, summoned the railway managers to appear in conference with
cabinet officials and representatives of the strikers. So quick-

ly did they come to an agreement assuring a just settlement that MacDonald authorized telegrams dispatched the very next morning calling off the strike.

As it was Saturday, many of the unions did not receive the summons until after they assembled to march to Hyde Park for the Sunday-afternoon mass meeting of the strikers. I was there when more than forty thousand of them were led by their bands and banners to gather around the many stands erected for the speakers. Few policemen in uniform were visible, none in squad formation, although well screened behind some hedges I discovered a platoon lying on the grass to keep out of sight. Great credit is due the details of police and soldiers for their patient, tactful, and even good-humored conduct all through this hard week, although on continuous duty and often under great provocation, sometimes in peril of personal injury. No attempt was made to interfere with the speakers, one of whom I heard threaten the extension of the strike "from the rail to the river and the road." What happened? Nothing except the exercise of British freemen's right of assembly and free speech, which when exercised without interference was the signal to disperse and go home— and, as it happened, the next day to go to work. When I informed an Irish policeman in Chicago that no bullet had been fired and no baton had struck a striker in all London, he replied, "Then there could have been no strike."

Mrs. MacDonald's death a fortnight after the settlement of the strike brought forth testimonials of the appreciation in which she was widely held. The daughter of a well-to-do family of social and professional distinction, Gladstone by name, and a niece of Lord Kelvin, the eminent scientist, she followed the example of her father, who while a professor of chemistry served on the London school board and enlisted in other civic and philanthropic movements. From her efforts to relieve the poor she was led to investigate conditions causing poverty. With experience and knowledge thus attained, she enlisted in the work of rallying women workers for their united struggle to improve their own working conditions. She thus became the founder of the Women's Labour League, and a director of the National Union of Women Workers.

Next to the economic freedom and advancement of women
the Independent Labour party laid claim upon her active
membership and that of her husband. Beyond these spheres
of action she not only shared but promoted his wider range of
reading, observation, and writing. Together they participated in the discussions of the brilliant group constituting the
Fabian Society. In their own modest apartment they held
"At Homes" when adherents of varying political and social
views met for good fellowship and the exchange of opinion.
In pursuit of the broadest basis for their own views and actions, they visited America, Australia, India, and South
Africa, on the problems of whose people Mr. MacDonald
wrote a volume. Mrs. MacDonald, meanwhile, read papers
before the British Association for Labour Administration and
contributed articles on social and industrial conditions to
many periodicals. From cabinet ministers and working girls,
members of Parliament and workingmen, distinguished clergymen and publicists, came testimonials of their appreciation
of her public services and personal qualities. Of what she
was to him and did for him Ramsay MacDonald wrote in
"one of the most beautiful tributes from a husband to a wife,"
as his memoir has been called.

When twenty years after his personally and politically
hazardous stand for industrial peace I heard Ramsay Mac-
Donald, in one of his epoch-making speeches at New York,
concede that by believing in international peace a nation lays
itself open to a risk, I was thrilled by his exclamation, "I take
it! I take it!" For I remembered what risks of peace he had
taken. In opposing the Boer War he risked, and for six years
lost, all prospects of a parliamentary career, which just then
was opening to him. Meanwhile, it cost separation from the
distinguished Fabian socialists, from whose society he and his
wife resigned when it would neither support nor oppose the
war. Yet again, he risked and resigned his leadership of the
Labour party, for which he had been spokesman in Parliament, by opposing Great Britain's entrance into the World
War, when all but four of his colleagues failed to follow him.
Thrilling it was to hear this twice-overthrown, twice-re-
instated prime minister recount his heart-to-heart interview

with our Quaker President Hoover, when interchanging their intentions to carry out the international treaty renouncing war by their policies of peace.[1]

At Birmingham and York I gained an illuminating insight into the practicability of combining industrial efficiency with social justice. It was exemplified by the proprietors of the two great cocoa-manufacturing plants located at these industrial centers. They had been founded and were managed by two leading families who were as well known in their homeland for their leadership in the Society of Friends as their names were known throughout the world wherever the products of their plants were in demand. Through the generous hospitality of both of them I was privileged to look out from their home life upon the ways in which they carried the family spirit into the relations they sustained to all enlisted with them in their great industries. The exactions involved in their management so far from obscuring seemed to impose the sense of social responsibility for the very success of their enterprises.

The Cadbury manor house and lands at Birmingham offered not only rare comfort and privilege to the family and its large staff of helpers, but also rare hospitality to the poor of Birmingham. Fortunate were Mrs. Taylor and I to be guests at the manorial home when Mr. and Mrs. George Cadbury received a multitude of summer-day guests on their beautiful grounds who were gathered for this occasion from the least-privileged quarters of the city. Although few, if any, of them were their own employees, they were made quite as much at home by their host and hostess as I found the whole body of factory workers to be later in the day. It was the May Festival at Bourneville, the outlying factory village, in the festivities of which the whole population and the proprietors of the plant heartily participated. The families of both were gathered on the ample village green for their games, dances, and refreshments. Such a day of simple, genuine, enjoyable fellowship I have rarely seen. It was at least an exemplification of

---

[1] Iconoclast, *J. Ramsay MacDonald—the Man of Tomorrow* (New York: Thomas Seltzer, 1924), pp. 55–132; *J. Ramsay MacDonald—Labor's Man of Destiny*, H. Hessell Tiltman (New York: Frederick A. Stokes Co., 1929), pp. 92–104.

social democracy, if not to the same extent an example of democracy in industry. An approach to that, however, was well made in the joint ownership and management of the village independently of the financial investment and operation of the manufacturing enterprise. The beautifully designed outlay of the village streets, the attractive and comfortable homes, and the permanent provision of educational and recreational facilities were all in keeping with the spacious and finely equipped shops.

At the old city of York the employees of the Rowntree plant found their own housing shelter. Perhaps its inadequacy and other adverse industrial conditions within the congested quarters of the walled town prompted Seebohm Rowntree to undertake the first survey of any city's poverty which was drawn from original sources by direct investigation. "The Poverty Line in York" has the distinction of being not only the first but one of the best original investigations of industrial and civic conditions. It gave initiative to many others. Its author has attained further distinction by subsequent authorship, by which, as well as by addressing bodies of commercial and industrial employers, he has promoted a better understanding of actual and potential relationships between organized industry and organized labor both in England and America.

The personality that most deeply impressed me was that of Charles Booth, head of the great freight shipping lines running from English ports to both American continents. I had anticipated much pleasure and profit in meeting him because of the recent completion of his great survey of *The Life and Labour of the People of London*, the publication of which had preceded that of Mr. Rowntree, but which had been drawn from secondary sources. Here was a man, who, though heavily weighted with business responsibilities, was yet so human and so good a citizen as to undertake the colossal task of finding and stating the actual facts involved in such a survey of the world's greatest city. It exacted all the time he could spare from his business through seventeen years, and large pecuniary expenditure. On presenting my note of introduction from Miss Addams, I found him seated at his desk in his large London office, surrounded by his clerks and accountants. A grave countenance, crowned with gray hair, the reserve of a cultivated English gentleman, combined with the directness of a business man of large affairs, characterized the personality of Charles Booth. My interview with him was memorable for the modesty of his manner and the scientific though human spirit in which he referred to his great achievement, almost in the language with which he closed the seventeenth volume of his survey, a copy of which he presented me with his signature. He talked of it as simply as he had written: "The spirit of patient inquiry is abroad; my attempt is only one of its children." The photograph of this civic patriot has ever since hung in my library, inspiring me with the hope that his type of spirit and service might come to be less rare in America, England, and throughout the world. Were it multiplied, our industrial civilization would be reborn and future generations would be heirs of a heritage of peace and progress.

PART III

INTERRACIAL BONDS AND BREACHES

CHAPTER XV

RACIAL HYPHENS—OUR OWN AND OTHERS

CHICAGO COMMONS was purposely located in the midst of a population of foreign birth and descent. Indeed the preponderance of the foreign born and those whose parents were born abroad is now greater than ever, when not more than 5 per cent of the ward's sixty thousand inhabitants are of native birth and parentage. While we located there because the people's heritage, traits, speech, and faith were then more kindred to our own, and therefore constituted a readier basis for mutual understanding and co-operation, yet the whole district unexpectedly became the scene of rapid racial transformations. Here in personal contacts and concrete situations we were confronted by swift changes that not only perplexed us but required a continual readjustment of our work.

The significance of this evolving situation is the fact that these successive waves of immigration were followed by the differing attitudes taken and legislative policies pursued by the nation. At first our neighbors belonged to the few Northern and Western races of the British Isles and Europe, from which had come America's colonists and early immigrants— the "old immigration" of the "Nordic" race stocks so called. After 1900, the Latin and Slavic races rapidly predominated in the population of our own and adjacent wards, representing the many racial elements constituting the "new immigration" of the "Mediterranean" stocks, whose vast preponderance accounts for the radical changes in our national attitude and legislation respecting immigration. Perhaps our experiences and impressions may emphasize some facts that were given scant if any consideration by our legislators, and which have begun to modify some of their legislative acts, under the pressure of unforeseen consequences that have somewhat changed public opinion.

Incidentally we American-born settlers received a larger and more varied share of the race life, while adjusting ourselves and our work to transitions which tested both it and us. Few of us earlier residents had any previous personal acquaintanceship with people born abroad, or any opportunity to observe their customs and manner of life. Personally, through youth and young manhood, my own contacts were only with those born and bred in America. The single exception was a little-boy playmate who was the son of a prosperous Italian merchant living in our Philadelphia neighborhood.

At home, however, and in the household of religious faith to which we belonged, our Holland-Dutch heritage was reverently cherished. All of us would have resented any challenge of our own "hyphen." At its far end it linked us with our family lineage in Holland. Motley's *History of the Dutch Republic*, in the minds of us boys at home, was the background which added glory to the story of our American Republic and coupled George Washington and William of Orange as fathers of free countries. At its American end our hyphen, through my father's ancestry, spanned the colonizing era when old Holland was founding New Amsterdam on Manhattan Island and the little fishing and farming villages across Henry Hudson's River. There his mother's family was long established, and my grandfather, Rev. Benjamin C. Taylor, though of English descent, was the *Domine* of an old Dutch Reformed church, founded by the settlers from Holland. I was thus prepared to appreciate the hyphens of other people, whose love of their old fatherlands made them no less loyal, but all the more valuable to their adopted country, into whose very fabric they weave themselves and their racial heritages.

Few, if any, locations in the city were better situated for first-hand contact with foreign-born peoples than the district surrounding Chicago Commons. Lying on the west bank of the Chicago River between the business center and the crowded residential area surrounding many industrial plants, it stretched westward across the prairie. It was the very gateway of the great Northwest Side. Through this point of arrival the representatives of one race after another, from one land and another, have come, gotten their foothold, and moved on. Those of one race moved only when, by the pressure of newcomers in the rear, they were overcrowded. Each national group in turn was enabled to possess larger space and better housing by increasing prosperity. Each one of these tidal waves seemed to lift up and bear onward the one before it. Yet each large group stayed long enough to become neighbors and friends and to constitute one of Chicago's most cosmopolitan family wards.

In the midst of this coming and going we at Chicago Commons were challenged to prove our capacity to make friends of these strangers and to understand and work with them. Although each individual among all these great racial groups was to us just another fellow-human like ourselves, yet differences of racial heritage, language, and customs lying between us had to be crossed, and by us first. They, like ourselves, are really to be understood only through personal friendship. They need to be known not only when at work but while at home, not only when with their fellow-workers but while with their families, not only under the heat and burden of the working day but while at leisure and at play in their own racial, neighborly, and church fellowships.

No native-born person can put himself quite in the place of the immigrants from any other land, however close their neighborship may be. But a native American can gain a truer impression of them by treading the soil of the immigrants' fatherlands, by breathing their native air, by learning something of the fears and hopes that led them to leave their homelands and family circles to become strangers in a strange land. Our resident group sincerely sought to be a neighborly household with every other in the neighborhood. Each of us cultivated the personal friendship of everyone with whom he or she came in contact through our clubs, classes, and larger gatherings. Members of our household, as well as my own family circle, together or separately as opportunity offered, traveled abroad partly to gain the added advantage of having first-hand knowledge of the background whence our neighbors came. To old Holland and England; to France, Germany, Austria, and Switzerland; to Italy, Poland, Russia, and the Far East, one and another of us went. And with those whose fatherlands and native towns we visited we always came into closer personal touch.

Forced into the steerage by the exigencies of the World War, I crossed the ocean from Europe to America under some of the conditions which test both the motives and the courage of so many of my neighbors in braving the ocean voyage between decks. And yet I would not presume to speak for any of them. The immigrant can speak only for himself—a fact which was borne in upon me by personal experiences of being myself a foreigner in a strange land. Thus too I learned how I need others to understand me, almost if not quite as much as do the strangers within our gates. In what follows, therefore, I propose to let my neighbors make themselves understood by speaking for themselves, so far as I am able to reflect what I saw them do, heard them say, and felt the impress of what they were. But the reader will not fail to offset what may appear to be detrimental to the reputation of any race by remembering characteristics and achievements which do not happen to have fallen within the experiences herein narrated, but which, though not forgotten, cannot be included in this narrative.

"Tenison's Corner," near my boyhood home overlooking the college campus, gave me my first impressions of Irish-Americans. Its noisy Sunday-night rows, due to the liquor dispensed too freely from the saloon of the "Boss" whose name claimed the corner, were somewhat offset by the genial, though boisterous, family life of nearer Irish neighbors whose children I knew. Our Celtic fellow-citizens and earliest neighbors at Chicago Commons, with few exceptions, more fairly represented their race and gave a far better account of themselves. The men were to the politician's and policeman's manner born. As a policeman the Irishman can be as inimitable in humor as formidable in courage. Often have I sought a touch of both these refreshing qualities in a good-night talk with the patrolman on our beat when he rang up the station from the telephone box on our corner. And scarcely ever did I fail to enjoy the ripple of his wit and the stroke of his wisdom. Mr. Dooley's shrewd comments to Mr. Hennessey on passing persons and events only re-echo what is to be heard wherever Irish good fellows get together. The byplay between the Irish boss and his *"Eye-talian"* laborers, which sings merrily in Daly's *Canzoni*, can be overheard at a street trench of the pick-and-shovel gang and at the fruit-venders' pushcarts. Sorry were we to hear one of our oldest Irish neighbors announce his departure from our ward with the lament: "The longer I stay here the more of a stranger I am."

As politicians, good or bad, the Irish readily won and controlled voting constituencies of other races long after they outnumbered the Irish contingent. In so doing, as in office also, they have registered a rare capacity for political leadership. But it led and misled them to leave records both of the best administrative achievements and of some of the worst partisan exploitations of public welfare in the history of American politics. At close range in our ward politics I saw how capably and courageously the best of our Irish local party leaders could wrest from the worst their control of party organizations and wield it for the public good.

The Scandinavians were our next neighbors, when we moved from the old Commons to the new building, a few blocks westward. The Norwegians had long been in possession of this region which they settled. Here were their great Lutheran churches, with a very few of other denominational connections. Here close by us were the office and printing plant of the *Skandinaven* newspaper, whose veteran editor, publisher, and printer, John Anderson, was then recognized throughout the Northwest as one of the foremost spokesmen of his fellow-countrymen. His partner, Iver Lawson, was the father of Victor Fremont Lawson, to whom Chicago owes its *Daily News*. The products of the pioneer printing shop, displayed on the sample shelves of its office, reflect the characteristics of the Scandinavian people. Histories and biographies recount the deeds of daring by which their heroes and leaders led the way to the discoveries and pioneer settlements for which their race is famous. A large proportion of religious

and missionary literature indicates the firm hold of their faith
upon them and their devoted loyalty to the Lutheran church.

Here in Chicago, as everywhere else where the Scandinavians have settled, they have attested their patriotic loyalty to American law and liberty. Their citizens in our ward,
however, failed to be as effective in local politics as they were
qualified to be by their intelligence and numbers. Although
for years constituting a large majority of voters in several
wards, they were not represented in the City Council or in
other elective offices as the city was warranted to expect.
Many of them, however, individually took high rank in commercial and professional circles and co-operated with civic
organizations and municipal departments in improving local
conditions of health and morals.

The arrival of the southern Italians especially discomfited
our Norse neighbors, who misinterpreted and suspected their
merrier and noisier ways. A delegation of northmen waited
upon me with a request to join them in securing police protection from what they suspected to be the attempt of their
new neighbors to depreciate the value of the houses they
wished to buy or rent, by making the neighborhood surroundings so disagreeable to the owners and occupants as to force
sales and rentals at low rates. When asked to cite specific
acts, the explosion of firecrackers, especially on Sundays, was
mentioned as the most grievous and intentional offense.
Advising delay until the reasons of the new neighbors' exuber-
ance could be sought, I reported the grievance to the good
priest of a neighboring Italian church. He said it was a custom in Southern Italy thus to celebrate events that pleased
the people, and that the occasion for the fireworks complained
of was the presentation of an oil painting to their church.
While this explanation of the disturbance of their Sabbath
peace dissuaded our Norwegian neighbors from demanding
police protection, it failed to reconcile them either to the
demonstrative ways of the warmer-blooded southerners or
indeed to my own disposition to be equally fair and friendly
to both.

Thus crowded out, the sturdy Scandinavian settlers of this
west bank of the Chicago River soon spread northwestward,

pressing the city limits across the prairie. The streets they opened, the houses they built, their shops and stores, and the great churches they reared were left to be occupied by the immigrants who followed in their wake. But we did not allow our Italian neighbors to forget that it was fully five centuries before Columbus set sail from the Spanish coast when Leif Ericson sailed due west from Norway until he made the first landing by Europeans on the coast of the new world—a tradition recently commemorated by the naming of one of Chicago's new lake-shore parkways "Ericson Drive." A big boulder in an outlying park bears the tribute of our fellow-citizens of Danish descent to the civic patriotism and social service of Jacob Riis.

With the coming of the Italians came fresh exemplifications of abiding loyalty to kinship and neighborship. Everywhere in Italy and here in America Italians are a family folk. Their kinship is real, vital, affectionate, and with few exceptions lifelong. Parents love their children passionately, if not always wisely. They work hard and long to give the younger generation better advantages here than they of the first generation of immigrants had on either side of the sea. Their children expect and are expected to provide for their parents in disability or old age. The Italian immigrant's first earnings are usually shared with the old folks in the homelands. There or here, the young man anticipates supporting his father, when premature old age, coming often before the fiftieth year, terminates the hard-working years of many who are worn out in gaining their first foothold in America. The married immigrant saves enough in earning his own living to support wife and children in Italy, until he can pay their way to join him in starting home life here, when the immigration laws permit them to follow him. As one and another of the family circle begin to earn, a son and daughter add their wages to the family fund. Often the mother receives the unopened pay envelope of father and children for household expenses, returning only a fraction of the week's wage for the personal use of each.

A short-sighted, self-centered Americanism reckons the money thus sent abroad as lost to America, failing to appreciate the gain of this thrift habit and the character value of family loyalty thus cultivated and expressed. It ill becomes any of us to complain of this trait since, from the days of Benjamin Franklin, thrift has been lauded, if not worshiped, as the very genius of America. Because of this premium put upon it, or the more perhaps because the opportunity to save incites the acquisitive habit, a thriftless thrift too often misleads the prosperous immigrant to sacrifice the personal values of his family to the acquisition of less valuable possessions.

Italians are neighbors to an extent that few if any people of other races exemplify. Rural villagers and city dwellers alike are possessed by this primitive human instinct. The emigrant clings to it the more consciously and tenaciously on leaving the fatherland. The immigrant shrinks from losing it, cultivates and seeks to perpetuate it in other lands. In most cases his only guidance in setting forth from the old home is to go where his kinsfolk or former neighbors have gone before him. He looks no further for his destination than where they happen to live. At whatever port he enters he really lands only at their threshold. He is hospitably taken in to the household circle until he gains his own foothold and finds his own shelter, which is usually selected as near them as possible. Long after they scatter they maintain their neighborly relations. This they do by sharing each other's joys at family festivals, the marriage, and the christening, and by expressing sympathy in sorrow at the house of mourning and the funeral. These neighborly folk literally transplant old-country neighborhoods across the sea. Many Italian societies bear the name of the old-country town from which most of their members came and in or near which their relatives and former neighbors live. The name of a patron saint is used in some instances to designate a society that gathers its membership from a wider old-country area whose people abide under the same saintly protection.

The keen interest of our Italian neighbors in our family trips to Italy was expressed by urgent requests to see their old home towns and neighborhoods, to call upon their kindred, and to place a lighted candle on the altar of their patron saint in the church where they and their kindred were at home. Our interest was as keen in so doing, and in bearing back the greetings of their friends and our own impressions of the scenes so dear to them.

High above inherited or acquired traits that in any way discredit them, our Italian immigrants in America are to be credited with an innate love of music and art and with a religiously devout spirit that finds expressions all their own. These survivals of their old inheritance are cherished and cultivated in their new experiences here. A first token of their aspiration for further acquirements is given by the new-comers in their intense interest in learning the English language, American history, and the practice of American citizenship—acquisitions which are perverted in the experience of too many of them who fall under the baneful influence of those who politically control the immigrants' livelihood and deliberately pervert their citizenship.

Among the masses of no other race among us, least of all among our American-born people, is there any such familiarity with operatic music and appreciation of sculpture and painting as among Italian wage-earners. The spirit with which they join in singing an operatic chorus is balanced by the almost reverential respect with which they listen intently and in silence, unbroken by whisper or action, at the first note from an instrumental or a vocal soloist. Perhaps to a greater degree than in other races the artistic temperament of the Italian is more passionate, finding keener expression both for love and jealousy, in quick temper and fine impulse. Surely such tone and color as they add should be welcomed in America, where so few of us comparatively have our lives enriched by an enjoyment of music and beauty such as lets the Italian share the world's greatest treasure—even in poverty.

Religiously the Italians are mystical and devout. While they identify their homes and neighborhood with their church, yet all within it and its rites is supernatural and mysterious. Nevertheless they are at home within its ever open door. Thither the babe is brought for baptism, and young girls in bridal attire come with their brothers for their first communion. There the maid and her man come to be married, accompanied by their families and friends. Thither men, women, and children enter at all hours of the day to kneel in silent prayer before the ever burning lamp within the altar rail, or at the shrine of a patron saint to which they bear a lighted candle. Thence their dead are carried for burial. Back to their homes they bring the observance of church festivals. At Christmas, under the Yule tree, the scenes of the advent are reproduced—the manger, the virgin and the child, the shepherds and their flock. With the encircling children and their parents it has been a joy for us to mingle in the merrymaking following the silent observation of the scene of mystery. Humble shop-keepers erect little advent shrines in their show windows, in front of which passers-by stand and even kneel.

The *fiestas* which benefit orders hold in honor of their patron saint, and for their own benefit, are colorful and impressive in many of their features. While the occasion is unhappily commercialized by granting concessions to sell refreshments and other articles, yet many tokens of religious feeling attest the sincerity of participants. With bands of music, banners bearing the name of the patron saint, and boys carrying lighted candles, the members of the Society in their regalia, followed by a multitude of men, women, and children, parade through the streets of the neighborhood. Vari-colored electric lights canopy their line of march. Across the street a cable is strung from the second-story windows of tenement houses. From each window on either side a little girl with cherub wings is drawn as though flying. Hovering over the middle of the street until the image of the saint passes under them, they drop their flowers upon the figure. From the throngs of onlookers, as well as from the ranks of the paraders, hundreds of devotees step out to pin upon the robes of the saint's image their offerings of one- and five-dollar bills. Sturdy men pay from ten to twenty-five dollars for the privilege of helping to carry the heavy platform bearing the weighty image of the saint along the long line of march. The money thus annually collected goes into the society treasury to pay the sick and death benefits of its afflicted members. But the reaction against the frequency and excesses of these occasions has set in, especially among the second generation of foreign-born immigrants. The parish priests also are conspicuous by their absence.

By attendance and floral offerings at funerals respect for the dead and sympathy for the living never fail to be shown by many friends of both. Local branches of many benefit orders which meet regularly at Chicago Commons assemble there to get their banners and regalia and to form their ranks for the line of march to the home, the church, and the grave of their dead. Extravagant as are these funeral expenditures, often pitifully so, they are expressions of sentiments worthy of sympathetic reverence. The casket and the gravestone appeal to the heart as the last token of family affection, with which it seems selfish and hard hearted to allow prudence to interfere. Often, if not always, the long-cherished hope of the last request of the dying for this little glory at death is faithfully fulfilled at any cost to surviving members of the family. Its loyalty and pride are judged by conformity to these standards. Insurance and benefit orders are satisfied with nothing less of a funeral display for their members than that which includes a delegation of their lodge marching in regalia preceded by a brass band, as many conveyances as can be afforded by the family and friends, floral tributes, the number and expense of which exhibited in the street procession indicate to the onlookers the public or personal regard in which the deceased was held.

The pathos of these funeral customs is that most frequently they are the one and only distinction of the whole life, and yet are conferred only after death. Their effect upon the living is not to be underestimated. Pride, display, and indiscriminating honor heedlessly bestowed upon the best and worst—the most spectacular scenes often attending the burial of the worst—are indeed to be deplored. But the dignity of death, impressed by the silent marchers, their bared heads, their furled and *crêpe*-enshrouded banners, the plaintive, solemn music, the still church, and its reverential service— all lend a superhuman, if not divine, sanctity to human life. By contrast, the unidentified or friendless dead at the morgue, by the very austerity of their loneliness seem to plead for human recognition. Denial of full religious burial rights to the executed criminal dead by the Roman Catholic church is a consistently just respect for the religion of the church and the law of the land, however severely it bears upon a doubly afflicted family.

The living need protection from being sacrificed for the dead by the extravagant indulgence of their own grief, as well as by the exactions of custom, the pride of benefit orders, and by the wasteful if not extortionate toll laid upon the bereaved by unscrupulous funeral trades. These costs are the first claim even upon the benefit for which the deceased was insured, though all of it or more is required to meet the expense of a funeral conducted by the order. Frequently nothing is left to meet the immediate needs of the widow and dependent children. Burdensome debts and a reduction in the family scale of living are incurred, which reduce the household below the minimum requisite for comfort and health. Undertakers too generally scale their charges to the amount of the insurance. The most unscrupulous among them have been known to take advantage of the distraught state of the bereaved mind and heart to demand in the very name of the dead expenditures cruelly excessive to the living. Recent fact-finding investigations have met with an encouraging response within the burial trade which promises to accelerate the initiative taken by a group of its responsible tradesmen. These surveys of the whole situation also encourage the hope of enlisting public opinion, and to a greater degree the influence of the churches, as well as that of insurance and trust companies, civic and social-welfare agencies, and probate courts, in keeping funeral expenditures within reasonable limits.[1]

[1] Three pioneer surveys interestingly and authoritatively reveal funeral customs and costs in our own and other lands: Frederick L. Hoffman (statistician of the Prudential Life Insurance Company), *Pauper Burials and the Interment of the Dead in Large Cities* (1919); Quincy L. Dowd, *Funeral Management and Costs* (University of Chicago Press, 1921); John C. Gebhart, *Funeral Costs* (G. P. Putnam's Sons, 1928), a survey initiated and financed by the Metropolitan Life Insurance Company, but independently conducted by an Advisory Committee of forty-two members, representing leading professions, religious and social interests, and funeral directors in many sections of the country. Its statistical conclusion, based upon 15,100 funeral

Only Italy fully interprets the Italian in America. Its everywhere present art accounts for the love of beauty prevailing more among Italians than in any other race. Italy's opera and music festivals enshrine songs and orchestral music in the Italian heart. In thrumming his own strings for his comrades to dance, or in accompanying his Romeo song to his own Juliet, the love of music wells up from his very life. Akin to his religious rapture is his thrill in hearing the stars and the chorus of an Italian opera.

Where else than at Venice can throngs be found such as from the embankments of the Grand Canal join the chorus afloat in midstream in singing Italian operas? Where else than in Italy's Umbria could St. Francis of Assisi have enamored so many to follow Lady Poverty? In what other land could he have loved and sung his way into the hearts of one generation after another? Where else is religion expressed so simply as in the wayside shrine at which the peasants kneel, and so grandly as in the ritual of St. Peter's at Rome?

We had scarcely become well acquainted with our Italian neighbors, five thousand or more of whom densely populated our end of the ward, when an overflow of the Polish population from the still more densely crowded adjoining ward set in. Rapidly it spread eastward and southward and soon became predominant numerically and politically. For some time we found our new neighbors more difficult to approach and far slower to respond than our friendly Italian folk. Temperamentally, they were more phlegmatic and reserved. Racially, their clannishness was more persistent. Nationally, they had good reason to suspect and fear the people of other nations from what they had suffered at the hand of Russia and under the heel of Austria.

An occasion came after a while that called forth an Ameri-

---

bills (incurred by estates, by industrial policyholders, by those filing claims with the U.S. Veterans' Bureau, and by widows applying for pensions), prove excessive proportions of small estates and the resources of persons of limited means to be absorbed by funeral expenditures, which range from 62 per cent of estates under $1,000 to 18 per cent of those of more than $1,000 and less than $5,000. Of 319 widows receiving pensions from the New York Board of Child Welfare the percentage of their net assets paid for funeral expenses average: for Italians, 50.7; for Irish, 44.4; for Jewish, 27.2; for all others, 43.8.

can expression of the high spirit of the Poles. It was their celebration of the one hundred and twenty-fifth anniversary of Poland's independence day, from which they dated their brief freedom from the repressive rule of their oppressors. One of the great West Side parks was the scene of their patriotic demonstration. Into it forty thousand or more of them marched with bands of music and the banners of their national, fraternal, religious, and social organizations. Gay was the colorful procession with society regalia, the jaunty uniforms of the men's and women's athletic associations, and not least were the bright dresses of many hundreds of the children from the homes and parochial schools of their district.

They marched to the monument erected to commemorate the service rendered America by Thaddeus Kosciusko in coming to the help of the Revolutionary Army and serving on General Washington's staff as the engineer who designed the fortifications at West Point on the Hudson. An American flag floated high above it. And as each battalion of the marchers reached the base of the flagstaff, the color-bearers made each of their Polish ensigns reverently bow three times to the flag of their adopted country. Patriotic speeches in both languages were preceded by the singing of the Polish national anthem and were followed by "the Star Spangled Banner."

It was through our settlement service to motherhood, that common denominator of all humanity, that we began to win the hearts of our Polish neighbors. To the baby clinic they brought their little ones. This led them to form their own Polish mothers' clubs, and then to invite their men folk and neighbors to their parties—invitations to which were extended in the name of the club. So now our largest hall is required to entertain our Polish guests on these occasions.

Sympathy with the Polish people both in their new and old homes during the World War revealed them and us to each other, especially during the draft for military service. Then their loyalty to the liberty of both lands stood the test of war risks to which they were exposed more than any other foreign-born men registered as eligible for military service. Visits to their emancipated homeland brought us still closer together. They were made by two of our Chicago Commons residents, one of them my daughter, Lea D. Taylor, the other Miss Mary F. Stone, who had spent a winter with the Sisters of a Polish Roman Catholic teaching order who conducted a school for girls. Embarking at Venice on a freight steamer, they visited peasant villages and their market places while the vessels docked along the Dalmatian Coast. Under the guidance of a young teacher they saw something of the cultural life of the towns en route, and for two days at Czestochova they witnessed the great midsummer religious festival. To it thirty thousand peasants, in groups numbering from ten to one hundred, tramped many miles from their scattered homes to this most sacred peasant shrine, singing as they marched along under the guidance of their local priests. The simple devotion, sincerity, and orderliness of these thousands of peasant folks, clad in their bright peasant costumes, was most impressive. In Cracow and in Warsaw they were fortunate to come in contact with groups of young people so well educated, earnest, and internationally minded as to interpret present conditions in Poland and thereby promising much for Poland's future. Enriching, yet intangible, assets were thus acquired for understanding the background and potentialities of our Polish neighbors.

A serio-comic incident introduced us to strangers next to arrive. Late one evening I saw a young girl running up our nearly deserted avenue terror stricken by the pursuit of a group of boys who were rapidly overtaking her. When stopped by me, she seemed more frightened than ever, but grew calmer as the boys fled away with loud laughter. Not until she ran from me to one of the women residents of Chicago Commons who came at my call did the child regain her composure. Neither she nor we could understand a word that we spoke to each other. By a series of signs we learned that she was going homeward up the avenue. So we accompanied her in an open street car for several blocks, until she darted from it as she recognized the tenement house in which she lived. Following her up to the top floor, we were met on the stairway by her father who spoke just enough English to make us understand that he was a Russian. Bidding us into the family apartment, he produced a *Russian-English Dictionary*, pointing to the words one after another which expressed his gratitude for befriending his daughter when returning from overtime work far later than usual.

Although the incident illustrated only the prank of playful boys indulging their excitement in the chase, yet it revealed the fear which caused the immigrants to dread what might happen to their children even at play with those of other races, and more still, what they might suffer at the hand of officials such as had abused them abroad where they had been unjustly ruled.

For twenty years or more the entire Armenian population of Chicago held many of their national, cultural, and religious society meetings regularly at Chicago Commons. Our assembly hall was the scene of most of their mass meetings, which were called to protest against the violence and injustice suffered by their families and race in Turkey. Funds for their relief were offered with the same self-sacrificing generosity by the poorest and the richest among them. So intense was the expression of their indignation called forth by the dramatic presentation of the outrages inflicted by the oppressors abroad that we sometimes feared vengeance would be wreaked upon the man who played the part of a Turkish pasha in carrying off an Armenian maiden. While democratically united racially, they were uncompromisingly divided in their political policies and by their religious affiliations. Between those of the old Armenian Gregorian church and the adherents of the Protestant missions the cleavage was sharp. Some of these groups would not hold their meetings in adjoining rooms. A memorable occasion on which they all came together was their three days' celebration of the fifteen-hundredth anniversary of the Armenian alphabet, the letters of which were strung above the stage, at either end of which were pictures of their two patriarchs who were accredited as the authors of their written language.

CHAPTER XVI

REPERCUSSIONS OF OLD-WORLD TRAGEDIES

REPERCUSSIONS of old-world tragedies from new-world experiences are illustrated by the following incident, and many another. Startled by pistol shots one midafternoon on our thoroughfare, I followed two men who were firing at a third running for his life. As he dodged into a tenement-house hallway they fired up the stairway. When they had emptied their revolvers they escaped around the corner where they discarded their weapons to avoid being in possession of incriminating evidence. Finding the pursued man in a family flat of a near neighbor having his bleeding wounds bound up, I sympathetically inquired by whom and why he had been shot. His only reply to me, and to the police officers who later appeared on the scene, was that he would attend to himself and his pursuers and needed neither hospital nor police care. Inquiries of the family, to whose top-floor apartment he ran for refuge, elicited no information. One and all they disclaimed any knowledge of who this man and his assailants were, why they had attacked him, or why he had fled to this home of theirs for protection. Their silence ended the episode. It thus became one of many such closed events, the sequel of which would almost certainly be followed in another shooting affray, which in turn would leave no trace of its connection with this occurrence.

Here we had our first experience with the primitive trait to take personal redress, or blood revenge, for injury suffered or suspected which had found customary expression in the *Lex talionis* of ancient history. It persisted longer in Southern Italy than elsewhere in Europe, as the Camorra spread from Naples, and the Mafia followed it in Sicily. Justified at first as a patriotic self-defense against the oppression of foreign domination and the exploitation of warring municipalities, the Camorra was tacitly accepted as the invisible government by the Neapolitans when rebelling against the misrule of the Bourbons. Then and long afterward, to take its vengeance was recognized to be a token of self-respect and self-reliance, in accordance with loyalty to accepted customs. But this historic precedent for taking the law into one's own hand was followed by a terrorizing banditry that resisted the restoration of law and the authority of the courts. And yet it had a semi-official recognized status in Sicily until very recently suppressed by Mussolini. While the administration of law was weak and distrusted there, not only political parties but also governmental administrations had recourse to bandit bands, as strong-arm auxiliaries in the crises of their careers.

Our Italian fellow-citizens and those of other lands, in denying such lawlessness to be the exclusive product of their race, have good reason to ask us to account for the duel, for our feudists and lynchings, for the Ku Klux Klan, and for the bandit and political gunmen that have been the excrescences of our American civilization, wherever and whenever our own administration of justice has been weak and distrusted. Although often tricked by unscrupulous politicians and misled by their own self-seeking leaders, the great majority of good American citizens of Sicilian origin justly protest against being suspected of having any part or lot with those parasites of their race from whose lawlessness they themselves have suffered most. When assured of protection by courts and the police, they have dared death to testify against these extortioners and kidnapers. Our citizens of Italian descent have not been conspicuous in the leadership or in the ranks of those who have menaced our industrial peace by revolutionary radicalism. Most of the many Italian workingmen meeting at Chicago Commons hail Mussolini for having "put Italy on the map." A Socialist minority, however, advisedly insists that the Fascisti dictatorship, however efficient, costs a loss of personal liberty and the freedom of the working class.

An incident occurred which showed the injustice of roughly handling the unemployed as though their presence was a breach of the peace. There had been an increasing multitude of unemployed men in the city for some time. At the call of a physician who had befriended many of them, several hundreds gathered on the lake front, most of them of foreign birth and language. Their avowed purpose was to make a public demonstration of their plight. Ordered by the police to disperse when found to be without a permit to assemble, they moved together in a straggling line along the adjoining avenue. As they did so, police reserves arrived and charged upon the crowd, using their night clubs and very roughly handling the marchers. The pitiful contrast between the illy clad and illy fed unemployed men and the robust, warmly uniformed, armed body of police, as they marched back to their City Hall station, deeply impressed me. It did so the more because of what some of the newspapers claimed to be their courageous suppression of what was gratuitously assumed to be a mob of dangerous radicals, largely, if not only, because the physician who had called the meeting was known to hold radical opinions. When he was taken to the police station, bruised and bleeding, a petition was found in his possession which read as follows:

We, the unemployed and destitute, call your attention to the fact that we are anxious, able and willing to work; that our only means of existence is to sell our powers of wealth creation. We do not own the factories, and therefore cannot employ ourselves. We do not own our homes and must pay rent. Without employment there are but two avenues open for us, suicide or crime. The state can employ us as criminals, why not as workingmen? You have the power of making appropriations for any calamity, and one exists now. The streets need cleaning and repairing. There is public work to be done sufficient to employ us now and continue until spring. If we were bankers you would help us. The whole force of your administration would respond. Your refusal to help must be evidence that we are less than bankers or business men, because we are workingmen.

A young Jewish unemployed workingman, nineteen years of age, Averbuch by name, was shot and killed by the chief of police in the hallway of his residence. The officer, who was a powerful man with long police experience, seized him on suspicion that he had come to take his life. While his prisoner struggled to release himself he was instantly killed although it was claimed that the chief might have arrested him with the aid of three members of his family and the policeman chauffeur who came to aid him.

The youth was found to have been living with his sister, who was a hard-working seamstress. In their humble Ghetto apartment the prayer paraphernalia of the Orthodox Jewish faith was found. They had fled from Russia after having witnessed, but escaped, the ghastly massacre of the Jews at Kishinev only three years before. By his sister and his employer the young man was credited with being industrious, quiet in manner, and of good habits. While said by a companion to have gone with him to the meeting of a radical group, to which neither of them belonged, and having been found to be in the possession of printed matter distributed by this group, he was not proved to have been an anarchist or an advocate of violence. His sister denied that he had ever owned firearms or had been familiar with their use.

Although the suspicion that this alleged attempt to take the life of the chief of police was a far-reaching conspiracy to assassinate other city officials, the widespread police dragnet failed to prove that any of the scores of suspects arrested had anything to do with this man or his errand. None of his few friends could account for his visit to the chief except upon the supposition that he had gone to secure from a police official what he would have had to get in Russia had he intended to seek employment in another city.

At its worst the tragedy proved to be an American echo of a European explosion, followed by a concussion of hysteria. It is a far cry from Russia to America, from Kishinev to Chicago, but what happened there must be taken into account to explain whatever happened here. While the Christian Easter and the Jewish Passover were being observed throughout Russia in 1903, absurdly false accusations were made of ritualistic murders of Christians' children by the Jews within the pale where they were forced to live. An alarmist newspaper, expressing the cruel ecclesiastical fanaticism of the Russian state church, raised the demon of persecution. From the frightful scenes of looting, ravishing, and massacre which spared neither property nor person, age nor sex, this Jewish youth fled with his family at the impressionable fifteenth year of age.

Regardless of this background, this tragedy was made the

occasion, both by the police and certain newspapers, for discrediting those who challenged their false alarms. The superintendent of police himself was reported in the press to have made the assertion that "social settlements are first cousins to the anarchists." The only occasion he cited for the calumny was that a meeting in the interest of the unemployed had recently been held at Hull House, and that I had previously charged the Police Department as corrupt. My reason for so doing, which was the publicly criticized connivance of police officials with vicious resorts which they not only tolerated but protected, he failed to state however. And it was this protection which aroused public indignation two years later to demand the suppression of the segregated vice district, as recommended by the Vice Commission.

A sample of editorial hysteria may be cited from one of the morning papers then well established. Although confessing that "information was not available to relate the course of this Jewish youth's life," yet the editorial wisdom did not hesitate to assert that he "doubtless heard apologies for anarchism at the Maxwell Street settlement." The editorial, under the title "By Their Fruits Ye Shall Know Them," closed with this melodramatic address to the resident groups in all the settlements:

Ladies and gentlemen, enumerate if you will your good deeds in other respects; asseverate your benevolence for the poor; glorify your every act in behalf of the weak—yet you cannot escape the responsibility for this boy assassin. Raise not your hands to confirm your innocence—they drip with his blood.

But of course in self-respecting newspapers counter editorials promptly appeared, two of which may be cited to attest the good repute in which the settlements were held by a prevailing intelligent and just public opinion. The *Chicago Daily News* made this caustic comment:

Because settlement residents living in the midst of the Italian, Russian and Jewish people naturally inquire of their neighbors concerning their knowledge and attitude toward the issues raised by these tragedies, and because the interpretation of these neighbors did not coincide with the suspicion against them entertained by the police and in other circles, the settlement interpreters were immediately charged with being in sympathy with the crime and even accessory to it.

Were not these the better citizens who claimed what they knew to be the fact that the suspected races in loyalty to law disavowed all sympathy with the deeds of violence, that there was no evidence of conspiracy and that there is less dangerous radicalism in Chicago now than there has been for many years.

The *Chicago Evening Post* made this rejoinder:

With respect to the newspaper attack, that may be discounted because of its source. Jenkin Lloyd Jones and Lincoln Center, Graham Taylor, Hull House, the settlements of Chicago need no defense in this community. But when the chief of police declares that settlements are first cousins to the anarchists, it is time that the official intelligence be brought to the realization of the nature of our institutions for social amelioration, their functions, their rights and the places they hold in the respect of the intelligent class of the community.

Because the settlements deal with conditions as they find them, and therefore are often associated necessarily with extremists, it is assumed that they encourage extreme views and support extreme acts. But the conditions are not created by the settlements. They are being studied and bettered by them. It is preposterous that any apology or any explanation should be called for in a community like Chicago on behalf of an institution like the social settlement.

Before this year of tragedies closed still another aroused Chicago and the Middle West to make the legal protection of the foreign born among us a national and international issue. Two years before a Russian workingman, Rudowitz by name, claiming to be a political refugee, sought the right of asylum in America. He was discovered in Chicago working at his carpenter's trade, and on complaint of the Russian consul was arrested, brought before a United States commissioner on the charge of having been implicated in the crime of murder in Russia, and was adjudged subject to extradition. This case greatly alarmed not only the many other Russian refugees in Chicago, but the whole Russian element in our American population, most of all those of the Jewish faith. One reason for this alarm was the fear which spread among these immigrants, many of whom had recently arrived, that the violence of police officials in the Averbuch case and the racial antagonism incited by some newspapers might endanger their liberty here as in Russia. Meanwhile, largely at the initiative of Jane Addams, the attention and co-operation of many prominent lawyers and other citizens of high standing loyal to justice and the American right of asylum, were enlisted in defending the prisoner's claim to be a political refugee, and not a fugitive from justice.

The decision of the commissioner to extradite him aroused a great public protest, which found able and vehement expression in mass meetings held not only in Chicago, but also in Milwaukee, Des Moines, Minneapolis, Omaha, Denver, San Francisco, and other cities, where branches of the Chicago Defense League had been speedily organized. Everywhere these meetings were very largely attended by mixed multitudes representing all classes, sects, and racial elements in the population. They were addressed by some of the most eminent men and women in these localities, whose condemnation of Russian official tyranny and whose assertion of American loyalty to liberty and law did much to calm the agitation of the foreign born and stir the patriotic spirit of our citizens. The denial of the Russian claim for extradition by Elihu Root, then secretary of state, not only confirmed faith in American institutions but also created a strong precedent for stricter procedure in safeguarding the right of asylum, which has always been recognized by the United States as a fundamental obligation of every civilized government.

The stand taken by the settlements and other groups of Chicago citizens in the Averbuch and Rudowitz cases did much to create public opinion that counteracted distrust then prevalent in our immigrant population. On the other hand, it both warned and encouraged officials to subordinate themselves to the laws which they were chosen by the people to administer. It was well worth while, therefore, to have incurred this misunderstanding and abuse to bring about this better understanding between classes and races.

CHAPTER XVII

THE WAR DRAFT'S DISCLOSURES

WHAT we had known of our own neighborhood at Chicago Commons before the World War shrank to small proportions in comparison with what we learned from the revelations of our selective-service experience. Appointed by the governor of the state as chairman of Local Board 39, with two neighboring citizens to act as clerk and examining physician, I turned over most of the space in the Chicago Commons' building, together with the telephone and other facilities of the house, without expense to the government either for this equipment or my services. My daughter, Lea D. Taylor, volunteered invaluable service as secretary of the Board. Many of our resident workers devoted much time in assisting the men to fill out their questionnaires, which scarcely any of them could do without aid. The steady work of some of the residents was required to tabulate the returns. Thus the whole household, and some of our non-resident volunteers, had the opportunity of helping the community through the perplexities and severe trials of war-time experience.

Like a great cleaver the examination of the registrants cut through all strata of the population, disclosing a cross-section of many conditions existing in the entire community. Eighteen nationalities were represented among the foreign-born registrants. In diminishing numbers they came from Austria, Italy, Russia, Turkey and its Armenian subjects, Germany, and from twelve other countries. They were employed in twenty-three occupations, most of them requiring manual, unskilled labor. The physical examination of all between eighteen and thirty-one years of age proved 17.64 per cent of them to be totally disqualified for military service, 69.04 fully qualified, and 13.32 as in the limited or remedial class. Of our younger men, eighteen to twenty-one years of age, only 66.12 per cent were fully qualified as against 76.89 for the country at large. And 16.93 were totally disqualified as against 9.93 for the country at large. The disqualifications of most of them were due to deformities, which stood first with us but second throughout the country. Conscientious objectors were few. Those that pled their own convictions personally seemed more sincere than those who seemed to take advantage of the creed of some small sect to which they belonged. So strictly did we conform to instructions from Washington to exempt family men that many registrants from other boards not so considerate applied to us to intercede for them if we could not register them ourselves. Not a few of our own registrants to prove that they were men of family brought their wives and children and their aged and infirm parents in evidence. So that on some occasions, two or three hundred people thronged our assembly hall where we were helping the registrants fill out their questionnaires.

There was not a little comedy to relieve the many tragedies. A truck farmer, who claimed exemption as essential to his productive occupation, was asked: "Why can you not easily be replaced by some other man in your business?" He answered: "My wife, she don't want some other man." And she proved to be both partner and spouse. Another man accused of marrying to avoid being drafted listed the reasons why he had not been married before: "I believe that the above facts, which are correct on my honor, do not show any yellow streak or cold feet, or afraid to go to war, and therefore got married to avoid the draft. No, far from it." When the unmarried son in a family with older married brothers claimed to be the sole support of aged and infirm parents, we sometimes summoned the whole family to appear. All too true, in many cases, was the insistence that the father was prematurely aged at about fifty years of age, and that both parents were too infirm to earn self-support. But in some instances we had occasions to chide married sons and daughters for not contributing to their parents' support, and in others we found that the younger son gave them too small a proportion of his earnings even to cover the expense of his own board and lodging. A few wives protested against the exemption of their husbands because they were delinquent in discharging home responsibilities.

We had very few wilful delinquents and always managed to deal with them better than the local representatives of the department of justice and its volunteer deputies. Occasionally, however, these latter officials insisted upon hastening our more deliberate procedure. In one raid they arrested the wrong man because he had the same first name as the one they wanted and it proved to be on the very day that the victim of their haste was to have been married. His expectant bride came to us in tears but we could not secure his release until the following day. Some who were suspected of deserting answered our questions for their whereabouts "from the trenches," having volunteered before the draft. Others who were casual workers had left their lodging-houses for the next job before their summons arrived and never received their notification to appear because they had hitherto received no mail and therefore left no order to forward.

To not a few aliens it did not seem fair to be exempted. One young Italian protested that it did not seem just for him and others who had enjoyed so many benefits in this country to be exempt from the obligations to defend it because they were not yet citizens or declarants. "If I stay at home and at work," he said, "while other young men who are citizens go to war, they will take all the risk and suffer all the losses while we aliens will have the jobs when they return from the war, and that is not fair." Personal, and even private, as such exemplary expressions were, they are significant in attesting a high sense of obligation to the nation. Strangely enough, the Armenians and the Turks experienced somewhat the same embarrassment in meeting the requirements of the war draft.

The few Turks whose first papers made them eligible for military service were well aware that although Turkey and the United States had not declared war against each other they themselves would be forced to fight against the Germans, in alliance with whom the Turkish government had opened hostilities against the British. While some of these registrants fled, others submitted to the requirements of the draft, presumably to protect their status as American citizens. The experience of the Armenians was far more tragic. While their hopes and sympathies were all with the allies, yet if found in their ranks they might be summarily dealt with by the Turks as traitors to the country of which they were subjects.

The Poles faced the same risks. Over eight thousand of the twelve thousand or more men who registered with the draft board at Chicago Commons were Poles from Austria, and over two thousand more of them came from Russia. When asked where they were born, they replied "Poland." When required to state whether it was in Russian or Austrian Poland, some of them proudly answered, "Not Austria, but Poland under the domination of Austria." Most of them said that they did not want to be soldiers, as they had left Poland partly to escape Austrian military service. But many who were exempt because they were aliens quickly added, "I go if you need me." Scores of them proceeded at once to file their declarations of intention to become American citizens. Returning from the City Hall with their first papers to be registered as subjects of the draft, not a few of them exclaimed, "I may meet my father or brother in the Austrian trench." All of them might have added that if captured they would have been shot as traitors. Of no American lad's patriotism was such an acid test exacted as these young Polish men so bravely stood. Notwithstanding the bitter experience of being classified as "alien enemies" when the United States declared war against Austria, the drafted men returned from Camp Grant, whither hundreds of them had been mobilized, not to sulk at home over the loss of their wages and jobs, but to volunteer in the Polish Legion. In pathetic contrast with their march to take the train for Camp Grant, led by martial music through cheering crowds, was their silent filing out of Chicago to be mobilized at Niagara and transported to the seat of war. Joining the volunteer Polish legion of the army of France, they fought through four years of the World War. Then many of them remained three years longer to guard the Polish frontier from the bolshevik Russians. Such loyalty to liberty speaks for itself and needs no comment.

To us who were registering these declarant aliens, as to the consuls of foreign governments, it did not seem just that they should be eligible to be drafted, after having only declared their intention to become American citizens, and while not yet absolved from their allegiance to the government which still claimed them as subjects.

The facts disclosed regarding the citizenship of the men registered by both draft boards in our ward were perhaps the most significant of all that these selective records revealed. The aliens who had not declared their intention of becoming American citizens numbered 9,588, and those with first papers certifying such declaration numbered 4,328. Studying the records of a large-enough proportion of these 13,916 men to be representative of the whole body, we found that about half of the non-declarant aliens had arrived in this country within five years preceding the war, and that the other half had been here five years or more. We also found that of the 4,328 men who had taken out first papers 33 per cent had taken them out within the first five years, while 75 per cent of them all had done so within the first ten years. The Russians led those who had most promptly done so. The Austrian Poles did so before they had been here ten years. Some Italians had been here much longer without claiming citizenship. One of them who received an appointment to serve our local board as an examining physician was found to be ineligible because he was not a citizen, although he had resided and practiced his profession in the city fifteen or more years.

Country-wide records prove that the people who emigrate in larger numbers from lands where economic and political repression prompt the quest for freedom elsewhere are readier to assume new citizenship than those who emigrate from more progressive countries and delay naturalization much longer in hope of returning to their native land. Inquiries as to why this privilege or obligation had been so long deferred elicited very different reasons from those who confided them to us. Somewhat reluctantly a few admitted that it was because they expected to return to their old homeland and kindred later in life but others admitted that they had abandoned this hope after their first visit to the old country.

Several confidentially informed us that the only person who ever suggested American citizenship was some saloonkeeper or political ward heeler to whom they did not want to become obligated. Many more extenuated their neglect by the fact that no one had ever spoken to them about it, or had offered information or help to put them in the way of applying for their papers. The uniformly eager response to our own offers of help to this end by many members of our classes in English and citizenship convinced us that our American citizens themselves were far more to be adjudged slackers by this test. The men were readier to meet them more than halfway than our citizens were to offer them help.

We Americans have thought of immigrants more as industrial assets or liabilities than as the fiber entering into the warp and woof of our national fabric. Foreign-born voters have been considered less as constituent elements of our permanent political life than as temporary gains or losses of our political parties. We knew that there were Italians, Poles, Bohemians, Russians, and people of many other nationalities among us, but as a nation we knew little and cared less about the heritages and traits which they brought with them. The folly of this stupidity is apparent, at least to those of us who at close range see its perverting effects upon the political attitude of many naturalized citizens. They were more inclined to accept better than worse leadership before they fell into the hands of these who preyed upon them as the spoils of industrial and partisan exploitation.

The American citizenship of very many of our foreign-born people is better or worse according to the good or bad influences under which they fall in the earlier years of their experience among us. The man through whom the immigrant secures his first employment, or under whom he works at his earlier jobs, usually interprets to the newcomer, either directly or indirectly, his first impressions of our political standards and practices. This boss of all public employment and in some private corporations is usually a partisan politician who leads or drives the immigrant to believe that his job depends upon his vote. Higher ideals of citizenship reach the foreign-speaking laborer, if at all, too late and too remotely to prompt his declaration of independence. The padrone, however, gradually loses control of the Americanized foreign-born workman, so that the political boss fails to exercise any such autocratic control upon those who become less dependent upon him for their very living. One of our political-ward bosses sang his swan song in this lamentation: "There's no telling what these immigrants will do when inside the voting booth."

The experience of selective-service boards all over the country where foreign-born inhabitants were registered was a trumpet call for a consistent and effective national policy for locally naturalizing, educating, and assimilating the strangers within our gates who seek the right to live and labor with us. First of all, we became conscious that it is unjust alike to the individual alien, to this country, and to the country from whence he or she came to allow men or women to expatriate themselves. We became convinced that they should be required within a reasonable period either to qualify as citizens of the United States or to give good reason to the government why they should be permitted to remain in this country as aliens. The justice of such a requirement has been demanded not only by native-born and naturalized citizens, from among whom an undue proportion of drafted men had to be drawn, but also has been affirmed by not a few of the foreign born who neglected naturalization, or were neglected by those who should have represented the nation in inducting them into citizenship. But this may be done far better without the compulsion of the boycott, the blacklist, or the menace of deportation by the due process of law and educational effort, which must draw more than they drive, if aliens are to become good citizens.

Since the war many more efforts have been put forth to this end by the Bureau of Immigration and Naturalization, judges of courts, and many voluntary agencies, especially the Immigrants' Protective League and the Foreign Language Information Service. The Carnegie Corporation of New York was prompted by many applications for contributions to such agencies to authorize and finance a series of studies of methods of Americanization being pursued throughout the country.[1] One of the most valuable results of these efforts is the enactment by half of our state legislatures of acts enabling boards of education to provide public-school instruction for persons over twenty-one years of age in the smaller as well as the larger communities. Yet strangely belated is this action in view of the facts of illiteracy and inability to speak English reported by the federal census and by other investigators. According to the census of 1920 there were in Chicago 97,547 illiterates, of whom 45,603 were men and 51,944 were women. Foreign-born white adults unable to speak English numbered 87,699, and there were 198,817 of them who had not taken out citizenship papers. *The Study of American Intelligence*, based upon army tests during the World War, urged the checking of its marked deterioration by restrictive legislation. Yet it suggested no educational measures to improve the millions of low intelligence in our permanent population, although it was conceded that "the group of immigrants who have been in this country from sixteen to twenty years have an average intelligence almost as high as that of the native born, while immigrants over twenty years test the same as the native born." The application of this experience to the newer immigrants, to any degree, is withheld.

Since the war immigration has been drastically restricted, especially that coming from Southern and Eastern Europe, by measures having such ill-considered effects as already to require modification. The facts bearing upon our industries were so forcibly presented in Provost Marshal General Crowder's report of the selective service that we might have been forewarned, but our Congressmen were heedless of them. The account that our immigrant workmen gave of themselves when registering for military service showed the proportion-

[1] "Americanization Studies" (Harper & Bros., 1922; 11 vols.). Chicago Commons was gratified to have two of its former residents identified with these studies: Allen T. Burns, as director of the series, and John Palmer Gavit, as the author of the volume *Americans by Choice*, which contains many findings and conclusions on the relative assimilability of the "old" and "new" immigrant races, i.e., those of the British and North European stocks and those of the Eastern and Southern European races (see esp. chaps. vii and viii). See also the volume on *Old World Traits Transplanted*, by Robert E. Park and Herbert A. Miller. For valuable summaries and comments on immigration legislation see Edith Abbott, *Immigration: Select Documents and Case Records* (University of Chicago Press, 1924).

ate order of their employments in the basic industries to be as follows: iron and steel, building materials and construction, transportation by rail, water and highway, metal and blast furnaces, food production, clothing manufacturing, leather harness, paper and printing. The "Carnegie Corporation Studies" reported three-quarters of our iron-miners, brass and copper men, coke dryers, and clothing workers to be not only foreign born, but to have been hitherto classified as unskilled. Coal-miners in most states would be found to be almost exclusively foreign born. From 5 to 7 per cent of the applicants for naturalization were found to be those who had succeeded in securing the steadier, better-paid, skilled jobs. Only 1 per cent of the lower-paid, less constantly employed, and more unskilled laborers who had been admitted from each nationality filed their intentions of becoming citizens.

The influx of unskilled Negro laborers from the plantation sections of the South, and the still less assimilated *peons* from Mexico, has precipitated upon our already overcrowded city populations problems of unemployment, housing, and health with which they were previously overburdened. The problem of re-employment was still further emphasized to the few of us who served with General Leonard Wood on the Bureau for Returning Soldiers, Sailors, and Marines at Chicago, through which nearly fifty thousand of them passed on their way from war to peace. Discontent prevailed among a surprising number of these men in returning to the occupations they had followed before entering the army. After coming into contact, many of them for the first time, with the great co-operative enterprises that made military operations possible, their former jobs, and even professional pursuits, seemed uninspiring.

Another effect of the sudden and drastic restriction of immigration was the infliction of much needless suffering upon immigrants coming from countries against which the discrimination was most severe. Many of these immigrants who had been earning their foothold among us were, without warning, prohibited from bringing their wives and children here. Many families were thus cruelly separated, and not a few of them permanently broken. The plea of the Immigrants' Protective League for legislation to allow the reuniting of these families, by the admission of the husbands or wives, the children, and the aged parents of immigrants permitted to remain in America, was indorsed by the President of the United States, the Secretary of Labor and the Commissioner-General of Immigration, who recommend the modification of the quota laws to this extent.

Basing the restrictive quota law upon the racial proportions registered by the United States census of 1890 discriminates against a whole group of races which it was aimed to exclude. Urged less by this injustice than by other objections to the quota basis due to its unforeseen defects, the Congress hastily shifted the basis for admitting immigrants to the proportions borne by those of kindred descent to our whole population. The discovery of these "natural origins" of our cosmopolitan population, after all these years of intermingling, is found to be difficult to trace and impossible to determine accurately enough to be just.

The World War's selective service suddenly awakened us Americans to the consciousness that individuals of many nationalities living in the land do not constitute one nation. Slowly but surely we are becoming aware that we have been self-conscious, but nationally only semiconscious. More slowly still this national consciousness and our relationships with other nations during and since the war are begetting the feeling that our nation is only one of many others having to do with each other in the family of the world's peoples. Thus our international consciousness is coming to its belated birth. So far, however, it finds far more expression in public opinion to which the churches and other organizations of the people give utterance than in the Senate of the United States, which with strange timidity stands aloof from the League of Nations and the Court of International Justice—the greatest achievements toward the "Parliament of Man and the Federation of the World" that history records.

CHAPTER XVIII

LOG OF A PEACE JOURNEY CUT SHORT
BY WAR

IN THE summer of 1914 the Carnegie Church Peace Union invited three hundred men as its guests to represent all nations and their principal church fellowships at an international peace conference called to meet at Constance, Germany, August 2-7. As one of the last ten of the fifty American representatives of Protestant churches to embark, I found myself on the ship "Philadelphia" of the American Line. Daily through most of the voyage we met in the cabin to discuss the scope and procedure of this first peace conference of its kind. Other men and women of different nationality and church relationship joined us in these informal conversational interviews. When nearing the shores of France this wireless message was posted on the ship's bulletin: "Austria declares war against Serbia." Surprising as it was to all of us, it was not taken more seriously by any than as another Balkan outbreak which would be quickly quelled by Austria. The improbability, if not the impossibility, of a European war was thought to be too great to warrant our fears. A business man thought so because capital could not afford it, and floated its traffic under any flag, as though it was too international to permit interruption by any belligerency in the name of patriotism. International federations of labor, more or less socialistic in consciousness and aims, were cited by another as a formidable deterrent, if not a positive check to the spread of hostilities. A Methodist bishop confidently declared that there were too many Christians on the Continent, with a goodly number of aggressive Methodists, to tolerate, much less acquiesce in, declarations of war! Despite all these reasons the ship's bulletin flashed this furtive message between our hopes and fears: "Germany declares war against Russia."

Every mile of the railway from the landing at Cherbourg all the way to Paris gave evidence of the hush before the breaking of the storm. We found the war clouds hanging low over the capital of France. Before we could leave for Germany the frontiers were closed. The railways were in the possession of the French government. Passenger stations were centers for mobilizing the army.

Messages wired to Constance brought no response from the conference which had already convened there with eighty-five delegates, official permission to open its session having been given after other peace assemblies of the people were prohibited. Then the terrible suspense increased its intensity by Germany's declaration of war against France. Our last little American contingent could get no farther. It could do no more than cable President Wilson its confidence that he would take the first opportunity, as the head of a neutral nation, to offer his good offices to bring about the amelioration of this impending disastrous international strife. He had already acted toward this end, and his offer was published in the Paris papers only a day or two after they printed our communication to him, but not before representatives of twelve nations appealed to the Czar, the Kaiser, the Emperor of Austria Hungary, the President of France, and the King of Great Britain to mediate peace.

Meanwhile, the conference at Constance adjourned. Safe conduct was assured the delegates applying for it across the border into France. They were forbidden to watch the mobilization of troops. The curtains of the car windows were spread to prevent any observation of what was going on along the route. Kodaks were confiscated, and those attempting to take snapshots were arrested en route, being held until they were acquitted of being spies when they were escorted over the border. Some of these delegates reassembled in London to discuss what they could add to their declaration from Constance. But the very men foremost in framing it objected to adding any specific references to the present complicated situation since hostilities had begun. The Society of Friends, however, issued a stirring message addressed to "men and women of good will in the British Empire." While standing firmly by their belief that the method of force is no solution for any question, they declared: "The present moment is not for criticism, but for devoted service to our nation." Their message dealt mostly with the reconstruction policies that should follow the war. It was prominently and repeatedly printed not only in the British papers, but was translated into French and German and widely circulated in leaflet form on the Continent.

To be sent on an errand of peace only to find one's self in the fury of war, to avow allegiance to an international court of arbitration and, on the way to advocate it, to come under martial law, is a strange experience to say the least. Only a person lacking a sense of humor would deny that it has a humorous aspect. The very errand seemed absurd in the cynic's view of the situation. And the irony of fate in it must be admitted. But both the humorous and cynical points of view are short sighted. They are taken at too short a range. The end is not yet either of war or of peace. Farther-sighted views of both justify not only peacemaking errands, but also the hope of the ultimate triumph of peace. No greater argument for the sanity, the reason, the right, the justice, and the triumph of peace was ever registered than by the insanity, the unreason, the wrong, the injustice, and the irreparable national losses of this fateful war.

While the outbursts of racial and national spirit silenced the voice of the churches, while the internationalism of capital did not make itself heard, yet it must not be forgotten that labor made the last stand for peace. Although borne down and fairly swept aside by the irresistible tide of feeling that reverted to a lower type of patriotism, the internationalism of organized labor had at least the courage of its convictions to hold out longer and more bravely against the barbarism of war than any other group in civilized lands. The two great socialist leaders in Belgium and Holland were the staunchest supporters of their governments in defending the neutrality of both countries. All labor groups in England united in opposition and held a demonstration of protest in Trafalgar

Square, London, on the Sunday before England entered the conflict. But when Germany invaded Belgium the labor party broke with some of its leaders in refusing to continue its protest. George Lansbury on behalf of the industrial unionism continued to declare Britain's war policies mistaken while denouncing Germany's aggression. J. Ramsay Mac-Donald held on and out in his opposition until the war was ended. Although he had resigned his chairmanship of the parliamentary labor committee when his continued opposition was not authorized by his colleagues, it is most noteworthy that he was restored to leadership, twice led his party to its triumph at the polls, and became the first and second prime minister of England's labor administrations.

Meanwhile, it was reported that the Welsh miners at Cardiff declined to work on two holidays to furnish coal for the navy, because they did not "consider it necessary and did not wish to encourage or in any way countenance the policy of active intervention in the present European conflict." At a session of Parliament which I attended the government was interpellated by a member who demanded to know whether this report were true, adding that if it were true of miners in Germany they would have been shot. Claiming its right to refuse to discuss the matter, the government sent its Welsh chancellor of the exchequer to persuade his countrymen there to abandon such forlorn hope. This incident re-emphasized in my mind the oft-recurring thought of the miner as the new antitype of old Atlas who bore upon his shoulders the weight of the world. Is not coal-mining the most basic of industries, underlying all others? If its workers should cease working for any length of time what other industries or utilities could continue? The fact that so large a proportion of miners constitutes the national section of the international socialist labor organization at least suggests the possibility that by concerted action they might prevent any international war from continuing very long or spreading very far.

The German socialists were the first to issue their public protest against a world-war. The manifesto of their section was proclaimed in public posters and by street demonstrations while the strife between Austria and Serbia had begun

to inflame the war passions of other peoples. Luridly pictur-
ing the fury of war in the Balkans, the manifesto expressing
the will of over a million members of the German social
democracy closed with this summons:

> The awakened proletariat of Germany, in the name of humanity and
> civilization, raises a burning protest against the criminal intrigue of the
> makers of war. The proletariat imperiously demands that the German
> government use its influence with the Austrian government for the main-
> tenance of peace, and, if the war cannot be prevented, then take no part
> in the conflict. Not one drop of blood of a German soldier should be sacri-
> ficed, either to the ambitious frenzy of the Austrian rulers or to the calcu-
> lating greed of imperialism.
>
> Comrades, we call upon you to express the proletariat's unchangeable
> will for peace. A solemn hour has struck, the most solemn in many dec-
> ades. Danger is on the march. The menace of universal war is upon us.
> The governing classes which enslave, despise and exploit you in times of
> peace, now wish to make cannon meat of you. Let the ears of the rulers
> hear from all sides your cry: "We don't want war! Down with war! Long
> live international friendship!"

These demonstrations were held throughout Germany
until prohibited by the government and until those who attempted further public protest were dispersed by force and
the social democratic papers were temporarily suppressed.

The manifesto of the French socialists was a clarion call of
the ninety-three thousand members of the section in France
to the French people:

> The socialists, the workers of France, call upon the whole country to give
> all its energy to the maintenance of peace. They know that the French
> government is making a sincere and definite effort to avert or to lessen the
> chance of a conflict. It is this strong, this imperious will for peace that you
> will affirm, citizens, in the meeting which we call upon you to organize. It
> is to arrange some vigorous common action that the International meets
> tomorrow at Brussels. In it and through it we shall struggle with all our
> might against the horrible crime with which the world is menaced. The
> mere possibility of this crime is the shame and condemnation of an entire
> régime. Down with war! Long live the social republic! Long live interna-
> tional socialism!

That morrow, when the International was to have met at
Brussels, never came. Jaurès' eloquent voice was silenced by
the assassin's bullet in Paris, just before it was to have been
raised in Brussels in appeal to the workers of all Europe to

unite in maintaining peace and making war less possible. When arrested, his assassin justified his act by exclaiming: "I killed him because he opposed the war." The streets of Brussels resounded instead with the tread of the invading German army.

If these workers in each land fell away from this their last stand for peace, it is no more of a defection from their anti-war sentiment than that which the churches, or any other groups, made from their commitments to the claims of peace. Either under coercion, or by the contagion of the war fever, all alike were either submerged or swept along by the tempest of fear and hate. Is it not to the credit of the workers, nevertheless, that they at least made the last stand for peace in the very teeth of war? And does it not beget the hope that the internationalism of labor and the reasserted catholicity of the Christian church may prove to be the foremost propagandists of peace and the most formidable defense against war?

The prompt and widespread acceptance of the multilateral treaty renouncing war demonstrated the prevalence of the peace sentiment among the people of all lands. Although an American citizen, Salmon O. Levinson, a Chicago attorney, had the honor of being the first to suggest this outlawry of war; and although the world-wide ratification of the treaty was due to its tactful formulation and advocacy by the secretary of state, Frank B. Kellogg, with the active support of President Calvin Coolidge, yet the opposition it met in the Senate disclosed how far some of the senators were from having any faith either in the peace goal of religion or in the good will of fellow-men. Nevertheless all but one of these belligerent isolationists yielded so far to the prevailing sentiment for peace as to be unwilling to vote against what they had derided as a mere "gesture," waiving also the reservations for which they had strenuously contended.

The date, January 15, 1929, on which the Senate of the United States, by a vote of eighty-five to one, ratified the treaty renouncing war as a legitimate means of settling international disputes promises to mark the end of our official isolation policy, and the beginning of an official expression of

the friendlier fellowship which our people have with those of
other nations, thus opening a new era promising international
peace by registering the world's will against war.

How archaic and incompatible with itself civilization has
made "civilized warfare" was impressed upon me by what
was to be seen of the preparation for it under the shadows
which its coming events cast upon the people of France and
England.

At close range and in human terms war loses the glamor
which may hide from those farther away its blood and tears,
its disasters and calamity. The first dark, silent, sullen shadow of war clouds which were to darken all lands and seas were
apparent as we sailed under them. The lights which civilization and humanity had kept burning were missing from the
coast and harbor we approached. We ran close by a French
man-of-war at anchor without lights. Then we read that
some of the friendly lights along other shores were being put
out. Friendly ports, which opened like welcoming arms to receive us from the great deep, were soon closed to passenger
ships and merchant vessels, and were left open only to the sea
dogs of war and the freight of destruction and death. In
crossing the English Channel a destroyer stood as a sentinel
athwart our bows until our colors proved friendly. Shortly
afterward our ship was warned off her course and away from
the deadly mines, which had turned this stream of all Europe's
life into a channel of destruction. A white-crested little ridge
in the sea was the wake left by a submarine, as it dived
out of sight. Held in leash thereby were some of the dread-
naught Titans of the sea, and swift cruisers were also deterred
from doing their best, or rather their worst. Instead of being
the highway of friendly peoples, the sea again shut the nations up to themselves and out from each other, prompting
prayer for the time when "there shall be no more sea." Instead of flashing their friendly lights and passing their electric
messages from one vessel to another, the great ships freighted
with human cargoes scanned the sea in fear, sailed in the
dark with lights put out or shut in. Wireless stations—those
new international signals of safety and fellowship—began to
be silenced far eastward. All at once there was such peril on

the deep, such sorrow on the sea, as civilized men never expected to experience again. And the worst was yet to come.

"Mobilization" has a far-away sound to American ears, but abroad it sounded startlingly near just then. Through peaceful harvest fields, fertile vine-clad valleys, simple peasant villages, and thriving industrial towns of France the railway rolled us into Paris. Over the French frontier and across the borders of Switzerland and Germany we expected to speed the next morning. But overnight "mobilization" began. And this is what happened as swiftly as lightning. War had the right of way.

Railway stations were picketed and garrisoned by soldiers. Sentinels stood at every bridge, viaduct, switch, and culvert. Trains were seized to move "reserves" in and troops out. Passengers had no rights to travel that the military was bound to respect. Thousands of them all day long, day after day, waited in forlorn hope to buy tickets and board trains. Automobiles were commandeered and were forbidden to be taken away. So were motorcycles. Soldiers supplanted chauffeurs at the wheels of private cars. Uniformed officers, with their arms and baggage, took the place of gentle ladies or joy-riders. Autobuses ceased to run on their public routes and ran reservists to their rendezvous, or regulars to the stations. Mails and telegrams no longer crossed hostile frontiers, and within national boundaries were sent only at the sender's risk. Cables were received only on the same terms, and no information given of when or whether they were sent.

Men disappeared from their work, waiters from restaurants and hotel dining-rooms and kitchens, causing them to close, porters from stores and depots, operatives from factories, clerks from stores, business and professional men from their offices, managers from marts and plants, farmers from the harvest fields. Little groups of peasant-like workingmen filed through the streets following a single soldier, in endless succession. Soon they were in uniform and under arms.

Silently they marched off to the railway station, without the tap of a drum or the note of a bugle to cheer them. Processions of young men paraded, singing the "Marseillaise" and chanting war cries, as did the hundreds of women clerks in the Louvre department store. But the reservists were silent, on their first march from home, as were the troops on their way to war. There was no hilarity, no "French vivacity," no bravado. All were impressively serious, determined, grim. That silent, steady tread of theirs, those set features, this wonderfully quick and effective mobilizing, entraining, and marshaling of a nation's workers into an army, betokened stern work ahead and a trail of tragic sorrow and suffering behind.

Out from the homes, along the street, at the thronged railway stations, and wherever the trains stopped at rural stations that long-drawn-out tragedy began. Such pathetic partings of wives from husbands, of children from fathers, of mothers from sons, were enough to break a heart of stone. Women with red eyes and tear-stained faces were everywhere. They followed their loved ones as far as they could. They exchanged farewells as far as possible across the cruel distance through which they disappeared from each other's sight. One trooper on the last file of a cavalry regiment held a woman's hand as she trudged along by the side of his horse. A young man approaching one of us strangers exclaimed: "War is inevitable. I must go and leave my wife and children tonight. God knows what is to become of them," and passed on into the awful night settling down over all Europe. Even in Germany it was the "War lords" and their military and naval bureaucrats, not the German people, who were responsible for this inconceivably awful catastrophe.

Most aliens living within the borders of any nation until then had been welcomed. But their plight became terrible. They were torn away suddenly from home and property, deported or corraled, suspected, terrified, and often robbed and abused, imprisoned, and even executed. Irretrievable disaster overtook them—most all of them innocent of any wrong, their only fault being their accident of birth—or their birthright. Thousands of peaceful families were thus torn up by the roots, cruelly separated, and ruthlessly hurled away by this frightful tornado of war. Even in London, where most consideration was shown them, the thirty thousand German residents in the city were in embarrassment as burdensome to the government as to themselves.

The economic and financial crisis brought upon native and stranger in war times is disastrous. Gold and silver coin suddenly disappeared. Paper currency of denominations equivalent to five, ten, fifteen, or twenty dollars was useless, as change could not be made when these bills were offered in payment. Banking was suspended longer at some centers than at others. Letters of credit and travelers' checks, if cashed at all, were honored only for small amounts. Citizens and tourists alike were without ready money. Strangers in a strange land were in desperate straits, out of which only the intervention of their governments could extricate them. As many as one hundred thousand Americans were said to be abroad. Most of them were unable to stay or get home without resources beyond their control. They were quick and efficient to help each other by volunteer committees cooperating with the embassies. Much consideration was shown them by police and other officials wherever they were. Even men of wealth and personal resourcefulness were in want and perplexity, and much more those who were inexperienced and of limited means.

Not only the soldiery, but the citizens of every land at war, as well as of every country trying to maintain neutrality, were borne down by a "state of war." The city of Paris under martial law became overnight the "entrenched camp of Paris." Wherever the enlisted or conscript men had gone to war territorials were drafted or recruited for home defense. The food supply became scarce and the cost of living rose, though every government intervened to prevent extortion and hoarding, to furnish work and relief. The British Parliament proposed to spend twenty million dollars in maintaining employment. Included among the purposes for which the great war appropriation of five billion dollars might be spent was the "relief of distress" occasioned by the war, security for the rent of the soldiers' families being specified.

But even these extraordinary measures to mitigate the miseries of war only emphasize the irretrievable losses and

intolerable burdens of war against which government raises
its futile protest.

War means the ax laid to the very root of progress, the
subordination of everything human to the supremacy of
force, the supersedence of law, reason, conscience, and humanity by violence, the triumph of passion over experience,
of mania over sanity, of barbarism over civilization.

To leave Paris or to stay there a police permit was demanded, after martial law had been proclaimed. All the foreigners were summoned by big government posters to get
their identification papers from the consul of their country
and have them "visaed" at the nearest police station. Germans, Austrians, and Hungarians, as citizens whose countries were at war with France, were given their choice, to
leave French territory or to go to "concentration camps" in
Southern France. They were in pitiful plight. At the German and Austrian consulates women and children stood for
days, bewildered, not knowing what to do or what would
become of them. Some scurried away from the only homes
many of them had ever known. They trundled their babies
and few belongings in every direction through the streets.
They swelled the hopelessly big crowds at railway stations,
awaiting the few chances to take trains across the borders of
their fatherlands. With such bundles of clothing as they
could carry, whole families silently, desperately huddled
together, awaiting transportation into exile until after
the war.

At the American consulate the crowd of tourist refugees
from all over Europe was as large, but less patient, though
more hopeful. They blocked the sidewalk, jammed the doorway, choked the stairways, and wedged themselves into the
offices. Half a day was required for the identification, certifying your personal appearance, your parents and place of residence, your wife and children, your past occupation and
present intentions. But the police stations were worse. Before them and within their narrow passages, winding stairways, stuffy deskrooms, from morning to night, day after
day, a motley throng of many nationalities and tongues, of
every class and condition, struggled side by side to get

stamped on their identification papers the police permit for staying or going. For three hours I stood there in line and moved across the hallway and up the stairs just thirty feet, only to be told that I must go to another station and begin all over again, as the place for those resident where I domiciled had been changed. At this station I found myself in line again, with one thousand people ahead of me. After spending nearly three days in securing my permit to leave, I actually left the city without being asked to show the permit to anyone.

At the railway stations it was still worse. Vast multitudes filled all the approaches and blocked the way to the entrances, which were guarded by troops, whose officers scrutinized every applicant for admission within the gates and doors. The ticket office was opened at noon and closed at six in the evening. From dawn to dusk, however, hundreds of weary men, women, and children stood four abreast, in a long line that scarcely moved, awaiting their turn to get a numbered ticket giving the next chance of admission to the ticket office and the trains. If not at the door when their number was called they lost the chance to get in and had to start over again at the foot of the line. It took days to pass up and out. By hiring a man to stand in line for us through most of two days, we cleared the railway station.

While waiting to do so a continuous stream of troops passed by us to be entrained. Officers whirled by in automobiles. Cycle squads, heavy laden with knapsack and rifle, sped by on their motorcycles. The clatter of hoofs and clanking of sabers cleared the streets before the cavalry. Solid bodies of infantry marched in almost uncanny silence.

Before lining up for exit it was necessary to have cash in silver or gold. To borrow it from a friend was the only way to get it. Letters of credit were refused cash by some of the largest banks on which they were drawn. A prominent business man of the Middle West had one for ten thousand dollars on bankers of international standing, and could not get a hundred dollars in specie. I could get only twenty dollars in French paper money when I presented Thomas Cook & Son with their own travelers' checks and informed them that I had nothing else to depend upon. That paper bill for one hundred francs was promptly refused at restaurants and even at the post-office, where it was claimed they had no silver change they could part with. The American Express Company, however, distinguished itself by cashing its own checks, dollar for dollar.

Friend borrowed from friend, and even strangers loaned to strangers, refusing security when offered. Such was the fine comradeship of common helplessness. The strong felt as helpless as the weak. Men of affairs were as distraught as the women traveling alone. At the Hotel Royal an elderly man who bore every evidence of prosperity and stability, mistaking me for a member of the American committee, exclaimed: "I want you to understand that I am a man of some consequence in New York City. I am president of such a bank, and director in such a trust company, and here I do not know what to do in order to get the money and the permits I need." When told he could only do what others did, he strenuously objected to "standing in line with the mob at the consulate." A woman near him was scarcely more hysterical in displaying handfuls of paper money, which she said would not secure her railway transportation back to her sick baby in the interior.

Loosing one's moorings from shore to put to sea in the steerage is a war-time experience which many American refugees shared and will never forget. Each one's story of what was endured strangely mingles situations in which laughter and tears were alike irrepressible. At Liverpool we with steerage tickets were summoned to the dock at nine o'clock in the morning, while the cabin passengers were called to be there at two o'clock. All day until four o'clock we stood in line to get our embarkation cards, giving to each of us immigrants our number in big red figures. With the one piece of hand baggage which each of us was allowed to take out of Paris, we crossed the gangplank, were directed along the narrow main deck to the forecastle, were pointed down steep stairs below decks, and wended our course around a hatchway flanked by coils of ropes and covered with the grating through which the light feebly struggled. Then steering toward the darkest hole ahead of us, I landed in Section B at Bunk 12. Under it was the only place for my belongings. There, too, I belonged, with fifteen other bunkers above and alongside of me.

Along the rail of the main deck six hundred other steerage shipmates—"cabin class" all of them except thirty former immigrants returning from visits to the old country—leaned and looked as the American liner "St. Louis" slipped her moorings and slid slowly down the Mersey to the sea. Soon we sought friends on the upper deck and found no barrier between us. Once at sea, however, dreams of "sublimated steerage" or "converted third class" vanished, as did the visions of sharing some of the cabin-table luxuries. Immediately all entrances and companionways between us and the "upper class" were roped off and afterward guarded night and day. A great gulf was fixed, across which some of them could pass to us, but few of us could pass to them. There they stood, those upstart friends of ours, looking down at us, with useless cabin-passage tickets in our own pockets! They even slipped into our pockets an orange or apple or a few nuts, purloined from their table and passed through the ropes—and we ignominiously accepted them. Down below we went to our mess—and a mess it was—the more so when not supplemented by those crumbs of comfort from above stairs, or by "surprise parties" from the larders which some of our more provident messmates laid in before embarking. One poor fellow ordered his meat thrown out the porthole, grimly exclaiming, "One shark less!" Another big man from Iowa was found in his upper bunk devouring a whole duck which, he said, "cost him a dollar and a half, and was worth it."

The sanitary conditions were inexcusably bad. Water was turned on only for an hour and a half each morning, an hour at noon, and an hour at dusk, with a sea full of salt water at hand. Smells of fifty-seven varieties, worst of all those from the dishwashing, brought seasickness to many without provocation from the sea. The ballroom of the second cabin was opened for the women to sleep on the floor, and the upper aft deck, over the propeller, was given over "to the steerage." There we were permitted to stay all night as well as by day. This space allowed some to spread the steamer chairs they had procured, and gave others a chance to use the camp chairs they had brought with them, but many had to use the deck itself as the only place to sit or recline.

Although I paid more than half as much for my steerage passage returning as for my cabin passage going over on the same line, yet I got a great deal more than twice as much for my money in the cabin than in the steerage. If the cubic feet of space used by each cabin passenger and the cubic feet of space to which each steerage passenger is restricted are rated by what each pays, there can be little doubt that the poor steerage passenger pays a far higher rate for every foot of space he occupies and every morsel of food he eats than the richer cabin passenger pays for every foot of space available for his use and every luxury on his first-class, or even second-class, table.

At quarantine we had to line up in the steerage again and again, once for the inspection of our embarkation papers, and again for the inspection of our vaccination marks, and finally pass muster before the government health officers. While the big ship was being shunted into her dock by the tugboats swarming around her, above their hoarse breathing, American voices from the steerage raised high notes of "My Country, 'Tis of Thee!"

I was greatly surprised the following year to receive a long telegram signed by Henry Ford, reading in part as follows:

NEW YORK
November 25, 1915

Will you come as my guest aboard the Oscar II of the Scandinavian-American Line sailing from New York December 4 for Christiana, Stockholm and Copenhagen? One hundred representative Americans are being invited. I am cabling leading men and women of the European nations to join us en route, and at some central point to be determined later establish an international conference dedicated to negotiations leading to a just settlement of the war.

With twenty-thousand men killed every twenty-four hours, tens of thousands maimed, homes ruined, another winter begun, the time has come for a few men and women with courage and energy, irrespective of the cost in personal inconvenience, money, sacrifice and criticism, to free the good will of Europe, that it may assert itself for peace and justice, with the strong probabilities that international disarmament can be accomplished. Full letter follows.

Two days later I received the letter, which was remarkable, as was the telegram, for the white heat of its fine feeling and the dim and elusive light of its weird judgment. Its amazing claims, apparently based upon the assertion of the most improbable surmise and without reference to proof, were as incredible as that a man of his business judgment could make them with unquestioning and unquestioned sincerity. The strange mixture follows, a few details being omitted:

From the moment I realized that the world situation demands immediate action, if we do not want the war fire to spread any further, I joined those international forces which are working toward ending this unparalleled catastrophe. This I recognize as my human duty.

There is full evidence that the carnage, which has already cost ten millions of lives, can and is expected to be stopped through the agency of a mediating conference of the six disinterested nations, Holland, Denmark, Sweden, Norway, Switzerland, Spain and the United States.

For fifteen months the people of the world have waited for the governments to act; have waited for governments to lead Europe out of its unspeakable agony and suffering, and to prevent Europe's entire destruction. As European neutral governments are unable to act without the co-operation of our government, and as our government, for unknown reasons, has not offered this co-operation, no further time can be wasted in waiting for governmental action.

In order that their sacrifice may not have been in vain, humanity owes it to the millions of men led like cattle to the slaughter house, that a supreme effort be made to stop this wicked waste of life.

The people of the belligerent countries did not want the war. The people did not make it. The people want peace. It is their human right to get a chance to make it. The world looks to us, to America, to lead in ideals. The greatest mission before a nation is ours.

It is for this same reason that I repeat my appeal to you to join a peace pilgrimage, with men and women of our country representing all its ideals and all its activities. The peace ship that carries the American delegation will proceed to Christiana, where Norway's valiant sons and daughters will join the crusade. In Stockholm the ship's company will be reenforced by the choicest of Sweden's democracy. At Copenhagen further harbingers of peace will be foregathered.

These various groups will add such momentum to the crusade that when the pilgrims reach The Hague, the moral power of the peace movement will be irresistible. There we hope to meet delegations from Switzerland and from Spain.

From all these various delegations will be selected a small deliberative body which shall sit in one of the neutral capitals. Here it will be joined by a limited number of authorities of international promise from each belligerent country. This international conference will frame terms of peace, based on justice for all, regardless of the military situation. It will be an agency for continuous mediation, dedicated to the stoppage of this hideous international carnage and to the prevention of future wars through the abolition of competitive armaments.

In case of a governmental call for an official neutral conference before the Peace Ship departs from New York, or reaches European shores, our party will continue on its mission, rejoicing that the official gathering has materialized. We will then place our united strength solidly behind those entrusted by the government to carry on the peace negotiations. At The Hague the members of the peace pilgrimage will be dissolved.

I respectfully beg you to respond to the call of humanity and join the consecrated spirits who have already signified a desire to make history in a new way. The people of Europe cry out to you.

Yours for peace,

[Signed]   HENRY FORD

In reply, under date of December 1, I wrote:

Since receiving your letter of November 27th, I feel obliged to inform you that were I free to consider your generous invitation, I would be constrained to decline it by my loyalty to the peace cause.

The unfounded claims that the desire for peace among the soldiers and the peoples of the warring nations "will add such momentum to the crusade that when the pilgrims reach The Hague the moral power of the peace movement will be irresistible" discredit the judgment, not to say the sanity, of those who make them. Claims of the intention "to reach the men in the trenches and have them out by Christmas Day" are so incredible that your friends cannot believe that you made them.

Thus far I have found no dissent from the judgment prevalent here that both the Pacifist cause and American intervention have been discredited seriously by this ill-advised project, which, however well-intentioned, proves to have as little representative support as the claims for it have foundation in fact.

While appreciating your sincere desire to do anything you can toward ending this fratricidal strife, I would not be true if I did not tell you how sincerely I deplore the words and acts which are so seriously embarrassing those who are truly the friends of peace.

Sincerely yours,

GRAHAM TAYLOR

Far more tragic than anything I saw or heard of the World War, abroad or at home, were the echoes of the revolution from far across the Russian frontier. They came to me in letters from my son, Graham Romeyn Taylor, through the three years during which he served his country there. He was one of several university-trained men commissioned by the Department of State to reinforce the staff of the American Embassy in Russia. This reinforcement was needed to enable the United States as a neutral power, which it then was, to befriend the German people in extending the relief of their government to the civilian prisoners interned by the government of the Czar. At first, when stationed at Orenburg, he told of his sledge journeys forth and back across the Ural Mountains with the temperature far below zero, accompanied by a Moslem driver and a German-Russian interpreter. He described the pitiful plight in which he found hundreds of the merchants and professional classes interned in small towns and villages, to whom he administered the relief funds provided by the Prussian government.

As the war was drawing toward its close his letters intimated as much of the whispered predictions of the revolution as he risked the censorship to mention. Although certainly expected, no one knew when or how it would come. When the storm broke, sooner and more overwhelmingly than could have been imagined, he vividly depicted the scenes which followed the announcement of the overthrow of the Czar and the autocratic bureaucracy whose corruption and inefficiency had betrayed Russia and ruthlessly led her peasant soldiers to their slaughter. He had been with the citizens of Orenburg when they all assembled in the great square of the city at the open-air mass celebrating the long-awaited dawn of the day of deliverance. While kneeling in the snow with bared heads they heard the Cossacks coming from the camp where fifty thousand of them were mobilized. No one knew what they might do. But as "thousands of heavy booted, overcoated, tramping Cossacks marched into the square, from the gray cap or bayonet of every one of them streamed the red ribbon of the Revolution, while citizens cheered the troops and the troops the citizens. Led by the military band, all together they sang the 'Marseillaise' and the 'Russian National Hymn.'" To my son it was "a day of profound spiritual stirring." From the scene "where the masses of citizens were radiant with a hope which shone from countenances that had been dull and melancholy" his mind turned "to the prisons all over the country, imagining the faces of the political prisoners who at one sweep had been released."

From Petrograd he wrote of the funeral of the martyr citizens who had been shot down on the streets and were buried —"in the 182 red coffins which were lowered into one grave, while the people sang the 'Marseillaise' and the Russian hymn to the dead." After the ambassador and his staff had withdrawn from Petrograd beyond the reach of the advancing Germans, my son wrote of being left there to continue the work of publicity which had been intrusted to his direction. On billboard posters and by moving pictures America's view of the meaning of war was portrayed in the Russian language, including the translation of President Wilson's message stating his "fourteen points."

Of this "hour of destiny" when the Duma was the new government he wrote: "How proud we all would be that America was the first to recognize it officially—this century's advance that has been made in a few days; how grateful I would be to take even the smallest part in whatever would help to prevent the lustre of this great, bright vista from being dimmed." When the bolshevik counter-revolutionists made their treaty with Germany, he was transferred to Siberia where the "White Russians" were making their stand under General Kolchak. The vista opened by the early revolution was dimmed even, more darkly under the chaos and cruelty of the White reactionaries than it had been by what he had seen of the Red régime only through its initial year.

CHAPTER XIX

CHICAGO'S RACE RIOT

POST-WAR conditions account for the aggravated race antipathies and conflicts that followed the Armistice. When, on the one hand, the war united different races in common defense against the common peril they feared, and, on the other hand, dissolved the artificial political and military bond of great empires, humanity reverted to its racial types and loyalties. This primitive, elemental instinct asserted itself all over the world. Here in America it created new cleavages between people of the white races as well as re-opened and deepened the old racial antipathies between our colored and white people. It even rekindled those fierce fires of religious prejudice, hatred, and persecution that are more irreligious and inhuman than all human passions.

Thus again this whole abnormal war psychology, which un-balanced all of us more or less, led to discharging the ill temper of the majority in the body politic upon any minority—black or yellow, Jewish or Catholic—by self-conscious, self-appointed defenders or champions of the nativity or faith of the majority.

With amazing virulence these old epidemics of hatred broke out anew between native and foreign born, black and white, Jew and Gentile, Catholic and Protestant. But their virulence proved them to be pathological, symptomatic of a temperature so high that it must either soon fall to normal or kill the body that was the prey of the fever. In fact, both these results happily were soon registered by these local outbreaks.

Some of these feverish organisms are dying of the tempera-ture which caused their cherished delirium, the anti-foreign, anti-Jewish, anti-Catholic, anti-American, anti-everything obsession! Wherever they asserted their class, sectarian or race pretension, and attempted to exercise their little brief authority, there the second sober sense, the normal judgment, of the real community began to reassert its balance and control. The spotlight of publicity is dissolving the mysterious Ku Klux Klan as the sun dissolves the night shadows and morning mists. The boastful "100 per cent Americanism" is no longer a single-plank platform as it was of so many wartime agencies.

But the experience of Chicago proves how readily partisan demagogues may array racial elements in a cosmopolitan population against each other. It also proves how the heedlessness of some citizens toward the racial self-respect of others may let them be the prey of such demagoguery. Here in Chicago the appeal craftily made to the pride of voters who had come with the "new" immigration from the south and east of Europe prompted them to assert the distinction of their old-world heritages as equal to those of the "old" immigration from the British Isles. The urge of the inferiority complex impelling these "Mediterraneans" to assert their power politically administered a rebuke to the superiority complex of the so-called "Nordic" stocks.

It also raised a warning signal against scare-head alarms of the white race's danger from "the rising tide of color." Lacking though the evidence is of the colored races of the world making common cause against the whites, yet there is no lack of experience to prove how readily the surviving racial antagonisms between the blacks and whites can incite them to strike back at each other riotously, as well as politically, where opportunity offers. Chicago experienced disaster from both of these back strokes. For a third time the votes of the Black Belt turned the scale favorably to the demagogue.

Back of this racial solidarity which gave the Negro voters the balance of political power lies the occasion for the tragedy of the race riot of 1919. It suddenly broke out on July 27, raged violently for seven days and smoldered for another week. Peace was restored by the police and the state militia only after they had been on guard a fortnight. Although the occasion for the local outbreak was incidental, it had been preceded by open warfare at East St. Louis, Illinois, two years before, and by minor clashes in Chicago. Both these industrial centers had attracted large Negro migrations while white workers had gone to the war. The Negro population of Chicago increased during the decade 1910–20 from 44,103 to 109,504. The failure to provide houses for this increase overcrowded the districts where Negroes had hitherto lived and forced many of them to seek shelter in neighborhoods occupied by whites. This had been the cause of irritation within and beyond these districts. No less than twenty-four houses occupied by Negroes, and also by white landlords who had rented them to these new tenants, had been bombed without any apprehension of those guilty of these outrages by the police.

The resentment against this failure to afford legal protection to the industrious Negro population incited the bravado of the more disorderly element. It felt itself to be immune from interference under the city administration's open-town policy which granted special privileges to illicit Negro resorts. Chicago had appealed, therefore, to both classes, as open alike to the industrious and vicious. Plentiful work and higher wages were made even more attractive by the report that the City Hall had become "Uncle Tom's cabin," on a racial scale.

The incident which provoked the riot, however, was the bathing of a few Negroes too near a crowd of whites gathered on the lake shore, close to the Negro quarter. Stones flew; a Negro boy drowned. Gun play began. But the first shot from a police gun was fired by a Negro officer who killed a Negro who had shot at the police. Hoodlum gangs, white and black, broke loose and ran amuck in street-fighting, bomb-throwing, and setting fire to Negro dwellings. About 1,000 were thus made homeless and destitute, 537 were injured, 38 were killed, of whom 15 were whites, during this race war which imperiled the peace and safety of the whole city.

Stirred by the city-wide, and country-wide, significance of this race antagonism, a few of us were moved to call a conference to consider the serious situation and the means of preventing its recurrence. Responding to this call, citizens representing forty-eight social, civic, commercial, labor, professional, and church organizations met at the Union League

Club. Among them were the Bar Association, the Medical Society, the Association of Commerce, the Packing House Industries, the two City Clubs and Woman's Club, the social settlements, the Federation of Churches, foreign-language groups, and the Urban League, with representatives from its Negro and white membership. The conference unanimously delegated a Committee of Six, on which I served, to wait upon Governor Frank O. Lowden, and ask him to appoint "an emergency state committee to study the psychological, social and economic causes underlying the conditions resulting in the present race riot, and to make such recommendations as will tend to prevent a recurrence of such conditions in the future." The governor promptly did so, naming outstanding representatives of each race to constitute the Chicago Commission on Race Relations.

Recognizing that emphasis should be placed not only upon investigating the facts of the riot, but also upon the study and interpretation of conditions of Negro life in Chicago and of the relations between the two races, the commissioners organized subcommittees to investigate racial clashes, housing, industrial and crime conditions, racial contacts, and public opinion. The published report of the Commission is widely recognized to be a most thoroughgoing, original contribution to the study of the relations between the two races in America. The high standing of the commissioners added significance to their findings and recommendations, which were specifically addressed to the following groups of public officials and private citizens: police, militia, state's attorneys, and the courts; the City Council, the park, and other administrative bodies; social, civic, labor, and church organizations; the public, its white and Negro elements; employers of labor organizations; places of public accommodation, restaurants, theaters, and stores; the street railway companies; and the press.[1]

[1] Chicago Commission on Race Relations, *The Negro in Chicago—a Study of Race Relations and a Race Riot* (672 pages, 55 illustrations and 18 maps), University of Chicago Press, 1922. The representatives of the white race were Edgar A. Bancroft (chairman) lawyer; William Scott Bond, real estate; Edward O. Brown, lawyer and former judge; Harry Eugene Kelly, lawyer; Victor F. Lawson, publisher and editor of the *Chicago Daily News;* Julius Rosenwald, merchant; and Francis W. Shepardson, director of the State Department of Registration and Education. Representing the Negro race were Robert S. Abbott, editor of the *Chicago Defender;*

The relation between the two races is slowly improving under the growing urge of self-respecting Negro citizens, who are discontented with the political prestige given the vicious element that exploit their own people and are exploited by politicians for personal and factional gains. The high civic and economic ideals of the Urban League win influential leadership and publicity. The Interracial Commission of the Chicago Federation of Churches, on which prominent representatives of the churches of both races serve, is valuably promoting better understanding by the conferences regularly held and the exchange of pulpits arranged annually on a Sunday devoted to race relationship.

The most promising co-operation between the two races, and between personal and public effort and resources for their common welfare, is that which is being effected by the far-reaching beneficence of Julius Rosenwald of Chicago. His belief in education as the hope of both races led to his acceptance of trusteeship at the University of Chicago and at the Tuskegee Normal and Industrial Institute in Alabama, and to his generous personal and financial support of both. Believing in the public schools as whole-heartedly as in the institutions of higher learning for each race, he helped develop the liberal and professional training at Fisk University and other colleges and the common schools for colored youth in the South. By contributing $3,230,000 toward the establishment of these schools during the past decade, the Julius Rosenwald Fund gave the colored people incentive to raise $3,800,000; interested white people to add $870,000; the taxpayers in fourteen southern states to appropriate $11,500,000 for the building and maintenance of 4,729 schools for colored children in 818 counties of 14 southern states. They constitute nearly one-fifth of all the Negro rural schools in the South, enrolling half-a-million pupils and ten thousand teachers.

George C. Hall, physician; George H. Jackson, real estate; Edward H. Morris, lawyer and legislator; Adelbert H. Roberts, lawyer; Lacy K. Williams, clergyman.

The Commission was served by a staff of sixteen investigators, seven compilers, and thirteen clerks, with Graham Romeyn Taylor as executive secretary and Charles S. Johnson associate executive secretary, representing each race, respectively.

Mr. Rosenwald's recent demonstration of his adventurous faith in the future of his city and his fellow-citizens is his investment of $2,500,000 or more in erecting an apartment building providing 400 Negro families with better homes than they have been able to secure, for rates of rent which yet are expected to yield 6 per cent on this investment. This second largest building of its kind occupies an entire block surrounding a garden. The "Michigan Boulevard Gardens" are ventured to demonstrate that dwellings for such wage-earning families may be commercially provided.

Another large investment by the Julius Rosenwald Fund gave initiative to the movement which provided $3,000,000 for the endowment and new building equipment of the Provident Hospital and Training School. Negro medical students will be given their full course by the University of Chicago and will be offered interneships and research fellowships hitherto seldom available to them. It is hoped that this promotion of health may lead to the reduction of the Negro death rate, 26.25 per 1,000, which is more than twice that of the white population of Chicago, 11.80 per 1,000.

Impressed by the work of the Young Men's and Young Women's Christian Associations, Mr. Rosenwald not only built the Sears Roebuck branch of the Y.M.C.A. to serve the employees at the headquarters of the great mail-order house of which he was president, but he offered $25,000 to any community in the United States which would erect and maintain a $100,000 Y.M.C.A. building for Negroes. So far eighteen of these buildings have been founded for young colored men and two for colored women, the Rosenwald Fund donating $500,-000, the colored people raising $425,000, and other citizens of these communities contributing $3,000,000 in response to the local campaign conducted by the Metropolitan Association.

When the funds for the Chicago building were raised, Mr. Rosenwald in addressing the colored men enlisted in the undertaking told them that he thought it only just for him as a member of the most persecuted race to lend a hand to Negroes as the next most persecuted people, adding that the Jews had grown gray under persecution before the Negroes had begun to suffer theirs. When I accompanied him on one

of his frequent visits to Tuskegee, we stopped over at Nash-
ville to visit Fisk University. Rabbi Emil G. Hirsch bade
the students remember that Julius Rosenwald did what he
did as a loyal member of the liberal Jewish faith. But his
parishioner elicited the rapturous applause of the chapel
assembly by characteristically declaring: "I have come to the
conclusion that any Jew who would not make a good Christian is not a worthy Jew; that any Christian who would not
make a good Jew is not a worthy Christian; and that anyone
who would not make a good Jew or Christian is not worth
much of anything." Then I wondered if any Christian had
ever done as much for Jewish institutions as this Jewish citizen was doing for Christian associations. Judging by the
spirit thus expressed, I have long felt and often said that some
of the most Christian-spirited persons I know are Jews, whose
catholicity of deed transcends the practice of the catholicity
of creed.

CHAPTER XX

THE FAR EAST AND THE NEAR WEST

MORE than fifty years before it was my great privilege to visit the Far East, the Orient was brought near to me in the persons of three young sons of Japan who became my schoolmates. Their unexpected arrival is still memorable in educational and missionary circles. They were the very first of their race to knock at the door of American schools for admission as students of Western culture. Two of these three came to the office of the Board of Foreign Missions of the Reformed Church in America with their friendly pilot, the captain of a sailing vessel that had arrived at the port of New York in the autumn of 1866. They bore letters of introduction from a missionary of that church, the Rev. Guido F. Verbeck, then entering upon his long service in Japan. He was distinguished for the influence he exerted upon the initiative taken by Japanese officials toward establishing modern educational methods. So far in advance of that initiative, however, were these youths that they ventured this voyage of discovery at the risk of their lives and under assumed names because their adventurous aspirations were so contrary to the traditions of their country. They entered the Grammar School of Rutgers College a few months before I was graduated from it, so that I was privileged to have Ise and Numagawa as my schoolmates, and later as my comrades. Sorry were we to hear of their early death soon after their return home. A year later Toro Kusakabé entered my college class, to be held in honor alike by his teachers and fellow-students as a man of high spirit, charming manner, and brilliant scholarship, especially in mathematics. Too frail to withstand the double strain of the change of climate and his intense application to his studies, he died in his

Senior year and was buried in the Japanese cemetery lot in
the college town, where a score of student fellow-countrymen
lie beside him. His name was retained in the list of the grad-
uating class on our Commencement program, and the enrol-
ment in Phi Beta Kappa was announced as having been
awarded in his honor. Its gold key, which he would have
worn, was presented to his father in Japan by another college
mate, William Elliot Griffis, who became an educational
pioneer there.

He was among the first of several young American college
graduates to be enlisted in the new educational policy which
was being introduced in Japan largely under the guidance of
Dr. Verbeck, who from 1869 to 1873 was superintendent of
teachers and instructors in the foreign department of the
Imperial University at Tokyo. Under his supervision Griffis
began teaching in the castle of the Daimio at Osaka in 1870,
only a year after his graduation. There he equipped the first
chemical laboratory for educational purposes. During the
two following years while teaching in the Imperial University
he supervised the establishment of the first polytechnic school
at the capital. In 1873 my esteemed professor, Dr. David
Murray, became educational adviser to the Japanese government. Thirty years after he had returned from Japan, at a
dinner given to honor his memory by the Peers' Club at
Tokyo, the Minister of Education declared that his name
would be remembered in Japan with the names of Commo-
dore Perry and Townsend Harris, for organizing Japan's system of national education, for nourishing the Imperial University, and for laying the foundation of women's education.

On our way across the Pacific in 1922, our most interesting
fellow-passenger on the American liner was Rear Admiral
Yamanashi, of the Japanese navy, who with a staff of four
officers had served at the Washington Disarmament Conference as Japan's technical advisers, for which he had received promotion to his high rank. Language was no barrier
to the friendly intercourse which Mrs. Taylor and I were
privileged to have, as he spoke English fluently. When asked
how he came to approve of international disarmament, to the
extent to which Japan had agreed, he replied by asking how

he could have felt otherwise after the early educational training he had received. And then he told us that his schooling
had been at the preparatory department of the Doshisha
University, which was established and conducted by American and Japanese Christians at Kyoto. "While at Washington," he continued, "I attended the Congregational church to
honor the memory of Dr. de Forest, the missionary who led
me into the Christian life and inspired and encouraged me
through my educational course."

He and others coming from the Washington Conference
gave their fellow-passengers a rare insight into the significance of that great event, addressing them at their request
one notable evening in the steamer's saloon. The following
quotations from the admiral's address gave token both of the
high ideals and playful spirit which gave charm to his speech
as well as to his conversation:

> From the naval point of view it is not an easy task in a sea fight to de-
> stroy a big capital ship of an enemy. You must expect at least an equal
> amount of damage yourself, together with a heavy loss of human lives.
> There in Washington, during those three months, under silent guns and
> with noiseless torpedoes, about seventy-five big capital ships of the great
> powers were doomed to the bottom of the sea, without prejudice to the
> safety and interests of the people of these nations.
>
> In that sense, one might safely venture to say that the Washington con-
> ference was by far a greater sea fight than any in the last war, with far
> better results.
>
> Posterity, perhaps, may be better able to judge the true significance of
> these results when far from the actual scene of the great drama. There
> has been much sensational talk about the future of the Pacific Ocean.
> Some even dared to say that it would be the theatre of great troubles.
> But now after this conference one may hesitate to profess such an evil fore-
> boding, to the keen satisfaction of everybody, and particularly to the
> people of the countries whose shores are washed by this great ocean, re-
> joicing as you all will in the bright prospect and clear horizon of these
> waters.

With many more expressions of his deep religious spirit
were we impressed, which if not avowedly were yet essentially
Christian. We were welcomed at Kobe by the son of the distinguished Matsukata family, who thirty-eight years before
had returned home from his course in Rutgers College and
the Yale Law School. Our good fellowship as fellow-alumni

led him personally to conduct me over the great Kawazaki shipyards of which he was the master and principal owner. The hulls of the great ships were on the ways. Machinery from all the best machine shops of the world crowded the vast plant covering many acres. More than fifteen thousand workmen swarmed about every center of the plant. They stopped a moment to see the big boss pass, some dropping their caps as they bowed to him, others calling the attention of their shopmates to his presence among them, he always saluting them in return. Pointing to a colossal crane towering above all others, he said, "That crane was used to lift guns on ships of 22,000 tons which we built here." Quietly he added, "It is of little use now." Passing a pile of castings, he remarked, "Those were for submarines, but useless now." Quickly he added, "The Washington Conference rightly seeks the peace of the world." With no little justifiable cynicism the editor of the *Japan Chronicle* had written by way of invidious comparison that at this great dockyard "battleships as massive and murderous as any floated by the most Christian and civilized nations in the West are builded and launched."

The extent to which large-scale production is carried in Japan is exemplified by the Kanegafuchi Spinning Mill at Kobe. It is one of the twenty-six cotton mills operated by the company running over half-a-million spindles, with fifty thousand more operating in its six silk mills. Its total payroll covered the wages of no fewer than 41,000 operatives, of whom 32,783 were women and girls and 8,300 men and boys. The ends of the earth meet among the bales of cotton waiting to be fed to the spindles. From India, China, and the Imperial Valley in southern California they come, and from our southern states, where "the finest fiber of them all is produced," the manager said in passing. When I visited the mill in 1922, it was conceded to have developed conditions of labor far in advance of the standards required either by law or public opinion in Japan. Promotion from lower- to higher-paid positions is opened and encouraged, 77 per cent then handling the machines having risen from the lower ranks of operatives. Higher technical schools and universities furnish most others for the work requiring greater skill. Prizes for efficiency were offered. Invention loans, on easy terms of repayment after ten years, were offered employees' families to encourage them to give their most capable children the advantages of the higher technical schooling. Although children of thirteen years of age were allowed by Japanese law to leave school and go to work, this company employed none younger than fourteen. Elementary technical courses were maintained for both sexes. Special training for clerks, matrons, nurses, and overseers was also offered. Books, stationery, and periodicals were furnished free. Scholarships providing for a year's food, clothing, and school expenses were available to those meeting certain requirements. Wages were supplemented by bonus and pension.

Care and encouragement were given the family life. Remittance of savings by single employees to their parents at home was facilitated, though left voluntary. The wedding day, or the day after, was granted any employee as a special holiday with full pay. A rest of seventy-five days at childbirth was given employed mothers, with money allowances in addition to medical and nursing service. Additional time was allowed for the complete recovery of working strength. Day nurseries and kindergartens were provided for the young children. A premium was put upon the home-building and family life of married employees, in preference to the continuance of the mother's work. Company cottages afforded homes for many hundreds of families. Training for their own domestic work was offered and urged. Varying but large proportions of full pay were continued to heads of families while absent from work on military duty. Not only were pension benefits granted in case of sickness, injury, old age, and death, but "conservation" allowances were given employees' families suffering from misfortunes or calamities for which the company was in no wise responsible. Following a Japanese custom, a farewell gift accompanies the departure from service, whether due to withdrawal or dismissal. At the death of any member of an employee's family, he or she was given three days leave of absence.

The health of each employee and of the whole company-community was safeguarded and promoted by doctors, nurses, examinations, tests, dentistry, hygienic and sanitary regulations and training, supplemented by sanitarium treatment. Ample light, ventilation, cleanliness, and wholesomeness were conspicuous in shops and offices. Many of these measures were taken for the prevention or arrest of tuberculosis, which prevails alarmingly among cotton mill operatives in Japan. In other mills 60 per cent of them were said to become infected while at work, of whom 20 per cent die within a year or two after returning to their homes. In this mill, at the discovery of the loss of weight or other carefully watched symptoms, the case was at once and progressively dealt with by way of prevention, isolation, and other means of recovery.

More paternalistic than democratic, with wages too low to justify high profits, these conditions at the time of my visit were far in advance of those prevailing in Japan and in most other lands. They were then due to the exceptional business ability, social intelligence, and human feeling of a manager, who was one of a few Japanese industrialists alertly observant of and sympathetic with social progress in industry. Since his transfer from this mill to another department of the company's work, these welfare standards are said to have been lowered and the labor exactions made more burdensome.

There is another and darker side of Japanese life, the deep shadows of which appear the blacker as seen in contrast with the white lives of two men bravely struggling to dispel their gloom, whose inspiring acquaintanceship I cherish. One of them is Toyohiko Kagawa, widely known as social worker, labor organizer and leader, formerly yet all the more now a Christian pastor. He is the son of a once wealthy father who was so prominent as to hold the post of a prefecture vice-governor, but so liberal in his views that he could not hold it long. The lad was said to be difficult in his home surroundings because critical of his elders and too lavish in his generosity to the poor to suit those upon whom he was dependent. To a rich uncle who adopted him after his father's death he became still more peculiar, because he became a Christian and insisted upon studying for the ministry. Failing to dissuade him, his uncle turned him off and disinherited him. The missionaries took him in, sent him through college, and several years later, with the help of many other friends, made it possible for the young man to take two years of graduate study at Princeton University.

Meanwhile, Kagawa sought to minister to the neediest of his countrymen and started his ministerial life and labor at first in Kobe, his birthplace, and then in the still deeper abyss of poverty and misery in Osaka, the great manufacturing center. Here he lived in quarters so small and poor as to rent for less than one dollar a month. His living seldom cost him more than one dollar and a half additional. Literally following the precept of Jesus, he gave a second coat if it were given to him to someone who had none. After his marriage he introduced his bride to over a hundred old men and women of his neighborhood whom he invited to meet her and presented her to them with the words: "My wife will be your servant." Assisted by Japanese and foreign friends, he established dispensaries, sick relief, mutual-help clubs, a co-operative brush factory, sewing classes, night schools, day nurseries, employment agencies, a builders' guild, consumers' co-operatives, Sunday schools, and a church.

These charities led him to take the risks of leadership in the cause of social and industrial justice. And risks there were. Whether preaching in his little church or to great crowds on the streets, he won a large following from among the depressed people, especially the unemployed and the illy paid wage-earners. He incurred dangerous opposition both from the upper and lowest classes. Robbed and kidnapped by street bandits who tried to force him to deliver to them funds from which he was giving to the poor, he was also under suspicion and surveillance by employers and the government. Intervening in a strike at the dockyards with the hope of securing conciliation, he was arrested and twice imprisoned. Although he was fined time and again for printing what the court considered dangerous opinions in his widely circulated publications, the *Labor News* and *Pillars of Cloud*, yet the more revolutionary radicals were so hostile to what they considered to be his conservatism that the police had to defend him from their attacks.

In later years both his thought and action have been better

understood and have long since been credited with the constructive influence which has won wide respect, more cooperation, and less opposition. The great circulation of his novel written in Japanese was entitled *Across the Death Line*, because after he thought himself as good as dead while suffering from tuberculosis, from which he unexpectedly recovered, he dedicated his life to the service of others with utter self-abandonment. This story of what his countrymen knew to be his own life was accepted by many thousands of them as a propaganda of his ideals of social justice. Its English translation, published in America and England under the title *Before the Dawn*, graphically describes the adverse economic and social conditions against which he still struggles. Personally gentle in appearance and calm in manner, he is simple yet forcible in public speech, and in action direct, courageous, and practically effective.

The other man seeking to cleanse his country from the still darker blot which stains its honor and fame is Gunpei Yamamure, who is in charge of the headquarters of the Salvation Army in Tokyo. Through his eyes and the literature he commands can best be judged the infamy of the Japanese Yoshiwara, which legalizes and attempts to establish government control of prostitution. Instead of proscribing the shame of it and curtailing its profits, its patronage has been invested with respectability. Its traffic in disease and spiritual death has been enhanced as an investment and given the status of a recognized occupation. Parents even indenture their daughters for a term of years, during which they can neither withdraw nor escape from the Yoshiwara district without paying the forfeiture or penalty of a breach of contract. The police enforce its payment by returning the fugitive to the resort; the courts by compelling the parents to pay for the service which their daughter still owes. In many towns this segregated district contains the best-built residences to be found within the city limits. Within the barred gates of Tokyo's Yoshiwara hundreds of these inmates perished in the fire following the earthquake. If anything were needed to prove the deception and futility of the pretense to regulate the social evil by segregating and protecting it, Japan

can furnish the evidence. The womanhood of Japan is raising a protest that cannot be unheeded much longer.

Along the protective and preventive line, stretching far
away from this abyss to the homes and happy childhood of
Japan, the missionary schools, the colleges for girls and
women, and the effectively progressive work of the Young
Men's and Young Women's Christian Associations invaluably
supplement the government educational and social institutions.

As an evidence of his appreciation of the latter Association's
personnel and service, Dr. Inazo Nitobé, professor in the
Imperial University of Tokyo, and his influential American
wife invited its staff to occupy their beautiful home during
the years of their absence in Geneva, Switzerland, while he
was serving the League of Nations as its secretary. To have
shared its hospitality for an evening's fellowship with the
socially intelligent staff workers and their native friends is a
memory that never loses its charm.

Dr. Nitobé has built for himself a greater home in the
hearts of his countrymen by interpreting the "soul of Japan"
as no living Japanese has done. What Lafcadio Hearn attempted in helping other peoples to understand the Japanese
their own interpreter did to help them understand themselves.
"Bushida," which symbolized the Knight-Ways, or the Pre-
cepts of Knighthood, that inspired and guided the chivalry of
the Samurai class in feudal times, he claims to be still the
animating spirit of his people's highest ideals, of which their
defaults are perversions. In his inspiring little volume he
wrote:

> Begun at first as the glory of the élite, it became in time an aspiration
> and inspiration to the nation at large; and though the populace could not
> attain the moral height of those loftier souls, yet the Soul of Japan ulti-
> mately came to express the *Volksgeist* of the Island Realm.[1]

Very wonderful is the development of the public educational system in Japan. In the compulsory attendance of
practically all children of school age, in the grading and thoroughness of the curriculum, and in the training for citizenship
Japan's schooling of her youth compares favorably with that

[1] Bushido—the Soul of Japan (author's 23d ed.; Tokyo: Teibi Publishing Co.,
1920).

of any other nation. The sight-seeing expeditions, which are a regular requirement of the schools, inspire the wish that they might be added to the all too monotonous routine of our American schools. I saw hundreds of pupils marched into the great railway station at Tokyo, seated upon trains and taken to see great natural scenery, large industrial plants, shipyards, port docks, public buildings, and shrines of worship.

The outline of official and privately conducted social work presented to the Prince of Wales when he visited Japan would have done credit to any city in Europe or America. Beautifully printed, illustrated, and bound, this souvenir prepared by the Bureau for Social Work of the government Home Department gave proof of a co-operation between officials and voluntary agencies which is even more promising for the future than deservedly creditable to the present in Japan.

My interview with Baron Goto when he was mayor of Tokyo greatly impressed me with the type of higher Japanese officials whom he represented. His familiarity with events of international interest was equal to his detailed knowledge of municipal administration. His approving references to the Washington conference for the limitation of armaments were indicative of his breadth of view. His keen interest in city planning was shown by his eager inquiries after the Chicago Plan and his announcement of his invitation to Professor Charles A. Beard, then of Columbia University, New York, to serve as the adviser of the officials projecting the plan for the Greater Tokyo.

On leaving Japan I brought no deeper impression than that which was made by what I saw and heard in the great Buddhist monastery garden near Yokohama. There stands the great Daibutsu, the colossal bronze image of Buddha. It has stood there under the open skies since 1252, a vast figure 53 feet high, 100 feet in circumference, weighing 400 tons. From all parts of the empire all classes come to bow in silence before this symbol of their ancient faith. A mother reverently approached it leading her little child, as I stood there. Advancing a few steps ahead of the little one, with downcast eyes like those of the great image, she prostrated herself before it as though sharing for a moment its eternal contemplation. When she arose the child faced about, took his mother's place, and, as reverently as she, bowed twice to the ground in childlike awe. For eight and a half centuries, generation after generation has thus reverently come and gone.

As I passed out of the gate through which I had entered, I read this call to my soul, which was inscribed in English and Japanese:

Stranger, whosoever thou art and whatsoever be thy creed, when thou enterest this sanctuary remember thou treadest upon ground hallowed by the worship of the ages. This is the temple of Buddha and the Gate of the Eternal and should be therefore entered with reverence.

Ever since, and the more because of this experience, what Dr. Nitobé wrote echoes within me:

To a philosophic and pious mind, the races themselves are marks of divine chirography clearly traced in black and white as on their skin; and if this simile holds good, the yellow race forms a precious page inscribed in hieroglyphics of gold. The very lost races are a palimpsest to be deciphered by a seeing eye. Christianity to my mind is "an old, old story," which if presented in intelligible words,—that is to say if expressed in the vocabulary familiar in the moral development of the people—will find easy lodgment in their hearts, irrespective of race or nationality.

While fully recognizing the justification of restricting Oriental immigration to avoid lowering the American standard of living among wage-earners and to prevent the amalgamation of races, which is unfortunate alike to the Occidental and the Oriental, yet with many others who favor this restriction I think the exclusion act of Congress unnecessarily offered an affront in discriminating against a progressive people, of whose government we demand commercial treaties due "the most favored nation."

The loss suffered, both by Japan and America in the early death of our Chicago fellow-citizen, Edgar A. Bancroft, so soon after he auspiciously began his services as United States ambassador to the Japanese, may be measured by these farewell words, which this comrade of ours addressed to the Chicago Association of Commerce as he was about to depart on his mission of peace:

The feelings of Japan have been hurt. That we were, and have been and are her friends only perhaps makes the hurt more keen. All these years of friendship between the two nations for the moment only make the hurt harder to bear. Their feelings are hurt not so much by what we have done as by the manner in which it was done. We know that mutual forbearance, mutual patience and abiding confidence in the good intention and friendship of both nations, as between individuals, will heal every hurt.

With this conviction I have accepted the mission to a land of natural artistic beauty, to a nation of strength and progress, to a people of great courtesy and of great kindliness, with the confidence that I shall be greeted as a friend and that there, in the quiet of understanding and through relationships that will continue the friendly relationships of all these years, all differences will be dissolved and there will be no cloud in the sky which bends over Japan and the United States.

My first impressions of the Chinese people fortunately were received through contacts with the educated classes. Respect and admiration could not be withheld by anyone who knew Yung Wing, one of the most cultivated and influential among the early representatives of his people in America. Both in China and United States he acquired well-deserved influence as a pioneer of the movement of Chinese students to take a part of their educational courses in American schools and universities. In order to help them maintain vital relations with the homeland and relate the learning of the Western peoples and their experience in the new world to the needs and opportunities of China, Yung Wing secured official sanction and support for the Chinese Educational Mission which he established at Hartford, Connecticut, in 1872. Thither came groups of young Chinamen, most of them to be guided to the educational institutions of their choice, and all of whom returned during their vacation periods for reunions with each other and to study the comparisons and contrasts between their old and new learning, under Chinese instructors.

In 1880, when I first became acquainted with the group, there were over a hundred students in it, including those from the higher grades of preparatory schools and from college classes. Their high reputation for studious habits, observant attitudes, courteous manners, and appreciation of what was new to them without loss of what they venerated in their older civilization was maintained through nine years without any breach or shadow falling upon it. In 1881 this great and

unique educational link between the Orient and the Occident
was abandoned, and all the students, then numbering one
hundred, were ordered to return to China, notwithstanding
that many of them were preparing to fill high positions similar to those in which their predecessors had rendered distinguished service to their country.

The closing of the educational mission was attributed to a
conservative reaction among Chinese officials then dominant,
whose reactionary policies gained support from the resentment felt in China over the practical abrogation of the Bur-
lingame Treaty of 1858 and because of the more recent rebuff
in the refusal to receive Chinese students into the Military
Academy at West Point and the Naval Academy at Annapo-
lis. Perhaps these reactionaries were still further moved by
jealousy of the leadership which these returning students had
attained in China, when they were supposed to be trained in
America only to provide translators and interpreters.

Impressions of the character and capacity of the household
in its ancestral home located among us, and most of all my
high regard for the native genius, acquired culture, and charming manners of Yung Wing himself and his American wife,
prepared me to look for like qualities in a race constituting
one-quarter of the earth's population, which has maintained
the stability of its civilization for thousands of years.

When late in February, 1922, our American liner arrived at
Shanghai, the seamen's strike was on at Hongkong. It proved
to be an epoch-making event, heralding and necessitating
great changes in the economic, political, and diplomatic relationships between Western nations and the Chinese people.
Incidents occurring then at this parting of the ways are of
unusual interest. My attention was first attracted to the
situation one evening while our vessel was docked at Shanghai, by noticing that the social hall of its first-class passengers
was being occupied by coolies who were taken aboard from a
steamboat which had run up alongside. Thus made aware of
impending trouble, I found it brewing in the dining-saloon
where I was the only passenger witnessing what followed.
There our Chinese steward's crew were lined up before the
ship's officers with the United States marshal of the port and

a Chinese interpreter standing in between. These stateroom attendants, helpers, and dining-saloon waiters were being questioned whether they would stand by the ship on its return from Manila to Hongkong. The men refused to promise to do so. The marshal thereupon ordered them to be off the ship within fifteen minutes and called the harbor police to enforce his order. Standing abreast with folded arms, the men demanded to be taken back to Hongkong where they had been shipped. On the arrival of the harbor police armed with batons and rope knots, the crew filed quietly down the gangplank to the dock. They stood there an hour or more in their white jackets without hats or coats with the chill wind blowing. Demanding their baggage, one of the men was roughly handled by the police at the top of the gangplank. Then the Chinese in the steerage began to show signs of interference. The baggage of the men was then put off the ship, many of the hand pieces being thrown on the dock, breaking open at the fall. Thus the eviction ended, with passengers seeking their serving "boys" to give them their fees and our ship starting off for the Philippines with an inexperienced steward's crew of landsmen to man the lifeboats in case of peril.

But the end was not yet. Passengers for Hongkong were officially notified that not only had that port been closed by the strike of the seamen, but hotels, restaurants, public utility, and many other lines of service had been crippled or suspended. Later it was reported that one hundred and seventy-two ships were helplessly anchored or docked in Hongkong harbor, while in the city five thousand coolies, house servants, cooks, and waiters had left work and gone to Canton, their home city. The guilds had called out the bakers, printers, and other employees. Seven weeks after the strike of the seamen had been called, the losses suffered by the shipping and business interests were estimated to be forty million dollars. The English papers published in China urged the government not to yield, warning that if it gave way it would be the end of its authority. But commercial interests required a settlement, which registered concessions never before granted—an increase of 15 per cent in the wages of transpacific seamen, and 20 per cent for those serving on coasting vessels, half-pay for the time they were off duty on strike, and the recognition of the seamen's union. Our ship on its return to Hongkong took back its old crew on these terms and gave each one of them a "farewell present," expected by every Chinese employee on withdrawing or being discharged from service.

Remarkable as were these gains to twenty thousand Chinese seamen on over two hundred vessels, yet the fact of this settlement was far more significant than its terms. It registered the fact that Chinese cheap labor could unite along racial craft lines to demand and secure from foreign exploiters a more human standard of living, more comparable and less competitive with that of workers in Western nations. That for the first time Western commercial and political control, wielded by Great Britain, its strongest representative, had yielded to native compulsion proved to be a much more significant and farther-reaching fact.

How far below a human standard of living a very large proportion of China's hardest-working classes exist can be understood only in the concrete terms stated by those who are in personal contact with actual conditions. One such witness, a professional expert, long resident in China and in governmental service, stated that multitudes of Chinese workers can afford as a luxury only a little sparingly used dressing, made of chickens' heads and feet boiled in peanut oil, in which they merely dip their chopsticks to flavor the rice on which they subsist. A United States naval officer confided to me his hope that the seamen would win their strike because he resented a standard of living so low that he had seen the refuse from the battleship caught by nets from junks to be sold and eaten, so that there was nothing left for the gulls. The manager of an American corporation with many Chinese employees also confided to me his opinion that within five years, or ten at most, the Chinese trade-union movement, reinforced and recruited by the old guilds and older family kinships, would wield a control never attained by the labor movements in America, England, or Europe. Still another judgment was passed by an American university graduate long resident and well acquainted in China. He said that the anti-foreign feeling then in 1922 growing in China was far

more prevalent than that which caused the Boxer Rebellion.
And he added, "God knows that it is due to indignities suffered by the Chinese at the hand of white people which no
self-respecting nation can tolerate on its own soil."

Here in the south I soon found myself to be at the source of
these great changes that had begun to come as never before
and are bound to develop a new China which will yet be as
Chinese as its people have ever been. At the old city of Canton as nowhere else are interwoven the China that has always
been and the China that is coming to be. Indeed almost anywhere else that initiative is being taken to improve native
conditions in native ways, especially to secure justice, industrial equity, and political peace and unity, the initiator was
found to be a southern man or group. Peking and the north
led in the renaissance of the Yangtze River Valley's basic industries, but Canton made good its claim to be the source and
center of the passion and struggle for democratic liberty and
national unity.

It will be China's own freedom in form and spirit. To attribute this vast revival of racial consciousness and the nationalistic movement for self-determination to the agitation or
leadership of any outside nation is to forget what China has
been and is. Conquerors and tradesmen from other peoples
have come, stayed, and gone for centuries, but China has remained Chinese. It still either gradually overcomes what it
does not absorb, as it did the Tartars and the Manchus, or it
isolates foreigners in their temporary concessions, which like
the island of Shameen are surrounded by the great sea of
Chinese life. Is it likely that bolshevik Russia can achieve
a transforming influence, in less than a decade, such as no
other race or modern nation has perceptibly wielded? An
American professor of Chinese literature answers: "Russia
is not at the bottom of the Chinese Revolution, but wants to
be on top of it." Interviews with three leaders in the southern
republic at Canton confirmed the claim of this progressive
spirit to be indigenous to Southern China. One of them, then
exercising a protectorate function in its state department,
had this to say:

The hope of this country is that China has a soul. It knows that material resources are no adequate basis for real national progress. Although as yet it has no national religion, there is a fundamental spirituality in China and there are standards of morality which will yet assert their supremacy. China cannot be helped from without. The Washington conference may prove helpful ultimately more than immediately. Foreign capital is needed to develop natural resources and will be protected, but it will not be accepted in exchange for China's rights. Her unification can be gained only by Peking resuming its allegiance to the national parliament which was dissolved there and driven south.

Missing the privilege of an interview with Dr. Sun Yat Sen because of his absence, I caught the spirit of his patriotic leadership of his people, the vast multitudes of whom revere him as the founder of constitutional government in China and its liberator from foreign control. What both Washington and Lincoln are to us Americans Sun Yat Sen is to most Chinese. More and more since his death, his spirit and teachings have inspired China's hope for the future. Perhaps I saw his spirit more clearly reflected by Dr. Wu Ting-fang than it might have been disclosed by himself. I had known of him as a scholar in the old classical learning and tradition, as a student of the law of the Western world at London, as gaining worldwide experiences in his diplomatic service in Japan, South America, Europe, and the United States, as a patriot in private life and public office both under the monarchy and the republic, and as a statesman who had earned the respect of his own countrymen and all who knew him abroad. "As no other statesman," wrote the leading American editor in the Orient, "Dr. Wu Ting-fang proved his ability to grasp, absorb and apply the principles of China's ancient civilization and those of the modern world." In the judgment of the foremost British journalist in China, "He contributed more than any Chinese, living or dead, to make for foreign understanding and friendship for China, and lived to hear the cries of the whole country ringing in his ears for his return to the premiership in Peking."

In the repeated interviews I was greatly privileged to have with him, I gained vivid personal impressions of the rare old man himself, who had packed his eighty years of life full of reflections upon his world-wide observations and interracial experiences. In appearance, as he entered his state-department office for our interview, he was tall and slender, alert in every movement, animated, and amiable in manner. Quaintly wise and witty in conversation, he strangely combined concentration upon the present with penetrating vision into the far-away past and the evolving future. His was a personality both impressive and winsome, a man of the whole world, yet a son of his own people, a seer with insight into his own times and outlook upon the coming centuries.

Mirthfully mindful of amenities, he greeted Mrs. Taylor and myself inquiringly: "So you come from Chicago and must know that it has one great blot." My hesitancy to admit that its one blot above all others was what he claimed it to be, "the slaughtering of animals and supplying animal food to poison the bodies and spirits of men," led him to attest the healthfulness of the vegetarian diet, upon which, like most Chinese, he had lived, and to commend the theosophist's principles underlying it in his own experience. As I deferred to the lady who did her part toward sustaining the conversation at this point, he remarked at my expense that "he had always observed that women were more intelligent than men about spiritual things." In contrast with what he held to be "the dark and dangerous passageways of Western civilization," he claimed that the Chinese still more highly appreciated spiritual and moral values and had far less brutal instincts. Their greater calm and cheer he held to be due "to the philosophy of life to which they were born and bred." Western people he considered "defective, in their craving and quest for material possessions and position."

Addressing me, he remarked, "I suppose you are aware that Americans are only half-civilized." With a merry twinkle in his eye and the laugh of undying youth in his voice, he responded to my inquiry as to the respects in which the Chinese were more civilized than we in the following remark:

In the filial reverence for age and in respect and obedience to parents, China's civilization is superior to America's. If our children associate with yours they will learn to defy their parents and break up the family foundations of China. In our dealings between man and man a Chinaman's word is so good as to need no bond. The persistent recognition of the corrupt administration at Peking by the United States and other foreign governments is the greatest impediment to the unification of China under an honest constitutional government.

At my last interview with Dr. Wu an amazingly illuminating event flashed a searchlight into the soul of China at its best, and let me see still farther into the soul of its greatest living seer. A "Purity Parade" was the culminating demonstration of a prolonged educational agitation against the licensing of houses of prostitution by the government of Canton. The movement was initiated by the native Chinese Christian churches. Their preachers had voiced the protest of conscience and faith against this degradation of womanhood, the desecration of childhood, and the demoralization of family and social life. Classes of adults and young people, registering over three thousand in attendance, had been conducted weekly for several months. Carefully prepared lessons had shown the deadly diseases and destructive moral effects of the social evil and what was being done to suppress and prevent it in other lands. This educational effort spread among the schools, enlisting the active co-operation of teachers and pupils. The native press vigorously spread the agitation and information. The newspapers in the English language, not only in Canton but in Shanghai and Hongkong, published full and frequent reports of the progress of this campaign with favorable editorial comments. Public attention was arrested and the conscience of the people was stirred still more by a survey of the vice conditions in Canton, initiated and directed by the Y.M.C.A., in whose spacious building the diagrams and pictures of the survey were exhibited for eighteen days with an average daily attendance of one thousand visitors.

Clearing the way for the procession along its line of march came the Boy Scouts, as trim and active in their appearance as anywhere else in the world. In long and bright array eight hundred students marched to the music of their many bands and drum and bugle corps; boys in their varied uniforms, girls in colorful summer dresses, medical students and nurses in white jackets and caps. Native members of Protestant and Roman Catholic church organizations, the Salvation Army, and Men's and Women's Christian Associations were followed by groups from forty labor unions and guilds that had co-operated in the campaign. Banners and cartooned placards were made impressive by many clever devices—a serpent strangling a man, a rat caught by pincers, a picture of better babies, a grandfather witnessing a dragon carrying off his descendants, a notorious resort depicted as facing a well-known Christian college, a scene of rejoicing at the burial of licensed prostitution.

Motor cars carried the delegation bearing the petition of eighty organizations to be presented to the government officials. As I stood beside the old statesman as he bent over the balustrade of the state-department balcony to review the marching hosts, I was profoundly impressed with his intense interest as manifested by his silent and searching gaze at every feature of the unique demonstration. Returning with him to his office when he received the delegation bearing the petition, I witnessed the earnestness with which it was presented and received. From Dr. Wu Ting-fang himself I learned that the spokesman for the petitioners claimed the government's right and duty to abolish licensed resorts because they degraded women, destroyed health, disrupted the family, demoralized soldiers, corrupted officials, and were subversive of public welfare. The old statesman concluded that "since the province had suppressed legalized gambling houses at the loss of ten millions of revenue from them, the city could afford to abolish licensed vice resorts as it did not need to levy revenue upon sing-song girls."

As we were leaving him at the end of this last interview he surprised me by asking me, "Are you afraid to die?" Before I could reply he solemnly said with childlike simplicity, "I am not. When God wants me to go, I am ready to say 'Thank You, I come.'" And yet it must have been hard for him to heed the summons when it came two months later. Tragic was the old patriot's figure in exchanging his toga for his shroud. Forced to flee with his colleagues from Canton at the invasion of a war lord's troops, he took refuge across the river in the Canton Christian College, now Lingnan University. Failing to resist the shock and exposure of the violent experience, he prepared for the rapidly approaching end with his philosophic equanimity. In loyalty to his comrades in their great cause he secured his seal of office and returned it with his resignation as secretary of state to his chief. Removed at his own request to the mission hospital, he arranged for his Christian burial service at the Anglican church, whose rite of baptism he had received at Hongkong in early manhood, although in later life he had accepted theosophy as "not inconsistent with Christianity." Such was the order and dignity of his going, as he passed out between what must have seemed to him and his countrymen to be the portals leading to the rebirth or reactionary overthrow of China's nationalistic hopes. In his death-stricken hand he held the recall from Peking to be the premier of what then was hoped to be reunited China. The old patriot's faith in the fatherland has been most happily attested by the appointment of his son, C. C. Woo, to fill the high station which his father so long honored as minister of the republic of China at Washington.

The improvement in local conditions and administration initiated by the leaders of the southern republic was strikingly exemplified at Canton. At the time of my visit Sun Fo was mayor of the city, having been appointed by the governor of the province, not only because he was worthy of his father, Sun Yat Sen, but because of his special preparation and qualifications for municipal administration. I found him in his quarters at the fine municipal building. In the full vigor of early manhood he does credit to his family breeding and his American education in his well-formed and poised mind, his direct English speech, his courteous manner, and his progressive spirit. The University of California may well be proud to claim him as a graduate from its four years' arts course and Columbia University of New York as its graduate student in economics and political science.

Mayor Sun Fo began our interview by reminding me that the municipality of Canton is the first municipal government to be established in all China. A little more than a year before it had acquired its provisional charter, secured under the act of the civil governor of the province, authorizing all provincial cities to organize their administrations separately from that of Kwan Tung province. This was to be done by the election of a mayor and commissioners of finance, safety, education, health, public works, and utilities, constituting the executive council, all succeeding to office those provisionally appointed. An advisory council of twenty members was provided for, ten to be appointed by the governor and three each by the chamber of commerce and the labor unions, one each by the educational association, the medical profession, the engineers' and the lawyers' organizations.

Pointing to a map descriptive of the *maloo*, or widened thoroughfares, twenty-five miles of which were then completed or being cut through, he invited me to inspect them. In the densely crowded sections of the city of more than a million inhabitants, designated as the area "within the walls," the sudden transformation from the old to the new thoroughfares was truly dramatic. Right around the corner from the narrowest passageways from ten to twenty feet wide one suddenly emerges to broad avenues or boulevards ranging from fifty to one hundred and fifty feet in width. Many of them are built on the foundation of the old city wall, which had been taken down to make way for traffic and better buildings. Other highways were made with the bricks and stones from these demolished walls which had hemmed in the city for nearly a thousand years. The *maloo* swarmed with jinrikishas, freight drays, hauled by teams of from eight to twenty men and women, while speeding past them were motor buses and private automobiles. Through almost all of the older streets there was no right-of-way for any wheel, nor indeed for sun and air. Commercial and public buildings with better dwellings were rising along these new arteries of the old city's trade and life, while public gardens and attractive residential suburbs were extending the *maloo* terminals and the city limits.

The city's sixty-one public schools provided for only one-tenth of the children of school age. But the Mayor said he appreciated and fostered the missionary agencies in setting the standard and creating the demand for the city's schools, while supplementing them to the extent of taking some forty thousand under their own instruction. The Canton Christian

College, with its courses in agriculture, horticulture, silkworm breeding, pursued by over four hundred bright and promising men and women students under the very competent American and Chinese teachers, impressed me greatly. It was one of the first to conform to the nationalistic requirement by changing its management and its name to Lingnan University.

Aged dependents without family care are cared for by a Roman Catholic institution aided by public funds. The only provision for the modern treatment of mental diseases in all China is the John G. Kerr Hospital in Canton, owned, and until recently managed by the Presbyterian mission with public subsidies providing for inmates committed by the courts, but now under government supervision.

The Mayor declared his intention to cancel licenses of houses of ill fame as the terms for which they had been licensed expired. He referred to *mui tsai*, the long-practiced and deeply rooted system of child slavery, as at once the source of the supply of prostitutes and the most persistent obstacle to the suppression of the social evil. It sanctions the sale of little girls by their parents, or by anyone having possession of them. Although ostensibly procured and trained for domestic service or other forms of labor, the little slaves are unprotected against cruel abuses and are sold into prostitution. Many are even brought up for that fate or for concubinage. Although prohibited by an edict issued in 1912, the first year of the republic, the law did not begin to be enforced until the southern administration at Canton proclaimed the practice to be illegal. "Meanwhile," the Mayor remarked, "it can only be gradually suppressed, because there are 25,000 *mui tsai* girls in Canton, without any public provision for other care or employment." He was gratified by the news just arrived from London that the British Parliament had enacted a law abolishing the practice of *mui tsai* in Hongkong.

I wondered whether this act would move the local authorities there to abandon the shame of protected commercialized vice which I found to be flourishing in Christian England's most conspicuous crown possession in the Far East, and also in the international concession in Shanghai very near the great churches of the Christian faith supported and attended

by the representatives of Western Christendom. The door-
plates on some of these higher-class brothels bore the names of
Russian young women inmates. They were said to have felt
this to be the last resort to which they had been driven after
they had fled from Russia, when the social classes to which
they belonged had been proscribed by the dictatorship of the
proletariat.

Both in China and Japan, as well as in the Philippines, I
was impressed deeply with the far-reaching significance of
the native and missionary religious movements as solvents of
interracial and international problems. In their fellowships
and work Orientals and Occidentals met and co-operated
on equal terms as nowhere else. Native control of missionary
institutions anticipated the demand for it by the Nationalists,
who at this time had not yet become dominant. Missionary
leaders had been thus far sighted, because in closer touch with
the native peoples, long before the diplomats abroad and the
statesmen at home.

I found those representing the international work of the
Young Men's and Young Women's Christian Associations,
both American and native, to be intellectually capable, ad-
ministratively qualified, socially visioned, and spiritually
devoted for their statesmen-like policy and achievement.
Their institutions occupied strategic locations at centers of
educational, industrial, political, and interracial importance.
Their personnel and buildings afford rallying points and common ground on which native and foreign representatives of
different religions and races meet and exchange values, thus
invaluably promoting mutual understanding and community
of interests.

The National Christian Council, at the organization of
which I was privileged to be present in Shanghai in May,
1922, brought to glorious fruition this spirit of interdenominational and interracial unity. It was exemplified and largely
due to the Apostolic leadership of the Rev. Logan H. Roots,
Protestant Episcopal Bishop of Hankow. Of its twelve hundred representatives then assembled two-thirds or more were
Chinese. Their demand, ably presented from the platform
by Dr. C. Y. Cheng, chairman of the conference, that the

Christian movement in China be entrusted to Chinese Christians met with no objection or demurrer from the representatives of Western Christendom, who accepted the suggestion that they become advisory as a token of their success in developing a constituency that had become willing and capable to assume the executive responsibility which they now claimed to be their prerogative. The native leader's ringing appeal for "a Christianity indigenous to China, a gospel naturalized to the Chinese and a united church of Christ for China," struck a prophetic note that then and there became historic.

In its reflex influence upon the home churches and lands of its supporters, the foreign-missionary movement yields rich return for all the money and lives invested in it. From this world-work of its churches Protestant Christianity receives more initiative and exemplification for its spiritual and federated unity than from any single source at home. That consummation devoutly to be wished has grown apace since Dr. Cheng on taking the chair of China's Ecumenical Council predicted: "The united church of China may give a new impetus to the divided churches of Western Christendom."

I found the situation in the Philippines seriously complicated. Personal and partisan favoritism, as well as disregard for social proprieties, under the preceding governor-general's administration, had discredited the hitherto-high prestige of the American official personnel. Political policies both at Washington and Manila had also impaired administrative efficiency and confused the governmental relations between native and American officials.

While Governor General Leonard Wood was fully aware that he would have no such authority in the Philippines as he had in Cuba to enable him to achieve the high success there attained, he nevertheless undertook this hard and hampered task. He did so against the advice of all his political advisers, and without any urgency from his personal friends. Referring to his decision to do so, he queried: "How could I have declined this unsought commission after having been urging and training young men all my life to serve their country at personal sacrifice?" This he said at his family luncheon table in the old Spanish Malacañan Palace, in which Mrs. Wood and he maintained as simple and hospitable an American home as they had with us in Chicago.

Interviews with the two outstanding Filipino political leaders interested me in their personalities and their politics. Manuel L. Quezon impressed me as alert in mind, vivacious and taking in speech, winsome in manner, a good mixer, with not a few of the arts and assets of a shrewd successful politician, some of which he had acquired while in America. He conceded many mistakes by Filipino officials, due to inexperience, but did not hesitate to assert his preference "for the worst Filipino government over the best American administration." Yet he volunteered the statement that "after long suspense of judgment he had become convinced that Governor Wood was wholly sincere and very capable."

Sergius Osmena combines the gentleness of the Filipino with the resoluteness of the Chinese, the blood of both races contributing the strength of his personality. In more statesmanlike manner he held that divided responsibility was the cause of past failures in the insular government and was the impediment to the future progress of the islands. While criticizing Governor Wood's veto of the Philippine legislature's acts, which he thought should be paramount, he welcomed the advisory relationship with the United States government, also unqualifiedly declaring his confidence in the "honesty and efficiency" of Governor Wood. Both men insisted upon the right of the Filipino people to immediate independence, denying any ground for deferring it.

While deeply impressed with the many attractive qualities of the Filipino people whom I met at Manila and elsewhere in the island of Luzon, especially the eagerness of all classes to take advantage of educational opportunities, and their courteous manners, yet they then appeared to be in the adolescent period of their political development even at Manila and Baguio, where I had opportunity to sound representatives of their most intelligent classes. I was the more doubtful of the readiness of the population as a whole for independent self-government when I saw the primitive Igorote mountaineers meet the lowland Filipinos on market day at Baguio. Clad only with "gee-strings" around their loins, these fine specimens of manhood in bronze brought barbaric customs into contact with the fashions and motors of modern civilization here as seldom elsewhere, except in South Africa.

The most depressing evidences of the unpreparedness of the ruling classes for legislative responsibility were the failure of the Philippine legislature independently to maintain the effective provisions they had made for public health and other progressive policies, to which initiative and guidance have been given by American officials. General Wood found an excessive death-rate from smallpox which had been practically eliminated while vaccination had been practiced. The insular government hospital for the insane was so hopelessly deficient in all modern equipment and treatment that many patients were found to be chained and otherwise cruelly maltreated. So pitifully lacking in both the comforts and the necessities of life were the hundreds of exiles in the leper colony of Culion that they gladly welcomed Governor Wood's visit by a procession in which their banners greeted him as "Savior of the Lepers." He had just made good their claim to that title by securing the return to the Philippines of Dr. Victor G. Heiser to re-establish the neglected public-health service of the insular government, which he had inaugurated when he was the first civilian commissioner of health. Although Dr. Heiser had produced cures warranting his prediction of the eradication of leprosy from the Philippines if the "Ethyl esters" treatment with chaulmoogra oil were strictly applied and followed up, yet the legislature was found so disinclined to provide adequately for the people's deliverance from this hitherto-incurable scourge that Governor Wood's appeal to America's benevolence for a leper fund of many millions was his last and perhaps greatest service attesting his sincere devotion to the Filipino people. The contribution of the first million assures the completion of the most fitting memorial to Leonard Wood, humanitarian administrator for America in the Philippines.

The summer capital at Baguio, the building of which was designed by Daniel H. Burnham of Chicago, was one of the far-sighted projects of the early American commissioners to the Philippines. The great Benguet highway they built provided access from the tropical heat of Manila to the mountain ranges, valleys, streams, and bracing climate of Baguio, only two hundred miles away, but five thousand feet above sea-level, in the Switzerland of the Philippines. Yet this greatest physical asset of the insular government had been allowed to fall into such disrepair that the legislature was moved by fear of its discovery partially to restore it before the arrival of the Forbes-Wood commission of inspection. Give these mentally alert, educationally progressive, and nationally aspiring people time and guidance to acquire experience in self-government and they will be sure worthily to maintain the independence which the United States has guaranteed them by act of Congress. When, however, I reminded a group of university students and graduates that we Americans had required twelve years to justify our Declaration of Independence by the adoption of our Constitution, the rejoinder which promptly parried my warning was that the Filipinos' present preparedness for independence proved how much more capable they are than we were.

PART IV

THE SOCIAL SETTLEMENT MOVEMENT

CHAPTER XXI

CHICAGO COMMONS AFTER THIRTY-SIX YEARS

IT IS now nearly forty years since the initiative of the social settlement movement in London, and subsequently in New York and Chicago, began to impress me. It stands in the clear for well-seasoned judgment, not only in its historical perspective, but also in the vivid memories of personal experiences through thirty-five of these years in which my family and I have shared settlement life and work.[1] Since my impressions came both from what I have read and observed of this historical development and from what has been so vital in my life and work, they blend in the retrospect of the movement. My judgment of what the settlement has been in the past and my forecast of what it may be in the future deal only with motives and methods most distinctive of the movement.

I was impressed with the impetus and status given it as an educational initiative by the favor with which the suggestion of the pioneer settlement for East London was received at Oxford University. Its founder, the Rev. Samuel A. Barnett, an influential alumnus, enlisted the sponsorship of men eminent in academic and public life; consecrated its building to the memory of Arnold Toynbee, the first of the fore-running student helpers; and inspired its motive with a broadly religious spirit distinct from any ecclesiastical order or control. While the pioneer American settlements shared the social and religious spirit and some of the educational aims and methods of these British initiators, yet in their origin, clientèle, and development they were less academic. Although the first two of them in New York City followed the British precedent in

[1] For references to these experiences throughout the volume see Index, Chicago Commons, especially pp. 7–10, 72, 83, 117–87, 210, 416, 422.

277

taking the titles of the "University Settlement" for men residents and the "College Settlement" for women, Hull House at Chicago, founded by Jane Addams and Ellen Gates Starr in 1889, soon after they were graduated from Rockford College, assumed the broader title of "Social Settlement," and was the first one to have women and men as resident and non-resident workers.

No academic leaders stood by our American pioneers as Dr. Benjamin Jowett, master of Balliol College at Oxford, stood by Canon Barnett, as John Ruskin and Thomas Hill Green prepared the way for Toynbee Hall, and as Principal Fairbairn of Mansfield College enlisted with Percy Alden at Mansfield House. No statesman here publicly backed our early settlement houses as Prime Minister Asquith, members of Parliament, and other men of public affairs indorsed and aided British settlements. American pioneers were left to blaze their own way and personally win their supporters one by one, with no official recognition and little influential patronage.

In both countries leaders in antecedent movements for social justice had held ideals aloft and created precedents for efforts to realize them. In England the social consciousness begotten by the Wesleyan revival still survived in the churches. The anti-slavery cause of Wilberforce still appealed for liberators. The social conscience kindled into flame by Charles Kingsley and Frederick Denison Maurice still called aloud for the further application of Christian ethics to industry, which Shaftesbury long before had begun to apply in his factory acts. For the sake of church and state, Thomas Chalmers had insisted that towns should have a "Christian and civic economy." He also exemplified ways of making charity more neighborly and less pauperizing by his epoch-making work in the slums of Edinburgh.

In America, Abraham Lincoln, by liberating both freemen and slaves, had done what William Lloyd Garrison and Wendell Phillips had agitated, what Theodore Parker and William Ellery Channing had preached, what James Russell Lowell had sung in and laughed out, what Ralph Waldo Emerson had reasoned away, and what Harriet Beecher Stowe did to make emancipation from slavery and other orthodoxies imperative. In neither land, however, had the settlement pioneers any immediate predecessors in moving in between dividing class, racial, partisan, and sectarian lines for a ministry of understanding, interpretation, and unification.

Coming into settlement experience with only a general knowledge of its underlying motive and these incentives that lay back of it, its specific aims and methods gradually disclosed themselves as we lived and worked at Chicago Commons. But what we thus learned proved to be what is most distinctive of the settlement movement, as indicated by the experience of others elsewhere.

Our earliest discovery was the potency of the group in influencing the development of the individual and the community. Each one of the twelve of us who came into Chicago Commons' first household profited not only by ideals that we shared with each other, but also by the differences which accentuated the individuality of each other. As the group grew to thirty or more, the ideals and capacities of every member of the household were developed far beyond what each one of us could individually attain.

We who took up our abode in the old rented house at Union Street and Milwaukee Avenue in 1894, which sheltered us and our work for six years, needed all the morale and cheer that the group life added to whatever capacity for endurance each of us may have possessed. It had seen far better days when a prosperous German-American family had built and occupied it as their residence in what was then a suburb not far from the west bank of the river. It long since had deteriorated with its surroundings when its location came to be on the lower edge of the West Side's Seventeenth ("River") Ward. Its spacious rooms, with their heavy hardwood trimmings, high ceilings, and large windows, survived the decadence into which the old family residence had been allowed to fall since it was rented to the proprietress of a lake seamen's boarding-house.

We felt ourselves fortunate, however, in finding such an old mansion. No other residence property in the district was so distinctive in its proportions and design for a neighborhood-home center. No other offered such possible provisions for public use, since an annex had been built for the office use of the Northwestern Railway, after its headquarters had been destroyed by the great fire. In the small rooms of this annex, wholly unfit for family dwelling, eight very poor Italian families lived, with only a glass door between their households and ours, until we could afford to rent this rear addition and move its tenants to better quarters. By incessant scrubbing, renovating, and repairing, the building became habitable though never comfortable. Its basement floors provided the only spaces available for the larger club groups. The space under the annex which had been used as a stable became our improvised assembly hall. There, beneath octopus-like furnace pipes attached to its low ceiling, our lowly and more highly privileged guests met on equal terms. Great gray rats challenged our occupancy of what had been their own preserve.

The old homestead, however, became more homelike than we could expect its surroundings to be. Next door on one side was a furniture factory with a buzz saw that rasped all day long. It caught fire every now and then, threatening the neighborhood with the conflagration, which two months after we moved to our new building swept away not only this old Union Street house, but all the other buildings on both sides of the street. Next door on the other side was a liquor saloon in front and a sausage factory in the rear. The grinding of the machinery of the latter gave undertone to the shrill crescendo notes of the buzz saw.

In front of the saloon was a horse trough, bearing the neighborly invitation: "Water your horses and don't forget yourself." A few steps away Milwaukee Avenue's trams and trucks roared by this corner, while down in the morning and back at night surged such tides of workingmen and working-women as were to be seen on only two or three other thoroughfares in Chicago. Such traffic as passed through our unpaved street to and from the railway freight yards at the other end of the block raised clouds of dust which rose as high as our roof. Smoke from the locomotives and the factory chimneys clouded the air and precipitated its soot on the walls of our living-room and all our belongings.

No sooner had we settled down under these discomforts than our friend who had christened Chicago Commons reappeared to reassure our confidence and inspire our hope. He surprised us by presenting carefully thought-out plans for a new settlement building. Our lack of funds and influence to raise them did not deter the prophetic vision of this citizen from moving him to declare with quiet earnestness: "It's a case of got to be, for which I want to help you get ready. For what needs to be comes to be, and this is nearer the bottom of the city problem than anything known to me." So he left us with this dynamic sentiment from which to charge our settlement motive with the energy and confidence of Chicago's will-power. But he did not return to help us get ready to fulfil his predestinating prediction. The qualities which prompted Edward F. Cragin to see our civic enterprise through led to his appointment as chief promoter of the Nicaragua Canal project. And the energy and devotion with which he urged this national enterprise, that may yet supplement its substitute at Panama, shortened his life, which came to an end in midcareer.

The adventurous spirit and devotion of the early residents loom large on the background of this retrospect. Worthy of all honor and long remembrance was the chivalric self-sacrifice of the women who braved the almost hopeless task of turning this old stranded house into the home it became at the very heart of this city wilderness. Worthiest of all these were the mothers of the two families, my own and one other, who themselves bore the risk of bringing up their children there. The safety of these children, as well as others who subsequently came into residence, proved to be as secure as their mothering was resourceful, fearless, and devoted.

Having often been challenged to justify the alleged hazards involved in family residence at settlements, I have always insisted that it was a question of expediency to be determined by the constitutional vigor and temperamental balance of the children, and of their parents also. I have protested against considering differences in occupational status, the property line or arbitrary social classifications, to be the test of the character of one's children's associates. The same discrimination is demanded of the parent among the richer as among the poorer classes, on the boulevards and in the suburbs as in the industrial residential districts, in the private school as in the public school, in the up-town as in the down-town church, among the native-born as among the foreign-born families.

In our own experience, a larger share of the race life was attained through such varied contacts and friendships as our settlement-residence offered. So far from realizing disadvantages feared by solicitous friends, our children profited by their acquaintances and experiences in the settlement household and neighborhood through their school years and college vacations, the youngest from her early years acquiring insight and incentive for her teaching at the Francis W. Parker School in Chicago, and her educational pioneering at the Shady Hill School, Cambridge, Massachusetts. Character and cultural values in our home life, and in that of the Commons' household, were enhanced and conserved by the calm equipoise, wise judgment, selfless devotion, and unassuming motherly influence of her who shared and steadied my own life's endeavor. Family groups always in residence have made the spirit of the house more homelike, both to its residents and the neighbors. Perhaps many settlements are inspired to exemplify and spread this spirit by having ever in sight upon their walls the "Madonna and Child" as the symbol alike of family and faith, interpreting and appealing for all they undertake.

The risks to health were found by us to be surprisingly slight. The exercise of ordinary sanitary and hygienic precautions proved sufficient to safeguard the health of the household to a noteworthy degree through the six years of our residence in the old location. Very few infectious or contagious diseases were contracted, even when infrequently prevalent in the neighborhood, which has been remarkably free from epidemics. Only such illnesses as might have occurred anywhere else have been suffered by our residents. Indeed not a few of them who entered the household depleted in body and depressed in spirit experienced early and continuous improvement, as they shared the good cheer of the house spirit in serving others.

To the oft-repeated inquiry as to how our neighbors regarded our residence among them, answers came to us from the neighbors themselves. Before they became well acquainted enough to understand why we came among them and what we were about, quite naturally they were doubtful and even suspicious of our motives and methods. We accounted for our presence in these simple words:

We have chosen to come to live and work here to be all we can to the people and receive all they can be to us as friends and neighbors; to share with them what to us makes life worth living; to assume the full obligations and claim all the rights of citizenship in a community with whose interests we identify ourselves, whose conditions we share, and for whose happiness, material welfare, political freedom and social progress we try to do our part.

Before we did so, however, we were given good reason to expect to be misunderstood, if not misinterpreted, by those who either from the hard and hardening struggle for existence, or from being selfishly acquisitive, would be unable to comprehend any other motive as actuating a human being. When we applied to rent the premises for our settlement residence, the brothers who owned it could not understand what gain we could get out of it, and therefore why we should want to rent it. "Did we expect to use it as a hospital?" "Could it be a dance hall that we intended to make of it?" When satisfied that we had neither of these purposes in mind, to which they objected, they inquired how we expected to get enough money out of the building to pay the rental. They could not imagine why anyone should rent such a property with the purpose of putting money into it for the good of the neighborhood as I told them we intended to do. When, nevertheless, they concluded to take the risk in renting the premises to persons capable of such folly, one brother addressing the other, while casting a witheringly pitiful glance at me, exclaimed in a considerately subdued tone, "Brother, there are some such folks."

Perhaps we ourselves quite as much failed to realize how unusual, if not unaccountable, to our neighboring family folk it must have been to see a score or more of young unmarried men and women form one household. They themselves lived

together as single families, to whose households a boarder
was admitted reluctantly, and all too often unhappily. The
family circles within our larger household, however, so relieved the strain upon their confidence that their neighborly
relations with us the sooner and more readily became confident and cordial. Even so, criticism was not withheld when
any of us were thought to have committed what was considered by them to be a breach of propriety, however in good
and usual form it might have been to us. Such challenges
were welcomed as giving us opportunity to correct any misunderstanding which was maliciously used to discredit Chicago Commons by the demoralizing groups of saloon proprietors and politicians, who regarded us as competitors and
dangerously observant critics.

More impressive than what any few critics among them
ever said is what most of our neighbors do to express their
confidence in our friendship. No more vital point of contact
between the settlement house and its neighbors is there than
its front door. No more important, responsible, and exacting
duty is required of the household than door service. Every
resident takes his or her turn "on door." The latchstring of
Chicago Commons has hung out and has never been taken in
all these thirty-six years, day and night, Sundays and holidays, summer and winter. And no one seeking to enter has
failed to find friendly welcome and counsel. Had the purpose
of these calls upon us been registered all these years, what
memories they would recall; what heart-searching they might
have prompted some of us to make as to the spirit and efficiency of our service; what tragedies and comedies would
have intermingled on the lists!

The need of such a permanent group rendering public and
personal service at an established center was demonstrated by
such human necessities and such ample public and voluntary
resources available to meet them as were thus registered.
Both the conservation and extension of social resources are
exemplified in the fact that the reputation of our household
group was so shared as to give a resident unknown to a neighbor ready access to the home as coming "from the Commons."
Our group thus came to be something like a corporate per-

sonality whose younger novitiates could extend the service made possible by the longer residence and larger acquaintanceship of their elders. But this economy of personal resources depends upon permanency of residence upon the part of the head resident and a certain proportion of the resident group. Personal acquaintanceship is the working capital for most of the settlement's local work as well as for its wider influence.

Emphasis upon the group, so far from lessening respect for the individual, increased it. Individual initiative and the personal resourcefulness of each resident worker have ever been relied upon to give influence and efficiency to the household group. Freedom to attain, maintain, and exert these qualities has been cherished and safeguarded within the settlement household. Organization has been subordinated to personality, and not allowed to restrict its free development. The spirit distinctive of the settlement can in no way perish more certainly and quickly than by being organized to death. The settlement must be simply a group of individuals, each one of whom is free to give personal expression to the spirit shared by all, if indeed its spirit is to be born or to survive. The earlier pioneers drilled into me the fact that the settlement is not an institution, but a state of mind and heart. Both for the development of these qualities and the unity of the group we have depended, therefore, upon cherishing the spirit of service and self-sacrifice, however invertebrate our organization may seem in comparison with institutional bureaucracy.

Inspiring confidence in the past and hope for the future are the facts that for thirty-six years young men and women possessing these qualities and capacities have come to us in unfailing succession; that they have come at their own impulse and from widely scattered areas; that, with very few exceptions, they have been attracted by the spirit of the service, or have quickly attained it; and that many of them have continued to serve with us for years, and many more have gone forth throughout the homeland and abroad carrying the same spirit into their service on widely differing fields. Very gratifying to me is it to be succeeded in the management of the work by my daughter, Lea Demarest Taylor, as head resident of Chicago Commons, and to be associated with her efficient leadership in continuing my own service as president and treasurer of Chicago Commons Association's Board of Trustees, and in sharing the fellowship and work of the resident household.

To grow together in the home life and work of the settlement household the conditions of fellowship must be there. The spirit of the house cannot be made; it must simply be. It may not be foisted upon any but can be fostered in all. Its atmosphere and ideality must exert their pressure unconsciously upon all, if the tone of the inner relationship and the standard of outward service are to be maintained. Upon this essentially religious spirit the settlement group depends for its unity and spiritual dynamic, which in turn require some medium of interchange and self-expression. The meal hour, especially in the evening, is one opportunity to make this fellowship real and personal. Since our residents of Roman Catholic, Jewish, Protestant, and ethical faiths, as well as those of several racial heritages, have lived and worked together with such equal devotion that no difference could be seen between the service and sacrifice inspired by differing faiths, we have needed no creedal test for admission.

We have also found it both possible and profitable to devote a half-hour to our household "vespers" before going to our evening classes, clubs, and other appointments. No one is required to attend, but we naturally linger for it in the residents' parlor. Someone plays a few moments on the piano or violin, a hymn is sung. Some selections from the greater scriptures are read responsively. The head resident or some other reads or says something that lifts and welds us together. Variety and interest are gained by commenting on the socially significant news of the week, by reporting some interesting occasion or address, by discussing some current literature and new books, and by getting guests to share with us their experiences, observations, and opinions. The informal interview merges into conversation. We unite in the Lord's Prayer. Then one by one we slip away to our evening's appointments, carrying with us into our work and life the glow of this fellowship, in which we always find something to share in common, however much we differ in creed and opinion. Many former residents in referring to their settlement experience mention vespers as their most cherished memory, exerting the deepest and most continued influence upon them.

By our respect for each other's personality within the settlement household we were constrained to show the same regard for that of everyone in the neighborhood with whom or for whom we worked. We had something to learn from each one of them. Those of us who were conscious of having the most to receive proved to have the most to give in this human reciprocity. No fellow-human was a mere "case." Everyone was a person, a somebody—a boy or girl, a man or woman, somebody's child, brother or sister, husband or wife. We found no normal individual detached, as a nomad or digit might be. Each was one of a group and part of it. The state recognizes no child as detached. If it has no parents it must have a guardian, and a public guardian assumes the care of it if the court has not committed the child to the guardianship of another. Even the homeless tramp is returned to the public care of the county in which he once may have had legal residence, if it can be discovered.

The early settlements helped personalize the "case," when the Charity Organization Society began to develop case work, which distinguishes the preventive, rehabilitating methods and results of modern charity from the temporizing, pauperizing almsgiving which preceded it. Thus also the responsibility and resources of the groups were laid under tribute to protect the personal rights and promote the personal interests of the individual having a claim upon any one of them. Later the courts were influenced to take account of the degree to which the person in the case before it is responsible for his own act, and how far others are responsible both for his act or for his restoration to normal life.

A deep and abiding personal experience drove home to my conscience and heart this wider view of the responsibility which others share with everyone for what he or she is or comes to be. Early in our home life at the old Union Street house my youngest daughter, then only seven years of age,

looked up in surprise to her mother from what she had just
seen across the street, asking, "Why did that lady over there
throw a stone at that little girl?" My child's query has been
ringing down to my heart's depths ever since. Why, indeed,
was the stone thrown at that little girl over there and not at
this one here? Their mothers differed so much that it was
impossible to imagine the experience of that poor, neglected,
unkempt child as possible to this better-born, better-bred,
tenderly cared-for child of the same age who nestled at the
heart of as good a mother as a child ever had.

But did either have any choice of a mother? Was either
asked whether or not she would be born? Would either have
chosen to be born at all, if of such a mother as could stone her
child in a drunken frenzy? Was it in any way to the discredit
of that child, or a credit to this one, to have been born so
differently and to such different fates? Is there any greater
mystery than that of the accident of birth? What philosophy
or theology offers any solution or even explanation of this
problem? Not mine. Who knows what to think or to believe
about it? Not I. But I did know what could be done about
it, and we tried to do it. That mother could be reasoned with,
and was to some effect. That child could be cared for, made
clean, and given at least a chance to be human. And she was,
when our kindergartner shamed the mother into some sense
of her duty by bringing the child home bright and happy in
clean clothing. When greeted by her child's exclamation
"See me, mother!" the mother replied to her neighbor, "This
shall never happen again."

The child's right to be born right asserted itself as the
birthright of every child many times, as at the sight of subnormal children of subnormal mothers; as at the still more
pitiful sight of a normal child born in the county hospital of an
unmarried mother, herself a child still in her early teens.
Thus the regenerating "second birth" was seen to be no substitute for a more normal first birth, but to involve it, if to be
"born again" is to fulfil its meaning.

Deeper toned than ever were those severest words of the
Christ as with a child in his arms he said: "Whosoever shall
offend one of these little ones which believe in me, it were

better for him that a millstone were hanged about his neck and that he were drowned in the depth of the sea," adding this all-sufficient reason, "It is not the will of your Father, which is in Heaven, that one of these little ones shall perish." This warning seemed to be applicable to communities as to individuals. Therefore we felt, and tried to prompt our neighbors and fellow-citizens to feel, that the degree to which any community safeguards and protects its children's welfare, its motherhood, and family life attests the self-respect and worthiness of the adult population even to survive.

Another experience was an impelling reason for being willing to learn from those we teach. One morning when starting to my distant classroom I noticed a little group gathering in the tiny side-yard of a neighbor across the alley in the rear of the old settlement house. Stopping to see what the matter might be, I found a strange woman to be the object of their baffled concern. She was evidently very ill and almost dazed by finding herself in this place strange to her, among people whom she had never seen before. She had been brought there by a small boy, who said his mother had found the woman on their doorsteps crying. It was late at night when she took the stranger in for sleep and shelter and now in the morning sent her around to my neighbor, hoping that in one of the several languages she spoke she might be able to converse with the stranger. But none of her polyglot repertoire proved to be the stranger's tongue. The county hospital seemed to me to be the only refuge that offered the rest and medical care so badly needed. So I offered to send for the police-station wagon, which I asked the Irish patrolman on our beat to call. Returning home at noon, I found the poor creature still where I had left her in my neighbor's still patient, considerate care. So I sought the policeman's reason why the wagon had not come to carry so sick a woman to the hospital. He said, "Come to the box with me." There he roared over the telephone to the desk sergeant at the police station, "You'd better be after sending that wagon, for Professor Taylor is raising the devil all over the ward."

Far easier was it for me to discharge myself personally from further obligation after soon seeing the stranger off to the

care of the county hospital than it was for my neighbor to
feel that she had done all she should, after doing a great deal
more than I had ever thought of doing. So she kept up her
neighborly care until she discovered the stranger's language,
found that she had been brought to our neighborhood to be
deserted, and stayed on the long trail until the stranger's
folks had been found and she returned to them. Of course,
then and ever since, we learned that to start in upon any
human service involves the obligation to follow it up to some
available solution. Thus was our first lesson in neighborly
case work taught us.

Our group could not have meant as much to our neighbors
as their groups have meant to us. In each of them we discovered standards and ideals of its own, which had the sanctions of heritage and custom. For these we felt bound to have
respect such as we had for the personalities of those who possessed them. Therefore we did not attempt to superimpose
the sanctions of our own or any other group upon any group
of our neighbors. Taking each as we found it, we sought only
to inspire its members with an aspiration for something a
little better and higher than what had satisfied them. What
they thus sought and acquired for themselves we knew would
be their own and might become part of themselves more than
anything received by them directly from others. This procedure, in being more indirect than direct and in exacting
more faith and patience, is distinctive of the settlements far
more than of all but a very few churches, schools, or other
propagandist and cultural agencies.

We had much more reason, however, to respect the family
group for what it contributed to us. It proved to be the common denominator containing what is shared by every other
group and relating each to the other throughout the whole
community. To the family folk around us we owed not only
the earliest confidence and co-operation which led the way
to all other alliances, but also guidance to the specific aims
and methods of our work. We were impressed and oppressed
by the fact that the very existence of the littlest children was
seemingly ignored by the city; that no place in the schools
was provided for the child under six years of age; that no foot

of ground was set apart for the feet of any children at play, except a few square yards leading from the sidewalks to the doorways of the school buildings; that no care was publicly offered the children of working women while earning their livelihood; and that little if any special provision was made either by the Health Department of the city or at the County Hospital to protect the children's health from conditions which caused almost the highest death-rate among children under three years of age registered anywhere in the city.

Our first duty, therefore, was to help the home to care for the child. We ventured to open the first kindergarten in our ward, which was preceded by only a few others that had been opened at public schools in other more favored parts of the city. It at once drew to us the mothers, who soon flocked to their clubs, which at first were limited to those of the same race or those speaking the same language, afterward expanding into the most interracial and democratic of all our groups. A day nursery seemed to be only a human response to the pitiful plight of the widowed and deserted mothers, distracted by the conflicting duties of earning the family living and protecting the health and lives of their children. It bears the name of the Matheon Club of young women, which co-operates in supporting it. A public playground soon seemed to be a human necessity for the children swarming the streets of our densely crowded family ward with no other place to play than where they were compelled to run the gauntlet of the dangerous traffic. So we rented two vacant lots on the crowded thoroughfare opposite the Commons. Immediately it was so overcrowded that the swings and the teeter-boards had scarcely space to operate. Summer-evening games were organized on less frequented residence streets, which proved to be popular neighborhood occasions, even after the larger playgrounds were opened by the park commission and the school board, few of which draw children from beyond three-quarters of a mile. To safeguard health, clinics were gradually developed in co-operation with city-wide charitable agencies, especially the Infant Welfare Society; one for expectant mothers, more of whom die at childbirth in America for the lack of proper care than in fifteen other nations; another to keep infants well by medical examination, by the regulation of diet, and by the nurses' instruction of the mothers both at the clinic and in the home. Special provision for the nutrition of underweight children supplements these efforts.

Up the line of advancing ages and differing needs and wants the settlement's clubs, classes, and other occasions provide a next step onward for the small groups of boys and of girls, each consisting of those who have grouped themselves in their "gangs" or "sets"; for the larger groups of young men and young women; and for the adult groups in membership organizations or assembling for special occasions. The family thus became, and has ever continued to be, the unit of our settlement work both for the neighborhood and the city. What other agency than the settlement, except the church, avowedly aims to promote and provide for the interests of the whole family group? Where else can the whole family go together and find such provision for the social needs of each member, from the babe in the arms to the school child, from the working boy and girl all the way up to the man and woman, the mother and breadwinner, and the aged as well? Very few agencies, and by no means all the churches, offer anything all at once to all of these, as most all settlements do, in proportion as their equipment and staff are at all adequate for their purpose.

The settlement house is really an addition to every little tenement home. Its books and pictures, the nursery and play space, the lobby and the parlor, the music and flowers, the cheery fireplace and lamp, the dancing floor and place of assembly, are an extension of the all-too-scant home equipment of most of its neighbors. If the settlement household and its individual residents have anything worth looking at or prizing it becomes more worth having if other folks share it.

Having been inspired and motived by devotion to the family and having centered their work at the interests of the home, it was annoying though not disturbing to the Chicago settlements to have a newspaper of the city, once claiming to be its chief financial journal, thus venomously misrepresent them in persistent attacks:

The socialist "social settlements" of this city teach that marriage should be abolished, that the "state" should own the children, and that their subsistence, education and destiny should be the concern of the state alone. Hull House, Chicago Commons, and other avowed socialist centers are necessarily committed to this doctrine, which is a fundamental of socialism. They proclaim themselves in the same breath as anti-Christian. . . . . They preach a creed whose theory if brought home to them individually they would reject with loathing. . . . . Is it a lack of chivalry to protest against the teaching which requires the reduction of womanhood to a universal state of helplessness and infamy? . . . . Should the "social settlements" of this city be sustained in their systematic effort to destroy the Christian theory of marriage and to abolish marriage, the family and the home?

The Chicago settlements could have had no more conclusive vindication from such bare falsehoods than the recognition for the part they took in the city-wide movements for the better housing of families; for safeguarding immigrant families from exploitation, especially women and girls arriving alone; for the protection of juveniles from those contributing to their delinquency; for adapting court procedure to the understanding and guidance of delinquent children, boys and girls, and of husbands and wives disturbed in their domestic relations; and for the establishment of the Federal Children's Bureau at Washington, which is the abiding acknowledgment of the nation's obligation to safeguard the childhood and motherhood of all its people.

All that the settlement tries to be and do with and for the family implies and requires the neighborhood. It was a surprise to me to find that the family was not more sufficient unto itself. Few memories of playmates outside the family circle and the homes of nearby relatives were registered in the experience of my youth. Where the family connections of others were numerous and strong, the home circle seemed likewise to be independent of its immediate neighborhood, at least for its companionships as well as for the supply of other wants. But when my manhood's work began, and through all the years since, the consciousness of neighborship as a heritage and a potent force for social progress grew with my sense of dependence upon it. Both in my country and city parishes I had found that much church work could not be done so well, if at all, from the church building as from the neighborhood centers, about which the homes, schools, work and play, trade and fellowship, of widely scattered parishioners clustered.

I had also found that where migratory and cosmopolitan elements were included in the population, detached individuals and households were dependent upon neighbors for most, if not all, of their companionships and other associations. If not offered, persons and groups are denatured by detachment. In the country I had found the tenant-farmer family, hired for the season or working the land on shares from year to year, to be pitifully and perilously isolated. The transient city family, without household belongings, moving from one "furnished room" to another, is the despair of our "family rehabilitation" efforts. The tramp is the specter of modern civilization, with which our charities and our city governments deal very inadequately in meeting the problem of the homeless, shelterless man.

The migratory family moving from the country into the city, or from its old homeland to this "new world," is likely to disintegrate if too long detached as strangers in a strange land. Cleavage between parents and children comes when the younger generation seeks association with schoolmates, playmates, and shopmates, and a share in the neighborhood life of the new land, while the old folks cling only to their old-country language, dress, customs, memories, traditions, and ever fewer friends. The very sacrifice of the more forward-facing parents to give their children educational advantages, of which they themselves were deprived, often leads to heartbreaking experiences, when the Americanized children either become ashamed of, or estranged from, their foreign-born parents. This tragic breach in the home life also occurs when the parents shrink from the children's different ideals and standards and take reasonable or unreasonable means of checking these departures from parental habits and authority, or of resorting to arbitrary ways of reclaiming them. This heartbreak in the homes of the first generation of immigrants is little realized, even by the teachers of their children, much less by others.

Even one to the American manner born does not escape intolerable loneliness in removing from where one is known to where one feels desolately lonely in a crowd. Twice we ourselves felt the homesickness of being strangers and not being taken in. Coming from the homeland of our country-parish community to the city center of Hartford, where family and neighborhood life was more or less disintegrated, we were so long in being "taken in" that the very street crowds thronging about us only increased the sense of isolation.

One Saturday evening when wandering along the crowded Main Street, knowing nobody, while heartsick for the hospitable, friendly countryside where I knew everybody, I received the first touch of neighborship that began to make this New England community akin to us. It came from such an unexpected quarter that I have never forgotten or failed to be grateful for it. I was passing the shop of a tobacconist on the bend of the thoroughfare near my home. Standing at his doorway beside the figure of his cigar-store Indian, he just nodded to me and said "Good evening." That was all, but it was enough to melt through what had seemed the icy chill of the New England social atmosphere and to make my heartstrings vibrate. Two years afterward I went to this first neighbor who took me in, so far at least, and asked him if he knew how much good he had done me. But he could remember no good turn whatever until I told him he was the first to recognize my existence in the neighborhood. That he had no motive to do so but friendliness impressed me the more, for I was not a patron of his shop or trade. I was just a neighbor and fellow-citizen. Perhaps the foreign descent, betrayed by his name and slight accent, accounted for the friendlier expression of good fellowship than the real New Englanders were bred and inclined to give the stranger, even though their hearts were warm with affection for their friends.

Again, our first two years at Chicago were spent in a nondescript district near the Seminary, which was flanked by the main West Side thoroughfare and a boulevard. Here neighborship had faded away at the incoming of a transient population. Only two neighbors called upon us. One was a colleague who was our first and best-known Chicago friend. The other was the landlord who came to see how we were getting along in this next-door house he rented to us, and incidentally to collect the rent, if its payment had not anticipated, and lost, his call.

After two years of this experience, we moved into the settlement neighborhood. Next door our nearest neighbors lived over their liquor saloon. The housewife of the family, who also shared with her husband the service at the bar, proved to be the first real neighbor we had. No sooner had we moved in than her cheery "Good morning" rang across the narrow passage between her window and ours. Somehow it made us feel at home again among real folks. Our neighborly regard for the next family to serve this saloon led to the suggestion that the children might fare better in a home disconnected from the saloon, such as the father could provide if he returned to his skilled carpenter trade. This led the mother to express the evidently long-cherished regret that we had failed to give token of our neighborly patronage. For she remarked, "Oh, our saloon would be all right if such folks as you would come to it instead of going to the toney saloons down town." So she thought we must do, for she could not imagine any family that did not frequent some saloon. Her sense of neighborliness was so strong she could not understand why the nearest saloon should not be the natural resort in which the nearest neighbors at least would be inclined to meet and associate.

What one household cannot do for another a neighborhood can provide for every family group within it. Its school building and playground may become the center for the social life, recreation, and co-operation of all the people surrounding it, both older and younger. Its branch of the public library can supplement both the school and the home in guiding the self-culture of the children and in promoting adult education. Its public bath supplies equipment lacking in too many tenements, and creates a public demand for hygienic and sanitary provisions in the home with which the builders and owners of family dwellings may be required to comply. The family and the neighborhood may thus intersphere. Motherhood and fatherhood may thus extend their functions through such self-respecting, protective, and progressive provisions which supplement parental care and home attractions. Families come to love a good neighborhood thus identified with their homes. Abuse of it is resented almost as much as insult to the family itself.

Finding our neighborhood lacking most of such equipment for the use of the home, we at Chicago Commons have sought to bring the resources of both into co-operation for the welfare of each. We have done so by being neighbors ourselves, individually and as a household group; by sharing with neighborhood families and organizations the use of the settlement buildings. The floor plans of the new building were drawn over the neighborhood needs which we discovered during our six years' endeavor to meet them in the old rented house. The neighborhood parlor is ever open to any family or other group wishing to share it. Our other rooms are shared not only by our numerous settlement clubs and classes, but also by sixty or more lodges, benefit orders, labor and employers' organizations, and church groups which hold their regular meetings within our walls, and their larger assemblies, dances, and political meetings in our assembly hall. Thus brick and mortar, floor plans and furnishings, dollars and cents, were so woven into the very purpose of our building as to make it, like human form and face, hands and feet, the embodiment of the very heart and soul of the service which it was meant to express and fulfil.

The wisdom of adapting a building to its purpose rather than to conform the work to the plan of the building has ever since been demonstrated by the serviceableness of our building equipment. In so doing we at Chicago Commons, as also several other settlement households in Chicago, were inspiringly guided by Pond & Pond, our architects. Allen B. Pond was inspired and equipped the more for this service by his sympathetic co-operation with Jane Addams in the development of Hull House. He was one of her earliest friends and advisers. Together they found the stately, but decrepit, old mansion bearing the name of its first owner, in remodeling which Mr. Pond gained some of the experience which led him to be the most distinctive planner of settlement houses in this country. As a trustee and architect of Hull House from the beginning he helped develop its properties until they covered the area of a city block. But each development was taken only in response to a discovered need, and every detail was designed with reference to its practical use. The Ponds thus came to understand the settlement from within and to mold its structure to conform to its purpose. Their designs for the Northwestern University Settlement, Chicago Commons, the Henry Booth House, and Gads Hill Center, in ways differing according to available resources and local needs, were highly distinctive.

By offering initiative and a rallying-point for neighborhood organizations, Chicago Commons and other settlements gave incentive to the community-center movement and the opening of public-school buildings for such use. The establishment of the Department of Public Welfare by the city of Chicago followed in the wake of these movements. The appointment of Mary E. McDowell,[1] head resident of the University of Chicago Settlement, as Commissioner of the Department, was a recognition of its source.

Neighborhood groups hitherto so locally restricted as to have little knowledge and less concern regarding the city at large were brought into participation with its social and civic interests. Neighborhoods of foreign-born populations which had been unknowing and unknown began to take their place and part in the city's cosmopolitan citizenship. Detached wards were thus reattached to the city's political and administrative operations, much to the advantage of both.

When confronted by the bad physical conditions in our own ward, we sought the co-operation of neighbors who shared our discontent and our desire for improvement. They were the heads of families and homeowners long resident in the neighborhood. While the women shared more deeply than the men the disgust at these conditions, only men could vote in those years. But as soon as they got together they realized how largely the neighborhood was dependent upon the city administration's sanitary, police, fire, and educational service for the protection of its health, life, and property. On the other hand, the city as a whole was seen to be what its con-

[1] See Howard E. Wilson, *Mary McDowell, Neighbor*. Chicago: University of Chicago Press, 1928.

stituent neighborhoods make or let it be. The alderman was seen to reflect the self-respect and political standards of the people of the ward. Yet the standards of the City Council, the mayor and his cabinet, were seen to lower or lift those of the ward.

Realizing more or less clearly this interdependence, the family men of our neighborhood organized their ward federation to promote better citizenship. Although co-operating with the central organizations enlisted in reforming the City Council, the local pride of our fellow-wardsmen kept their own organization entirely independent. Younger single men, inspired by this example, organized their own Community Club. Aldermanic candidates recognized the political influence of these organizations by appearing before them to state their claims for indorsement. This was given without regard to the national party affiliations of the candidates. Between campaigns their members were held together by the good fellowship and recreative attractions of their clubroom at Chicago Commons. They served as judges, clerks, and watchers at elections, as men and women residents also do at the polling place of the precinct located in the settlement building.

The vivid neighborhood experiences accompanying the effective political campaigning of these organizations registered results which distinguish our ward and were noteworthy in the city-wide movement for political reform. Party voters who had suffered the domination of the "boss" became free citizens of their ward and of all Chicago. For fifteen years the aldermen representing the citizens of our cosmopolitan ward were as worthy to serve it and the city as their boss-controlled predecessors were unworthy, disgracing both by their disreputable characters and their political corruption. The first of the better aldermen was an American-born Pole, John F. Smulski, who, after representing the ward in the Council, became city attorney, treasurer of the state, and the foremost representative of his fellow-citizens of Polish descent in the nation. His successor in the Council was a young lawyer of Irish descent who studied law evenings while employed during working hours in a tannery. After representing the ward through five terms in the City Council with inflexible integrity and distinctive ability, he was elected and re-elected judge of the Superior Court of Cook County. During his second term on the bench his nomination for mayor by an influential group of citizens affiliated with both parties was accepted by one of them, and he was elected by a plurality of over one hundred thousand votes. Nothing has given us at Chicago Commons greater satisfaction than the encouragement we were privileged to give to William Emmett Dever to enter upon his political career, the distinguished services of which were consummated in giving the city of Chicago the best administration it had secured during the lifetime of most of its citizens. A good alderman of German descent followed in this worthy succession for several terms. The prevalence of a racial loyalty in the next predominating influx of immigrant citizens for several years has lowered the capacity and service of our ward's representative in the Council, requiring the renewal of educational efforts such as had raised civic loyalty above mere racial preferences. By such experiences the settlements are amply justified in basing their social and civic work upon the neighborhood as the central group of the body politic which relates individuals and families to the larger community and to the nation.

Bitter as was the antagonism of political groups during aldermanic campaigns, the good fellowship and co-operation of our partisan neighbors were more readily maintained than with the clergy of rival sectarian churches. Their sensitiveness and suspicions were more acute because religious convictions are deeper and more abiding than political predilections. We ventured, however, to welcome the Tabernacle Church people to share our new building, as it was built at their urgent request on the site of their old edifice where this oldest group of neighbors had fellowshiped each other for half a century. Our offer of equal hospitality to other churches has been more readily and continuously accepted by those of Roman Catholic than by those of Protestant affiliation, since the former predominated over the latter when the South European immigration superseded the Northern settlers of our Lower West Side wards.

The settlement and neighborhood fail to realize their civic function and wider influence if the whole community is not recognized to be the circumference within which their local work is centered. Indeed, the settlement can in no way more surely lose its distinctive significance than by being content to restrict its sphere to its immediate locality, however essential such neighborhood rootage is to it. What Robert A. Woods added to the title of his volume on *The Neighborhood and Nation Building*, describing its contents as the "running comment of thirty years at South End House," strikes the keynote to which the distinctive work of all settlements should be attuned.

And yet so loyal were some of the settlement pioneers to the personal and group independence of each of their households that he and other residents in Boston and New York very slowly came to favor the federation of the settlement houses. But the western pressure for closer fellowship and co-operation gradually resulted in the organization of the city, the national and the international federations, which have greatly extended the wider influence and activities of the settlement movement, without loss of personal freedom or local loyalties. The gains thus to be achieved are exemplified by two country-wide investigations undertaken by the National Federation of Settlements in the United States.

Challenged by an expert on community health conditions to share with the public what we knew of the ways in which persons and families in our neighborhoods have been affected by prohibitory legislation, our federated settlements undertook to do so. Each local settlement was enlisted to ask its neighbors what their experience and observation had been. To test and supplement impressions thus secured a questionnaire was put up to workers and observers in many other fields of philanthropic, civic, educational, and religious work, containing the same questions which each settlement group was expected to answer. They inquired after what good or bad conditions were known to exist before national prohibitory legislation was enacted in 1918, while it was better obeyed between 1918 and 1921, and since it had been less regarded. An experienced social investigator was also sent to interview these and other informants, in and beyond the communities where settlements are located. Returns were thus secured from 41 states and Canada, and in 95 cities and towns. They came from over 200 public officials, private citizens, and groups in closest touch with situations where the effects of the liquor traffic upon family life were to be more directly observed, as in settlement localities.

Rightly regarding prohibition as a distinctly American product, the outgrowth of seed planted by American farmers and village churches, it seemed fair to start on the trail in the Middle West where the American stock predominated, upon which immigrant stocks had longest and most successfully been grafted. Following the trail farther afield, facts were found warranting these conclusions: That northern races best observed the law themselves and enforced it upon the blacks in the South and the Indians in the West; that the population of Latin and Slavic descent most disregarded it; that geographical opportunities to enforce or violate the law account for its success in interior rural states of the West and South and for its failure in states on the coast and the border.

Unemployment and poverty create problems which were found to be unsolved by prohibition. Where the standard of living had risen there was less drinking to drown misery. But the illicit traffic was found to be reaping everywhere its harvest of crime and death, especially among its more prosperous traffickers and patrons. Financing the underworld, enabling it to weaken or defeat the enforcement of law protecting life and property, peace and order, was found to be the most serious ill effect of prohibition.

In their own neighborhoods most settlement houses reported better health and habits of the children, improved home conditions, less waste and more saving, fewer marital quarrels and street brawls. The conclusion of the Federation was that "things hoped for by advocates of prohibition are being realized in some places, and even where the law is least observed some of them have come true." Notwithstanding the illicit manufacture and sale of poisonously inferior liquor, enriching and emboldening the worst people in every community in their defiance of law, yet their traffic was so driven to cover that instead of publicly seeking its patrons they had to seek its product privately. This, perhaps, is the greatest gain which prohibition has brought to settlement neighborhoods, if not to the country at large.[1]

Encouraged by this experience and the somewhat uniquely practical information it obtained, the settlements through their national federation have undertaken to ascertain the effects of unemployment upon the families of their neighborhoods.[2] This inquiry will search intensively for what family life suffers from irregularity of employment, both directly and indirectly, immediately and remotely. Through their confidential neighborly relations settlement residents may secure human facts and factors revealing farther-reaching effects of unemployment upon family life than their own casual observation or expert statistical researches could disclose.

Long before, Raymond Robins and James Mullenbach, while in residence at Chicago Commons, pioneered the establishment of Chicago's Municipal Lodging House, and for two years personally managed the free shelter it offered to multitudes of unemployed, homeless men.

Settlements in the several lands to which they have now extended are promoting their fellowship and co-operation through their International Federation. Far beyond the influence that either of these federations have been able to exert upon international relations is that which Miss Addams of Hull House is widely recognized to have. Exemplary and inspiring has been her advocacy of world-peace, because of her studious reliance upon accurate knowledge of international relations, her unwavering faith in democratic social progress, and the tolerant patience and high courage with which she has maintained both the pace and the poise of her reasoning. Still more effective is the leadership she has contributed and rallied for the organization and guidance of the Women's International League for Peace and Freedom.

To very many, as to me, she has been what Professor Charles E. Merriam described her to be: "A great professor

---

[1] Martha Bensley Bruere, *Does Prohibition Work?* (For the National Federation of Settlements.) Harper & Bros., 1927.

[2] See *Neighborhood*, a Settlement quarterly, December, 1929.

without a university chair, a great statesman without a port-
folio, a guiding woman in a man-made world, a brooding
spirit of the mother hovering with gentle sympathy over the
troubled sea of poverty, of weakness, of arrogance, of pride,
of hate, of force." To her I owe more than to any other comrade, a deeper insight and a closer grip upon life, and a vision
of a world grown greater yet nearer, more human yet more
divine, since I have shared her understanding of it.[1] Through
all these thirty-five years she has helped us guide the development of Chicago Commons as one of its trustees, and still
more helpfully as the comrade of those of us who have led it.
No one has been more intelligently sympathetic than she
with the hope of making social and spiritual ideals and resources tributary to each other in my teaching and practice.
None has been so suggestive and practically helpful in the
whole endeavor to initiate and carry them out.

[1] Jane Addams, *Twenty Years at Hull House.* New York: Macmillan, 1910. *The Second Twenty Years at Hull House.* New York: Macmillan, 1930.

CHAPTER XXII

SETTLEMENT INITIATIVE IN TRAINING
FOR SOCIAL WORK

A VERY definite educational purpose played an essential part in the founding of Chicago Commons and guiding its development. My forecast of needing first-hand knowledge of actual conditions, in order to train young men and women to apply religion to life, at first prompted the intention to provide what would serve me as a laboratory or clinic for my classroom. The failure of the Seminary to secure special funds for this purpose fortunately left me free to establish a center, independent of institutional control, to fulfil a more human and therefore a broader educational purpose. I was enabled, therefore, not only to supplement the academic teaching of my classroom, but also to provide educational opportunities and facilities hitherto described, for teaching men, women, and children of a great cosmopolitan community how better to live and work together as neighbors and American citizens.

Reflexively, through the training of its resident workers for other widely scattered fields of service, and through the farther-flung influence of the work itself, Chicago Commons, as have other settlements, spread an inspiring spirit that has permeated many levels of life. What was done in the first kindergartens to be established in settlements inspired so much interest that training schools developed from them. From our pioneer kindergarten at Chicago Commons grew the Pestalozzi-Froebel Kindergarten Training School, now Teachers' College, which since 1897 has sent forth annually scores of well-trained teachers, some of whom became club and play leaders. Training for social work, however, came at first from what the residents did at the house and in the neighborhood, with such interpretation as was given personally by the head resident or by exchanging views with each other. After a while the varied social work in hand at the settlement was seen to exact more systematic instruction. The demand for workers, trained in this more or less desultory way, increased so much that we could neither retain our own staff nor furnish recruits for other fields.

Bearing this burden with me on a trip to England in the summer of 1903, I was deeply impressed with what I found some of the settlements were doing to train their own resident and non-resident workers. Fortunately this training was the subject of discussion at one of the first intersettlement conferences, which long preceded and suggested the federation of settlements. This third session of the provincial settlements' conference was held at the Woman's Settlement in Birmingham. The training reported and discussed ranged all the way from the fragmentary and occasional efforts adapted to the smaller settlements up to the well-planned and directed two-year course which was successfully conducted at the Women's University Settlement, London, then under the guidance of Miss Gladstone, daughter of the great prime minister. Its graduates not only made the personnel of that settlement distinctive, but had furnished head residents for several important provincial settlements and other influential positions in social work.

I was particularly interested in the suggestive participation taken in this conference by two prominent professors of the University of Birmingham. Professor Ashley, who had recently come from Harvard to enter upon his long service as dean of the School of Commerce, confessed with shame the little help which economists had given to social workers or had received from them. Between them, he said, "a system of understudies could be arranged which would invaluably supplement the work of each." Professor Muirhead tersely summed up the results of the session. Among many other equally direct suggestions, these answered some of the silent queries:

Candidates for residence should be enlisted and trained. Professor Ashley could easily relate the Department of Commerce to the settlement if he would offer himself as a resident. Seriously why not, when schools of

mining, engineering and metallurgy are being located at the mines?
Definite investigations should be undertaken with scientific spirit and
method and for practical purposes. To succeed we must dare to fail, for
they who make no mistakes make nothing else.

Inspired by these examples, I brought home with me the
determination to "dare to fail" in attempting to initiate
training for social work by courses run at least through the
academic year. A summer school had been opened that very
season in New York under the auspices of the Charity Organization Society. Soon after my return I had an opportunity to suggest the obligation of educational institutions located in or near Chicago to make some return for what Chicago had done for them. It was at a meeting of the Faculties
Union of Seminary professors. The only response to my
suggestion then and there received came silently in the form
of a visiting card, bearing the name of William R. Harper, on
which were penciled the words: "When you want to talk business about this, call upon me." Reporting to him my observation abroad and presenting the need at home for a more diversified training to meet the insistent demands for efficiency
in the administration and operation of industrial, civic, social,
and philanthropic work, both public and private, I found
him to be alertly alive, as he ever had been, to every opportunity to extend the service of the University of Chicago not
only within but beyond hitherto-prescribed limits. He
promptly offered a classroom where the classes of the Extension Division were held at the business center of the city, and
included the announcement of the new courses in the publications of that department.

Aside from these initial provisions for shelter and publicity,
no financial provision was for some time available for instruction. When, therefore, the Social Science Center for Practical
Training in Philanthropic and Social Work opened its first
course on "Dependency and Preventive Agencies" in October,
1903, it ran one evening a week for twelve weeks, with Professor Charles R. Henderson of the University of Chicago and
myself as volunteer instructors and with twelve students, all
of whom were actively engaged in social work. The next year
two evening classes were held each week, one on "Personal,

Institutional, and Public Care of Dependents," the other on "Preoccupying and Preventive Methods and Agencies." Our slender teaching staff was reinforced by Miss Julia C. Lathrop, Alexander Johnson, Robert Hunter, and Dr. Hastings H. Hart, who offered two or three lectures each. In simple self-defense of the local work, its leaders volunteered to help us train staff workers for their office and field work. It is interesting to note that the commissioner of public health of the city of Chicago, Dr. William A. Evans, Judge Julian W. Mack, then of the Circuit Court of Cook County, and the president of the Cigar Makers International Union, George W. Perkins, were among the volunteers from the field.

At the opening of the third year of our adventure of educational faith, which had come to be known as the "Institute of Social Science and Arts," President Harper was favorably considering my suggestion that the success of the Institute might warrant taking it over. His further consideration of this proposal was prevented by his illness, from which he died January 10, 1906. Thereupon I was informed that the Institute had never been on the budget of the University for an appropriation, that the few hundreds of dollars it had received from President Harper must have been privately solicited by him, and I was, therefore, free to do whatever seemed best for the future of its work.

The trustees of Chicago Commons Association at once took the Institute under its auspices, Victor F. Lawson underwriting its expense to the extent of two thousand dollars per year. Its educational and financial resources were greatly increased the following year by an appropriation by the Russell Sage Foundation of ten thousand dollars a year for five years to establish a department of investigation and research. This enabled us to secure the invaluable services of Miss Lathrop as its supervisor, and as co-director of the Institute. On May 10, 1908, it was incorporated as the "Chicago School of Civics and Philanthropy," "to promote through instruction, training, investigation and publication the efficiencies of civic, philanthropic and social work, and the improvement of living and working conditions." To its board of incorporating trustees the Chicago Commons Association turned over the responsibility for the school. They included men and women widely recognized for their interest in educational progress and their active participation in progressive social movements. Professors in several state universities personally acted as active or advisory members of the Board of Trustees.

To Julia C. Lathrop the school owed much of its initiative and development. Having served for twelve years on the Illinois State Board of Charities, she was as conversant with the administrative standards of public institutions as she was sympathetically acquainted with the people from which their inmates came, having long lived as a neighbor to many of them at Hull House. The help she got from the school and gave to it after leaving us to pioneer the Children's Bureau under the United States Department of Labor at Washington is best expressed in her own words:

When we held our first civil service examination, we wanted people who could make some scientific inquiry, with a statistical basis, which the government required under the organic law of the Bureau. A number of students from the School of Civics took the first examination and passed triumphantly. Forty of them did well in the work, largely due to their field work. Some developed executive ability and ingenuity in research and in presenting reports which they had written. Contracts with the school for some investigations enabled it to give its scholarships in social research, from which rich dividends on the investment were returned to the government in the reports, which were included in the publications of the Bureau. Here is a school whose great usefulness should offer universities the kind of field training which can be given only at the center of a great city.

These and many other achievements of the school, especially of its Research Department, were due to the rare ability and distinctive service of Miss Sophonisba P. Breckinridge, who succeeded Miss Lathrop as director of this Department and became dean of the school, and that of Miss Edith Abbott, who directed the investigations. The scientific thoroughness of the training thus offered to graduate students in methods of modern social investigation and research; the wide range, statistical accuracy, and practical value of the publications reporting these investigations; and the exacting positions for which graduates were sought and in which they rendered distinctive public service—all contributed much to the growing reputation of the school. For the effectiveness of the field work, which contributed so much efficiency to all the studies in the classroom, credit is due to the generous co-operation of the privately and publicly conducted local social agencies in providing supervised work on their fields for students whose experience was checked up and correlated with their courses by the school's own supervisor of field work. The service which the students and teachers of the school rendered to these agencies was publicly and appreciatively acknowledged by their executives from time to time.

Among such recognitions none is more interesting than that officially given for its war-time service. The school was found ready to offer training and furnish helpers for the local and national Red Cross; for the direction of recreation in camps and community centers organized by state councils of defense; and for women in protective work with girls such as was conducted under the auspices of the Fosdick Commission. During the war and after the Armistice nearly six hundred helpers were trained for these agencies, without requiring tuition fees, and for the still more exacting service of the War Labor Policies Board, and especially for the Ordnance Department of the army.

After eighteen years of steady progress, the Chicago School of Civics and Philanthropy faced the crisis of its success. Its trustees and faculty realized that the weight of its work in meeting country-wide demands for its service could no longer be borne either by the generosity of the few contributors to its financial support or by the loyalty of its students and alumni, whose tuition fees covered a remarkably large proportion of the budget, and whose contributions from their scant early earnings expressed their estimate of its worth. Then the feasibility of affiliating the school with a university was considered. The University of Chicago was found to be favorable to the overture. By action of the Boards of Trustees of both institutions in August, 1920, the school was taken over by the University and became its Graduate School of Social Service Administration.

The successful operation of the former department of

recreation was independently continued as the Recreation Training School of Chicago, under the directorship of Miss Neva L. Boyd, who had conducted its courses from the beginning. After seven years of distinctive service in this field at Hull House, the Northwestern University added it and its director to the College of Liberal Arts, placing its work under the Department of Sociology. Thus permanent provision was secured for the continuity and development of the whole work initiated and carried by the Chicago School of Civics and Philanthropy, which had the distinction of being the first school for social work with an all-year-round curriculum to be established in this country. Since this initiative was taken, schools for social service have been introduced by many colleges and universities.[1]

[1] *A Study of Education and Training for Social Work*, by Professor James H. Tufts, vice-president of the University of Chicago, was made and published under the auspices of the Russell Sage Foundation. It critically surveyed the educational status of this training and its relation to the university curriculum.

CHAPTER XXIII

SETTLEMENT SAFETY VALVES
VINDICATED

THE struggle to improve living and working conditions and the relations between the two industrial groups involved has been at once the supreme opportunity and the severest test of the settlements' loyalty to their mission. Failing to function to this end, a settlement stultifies itself by trying to play its *Hamlet* with the Hamlet left out. It was his first-hand contacts with the casual laboring class of East London, which had sunk below any normal standard of living, and the inhuman odds which his parish work thus encountered, that prompted Canon Barnett to suggest the founding of Toynbee Hall and enlist the help of the university in investigating and ameliorating these conditions. It was in seeking to make known his own and others' findings that Arnold Toynbee, the first Oxford man to volunteer assistance, struck the keynote to which resident workers at Toynbee Hall subsequently endeavored to make their work respond. He asserted that "it was the labor question that revived the method of observation in political economy, which was thereby transformed by the working classes"; that "it was the pressing desire to find a solution of problems which the abstract science treated as practically insoluble, which drew the attention of the economists to neglected facts"; and that they were thus enabled "to ascertain, from actual observation of the industrial world in which they lived, in how far their assumptions were facts, and from the knowledge thus acquired to state the law of prices, profits, wages and rent in the actual world."

During the late eighties and early nineties in Chicago the cleavage between the industrial classes, and the discontent over the restriction of the freedom of speech and the right of

assembly following the Haymarket Riot, became alarming.
It was then that Jane Addams in the early days of Hull
House encouraged the organization of the Working People's
Social Science Club, which was open to both men and women.
She did so in order "to give opportunity for representatives of
various economic theories to modify each other, and at least
to learn tolerance and the futility of endeavoring to convince
all the world of the truth of one position." In justifying this
purpose against the charge of radicalism, she truly wrote:
"Fanaticism is engendered only when men, finding no contradiction to their theories, at last believe that the very uni-
verse lends itself as an exemplification of one point of view."
Free speech and frank discussion were promoted among representative business and professional men by Lyman J. Gage,
then president of one of the city's great banks and later secretary of the treasury in the cabinets of Presidents McKinley
and Roosevelt. With this purpose he founded and presided
over the Sunset Club, which gave precedent and impetus for
other free forums.

I could scarcely have realized what a venture it was to offer
another such safety valve by opening our free-floor discussion
at Chicago Commons, after only a year's residence between
the lines of class conflict. But we felt well enough away from
the wild prairie fire of nine years before not to be likely to
kindle into flame any possibly smoldering riot resentments,
which indeed we found to have cooled sufficiently to be only
incidentally referred to and calmly discussed. We published
the call to it among the special announcements in the *Chicago
Daily News*, inviting "all sides to free speech with no favors"
every Tuesday evening. From a score who came to the first
meeting the attendance grew to an average of one hundred or
more, most of them men of our own neighborhood, with an
increasing proportion coming from other parts of the city. In
accordance with our proposal to make the occasion frankly
democratic both in spirit and procedure, they agreed to limit
the opening speech, by a speaker of their own choice, to
twenty minutes, and all others taking part to three minutes,
unless any speaker's time was extended by vote. The only
limit to the freedom of speech was against the advocacy of

violence, which was declared to be "out of order." The only
concession to Chicago Commons was that the chairmanship
of the meeting should be filled by myself or by my colleague,
John Palmer Gavit. But we held ourselves and were held
strictly within the limits of debate prescribed from the floor.
Equal freedom of speech was assured for personal opinion on
all sides of economic, social, political, and religious questions.

Although speakers representing widely differing views were
chosen and respectfully heard, yet the topics they presented
were discussed mainly by radicals, far less by trade-unionists,
and least of all by the few representatives of the employing
and professional classes. Many students and some professors
from universities and seminaries in and about Chicago frequently attended in groups, which with other onlookers occasionally doubled the number of these silent but eager listen-
ers. They were often challenged "to assert their convictions
if they had any," since they might not "always safely hide
under silence."

The radicals were either individualist anarchists or socialist collectivists. The single-taxer never failed to oppose both
of them more vigorously and more intelligently than those
extremists antagonized each other. Only occasionally did
trade-unionists break their silence, dissenting from all these
"theorists," in pleas for something practical.

As the anarchists, one and all, claimed self-interest to be
the only motive that does or should move anyone, I privately
challenged two of them to prove it. To one, who was the
dignified, studious, and ever courteous editor of the anarchist
paper, *Free Society*, I put this question: "Supposing you saw
a ruffian beating a little girl, what would you do and why
would you do it?" He replied, "I am so sensitively constituted that the injury inflicted on the child would cause me so
much pain as to impel me, in self-defense, to make the ruffian
desist." Of the other, a German cobbler, I asked: "If that
tenement house across the street were on fire and you saw a
woman with a child in her arms on the top floor with no way
of escape, what would you do, and why would you do it?" He
started to answer me by inquiring: "What would you expect
me to do? What do you take me for?" I promptly replied:

"As the big-hearted man I know you to be, I would expect you to risk your life in trying to rescue the lives of the mother and child." His rejoinder was: "Of course I would, and because under those circumstances I would rather do that than anything else." Then he turned challenger, demanding: "What for do you live at Chicago Commons? Is it because you don't want to? Then it must be for self-interest."

This man gave me two other reasons for respecting his motive, if not his judgment. When asked on first acquaintance what his occupation might be, he made this memorable reply: "By occupation I am a cobbler but my calling is that of an anarchist propagandist." Ever since, I have wondered how much faster the pace of human progress might be if others made their occupations tributary to their higher calling as self-sacrificingly as this man did. For I have known him to scrimp his living expenses to the lowest limits in order to pay the traveling expenses of fellow-propagandists to come from New York to Chicago to help advocate his cause. When I asked him "why," his eye gleamed with the fire of sincere enthusiasm, as he exclaimed: "For the sake of the redemption of mankind and the salvation of the world." The other insight into his sincerity and tender-heartedness was given me in a private interview sometime after the assassination of President McKinley. He began by telling me that when younger in the fatherland he had thought the church to be the chief obstacle to the liberty of the masses of the people. Therefore he thought it his duty to rid the world of one of its clergy. So after buying the only gun he ever owned and starting out to find the victim, he met a friend in crossing a bridge. The friend inquired: "Where are you going?" The man replied: "I am going to kill a priest." Halted by the rejoinder, "You big fool, a hundred will come to his funeral," he dropped his gun from the bridge into the river. As the sequence of this story he added: "While sitting at my cobbler's bench one day a soft-spoken young stranger called upon me as a comrade, but said nothing of himself or his purposes." A few days after this stranger was reported to be the assassin. The cobbler confided to me the regret which he remorsefully felt after reading the news. "Had I asked the young stranger where he was going and he had told me of his intention, I would have talked to him so that he might not have killed the president." Long since this man switched his propagandism to that of a vegetarian philosophic cult of oriental mysticism.

The anarchist-editor also bared his heart in defending comrades against what he considered a false imputation. It was at a meeting on our free floor, after the excitement over President McKinley's assassination had subsided sufficiently to allow a calm discussion of the question: "What is law and why we need it?" A judge was sought to open it, and an Irish judge was selected because his sense of humor might tide over any emergency. Special effort succeeded in attracting many more radical leaders and their adherents than usually attended the meetings. When the judge expressed his surprise that such well-appearing men should be enlisted in a propaganda involving violent and destructive action, the editor asked if His Honor would pardon an interruption. Assured that it would be welcome, the editor deferentially endeavored to correct what he considered to be the judge's misunderstanding. "Many of us individualist anarchists are as non-resistant as Leo Tolstoy," he said. "And some of us are vegetarians, because we cannot conscientiously live on food which costs the life of sentient beings." The idea of vegetarian anarchists was so contradictory to all the judge's preconceived notions of this strange variety of the human species as to cause his Irish sense of humor to break forth in loud laughter, which brought the house down to join in the mirth of the jolly judge. An Irish anarchist, and the only one known to us, thereupon confessed: "I came here to have a scrap with the judge, but there is less to scrap about than I thought."

Years after this heart-to-heart occasion, the former editor wrote me from his far-western home, where he had become chairman of the school board: "I shall never forget you, nor fail to appreciate your respect for what then were my deepest convictions and for giving me the same freedom to express them as you claimed for the expression of your own." In response to our Christmas greeting he wrote from his orange-grove home of which he and his wife, now both aged, are very proud: "I still think often of Jane Addams and you, especially when inclined to become pessimistic as to the advancement of mankind for the better." Referring to the advent sentiment, "Manward to God and Godward to Man," with which our Christmas card closed, he added: "The sentiment expressed appealed to me very much, with only one exception. Incorrigible as I am—I still cannot believe that there can be 'Liberty with Law,' but I know that you will forgive me."

There were others in this anarchist group of a far different type and temper, bent only on destruction with little or no vision of anything farther ahead than for each one to do as he pleases. One of the worst of these was an Englishman who had been a choir boy in an Anglican church. With difficulty the chairman restrained this man's bitter spirit from violent speech. Anticipating the World War experience, this savage once boasted before he could be checked: "With a balloon and a stick of dynamite I could bring any town to terms." He was never taken seriously, however, either by his "comrades" or by other hearers, none of whom had yet dreamed of bombing cities from aeroplanes, sinking passenger ships by submarines, or poisoning multitudes by gases, as authorized weapons of "civilized warfare."

And yet had Peter Kropotkin spoken in Chicago after the World War he could have cited it to prove what he said there long before, that the violence of Russian Nihilists was not to be compared with the wholesale slaughter of organized warfare. When asked by me whether nothing short of violence could deliver the Russian people from oppression, he declared that the despotic bureaucrats could be overcome only by being blown off the face of the earth. To such a philosophy of despair had been driven this man of such widely recognized personal qualities, eminent academic service, and international repute as to have been secretary of the Royal Geographic Society of Russia. Governor Altgeld throughout the interview, which he shared with me, filed exceptions to any justifications for such conclusions in America. His reserved judgment and conservative attitude toward the existing order here interestingly offset the prevalent exaggeration of his alleged radicalism.

The Socialists appeared to much better advantage on our free floor. Their pioneer leader in Chicago for nearly forty years was Thomas J. Morgan. Born and brought up in England before child labor had been outlawed there, he attributed his failure to attain full stature to having been put to work too early. He extenuated his askance attitude toward the church by having been sent to a "ragged school," as early Sunday schools were called, resenting the emphasis thus laid upon his ragged clothing rather than upon his boyhood. After working for thirty or more years in a machine shop in this country, he found his skill as an expert mechanic less in demand, and of less wage-earning value, in the shops where he worked. Studying law after working hours, he was graduated with credit from the full course of a well-established law school, and became a practicing attorney specializing in labor cases.

He was a man of vision, and was yet content to die without the sight of realizing what he had faith to work for all his life. Meeting me one hot summer day in one of Chicago's breathless canyon streets, he greeted me with the question: "How are things?" His rejoinder to my reply that they were sometimes better and sometimes worse was as characteristic of him as it was chiding to me: "We must not judge by the days or by the years or the decades, but by the centuries and the millenniums," he said. Looking still farther beyond this far-flung horizon, he musingly added: "You Christians must be happy in the hope of reward in the future life for doing no more than your duty in this life, but we poor fellows must do right just because it is right."

He could urge his cause with impassioned eloquence reinforced by stinging sarcasm. His oratory rose to its full height, and reached beyond the heights previously attained by anyone on our free floor, on its most memorable occasion. He had opened a discussion on socialism in which a stranger, whom we had never seen before, took a startling part. Claiming the "philosophy of power" to be his belief, he said he was "tired of hearing brotherhood talk among workingmen, and socialism offered the world to protect the weak from the strong." Then affirming that "the survival of the fittest is the law of nature and competition is the law of trade; that might is the only right and that the biggest bone belongs to the strongest beast," he exclaimed: "For preaching his 'Golden Rule' the creeping Christ deserved to be crucified, and if he came to earth again I would help nail him to the cross!" With the accent of an educated man, but with the emphasis of a brute in the cosmic struggle for existence, thus spoke this stranger.

By this shock to the human that is in us all, this group of radically disagreeing men was welded, for the moment at least, into unanimity. They expressed it at once by the hush of silence, strange to this arena. Murmurs of dissent rose to exclamations of protest. Then arose Morgan to close the discussion. Advancing as he spoke in the direction of his over-towering challenger, he was a reminder of David meeting Goliath. Beginning with the claim that there is in nature "a struggle for the life of others as well as for the survival of self," he cited for proof Henry Drummond's chapter on "The Evolution of a Mother," in his volume on *The Ascent of Man*. And then he brought this claim to bear upon himself and his hearers with an eloquence born of the deepest feeling, saying: "Without a mother's struggle for our life and her own, not one of us was born. I have heard that there was less of it in the hyena breed." Pointing toward his opponent, he scornfully exclaimed: "That man's evolution seems to have been arrested at the hyena stage." Turning to his audience, he fairly flung his whole soul into his final appeal, pleading in subdued and tender tones: "You know I am no churchman but it fills my heart full of tears to think that the Carpenter of Nazareth, who gave us the Golden Rule, had to die on the cross to get the beast out of us all, so much more of which is in that man yonder."

This could have been no "scene" staged for effect. The shock producing the real sensation was so sudden that the reaction to it was spontaneously sincere, baring the instinctive, elemental feelings common to the human heart and conscience. Neither spokesman had any chance to "play to the galleries," for this gallery crowd was as averse to any philosophy of mere "power" as it was to any claim of authority for the church. Both spoke out what was within. So did the crowd by a silence and an applause more expressive than speech.

It is unfair, however, both to Chicago Commons and to its free floor to characterize either by the extreme expressions of radical opinion, or by the presence of their extremist propagandists at a weekly meeting. These instances have been narrated because they fairly characterize both persons and ideals seldom heard, much less understood, by most of those who make public opinion, and make it so intolerant as to be incapable of offering anything in reply except denunciation. We tried, however, to counteract the tendency of radicals from other parts of the city to monopolize the discussion. This tendency was not wholly due to them, but also to an increasing proportion of the audience which likewise came from outside our neighborhood to be amused or startled by the extremes to which the speakers might go. These speakers became still more extreme in responding to the stimulus of such applause, which was often loudest when they were at their worst.

The topics and speakers of the free floor ranged almost as widely as the all-year-round human service of the Chicago Commons household. The programs included topics dealing with the manhood and womanhood of the individual, the family, marriage and the social evil, health and housing, thrift and spendthrifts, law and citizenship, interracial and international relations, peace and war, ethics and religion, destiny in this world and the next. Indeed, as Mr. John Palmer Gavit wrote:

The most intense interest and feeling always attaches to the deepest ethical and religious questions, which will not down. The discussion of the historicity of the life of Jesus lasted until past midnight, and nearly every meeting elicits some aspect of the ethical problem. The first meetings generated tremendous heat and personal bitterness, now long since past. Mutual toleration and respect as shown to all by the chair and demanded of each other from the floor have modified opinion. The ability and the give-and-take spirit of most of the speakers also contributed much to this result. Among them were men and women of high standing in industrial, commercial, professional, political and religious life not only of the city, but of the nation and of foreign countries. While little respect was shown persons, or their standing elsewhere, apart from what they said and were on this platform, yet they did help counteract certain tendencies which qualify and often destroy the effectiveness of free forums.

To men of such eminence as Lyman Abbott and Washington Gladden, the unterrified democracy listened respectfully, but its spokesmen hesitated no more to challenge and controvert what they said than what was said by speakers from their own ranks, when discussing the same topics of "human rights" and "industrial ethics." A noted theological professor's claim for the Christian initiative of most charitable and philanthropic movements was vigorously denied by speakers who cited the pre-Christian establishment by Jewish and other peoples of provisions for the care of the sick, the widow, the orphan, the aged, and the stranger, as well as for justice to wage-earners and tillers of the soil. The measure of a speaker's manhood was taken by such tests. Men of large yet humble spirit proved themselves to be such by happily meeting fellow-men on a man-to-man equality. Other men, smaller by nature, or self-assertive by habit, did not fare so well. Some judges and clergymen resented the contradiction from which both the bench and the pulpit protected them. But here the dictum "Thus saith the Law" did not allow a jail sentence for contempt, nor did a "Thus saith the Lord" silence the challenger.

A well-known professor of economics finely exemplified the best academic spirit in a debate on the theory of value with a Russian Jewish socialist. So confident was he of his ability to defend his own theory that he asked me to get someone from the University of Chicago to debate the question with him. When they met, the professor stated and defended the theory as taught in the text, from whose most authoritative authors he quoted. This prompted the impatient challenge of his opponent: "No matter what others say, what do you think, and why do you think so?" In restating his argument the professor paid tribute to his opponent's independent thought and forceful defense of it, verifying my warning that he would meet a foeman worthy of his steel. And yet this man, who had immigrated only a few years before, acquired a fluent use of the English language by his own effort, aided at first by his observation of advertisements on billboards and handbills. He showed me the metal of his mind by seeking my help to secure a position as a night ticket-taker on the elevated railway, in order, as he said, to get a chance for consecutive reading when less interrupted in the early morning hours.

Mr. Gavit also conclusively justified the motive of our free floor in rejoinder to those who misunderstood and misrepresented it:

In the saloons of the poorer districts, as in the clubs of the more prosperous, men gather in groups to discuss topics and interests of the day. These discussions are characterized by absolute freedom of speech and democracy of personnel. Every shade of belief, social, political, religious, from laissez faire individualism back to force-anarchism, from communist socialism to survival of the fittest, from ultra-conservative catholicism to "free thought," find expression in those hand to hand disputes of neighborhood opinion. It was the most obvious opportunity of the settlement, as regards the men of the community, to offer place and occasion for just such a free discussion, apart from the environment and temptations of the saloon.

It is at once a most useful, a most far-reaching and least understood feature of the settlement's work. Those who characterize it as a "nest of anarchists," those who think of and visit it as some sort of social circus, and those who regard it as a weak-kneed apology for a religious meeting, alike fail to discern its purpose and its value, alike misunderstand and misrepresent it. The "Tuesday Meeting" is none of these things. It is the settlement's deliberate proposition that all classes of men, all shades of thought, all degrees of prosperity and of culture, shall come face to face, and "have it out." It calls men out of their corners where they nurse their grievances and brood over social salvation into the light of day, for full examination and frank discussion. Assuming the good faith and good intentions of the average man, it offers one of the few cases of self-conscious democracy in the wilderness of social confusion and industrial chaos, where distinction of class and caste may be ignored, and mere human manhood may be the title to free speech and frank opinion.

The sensational, and often intentionally distorted newspaper reports, scare heads, and editorial comments tested the courage of all connected with Chicago Commons in loyally continuing this mediating service to the whole city. So long as it fulfilled this purpose the free floor was steadily and stoutly maintained. When, however, extreme radical spokesmen and their retainers from other parts of the city preponderated and monopolized the occasion, when the play to the galleries impeached the sincerity of the discussion and the applause it evoked then the men of our own neighborhood resented the misrepresentation which it was giving us, and agreed with us that it be discontinued.

This and other readaptations of our methods were required by rapidly changing conditions due to the racial transformation of the population surrounding us, from predominantly English-speaking peoples to recently arrived immigrants from Italy and Southeastern European countries. They needed more direct educational aims and methods than had been required by the agitated public opinion previously prevailing, of which they were unaware and from the discussion of which their ignorance of the English language debarred them. Recent reversions to the narrowest prepossessions against the advancement of scientific learning, and to the most chauvinistic patriotism, provocative alike of internal racial antagonisms and international strife, add startling emphasis to the urgent necessity of adult education among our native, as well as foreign-born, people in America. The success of our "community meeting" in attracting to it and our educational classes more men than ever before rallied to Chicago Commons amply justified this ready response to their needs.

That open and free discussion would prove to be a safety valve was demonstrated, however, not only by seven years of experience in conducting our free floor, but stands amply ratified in the longer retrospect. It gave vent for one extreme to counteract another. It offered opportunity for reason to justify safer means to realize saner ends in achieving social justice. The danger of driving men to discuss their grievances in secret assemblies of those holding one and the same opinion was surely demonstrated by tracing the Haymarket tragedy, as many another has been traced since to such enforced secrecy.

The impressions of the free floor made upon him as a neighbor were publicly restated and confirmed by Mayor William E. Dever twenty years later in these words:

About the time I was being urged to run for alderman, Chicago Commons was established in the old Seventeenth Ward. It was a new development, a new venture, entirely new to me. Those of us who were living there were leading extremely practical lives in those days. We went to the Commons with some misgivings, wondering, certainly not knowing, just what the advent of that institution meant or was intended to mean in that community.

In those days Chicago Commons had an open forum where every sort of opinion was expressed, however extravagant. It did many a great deal of good and meant much for the community. It was a wonderful safety valve for a community which had in it many things that might, if not properly cared for, become dangerous to the social order. What we needed at that time, and what we need at this time, is that tolerant, thoughtful understanding of what human nature is and how necessary and possible it is to reconcile the apparently conflicting opinions that grow out of different habits, different customs and different conditions.

Notwithstanding such support as one and another within and beyond our neighborhood gave us in attesting their personal observations, the motives and methods of all identified with Chicago Commons continued to be viciously attacked through its earlier years. It is due the pioneer residents, as well as friends who assumed responsibility for our work by participating in its management and support, to recall the opposition that was silently and steadfastly faced. The radicals on our free floor charged that we were there in the midst of a working-class population, perhaps unwittingly, as spies or propagandists of capitalistic supporters, or of sectarian propagandists. When disabused of this suspicion, by the freedom and frankness of our speech and attitude toward them and their views, they good-naturedly held us accountable only for advocating and exemplifying what, though good in itself, was the enemy of the best.

We did not fare so well at the hands of the spokesmen for certain partisan and predatory special interests, whose attacks in the public press were as bold as they were false. From my file of clippings I cull the following brief quotations from whole columns of editorial attacks in the *Chicago Chronicle* and the *Inter-Ocean*, then widely circulated as aggressive exponents of certain financial and political interests, but long since happily deceased and deeply buried under the discredit into which the principal proprietors of both of them at last fell:

By some mystical lunacy the social settlements in this city have been made identical with opposition to the constitution of the United States and hostile to the laws of Illinois. The patrons and benefactors of Hull House and Chicago Commons should kindly ask their conductors whether or not it is consistent with conscience and integrity to accept subscriptions, in fact to solicit subscriptions, in the name of charity and apply them to inculcating this hostility. If the conductors of these now openly avowed schools of socialism and anarchy admitted frankly to their benefactors that the money solicited was to be used against the institutions under which life and property are protected in this country, would the treasury be so full? Is it not reasonable to assert that so far as political propaganda of these places goes, the monies given for their support are largely secured under false pretenses? . . . . The perversion of a few Chicago social settlements into centers of socialism and anarchy is deplorable but it is not without cure.

Anarchists, as Professor Taylor correctly says, believe the world against them. But when he says "These people must be taught that the law is not against them," he embarks upon a hopeless task and exposes his own error. To attempt to teach them by ordinary means is as useless as to read the Riot act to a pack of wolves. There is no middle way of dealing successfully with the anarchist. He must be wiped out or allowed to wrap the world in flame. He himself has decreed it, and Professor Taylor and Miss Addams are in poor business when they try to conceal this fact, and thus become the apologists of such a hideous creature.

Ignoring all that we had said and done to the contrary, all that was said and printed about the purpose and work of Chicago Commons by those who had the right to bear witness from personal observation, and all the denials that might have been obtained from neighboring families whose motives, as well as our own, were aspersed, these newspaper editorials thus melodramatically appealed to prejudice and passion, notwithstanding all the facts were directly to the contrary:

The parents who seek the charity of the socialists' "settlements" are generally foreign born, often illiterate and inoculated with hatred of government as immigrants from countries in which they were oppressed. At Hull House and Chicago Commons, and in all similar settlements, they are taught that it is the duty of the government to take their children from the parental care and provide for all their wants. Thus the parental instinct, generally correct, is strained. The deluded parent waits for the officer of the "state" to come and put an end to the piteous struggle for existence. But the expected visitor does not arrive. Slowly but resentfully the deluded immigrant comes to the conclusion that the "state" is treating him with special neglect or wilful tyranny. . . . . Hope deferred makes the heart sick. The word of promise is unkept. But if the "state" owns everything in this country and is bound to provide for him and his children, there can be no impropriety in taking what is not given to him. It is not crime as he understands the word. It is only taking what Hull House and Chicago Commons teach belongs to them. . . . . The child meanwhile has been caught stealing. A correctional sentence is inevitable. The state has interfered for restraint instead of for indulgence. Now the state must be hated for treachery.

Thus the immigrants and the children they bring or bear after arrival are trained by the "social settlements" in hostility to the lawful institutions of the country in which they seek liberty and the pursuit of happiness. Of all the victims, the child is most to be pitied, because its destiny is marred from the start, and they betray who ought sacredly to have cherished its confidence and honor. It is a cruel fate which guides the ignorant immigrant into the socialist precincts of Hull House and Chicago Commons. It is a sad misuse of Chicago money which maintains these alluring pitfalls for the trustful and helpless.

Under all such annoying notoriety, and the askance attitude of their reactionary uninformed friends in business and professional circles, which may have been harder to bear, the trustees of Chicago Commons never wavered in their loyalty to its residents and work, which was expressed in their first public appeal for the support of the settlement in these attesting terms:

The trustees desire hereby to bear testimony to our faith in the efficiency and great usefulness of the work accomplished through the settlement by those having it immediately in charge. We know of no place where so small an investment of money makes possible and secures larger expenditure of concentrated effort, nor are we aware of any service of greater practical value than that in which these faithful workers are engaged. . . . . It offers a spirit of initiative for the expression of the best impulses of the community, and provides a neutral meeting ground for the unification in American citizenship of the heterogeneous population in a densely inhabited industrial district. It is our conviction that the achievement of the Commons in its local field, in its wide influence upon persons and communities throughout the country, and not least, in its general endeavor for civic and social progress justifies us in the appeal for support and co-operation.

Neither then nor since did I make any public rejoinder to such newspaper attacks or anonymous letter-writers, although I seldom failed to reply to sincere critics, conversationally or through correspondence. Friendly and constructive criticism I have always regarded as something to be grateful for and to profit by. Moreover, experience proves affirmation to be better than denial, demonstration better than defense, formative thought, speech, and action than reformatory effort, however necessary they may be.

This attitude succeeded in winning recognition which more than disproved and rebuked defamation. Influential newspapers promptly came to our defense in editorial comments such as this one: "The ignorant or designing abuse which has recently been wantonly heaped upon these little groups of citizens in settlements is as grotesquely absurd as it is outrageously unjust." Better still were the unsolicited requests we received to be interviewed. Opportunity and material were thus furnished for reporters to describe the aims, methods, and results of the settlement work and to explain the teaching which it exemplified. Many illustrated articles, generously spaced, fairly and fully interpreted our work in narrative form. The *Chicago Daily News* helped most of all by assigning to me a column on its editorial page every Saturday. Meanwhile, our settlement monthly, *The Commons*, combined with *Charities*, the publication of the New York City Charity Organization Society, to develop the *Survey*, long since accredited as the leading authoritative journal covering current developments on the entire field of social work.

Despite persistently continued attempts, earlier and later, to cut off financial support, responses to our appeals, made almost exclusively through correspondence, slowly but steadily increased. Had not a large proportion of these earlier responses come from other towns and cities farther afield, our initial efforts could not have grown sufficiently to attract many more and the larger contributions from Chicago and its suburbs. Even yet the budget is covered annually by about six hundred contributors, some of whom are scattered over a score of states, although four-fifths of our contributed income now comes from the metropolitan area and a goodly proportion from or through our trustees. The personal solicitation for the erection of the new building exacted of me more sacrifice than anything else called for. Alone at first, and almost to the last, I had to solicit persons with whom I was very slightly acquainted, if at all. Lack of confidence in my ability to make an impression was so great as sometimes to turn my feet away from office thresholds, although no such heart-failing was experienced in meeting other exactions.

The need of an endowment was increasingly emphasized by the fear which haunts faith that illness or accident might interrupt or end the continuous personal endeavor to raise funds, while pressed so hard by professorial and other exactions. It was therefore with a thrill of new confidence in ultimate success that the first announcement of an initial contribution toward an endowment fund was unexpectedly received. It came to me over the telephone from Dr. Frank Wakeley Gunsaulus, whose early and continuous fellowship relieved a loneliness under the solitary load. Informing me of a bequest in the last will of one of his merchant parishioners he said it was due to one of the newspaper attacks that had been made upon us, which had so outraged his parishioner that he had added ten thousand dollars to the fifteen-thousand-dollar bequest which he intended to leave Chicago Commons, and also added another five thousand dollars to his bequest to Hull House, since Miss Jane Addams had been slandered by the same editorial.

The occasion taken to discredit us was the hanging of four young bandits for the crime of robbery and murder. Although it occurred in a part of the city far distant from us and although we had never even heard of these criminals before the commission of their crime, the editorial comment on their fate had the hardihood to assert that at a certain stage of their youthful waywardness they visited Chicago Commons and were inoculated with anarchism by me! My lifelong practice never to defend myself from such slanders in the public press, but to depend for defense upon their incongruity with personal character and the spirit of our public work, was all the more justified by this strange experience.

The largest gift to the endowment fund surprised us almost as dramatically. A trust company announced over the telephone that Chicago Commons was one of ten beneficiaries of a memorial fund in honor of the donor's parents, Eli B. and Harriet B. Williams. A few days before, Hobart W. Williams, the old gentleman who founded this fund, devised still larger

gifts to the University of Chicago and other institutions in
Illinois. Never having seen or even heard of him, I sought his
home in Connecticut to thank him for his public benefactions.
After seeking in vain to locate his residence by telephoning
and by inquiring of some residents of the little town where he
lived, I was directed by the post-mistress where to find him.
The personal appearance of the old man of nearly eighty
years matched well the plain village house in which he lived,
both typical of an interior New England locality. Diffident
and shy in manner, scant and hesitant in speech, ill at ease in
company, he was yet the captain of his own soul and fortune.
His only response to my grateful congratulations upon his
generous loyalty to his native city and state was to remark:
"As the money came from Chicago and Illinois it should return there," adding almost in a whisper, "I am glad to have it
do any good."

That a man so little known in the village town where he
lived his quiet almost recluse life for nearly half his many
years, and still more unknown in the great city which he
visited only occasionally on business errands, should come to
Chicago to make these entirely unexpected beneficent gifts is
nothing less than an idyl of America's simplest life. By returning property accumulated by the growth of a great city
around and over his father's farm, whose many acres had long
since been a most valuable part of the city's main business
section, this last surviving heir was prompted only by his
"New England conscience" to deal justly with the public
claims to the "unearned increment" of which he probably
had never heard. His Chicago attorney who drafted the legal
document devising the fund aided him in selecting its beneficiaries by making some of them known to him. Two or
three years later his body was brought to his native soil to be
laid alongside his father and mother—to whose memory
rather than to his own he had left so much to benefit the on-
coming generations of his native state and city.

The additions to the endowment fund have come from the
gifts and bequests of our trustees and other citizens of such
character and standing as to give the highest indorsement of
the spirit and service of Chicago Commons and to express

most significantly their confidence in the future of the settlement movement. Most of them, having co-operated as trustees or advisers, were prompted to assure the development and permanency of its public service by thus attesting their personal knowledge of its worth. Outstanding among them was Victor Fremont Lawson, not so much for the amount as for the continuity of his support through more than thirty years, and still more for opening the editorial page of the *Chicago Daily News*, which he owned and edited, to my freely expressed comments on current events from the settlement point of view every Saturday for twenty-eight years.

CHAPTER XXIV

THE SETTLEMENT'S DISTINCTIVE FUTURE

AMONG the influences exerted by the settlement which stand attested as essential is the reflex influence of its spirit upon the life of its workers and upon the ideals and methods of religious bodies. Residence in a settlement brings to many of its workers a crisis in their spiritual experience. Facing actual conditions which they can neither tolerate nor eliminate, they may at first impatiently feel driven away from what seem to be temporizing efforts merely to ameliorate the effects of insufferable evils, the eradication of which appeals only for radical action. Experience demonstrates opportunism in action to be the only practical way of realizing idealistic hopes for progress. Sooner or later faith and hope, essentially if not avowedly religious, prove to be the only alternative to despair. Such has been the experience of most of the many settlement residents of widely divergent antecedents and convictions with whom I have been affiliated. Recognizing and respecting religious and other differences, the settlement aims to offer common ground to all in their own and other groups, where without compromise of principle or preference their members can meet, mingle, and exchange values in co-operation for the common good. In so doing they learn to emphasize the universal in distinction from the exclusive, the essential above the accidental and circumstantial, what is common to all humanity above everything that separates fellow-men.

Respectful toward the distinct prerogatives and functions of the church and the synagogue, the settlement never claims to substitute anything for them, much less to supersede them. On the other hand, it is surely no discredit to church or mission that it is not and cannot be a settlement, in strict accordance with its original purpose. Each would abandon its distinct function if it attempted to fulfil that of the other. If a church ceased to press the propaganda of its faith, it would cease to be a church of that faith. If the settlement enlisted in propaganda for any one cult or creed, it would forfeit its prerogative of being common ground, a clearing house, a cooperative center of the whole community, and also would be surely ostracized or boycotted. Many communities would thereby lose their only place of assembly where those of all faiths and none, of all parties and classes, can fellowship and work together for the common welfare.

The settlement, therefore, is shut up to one of two courses: it must either try to take the whole community along with it as far as its groups will go together, stopping short of divisive points in religion, or be content to go with far fewer as much farther as it might wish. It would run the risk of having no following at all, in case the racial diversity and transformation of the community become more rapid and radical. The broadly religious spirit shared by Protestant, Catholic, Jewish, and ethical affiliations is shared by the settlement also. But it can offer no creed or ritual as a common denominator relating them to each other. The church, on the other hand, accepts those who will go farther and leads them as far as it can get them to go in the direction of its distinctive tenets. The settlement comprehends and unites all these groups, and others besides, on the common ground and with the all-embracing framework of neighborship and fellow-citizenship.

There is no reason why this periphery of a circle should be discredited for not being one of the greater segments which converge toward a supreme center. There is no more reason why a settlement's right to be and room to work should be challenged because it is not a church or mission than that a public school should be denied its function because it is not a parochial school, or that a parish should be discounted because it is not organized as the ward of a city. No more should the church communion be minimized because it is not the community, or the ecclesiastical denomination suffer from invidious comparison because it is not the body politic.

Church and settlement, however, may each contribute to the other's fulfilment of its own function.

Churches necessarily divide a community by the very depth of the religious conviction which their denominational differences emphasize. These differences are more persistently divisive than those of party or race. So at least we have found them to be in the neighborhood of Chicago Commons. Therefore no one of the churches nor all of them together can become the center at which a whole heterogeneous population will or can come into fellowship or co-operation. But the loyalty to ideals, to truth, and to standards which the church begets in each true member is susceptible of being developed into those neighborhood, social, and civic loyalties which the settlement weaves into community spirit and action, from which too many churches stand detached. Thus at Chicago Commons, under the same roof, on the same common ground, and on the same day have statedly gathered in separate groups and rooms a Protestant church and many Roman Catholic orders; Armenians, converts of the foreign missions in Turkey and others who adhere to the old Armenian church; Greeks, some of whom are still sons of the Orthodox Greek church, others who belong to the old Uniat branch of the Roman Catholic church, and still others who came from their fatherland as Protestant converts. But they could not be drawn or driven together in any religious service, yet representatives of all of them could unite as neighbors and fellow-citizens.

Sacred is the confidence reposed in the settlement by parents of so many faiths in committing their children to our care and guidance. Deeply would any parent resent the breach of such a trust if those to whose social care his or her children had been committed were found to be covertly using the settlement building and its neighborhood fellowships and activities to estrange or detach the child from the faith of its parents. On the other hand, it is entirely fair, and highly desirable, for a church or a mission openly and avowedly to use social methods and equipment as tributary to its distinctively religious purposes and services. But the church which adopts such social methods does not thereby become a settle-

ment and should not, in justice either to itself or to the settlement, call itself such. Recognizing the "diversities of operation" of "the same spirit," the church may wisely and well
acknowledge that its own organization can seldom be considered the best executive of its own ideals. Relying upon
other agencies to carry on and out many things it initiates
and helps support, the church may gladly inspire individuals
and groups to co-operate with them in resisting the evils and
realizing the common welfare of the whole community. Certainly citizens who face the stern facts of the racial, sectarian,
and class cleavages in our unprecedentedly mixed population
should appreciate the ministries of understanding, mediation,
and good will fulfilled by the settlements sufficiently to safeguard them from being misunderstood and suspected because
of any confusing misuse of their name.

In distinction from sectarian propaganda and its ecclesiastical expression religion finds broad yet intensive expression
in settlement life and work. The religion of relationship, Godward and manward, is interpreted, exemplified, and incar-
nated by the settlement household. It stands for nothing
higher and nothing less than to realize those divine ideals of
relationship between God and fellow-men which both Judaism and all forms of Christianity seek to inspire. But where
they cannot be preached out and prayed in, the settlement
worker can live them out and love them in. Settlements express their religious spirit in deed if not in words; by reverential ministries to the commonest human needs; by simplify-
ing, sweetening, strengthening, and fulfilling the common relationships of the family, the workaday and the community
life; by applying the common faith to the social conditions of
the common life; by inspiring and encouraging each neighbor's development of his or her own ideals, where those of
others cannot be superimposed—thus in Channing's fine
phrase, and with Felix Adler, "letting the spiritual, unbidden and unconscious, grow up through the common."[1]

Deeper and more far reaching than any other settlement
influence has been the effect of its permeating spirit upon
religious feeling, thought, and work. This influence has medi-

[1] *The Reconstruction of the Spiritual Ideal.* The Hibbert Lectures, 1923.

ated between form and spirit, the material and spiritual, the
secular and religious. It has discriminated between the ex-
crescent and the elemental, the divisive circumstantials and
the unifying essentials, sectarianism and catholicity. It has
helped ally the church and the community and to relate
religion to the life of the world. Reciprocally interdependent
and serviceable to each other, therefore, are the church and
the settlement both in realizing the social ideals they hold in
common and in the co-operative service they may render in
their distinctive spheres of influence and action.

In rounding out its first half-century, the settlement movement raises questions as to how it may meet the needs for its
work in the future. But its experience through all these past
years challenges any doubt either of the continuance of the
needs which called for its initiative and development or of its
way of meeting them. In prompting other groups and agencies to enter its field, the settlement has never feared nor failed
to welcome their co-operation, nor to turn over to one and
another of them what they might do better or on a larger
scale. Even so, the settlement may still supplement their
work. Public schools and other buildings may be used by the
neighborhoods as the settlement houses now are, but they
will not shelter a resident household of neighborly workers,
unless teachers unite to live among their pupils in settlement
households of their own. Community centers may undertake
many of the organized activities now conducted by the settlement. Then the settlement, relieved of the expenditure of
time and money thereby exacted, may be left free to let its
resident workers be more to their neighbors personally and in
their homes, and be better equipped for more thorough investigation of social, civic, and industrial conditions. District charity visitors may fill out their case-work schedules
accurately, but the settlement group, more than fulfilling the
function of resident friendly visitors, may add what no investigator who comes and goes can acquire for understanding the
whole human situation involved. Universities may forward
their own and their city's interests by co-operating with civic
and social agencies as laboratories for research and fields for
practice, yet settlements will continue to be outposts for in-

sight and outlook such as no laboratory can claim to be. Their human touch is a medium of observation still quite distinct from all laboratory apparatus for social research and education. Churches are equipping and extending their ministries with social-service buildings and commissions, but the settlement offers common ground for making common cause to those who may act together when and where they can neither believe nor worship together.

But if these agencies should attain such qualities, and no longer need the co-operation of the settlements, they would have faith, as they always have had, in their own capacity to find something that needed to be undertaken. Daring to fail in seeking to demonstrate what might or might not prove worthy of acceptance and support, they have not feared to lose their life in finding it.

Even though many of the functions which the settlements have hitherto fulfilled should prove to be outgrown, as a better social order eliminated the need of them, there will always remain limitations of human nature that will continue to call for such unique service as the settlements have effectively rendered. Between groups separated by natural or acquired distinctions, living links such as settlement households provide will be needed. As long as there are differences of race, class, sect, and sectional areas which estrange and divide communities, so long will the settlement's ministries of understanding and interpretation be needed and supported; so long will its distinctive group be called to live and work between the lines of these divergent groups to mediate mutual understanding and co-operation for the common good. As long as there are self-centered or antisocial individuals and groups, so long will it be necessary to develop social consciousness through such an influence as the settlement exerts upon older and younger members of family and neighborhood groups. As long as the spiritual potentialities of the individual, the group, and the community are known not to be fully expressed, so long may the settlement inspire the spiritual element in each to grow up, unconsciously and unbidden, through the common round of life and the daily task—thus religiously supplementing the church's bidding for a definite acceptance of its faith, attested and expressed by a sacramental act.

PART V
THE EVOLVING SOCIAL CONSCIOUSNESS

CHAPTER XXV

FROM INDIVIDUALISTIC PREPOSSESSIONS

I FIRST experienced as a child what I learned in manhood from books, that the consciousness of self is born and grows as one becomes conscious of other selves. My young mother died in her twenty-sixth year, only a year after giving me birth in 1851—sinking under the double strain of keeping her puny babe alive and nursing my father to health from a long and dangerous illness. I have no memory of her brooding love and her gentle touch. And yet I owe her at least the beginnings of that development which Alfred Tennyson's seer-like insight visioned long before modern psychologists scientifically described it, in his well-known lines:

> The baby new to earth and sky,
> What time his tender palm is pressed
> Against the circle of the breast,
> Has never thought that "this is I."

> But as he grows he gathers much,
> And learns the use of "I" and "me,"
> And finds "I am not what I see,
> And other than the things I touch:"

> So rounds he to a separate mind
> From whence clear memory may begin,
> As through the frame that binds him in
> His isolation grows defined.

It was through my earliest and continuous companionship with my father, William J. R. Taylor, whose gentle, strong spirit was as motherly as it was fatherly, that I "rounded to a separate mind." I cannot recall any consciousness of existence through childhood, and very little ever since, apart from the home life of the family group. It has always been as truly a part of me as I have been of it. Outside influences intervened less through the earlier years of my boyhood when frail health kept me within the doors of our Philadelphia home through much of every winter. The beauty and fragrance of early spring flowers, which greeted my first trips with my father to the city market, still linger in my memory as a part of the brighter horizon of my midcity life. Joyous memories of a city boy's paradise, lost and regained, still hover over Bishop Hill at New Brunswick, New Jersey, where my seven cousins and six of theirs welcomed me as their summer play-mate to the spacious grounds of their beautiful homes. Across the span of forty years Isabella Bishop brought the charm of our early youth into the comradeship of our later life.

Very gradually the consciousness of selfhood as separable from the home life dawned upon me. The first separating streaks of that dawn came to me when I went to a small private school, where I was seated alongside of other boys and away from my elder brother, Van Campen Taylor. My first playmate in the neighborhood of our Philadelphia home was a little Italian boy whose difference from me disclosed my own difference from others. I remember to have felt alone when on our family summer outings the open sky and the spaces of the sea seemed to single me out even from those nearest and dearest.

Never was I so conscious of isolation and loneliness as at church. At home, religion always blended with our family life. We had family worship daily, with responsive reading, Bible stories, and the singing of hymns. Sunday at home was different from other days, chiefly in having more companion-ship with my father, and stepmother, my mother's sister who mothered my older brother and myself as tenderly as she did her own two boys, so that I would never have known that she had not borne me had I not been told. Sunday afternoon was the gladdest time of the week, toward which we four boys looked forward joyously, not only because our treats of candy or fruits, of a new toy or picture-book, were kept in store for that day, but the more because in the afternoon and early evening play and merriment mingled with instruction, story-telling, vesper hymns, and dear home-companionship. The Sabbath was more of a holy day because it was so much of a home holiday. Religion was the more real because it was what we all shared at home, as we did everything else. Because of the sacrament of the daily meal at home, the sacramental table was the more homelike at church. We were brought up never to know any time or act that was not as religious as any other.

Yet at church I felt separated even from the family, although we sat together in the same pew. Even as a boy I came to be a "soul" at church. And yet the soul was not me myself, but some part of me more precious than all else in me. Although my father was in the pulpit which I first faced and until I was ten years old, even he when robed in his black gown and standing behind the marble pulpit seemed different from what he was at home. On the wall of the church I attended in later boyhood the Ten Commandments were inscribed. Although their golden letters shone on a background of heavenly blue, yet their tablets faced me like the stone tables of Sinai, casting the shadow of fear over the "new commandment" to love one another, which, with other gentle promises, supplemented the law with the glad tidings of the gospel.

The preaching seemed sterner than my father's, perhaps because it was that of any other man. The pulpit seemed more the judgment bar than the mercy seat. Some preachers seemed to be more like prosecutors of their fellow-men before the high court of heaven than messengers of heaven's peace and good will, calling for repentance. At the communion service, which was held every three months, the communicants were seated in the middle block of pews in order to facilitate the distribution of the bread and wine. To make room for them non-communicants were expected to occupy other pews. When at twelve years of age I took my seat across the aisle from my parents, that aisle seemed as wide as the gulf fixed between the "saved" and the "lost" and as long as eternity. Yet the old Genevan sacramental liturgy, in prescribed use by all Reformed Dutch churches, had many winsome words which then and ever since have won my heart's response and hope. Although it sternly "fenced" the sacrament against all defiled with very specifically listed sins, yet this warning was said not to be designed to "deject the contrite hearts of the faithful, as if none might come to the supper of the Lord but those who are without sin." Therefore it helped me to "rest assured that no sin or infirmity which still remaineth against our will in us can hinder us from being received of God in mercy, and from being made worthy partakers of this Heavenly meat and drink." These oft-repeated words became the straight gate to church membership, through which I passed farther on the narrow way, in which I had been brought up from birth to live and grow.

What really sent me across the aisle to take my place with the family at the communion table came from my father, in the form of a tenderly yearning letter, which I found on my bureau at bedtime one evening. Although he was at home, he considerately made his appeal to me silently when it could reach me alone. It was simply the affectionate expression of his hope that I might feel like taking upon myself the vows which he and my mother had taken for me at my baptism in infancy. When admitted to the communion by the elders of the church, my parents' fulfilment of their baptismal vows to bring me up "in the fear and admonition of the Lord" was taken for granted. Therefore I was asked only such questions as a boy fourteen years old could intelligently answer, if not overawed by the procedure. Had I been a candidate for adult baptism, even at this early age, my assent would have been required to "all the articles of the Christian religion as they are taught here in this Christian church." Yet they were all far beyond the understanding and experience of a child, as I realized later when welcoming unbaptized children to the care and fellowship of the household of faith. Had I been asked as a prerequisite to ordination to give my own assent to these very same articles I could have done so neither intelligently nor indeed conscientiously if even then I could have understood them.

The fear that was driven home to me by being constantly reminded that I was on a lifelong probation made me afraid of myself lest I might make the fatal misstep unwarily, through weakness or waywardness. It was cruel enough to be silently reminded of it from reading misapplied Bible texts, but still more heartless to have it sung into you by those who with unheeding cheerfulness sang:

> Lo! on a narrow neck of land,
> 'Twixt two unbounded seas I stand,
> Yet how insensible!
> A point of time, a moment's space,
> Removes me to yon heavenly place,
> Or shuts me up in hell.

In our collections of Sunday-school hymns, though entitled *The Golden Chain* and *Happy Voices*, the mortuary hymns attuned to death and the world beyond far outnumbered those in any way referring to the life we youngsters were just beginning to live. We sang "There is a happy land," but it was "far, far away where saints in glory stand"; "Joyfully, joyfully, onward we move," but it was "bound for the land of bright spirits above"; "Beautiful Zion," but "built above"; "Shall we gather", but it was "at the river"; "River of Death, thy streams I see"; "Around the throne of God in Heaven, thousands of children stand," but children "whose sins were all forgiven." Yet each of us was supposed to sing as though gladly intent only upon leaving this green earth, in these un-childlike strains:

> I'm but a stranger here,
> Heaven is my home,
> Earth is a desert drear
> Heaven is my home.

> Do not detain me for I am going,
> To where the fountains are ever flowing,
> I'm a pilgrim and I'm a stranger
> I can tarry, I can tarry but a night.

Few though cherished were the hymns referring to Christ's life on earth or ours. At Christmas we sang:

> We three kings of Orient are
> Bearing gifts, we traverse afar,
> O'er field and fountain, moor and mountain,
> Following yonder star.

Of Jesus' life we sang as it was lived on earth:

> Galilee, Bright Gallilee,
> Hallowed thoughts we turn to thee,
> Woven through thy history
> Shines the charming mystery.

Of our own lives we sang even less, but loved to join in singing:

> Savior like a Shepherd lead us,
> Much we need thy tender care.
> In thy pleasant pastures feed us
> For our use thy folds prepare.

Closer to our ways and waywardness came the mellowing refrain:

> Kind words can never die.

My Sunday-school teacher, John Van Nest, did much to make religion seem to have more to do with our life in this world. He was a plain carpenter. His character and speech were as upright and downright as his daily work. Although he knew little of the Bible as a student, yet he knew it well as the way of life. He showed us boys the difference between right and wrong and why we needed help from above to make the choice between them. My respect for his manly Christian character and my gratitude for the interest he took in us have stayed by me and influenced me ever since.

The only books I remember to have read in early boyhood were *The Peep of Day* and *Precept upon Precept*, one of which glorified the bears that ate up the children who called Elisha "bald head"; *Reading without Tears*, which did not stop the flow of mine; *Ministering Children*, which made helpfulness winsome; and *The Shady Side*, which strangely was read to us by mother, though it told the doleful story of a pastor's unhappily impoverished home. There were no periodicals for children's reading, except the Sunday-school papers, which were of the same tone and type. Picture prints were few in these papers and fewer still in the books for children. Such as there were had little to do with fiction or fact. Two sets of books, the "Jonas" and the "Rollo" series, were cherished for the stories they told of children and their travels, with illustrations which illumined the text, however sparse and crude they might have been. The rediscovery of child psychology since Pestalozzi and Froebel led the way of the school and the church to impart what they have to give "as," Jesus said, "a little child receives," thereby creating a happier childhood and a new hope for the race.

While all these anachronisms and paradoxes contradict the whole modern psychology of child study and religious education, yet even such teaching of religion is to be credited with a distinctive educational value. What the higher education does for the few in creating the capacity to detach one's self from others and from one's immediate surroundings religion does for the many in doing much more. It summons the single self before the one God. It faces the soul with time and eternity. It bears home to the conscience the sense of individual accountability. It leaves us alone to reckon with destiny. The experience of spiritual detachment thus begotten by religion, and the capacity for intellectual detachment created by higher education, are essential to full-orbed consciousness of self, fellow-man, and God. Without it the individual is so closely identified with his immediate surroundings as to be unable to distinguish himself or anyone else from them. Only as one is thus intellectually or spiritually enabled to back away from self can one judge one's self. Only as one is capable of viewing his own times in the light of other ages, in contrast or comparison with the experiences of other generations, can contemporary movements be understood and their achievements estimated.

However these early impressions at church might have repelled me from entering the ministry, yet I cannot remember that I ever thought or wished to prepare for any other calling. My "call" to it must have come through influences as unconsciously exerted as they were received. All along those early years, and ever since, the life and teaching of Jesus were within reach of the heart's understanding, if not within the comprehension of the intellect. His communion with God as his father and his bidding us call him "our Father" brought the only idea of God I have ever been able to attain, at least within the range of apprehension. By his own sonship Jesus taught how much more fatherly the heavenly Father is than the best of earthly fathers can be. Since, therefore, "like as a father" God was shown to love, pity, and care for us all,

I learned to measure him up by "how much more" he must be than my father.

Thus my father became my theology, and his life and love the trellis over which the vine of mine grew upward—above all doubts that come when knowledge vanishes away, above all fears that arise when prophecies fail. Therefore those whose earthly parents are unknown or bear no resemblance to the heavenly fatherhood have ever appealed to me for suspense of judgment, patient consideration, a love that never fails, and hope that cannot make the heart sick by being long deferred.

The sanction thus given to my natural inclination to follow my father must have been strengthened by what came down the line of descent to me from my forebears. Although scattered in several widely separated centers, their professional achievements seemed to belong to, and be shared by, all of us. Callings to the medical, legal, and ministerial professions seemed to link together the generations in our family. I have always been grateful that my grandparents lived long enough for me to be very fond of them and to profit very much by my companionship with them. My mother's parents were farmer folks, Cowenhoven by name, descendants of old Holland-Dutch settlers of the soil. My father's father, Benjamin C. Taylor, was the son of parents born in England. Although he might have shared the success of their pioneer importing enterprise in Philadelphia, he felt called to the ministry when at school and prepared at college and seminary to enter that of the Reformed Dutch church. He was in the closing years of his widely honored pastoral service extending over fifty-eight years, through forty-two of which he served one historic church. My grandmother's father and grandfather, and her brother also, had served the old Dutch church in its ministry. So in this "apostolic succession" I found myself one of the fifth generation of ministers, if the transmission is conceded to have come through her.[1]

[1] One hundred years ago, in 1828, my grandfather, Benjamin Cook Taylor, became the pastor of the Bergen Reformed Dutch Church, located on the New Jersey side of the Hudson River, opposite New York City. The church was then one hundred and sixty-eight years old, its founders having taxed themselves 417 *guilders* to erect their first house of worship, which was built in 1662. In his *Annals of the Classis and*

mented with only a very few occasional visits to the scantily equipped observatory. Systems of government were taught, from the top down, while the practice of citizenship was ignored. Economics whipped facts into line with theory, ignoring industrial history and human experience. Ethics was almost exclusively individual, neither the group mind nor conscience having found expression in social psychology.

Even in the seminary curriculum the Bible as literature, or as a guide to character and conduct, failed to find space, which was chiefly devoted to defending and interpreting a "rule of faith" or a system or doctrine. The "natural" was held to be antithetic, if not antagonistic, to the religious. Nature, in man, in flora, and fauna, and even in the stars above the green earth, was ever subordinated to, if not considered subversive of, revelation. It was seldom or never referred to as revealing the invisible, except when we read in Hebrew some of the psalms and prophets. Indeed, as late as the nineties, in a seminary chapel prayer I have heard the Creator thanked that "we do not have to deal with dull, dead matter." This same father in Israel also defined homiletics as "mathematics applied to preaching." Preparation for preaching but not for teaching emphasized the lack of knowledge of religious pedagogy, or attention to this primary function of the church and its ministry. The dictation method of lecturing and the reproductive recitation laid no stress upon, and gave little incentive to, collateral reading, original inquiry, firsthand observation, or independent thought upon the part of the student. Such curricula were as dominant in other colleges and seminaries of the period as in Rutgers College and in the Theological Seminary of the Reformed Church in America at New Brunswick, New Jersey, from which I was graduated in 1870 and in 1873.

In the breach between religion and life, church and world, stood the pastor of my college and seminary years, Dr. Chester D. Hartranft. In his learning and preaching he towered as far above us all as he did in his height. Although in the pulpit he was as much of an ecclesiastic as any of his older predecessors, yet his culture and human interests were more varied and profound than those of anyone else in town or gown.

From both he won devoted response to his musical leadership. The Choral Society, which he personally conducted, rallied the young people from within and beyond his parish. His effort to establish a conservatory of music enlisted the personal co-operation of leaders in the musical profession from New York City and elsewhere, and attracted students from near and far. Profoundly impressive were the church services at which the oratorios were rendered. In Holy Week Haydn's cantata, "The Seven Words," was sung by a large chorus, supplemented only by the reading of these last sayings of Christ from the Cross; and at Christmas, when Handel's *Messiah* began to be to me a fifth gospel, as it has been ever since.

Still more humanly was my conception of the Christian life broadened beyond the limitations of church fellowship by being taken into a personal friendship such as this reserved man could maintain with very few. It grew apace during my seminary years, from the time he pulled the stroke oar and I the bow oar in the six-oared shell of the "Septemviri" boat club, which he christened and captained on the Raritan River. More even than then I felt myself to be the lightweight of the crew when called to keep pace with his mighty stroke in pulling Hartford Seminary into the current of modern scholarship and life.

Through all the intervening fifteen years, however, I keenly suffered from having been deprived of such academic studies as would have interpreted fellow-men and Mother Nature; studies which long since have been included in the curricula of my own college and seminary and in those of every other institution claiming to give a liberal education. It required a trying experience in preaching to make religion relevant to the lives of my fellow-men, as I found them to be lived in the real world. The painful consciousness of failing to make religion as real in my preaching as I did in the personal contacts of my pastoral work, in my Bible class, the week-day and Sunday-evening meetings, carried this pulpit inhibition through these earlier years into most of my subsequent experience. From any such self-conscious obsession I have been free in speaking from the platform and writing for the press.

I account for these contrasting experiences partly by the extent to which I personally appropriated the divine spokesmanship with which the preacher was theoretically invested. It let go of me, however, when feeling free to be just human in my face-to-face, heart-to-heart contacts with fellow-men, when talking with them, or addressing them from the platform and through the press.

The transitions from a Pennsylvania city and a New Jersey college town to a country parish in the Hudson River valley; again from this rural family community of Holland-Dutch descent to Hartford, one of New England's oldest and most influential cities; and thence to Chicago, the metropolis of the great West, and to the hidden heart of its cosmopolitan population—may seem too radically changeful to have been in any sense a progressively developing experience.

There were, however, overlapping experiences which prepared the way from one to another of these transitions. The most perilous of them all, that from personal to ecclesiastical relations, from evolving student life to the ministerial status, was fortunately made less formal and more humanly real at my ordination service. Professionalism had been emphasized at every step between the seminary and the ministry. For licensure to preach I had passed a public examination by one Reformed church classis in Hebrew, Greek, biblical criticism, and church history. To qualify for ordination, I had been examined by another classis in theology, liturgics, pastoral care, and ecclesiastical polity. In both examinations I was expected to conform to the standards of the church and did. But it was more by rote than by thinking my own way through to these formally accepted conclusions, which were then far beyond my intellectual grasp or spiritual experience. They included the Belgic Confession of 1561, containing 37 articles; the canons of the Synod of Dort, 59 in number, which were ratified in 1618; the Heidelberg Catechism, drafted in 1563, covering 129 questions and answers. The liturgy, derived from Calvin's forms for his congregations at Strasburg in 1541 and at Geneva in 1543, was revised and adopted by the Holland churches in 1568 and 1574. The only touch upon the heart which I found any of these articles to have was in the first question and answer of the Catechism, which read: "What is thy only comfort in life and death?" "That I with body and soul, both in life and death, am not my own but belong unto my faithful Savior, Jesus Christ." Thus prefaced the standards of the Reformed church in the Netherlands and in America have always seemed at least somewhat more interpretable to the heart, and transmutable into personal experience, than those of Westminster, which start with a challenge to the head so abstract and philosophical as to daunt the wisest brain: "What is the chief end of man?"

Engraved upon my heart from earliest years, and later inspiring the evolution of social consciousness, are these words of the sacramental liturgy, which became symbolic of the body politic, as well as of the mystical body, in which the spirit of Christ dwells on earth:

> As out of many grains one meal is ground and one bread baked, and out of many berries being pressed together one wine floweth and mixeth itself together, so shall we all, who by a true faith are ingrafted into Christ, be all together one body, through brotherly love, and not only show this in words but in very deed toward one another.[1]

My ordination service at Hopewell, New York, was a homelike occasion, but none the less churchly than it should have been. My father, Dr. William J. R. Taylor, preached the sermon; my father-in-law and beloved teacher, Professor David D. Demarest, charged the people to be gracious and helpful to me; and my venerable grandfather, Dr. Benjamin C. Taylor, offered the ordaining prayer, while he and all the ministers present laid their hands upon my head as I knelt. These very human expressions of faith, hope, and fellowship, not only by my kinsmen, but also by all others participating in the service, impressed me with the fact that these and most other churchmen were more humanly Christian in spirit than their creeds. My good people also made it their family affair, by

[1] Remarkably similar phrasing is found in *The Teaching of the Twelve Apostles*, dating prior to 100 A.D., but not discovered until 1873. Under the section devoted to the Agape and the Eucharist these words appear: "We give thanks to Thee, our Father, for the holy Vine of David. . . . . And for the broken bread, we give thanks to Thee. As this broken bread was scattered upon the mountains and gathered together became one, so let thy church be gathered together from the ends of the earth into thy kingdom."

having their whole households in attendance and by extending the hospitality which they offered their visiting guests to all present from the entire community.

Better precedents and examples could not have opened and marked my way in entering upon my ministry. Both inspiring and instructive were the evenly able and wholly devoted pulpit and pastoral ministries of my father and grandfather. The spirit of the former loomed the higher as seen from the home while he was on his daily round and special tasks. Two features of my grandfather's ministry valuably exemplified to me his never failing consciousness of ministering to the community through the ordinances and service of the church. The accuracy with which he kept its records gave them an authority which was never challenged in the probate and other proceedings of the courts, in which they were frequently cited as evidence. Perhaps on this account he was invited by the court to offer the invocation at the opening of Hudson County's new courthouse and jail. So impressed were all who heard his "solemn and appropriate address to the throne of grace" that members of the bar, the Grand Jury, the Board of Free Holders, and other citizens united in requesting a copy of his prayer for publication, to inspire them with the highest ideals in the discharge of their respective public duties. As published in the proceedings of that occasion, the prayer justified their request by its reverent and pertinent petitions for the maintenance of justice, for the righteous judgment of the judges, for the guidance of juries, for the fidelity of lawyers, and for all to whom justice would be administered. As considerate yet more unusual were his thanksgivings for the good work and the health of the workmen, contractors, architects, and inspectors who had been employed in the construction of the building.

With such background in recent and long-past memories I was the better enabled to recognize the emphases which, in significant succession, were laid upon the family, the neighborhood, and the citizenship of the local community, both as the fields and resources of ministerial and church work. From the first each one of these relationships asserted itself as a factor that had to be reckoned with and might be utilized.

Later all three were discovered to be the primary units of human association, which are woven through all sociological theory and social action.

The interrelated Hopewell parishioners emphasized, as my early home life had, the family unit as primary also in religious work. In calling upon every family in the entire community as the pastor of its one church, and in using the neighborhood schoolhouses regularly for religious and other occasions, I was the better prepared to carry from house to house the religious sanction with which each of these human relationships is invested. Neither then, nor since in cities, have I failed to feel the shepherding of the family flock and the promotion of good neighborship to be as great an opportunity as it is an imperative obligation. Fresh and grateful are my memories of the personal fellowships I had with the whole family on each farm, with the women and the children at the house, the farmer on the field, the hired man at the barn, as well as with his family in the tenant-house on the rear lot. Still precious are the recollections of the confidential counselings with parents about their children; with the boy or girl leaving home for high school, college, or business; with young couples about to be married, or when visiting in their new home after the birth of the first child. Still sacred are the companionships with the bereaved in the loneliness of their grief.

Reverential, yet inspiring, were my friendships with the aged people whose gray heads surrounded the pulpit, to which they voted to call me, a youth of only twenty-two years of age. For the intimacies to which they welcomed me at their quiet homes I was better fitted by my fondness for my two grandfathers, one of whom had been a farmer and accustomed to have too much his own way with his family and hired help, as some of these farmers had.

Not a few families of my Hopewell parish, in the old township of East Fishkill, lived upon the very soil which their ancestors had settled, the original "patents" and deeds to which were still held by their descendants. It is not perhaps surprising that some of them felt like lords of the manor, or that their family customs, fixed by long tradition, should yield slowly and reluctantly to changing conditions. Some of these customs, however, were obstructive to the attempt to adjust the church's efforts in endeavoring to serve the whole community. The tenure of the larger farms had always passed from the head of the family to the eldest son, by a custom almost as exacting as the old English law of primogeniture. While it was often unjust to the daughters, the younger sons frequently secured the division of some of the land among them.

Custom also restricted any marked variation or advance in the tilling of the soil or the operation of the dairy. Consequently the subdivided land lacked intensive cultivation and therefore yielded diminishing returns in crops and in income to the household of the younger generation. Gradually some of the tenant farm hands succeeded in working the land on shares until they acquired ownership of a farm after years of struggle to pay off heavy mortgages.

In offering seats and welcome to these permanent but "outside" landowners, as well as to the many families of the poorly paid and badly housed field hands, the church had many difficulties. The most obstructive and persistent of these obstacles was the family ownership of its ancestral pews. They were held as much in "fee simple" as their hereditary farms and homesteads. These pews in the church were willed to the heirs with the estate. Those who inherited two or more pews privately rented those they did not occupy. Requests to return these rentals to the church, or to increase their subscriptions for its support, were refused by some, even after they removed their residence to neighboring or distant cities. One man of large means based his refusal upon his reluctance to part with his pew "as it was the last piece of real estate he owned in Dutchess County." An elder upon selling his farm and removing from the parish somewhat indignantly regarded such an appeal, even though he himself had been impatient over the difficulty of raising the very small amount required to cover the annual budget of the church. Nevertheless, he retorted that "he might as well have been asked to give his horse."

The only escape from this absentee landlordism, which held

the most desirable space in the church partly vacant or deprived its treasury of the income from the most rentable
pews, was to utilize the galleries, which had always been free.
To do this effort was made to inspire those who had no other
church within reach to make room for themselves in this one.
They did it by lowering the ascending floors of the galleries
and turning their high-perched and uncomfortable seats into
the most attractive sittings. Thus it soon came to pass occasionally that more of my hearers were in the galleries than
on the ground floor, giving our Sunday assemblies a somewhat top-heavy appearance. After several years this innovation succeeded in clearing most of the first-floor space from
private ownership, so that voluntary weekly contributions
were substituted for pew rentals as the better system of
church support. It required, however, seven years of patient
diplomacy in working between the church and the community
before some of the most spiritually helpful and influential
of the newcomers, as well as many of the humbler people,
found seats in the community's only church.

These obstacles which obstructed work at the church center were largely offset by the neighborly fellowship of these
old families with each other, and with those who had come
into the neighborhood from the outside. Thus neighborship
became invested with a vital value to each individual and
every community, which I found to be equally valuable in
religious work. There were no less than eight neighborhoods
within the one hundred and twenty square miles covered
by my parish in which the people were related to each other
more than at church. So I learned that neither the church
nor the community life would be strong at the center unless
supported by the spiritual and patriotic loyalty of each lesser
neighborly group. This neighborhood fellowship centered at
its district schoolhouse. There everyone had a right to be and
was free to meet and mingle in social, recreative, and political
gatherings. Their children came to the schoolhouse as regularly to Sunday school as to the day school. Whole families
attended the monthly preaching service, held in each schoolhouse, more regularly than they came to the Sunday-morning
service at the church. Fewer but faithful souls met their

pastor also in each school district for week-night religious fellowship and instruction. Because of this warmth at the extremities, the heartbeat at the center was stronger. The centrifugal movement toward the farthest circumference and the centripetal movement toward a strong church center thus became equally important as methods of work for religious and community welfare.

Although the loss or lack of such family and neighborly unity in my two city fields made the use of these units more difficult, yet the effort to utilize them proved to be encouraging. In Hartford the little neighborly groups which gathered in the small living-rooms of family apartments sometimes yielded as large returns, for the time and energy they cost, as was gained by the far greater effort expended upon the larger gatherings. And in Chicago, the revival of neighborship through the settlement centers seemed vitally necessary to the religious stability and the social safety and progress of the city.

While striving in these ways for a more adjustable spirit among the farmer folk, the framework riveted upon my faith by my theological training remained so fixed that I have since wondered whether it did not positively obstruct my ministry of the gospel. The framework was that of the "Covenants," successively made by God with Adam, Abraham, and Christ, each representing the whole race, yet the Covenant included those few only who accepted the call from the fallen race into God's adopted family, and those whose sins were "imputed" to the Savior, and to whom his righteousness was imputed in exchange. Conscientiously and persistently I sought to realize this "plan of Salvation" and to make it real to others by preaching, teaching, and personal appeals.

But while very gradually realizing my failure to do so the personal consciousness of the personal presence of the personal Christ dawned more and more upon me, and upon others who sought to keep company with him, as the essence and effort of the Christian experience. Beholding as in a mirror the glory of his personality, the experience of being changed into the same image became more possible and actual. Being with Jesus and learning of him in going about

doing good became the simpler and more effective way to get
and live his life. Again, it was in trying to introduce him to
others, whose companionship with him I sought, that I was
led forth from a very artificial and mechanical to a more
natural and vital view of relationship with the Father. Then
it seemed too incredible for belief that any disciple of the
Elder Brother of us all should think and say what a gentle
pastor of a neighboring flock declared to me: "God, the mak-
er, is no more a Father to the sinner than a wagon-maker is
the father of the wagon he made."

As I realized God's fatherhood to all his children, deliverance came from the unreal, if not cant, misconception of
"the world" as entirely "evil" and wholly "lost," as something to be shunned while in it and fled from through life and
escaped at death. This deliverance came at first through
sharing with some of the saintliest souls I ever knew their
reverence for the world of nature as the handiwork of God;
their faith that "the earth is the Lord's and the fullness thereof, the world and they that dwell therein"; their joy in the
life that now is; their prayer and work to make "the kingdoms of this world the Kingdom of our Lord and of his
Christ." They sent me back to my Bible to learn how to
preach and teach that the world is the subject of redemption
as the object of God's love. May I be forgiven for having
preached such a sermon as my nature-loving farmer folk
once endured, on the terror of being "in the world"—the
world of nature, "red in tooth and claw," the world wholly
possessed by evil and hurrying to complete destruction—the
terror being used as a persuasive warning to risk no longer
being "without Christ."

And yet had I acted upon the knowledge then which has
since impelled me to act, in bringing church and world together, in a co-operation essential to the safety and progress
of both, these good people would have probably resented it as
an intrusion of the minister into politics and an attempt to
secularize religion. For instance, the spiritual and economic
odds were stacked against the tenantry by the wretchedly
built, poorly equipped, and rundown tenant-houses, in which
large families were so overcrowded as to imperil health and to

leave too little space for modesty or even decency. Yet had I been moved to call attention to that fact, however tactfully, it would have been resented as an impertinent interference of the *domine* with private business. Had I taken part in school meetings to secure the repair or rebuilding of the neglected schoolhouses, it would have been regarded as an intrusion upon politics, with which neither women nor ministers were then expected to meddle. Indeed, the mother of one of the most influential church families admonished me to "confine my attentions to those who paid my salary, instead of calling upon every household in the community." I meekly replied that "I presumed that I was the minister of the whole parish and never imagined that I was only the pastor of the subscription list."

It required breaches in the peaceful order of local life to impress upon me the sanctity of the common welfare, and the obligation of the ministry and the church to have a community consciousness. The first instance of lawless lack of it was brought home to my conscience by the objection of a plain farmer parishioner to the installation of an outstanding young man whose nomination for the office of deacon had been publicly announced in church. To my inquiry why he objected he laconically replied: "Because he bought his father-in-law's election as county commissioner." Upon his assurance that he would make and sustain this charge before the church officers, I personally informed the very well-connected young man of hitherto high repute that his nomination had been challenged. To my surprise he frankly admitted "handling the money." When asked if he did not know it was against the law he replied, "Yes, but they all do it." When reminded of its inconsistency with what the church stands for, he withdrew his acceptance of the nomination and with his whole influential and deeply offended family connection ceased to attend the services of the church and to contribute to its support. But several years later he and they resumed their attendance and support, he thanking me for turning him away from political practices, the prevalence of which had blinded him to the personal wrongs and public peril they involved. Yet this wrong was so generally accepted as a political party's right that a warden of the state prison, also a member of this church, did not hesitate to stand at the door of the polling place with two-dollar bills in hand which he paid out to voters as they left the polls. Upon hearing of the other case he expressed his regret that the *domine*, with whom he was personally friendly, "had interfered with politics."

Then and ever since I have always felt and often publicly insisted that it were better to have the church, or any other institution, go down with its moral standard flying at high mast than to float on any bottom with lowered ideals. For thereby the end which it claimed to serve would be sacrificed in order to maintain the means of institutional existence. And yet, the hoodwinking of conscience to evade this axiom of common honesty is strangely prevalent in high circles.

This rural experience marked the beginning of my transition from a sense of individual responsibility to a community or civic consciousness. Nevertheless this and many other intimations that as a minister I was not regarded as much of a citizen as any other man in the community always raised the question whether manhood and the ministry were incompatible. Through all the after-years I learned that a minister is only a man ministering, and that the measure of one's manhood measures his ministry. I have often wished that I might return to the family folk of my first-loved parish "to do works meet for repentance." Patient and long suffering as they must have been with my preaching, they probably would have thought even less of it and surely less of me had I known enough to serve that dear old church and its friendly community better. I have also wished that every minister might prepare for rural work by taking part of his training at an agricultural college, especially if he were city born and city bred, for no more of a greenhorn ever came from the country into the city than I was when I came from the city into the country.

It was such a heart wrench to leave this family church and community at Hopewell, after seven happy years of home life in the dear old Hopewell parsonage, that I often wondered how and why I came to consent to be a stranger in a land so strange to me as was all New England at the call of the Fourth

Congregational Church of Hartford. Drawn, perhaps, by the adventure of the change, I yet withheld my letter of acceptance until the very last mail by which my decision could reach the church when it was due. Even then I got the railway conductor to hold the train at the station until the arriving messenger from my father could deliver his message. It was that I should not let loyalty to the church fellowship of my forefathers dissuade me from obeying what might prove to be a call to render a larger service beyond its bounds. As this fatherly foresight confirmed my own very dim, yet urgent vision, I handed my letter of acceptance to my friend the conductor to deposit in the mail car as he signaled his train to start east. Thus the die was cast by a decision so blind that it ever afterward seemed to have been made for me by one who could devise my way, which I could only follow by an adventure of faith.

Far reaching as were the influences and effects of going from rural New York to city life and work in New England, from the conservative, organically united church of my fathers to the much larger, wider-spread, more liberal, and independent "fellowship" of Congregationalism, yet the outleadings of this great transition were recognized and experienced very gradually.

CHAPTER XXVI

INFLUENCE OF NEW ENGLAND CONTRASTS

BEFORE and after my arrival at Hartford, in 1880, the cultural spirit and advantages of that far-famed city appealed to a deeply cherished hope of increasing my intellectual equipment, by pursuing long-deferred studies, for which I found less time than I had expected in the country. The presence of my former pastor, Dr. Chester D. Hartranft, then president of Hartford Theological Seminary, rekindled this hope, as I owed to him the greatest intellectual and spiritual stimulus I had ever received from the church. Soon after I was settled in my new parish, I resumed work on the German language with a private tutor, in order to undertake more technical biblical studies that I had not yet found either time or facilities to start.

I had scarcely made a beginning of this work in my study before the present demands of my needy church and its neglected parish began to claim the right of way over the prospects of a more alluring future. Before I sensed this situation, the junior deacon remarked to the senior deacon, on catching his first glimpse of me in the pulpit, "I guess the man couldn't come and sent his boy," thus perhaps expressing his doubt of my youthful capacity to undertake what he knew to be a harder job than I could have foreseen.

I found the Fourth Church to have more of a history than a hope. Although on Main Street at the center of the city, its spire rose above a district covering one-quarter of the city's area, into which three-quarters of its poor and delinquent people were densely crowded. Their need to be served appealed to me so much more than serving the church that I challenged it to devote itself to the people surrounding it as the only hope of saving itself. The few survivors of its "Old

Guard" had memories which predisposed them to accept such a challenge. They and others who shared their pride in the courage of the "Old Fourth" to stand alone for what had been unpopular causes that other churches had been slow to espouse were ready to enlist in a new adventure of faith.

Long before, these plain people of "The Free Church," as it was called by its founders, had shocked the proprieties of the other congregations by freeing their pews from sale and rental; by daring to preach abolition from slavery, under the able and courageous ministry of their pastor, Dr. William W. Patton; by organizing one of the first Sunday schools in town; by aggressive advocacy of the temperance cause; and by agitating for woman's suffrage. To me the duty of the hour called for a democratic evangelism, in which my people were better prepared to follow than I was to lead. The more my preaching scaled to previous standards, the less it attracted those without. So from the empty spaces providing twelve hundred sittings, only forty-five of which were occupied, we went out to find the people where they were. Our outreaching was through open-air services on the streets under the big elms, on the baseball grounds where the bleachers were almost as crowded with men as at the week-day games, and from the church porch past which throngs surged along the main thoroughfare. Personal appeals were made through the cell bars at the police station, the jail, and state prison. House-to-house visitation discovered many unchurched families, which later led us to undertake with the aid of some seminary students a religious census of the whole city.

When from the highways and byways "strangers to the covenant of promise" began to arrive and seek shelter in our household of faith, its family fellowship steadfastly stood the test which severely tried its loyalty. We owed the organization and place within which to gather and hold those recruits from the "far country" to a gambler who had left his game, to a drinking man who had conquered his habit, and to the saintly widow of Horace Bushnell, Hartford's greatest prophet preacher and most distinguished citizen. Touched by the death of his child, the gambler "came to himself." He wrote me:

I have determined not to go back into the old business, come what will. I trust that there will be an opening so that my wife and child will not starve. But I do long to associate with good and Christian men and women. I am starved for that association. If I could have it I believe I could soon be willing to leave all to God. You can hardly imagine the darkness, almost despair, that at times I have been in. For years I had no one to talk with, as I now do with you, and I have had to bear it all alone, without human help. Words cannot tell you how I long to be out from all low and wrong associations. They, none of them, have any pleasure for me and I do not believe that I shall be compelled to have any more of them.

Finding no place to be at the church between its Sunday and week-day services, he took refuge and sought companionship in the only place he knew he would be welcome, which just then happened to be my home study. And I may add, that when his need was more fully met, he kept his word, leaving all, even life itself, exclaiming when dying from an occupational disease: "Had I not borne this cross, I would have lost my crown." The other man, who had felt the same need in breaking away from the associations of the saloon, offered the first hundred dollars toward building an addition to the church, where such men could be at home with one another while finding their own place in the church household. "Cannot something be done," he wrote, "to lessen these odds, to even things up, to give the Lord a fair show with a man who wants to be saved?" The second hundred dollars toward the building of the ever open clubroom for the Yoke Fellows Band was given by Mrs. Bushnell, thus exemplifying, as she did in many another way, her husband's supreme aim—"to justify the ways of God to man."

Through this ever open door on the street level and from the increasing numbers gathered into our Sunday-evening evangelistic service so many sought our friendly guidance and spiritual watch and care that office hours twice daily were required by over a thousand individuals a year who sought conference with us.

The ingathering and homing of these many disconnected people required stronger organization and more funds. It therefore became necessary to explain our continuous evangelistic efforts in order to win sympathy and support. Opportunity to do so was offered in the fourth year of our struggle by an appointment to present a paper on "An Evangelistic Church" to the annual conference of the Connecticut Congregational churches. In so doing, the function of the whole church was claimed to be evangelistic. A disclaimer was made that any local church endeavoring to fulfil in its field this function of the "great commission" was to be considered a different kind of a church. So dependent was the whole church shown to be upon evangelizing and nurturing that her very faith and life failed with her failure to do both. The interdependence of evangelism and nurture was held to be such that when the church ceased to evangelize she well-nigh abandoned the nurture of her own children, and when she neglected their nurture in dependence upon evangelism she failed to win those without. The house not made with hands but of hearts is the only home of the soul. Missions are not churches. At best they can be but their vestibules. Though necessary they never can be sufficient. Men and women cannot live and be at home in them. Most self-dependent people will not come to them. Newborn souls are like foundlings when left outside a nurturing home church. They are exposed to what Cardinal Manning called the "last peril of the spiritual life, the storm in the harbor."

Therefore the first prerequisite to the permanent success of evangelism was claimed to be a people who incarnate the Christ, not only in their own human lives, but in their church fellowship; unto whom, singly and together, like the Christ himself, those being saved are added day by day, as they were to the fraternal fellowship at Pentecost. Such a people those of the Fourth Church really endeavored to be—Christ's ministering body among his fellow-men and theirs.

For what it came to be and do the Fourth Church owed most to my two colleagues. From his small farming on a Connecticut hillside came Henry J. Gillette at our call to be a sower and reaper of fellow-men on our stony field. His Christlike love and human touch more than compensated for his scant schooling. His man-to-man ministry found access which we minister colleagues could not even approach. His irrepressible sense of humor tempered the intensity of his spiritual devotion. In our own and other church gatherings he breathed a humanly divine spirit that kindled altar fires such as he made glow in lowly hearts. And when he entered into his rest his works followed him from a multitude whose lives he inspired, mine not least among them. To the educational and musical leadership of Henry Hopkins Kelsey, my brotherly associate pastor, was due the enrichment of public worship and the large Sunday-school development, which attracted a multitude to fill the church and to be welded into its household of faith, through the twenty-two years of his ingathering and upbuilding ministry.

Intellectually stimulating and broadening as the distinctively New England influences proved to be in later years, my earlier identification with the masses of the people on the hardpan of life really trained me more both for the religious work then in hand and for the sociological study and teaching awaiting me. As men came up from the pitfalls dug by themselves and by others, they taught me, on the one hand, that the fallen could rise, and, on the other hand, that the conditions under which they fell could and should be changed so as to make it easier to live right and harder to go wrong in every community. Meanwhile, I was prompted to say with old John Bunyan: "Oh, then come hither and lay my book, thy head and heart together." For I had learned that the knowledge of the head and heart had at least to be equal to that of the book in order to bring them together. Dr. Bushnell's vision of the "grandeur of human nature as seen in its ruins" grounded my faith and hope in the innate capacity of fellow-men to be restored to the likeness of their Creator. So we sang more intelligently, and with faith both in God and man, the gospel hymn:

> Down in the human heart crushed by the tempter,
> Feelings lie buried that Grace can restore,
> Touched by a loving hand, wakened by kindness,
> Chords that were broken will vibrate once more.

Fallow spots on stony ground were found for the seed of the Word, as forth we went to sow it. Experiences in so doing precipitated a flood of challenging questions upon every mind capable of any reverent apprehension of the mystery of good and evil. Psychological and moral reaction to social conditions become sources of information and inspiration to action. But far beneath the surface of each of these very human types of experience to be narrated surge the deepest problems for scientific inquiry and religious faith to fathom. When up against the "crannied wall" of each such stony soul, I have ever been moved to murmur to myself:

> If I could understand
> What you are, root and all—and all in all,
> I should know what God and Man is—

and what and whose is sin.

From many stories of rare human interest these which follow reach farthest down and up.

Timidly inquiring for me at the door of my Hartford home stood a young man of twenty-two years. He came seeking only friendly counsel and encouragement, fulfilling his promise to a neighbor of mine who chanced to recognize him, when he asked for aid at her door, as a boy who had been in her mission Sunday-school class. He had passed back and forth while "screwing up his courage" to come in to see me. Put at ease by my welcome, he let me know that all went well with him "until mother died," but when at his fourteenth year he had been arrested and jailed for carrying a coil of rope which a thief had hired him to sell, and after he had been driven from home by his father, he felt, "If father was against me everyone else would be." So he became a sneak-thief, a "drunk and disorderly" police-court rounder, a burglar, and a convict. "Now I am tired of myself," he said.

When told that his teacher and I cared for him, and that Jesus bids all who are weary and heavy laden to find rest by taking his easier yoke and lighter burden, he dreamily replied, "I tried to remember that while in my cell, but I never knew it meant me." As he was in danger of falling into crime through drink, I had him call upon me daily, as did many other men to encourage themselves—and me. During his first absence from town he wrote me a postal card each day, one of which read: "I now take up my pen to write to you, hoping you are well as I am. I went to the mission last night.

The leader said he would rather have one righteous man than fifty sinners. Then I thought that you would rather have fifty sinners than one righteous man." The police had so often locked him up, suspecting that he would do wrong if opportunity offered, that I begged them to give him a chance to do right by leaving him with me on the first circus day after he and I became friends. That was the first such day he had been free for several years, and it helped make a man of him. His former life receded from his own and others' memory as he rose into wage-earning self-respect, married and had a home of his own, and was respected and fellow-shiped by the Yoke Fellows and other new friends at church. But he did not fail to expect the same welcome to be given others coming up from the depths as he had received. The remark reported from another church, that it "was not a church for ex-convicts," drew from him the soft-spoken response, "I would rather belong to a church of ex-convicts than to a church of ex-converts." To the amazement of the police and to all who had known his past, he stood uprightly a man among men and in the fellowship of the church for eight years. Enfeebled in strength and in will, he yielded to a temptation to drink, arousing the long-conquered appetite which overwhelmed him with despair, despite all he or we could do for his recovery. Here was a man who as earnestly struggled to be saved as we to save him. If "lost" to this world, had the next world no hope for such as he?

A more heartening experience was that of a fine type of young Irish manhood. Unable to stop drinking, he asked the judge of the police court to "shut him up where he could get no liquor for ten days," and there in jail we found him. He was a railway freight brakeman, and had barely escaped with his life in a recent accident. When expecting death under the wreck, a little prayer which his good Roman Catholic mother had taught him in boyhood came back in memory to awaken him to his danger of making a wreck of himself. We welcomed him to our fellowship, while encouraging him to maintain his birthright in the old church. When he got in the clear from the habit and associations of drinking, we recommended him for appointment in the Hartford Fire Department. In its service he rose steadily until he became the driver of its largest motor fire engine. His strong physique and early religious training were prime factors in the stead-fastness of his recovery.

At state prison I found a hard-featured, rough-handed man of twenty-five years who proved to be boyishly gentle at heart and manly in action. When I read to his fellow-prisoners some verses he had written in his cell descriptive of his way into crime and what he hoped would be his way out, he "felt like fainting away" for fear I would mention him as the author. After his discharge in starting to live a better life, he felt unworthy to continue because he struck a woman for laughing at his attempt. So he produced the New Testa-ment I had given him, as unworthy to have it. Surrendering another which I had given to a man he knew, this militant penitent declared: "He is not fit to have it either, because he made fun of it in a saloon, so I knocked him down and took it away and here it is." Rough as he was on the surface, he was sensitive at heart. Because the scars on the back of his head, like John Brown's dog Rab, formed a map of the battles he had fought, this man never took a front seat in any assembly where he could be seen from the rear. Years after I had gone to Chicago, I heard someone timidly call me by name while standing in front of Chicago Commons. In re-sponse to my greeting he said: "I beat my way here to see you because you are the only one who ever took stock in me." Assured that I always would, he intrusted to me his savings from the harvest fields, his last remittance following his tramping through an alkali desert, where he nearly died, as he probably did not long afterward since we never heard from him again. What more could have been expected from one who had never known any mothering or fathering and whose life was launched upon the sea with no knowledge of any port of departure or port of entry?

Another fellow-prisoner of this man, although with better background and more to live for, cared less for what became of him after his discharge, because he despaired of recovering what he had lost. "No one cares what becomes of me," he bitterly exclaimed. But when I produced a letter from his sister welcoming him to her home as proof that she and I cared, I noticed moisture come to his eyelashes and that something seemed to swell in his throat. Through these openings to his heart I found the man behind the convict. He became the sexton of our church and honorably rounded out in the fellowship to which he was welcomed the few years surviving a misspent youth.

One Sunday morning there stood at my door a man twenty-five years of age. He had delicate features, the lines of which had grown somewhat hard and sharp. His manner revealed him to be of a high-strung, nervous temperament, showing some signs of neurotic excitement. In quickly spoken phrases accompanied by penetrating glances from a keen, lustrous eye, he inquired: "When speaking to us men at the prison a few Sundays ago, you said you would take an interest in any of us when we came out, did you not? Did you mean it? If you did and meant me you will have a hard time." He kept his word. Again and again he fell into drink, but never into crime, although his previous criminal career, into which I did not inquire, was suspected of being long and persistent. Whatever it was, he abandoned it when he came to us, his only fear and ours being that he might do something criminal while intoxicated. Out of those depths he would write from some saloon at 2:00 A.M.: "Would God you were awake and I could reach you." However many times he went down, he always came up again, and we always took him back, not only to our watch and care, but into our personal fellowship. His last fall, however, caused all but a very few of his comrades in the Yoke Fellows Band to fall away from him. They warned me that if he were taken back some of them would leave. Promptly and decidedly I replied that while I would be sorry to part with them, I would obey our marching orders to give him, and any next man after him, the same welcome to take a new start and another chance that had been given to all of them. None of them left when he came back, but it was harder for him to return than it was for them to receive him. "Let me go, I cannot help it. I am no longer worth your time," he cried. I told him I would not do so, that we were all saved by hope, and that if we did not hope for ourselves someone else could hope for us, as I did for him. Slowly he recovered his better self with better health. Under the tutelage and friendship of an elderly, invalid, spiritually minded woman, who watched over him like a mother, he gradually rose into his spiritual manhood. Meanwhile, he won our hearts, and our admiration also, by the tenderness of his heart and his intellectual appreciation for truth and beauty. These qualities he expressed in quoting the choicest scriptural treasures, which he discovered, some of which none of us knew so well if at all. So hopeful were we of the progress he might make if afforded educational advantage that we secured his admission to the Mount Hermon School, founded by Dwight L. Moody. Although for a half-year or more his conduct and spirit were such as to win the confidence of his teachers, the old wanderlust so repossessed him that he begged me to let him go from the school. "I have never stayed so long in any one place, except in prison, since I was a boy," he said, adding, "I could more easily stay there where I had to than here where I am supposed to want to remain." Nothing in my experience or reasoning could cope with this obsession. But after moving about for a brief period, during which he visited a sister whose love he had not requited for many a year, he returned to Hartford, never to fall again during forty years from high standards of conduct and character. These he maintained in the little family circle of his own home, in the fellowship of the Fourth Church, and among his fellow-citizens, rounding out the full length of an honored life.

While the bright lights of hope prevailed over the dark shadows, yet so stern were the struggles encountered in these personal experiences that they emphasized the need of an evangelism no less personal for seeking to evangelize conditions adverse to the aims and hopes of the Christian faith. The zeal with which lifting the hand, rising for prayer, or shaking the hand of an evangelist is hailed by singing "Hallelujah, it's done," seems so devoid of knowledge as almost to be a mockery. The "sawdust trail" may start some out, but if efforts to follow up do not exceed and long outlast the effort to start converts out, a very great responsibility is assumed which falls far short of being discharged. The early nurture of religious life, by progressive educational training in the home and in the church school, rises far higher both in the quality and the extent of its effects than those achieved by evangelism without it.

Surely no observant, inquiring mind can follow such experiences back to what lies behind them, out to the physical and social conditions surrounding them, and forth into the farther future which tests them without encountering all the problems which modern psychology and psychiatry, the social sciences, and civic reform seek to understand and solve. For the lack of this knowledge, or the sources and methods of acquiring it, our religious, moral, and even judicial appeals have all too vainly been made to those who lacked the capacity to apprehend, much less respond to, them. From this point of view the neglect of education for parentage looms large in the retrospect and the prospect of the years. Even more fateful is the failure of the state to prevent by the custodial care of subnormal girls the alarming increase of subnormal births. Our courts and correctional institutions are aware of these facts and are reliant upon psychiatric aid in dealing with problem children, far more than parents, teachers, and pastors have been.

My contacts with industrial conditions in Hartford were either with self-reliant skilled workers or with those who through faults of their own had lost or never gained foothold for self-support. Yet I saw and heard enough in my pastoral work to awaken me to the vital connection between character and industrial conditions. A sturdily independent mechanic and a leading official in my church complained of the shutdown of the shop in which he had worked for a score of years, with no notice other than that served at a week-end pay day that there would be "no more work until further notice." And he asked, "Why should no more consideration be shown a man and his family than to have their income cut off suddenly and indefinitely, with no chance to adjust their present expenditures for future obligations?" I could not see "why" then nor since.

A simple-hearted, industrious, and devoted man so vividly

spirit exerted a transforming influence upon me. Although it was unobserved at first, it followed me through all these intervening years, looming the larger in the lengthening retrospect. The spiritual vision of Horace Bushnell had clarified the religious atmosphere. Although he had been translated a year or more before my arrival, I felt his surviving presence in the life of his home, which was not far from my own. Its atmosphere was radiant with Mrs. Bushnell's refinement of spirit and serene assurance of faith. The park surrounding the state capitol, which the city owed to his vision and called by his name, seemed to recognize him still as the first citizen of Hartford.

Worthily recognizing him as such, this fifty-fourth year after his death, was the gift of the Horace Bushnell Memorial by his venerated daughter, Mrs. Dotha Bushnell Hillyer, and the acceptance of the great building by the citizens of Hartford. Dedicated to what his family knew him to be devoted, it was accepted as a "center for public educational and cultural activities to encourage public appreciation of music, art, science and all benevolent, religious and other public activities." The Mayor claimed its great auditorium to be a "splendid substitute for continuing the functions of the old outgrown New England town meeting." And the City Council registered the commonwealth's appreciation of the "memorial to the life, hopes and services of her beloved father, leader, orator, pastor, prophet and citizen of Hartford and the world."

Fortunate was I in sharing the fellowship of Dr. Nathaniel Burton, who had been chosen as Dr. Bushnell's successor in the Park Church, after serving the Fourth Church as one of my predecessors. Those of us under the spell of his personal charm could feel what perhaps his auditors only heard. We caught the tones of his voice and the flavors of his speech in reading his "Yale Lectures on Preaching." They scintillated with the genius which gave vision to his conduct of worship, wings to his words in preaching and prayer, comradeship to his conversation, vividness to his wit, and atmosphere to his personality. Through his introduction to the Liturgical Club, I found inspiring fellowships with men of rare spirit and scholarship in the Episcopal and Catholic apostolic church ministries.

He was one of three minister citizens whose triumvirate partly succeeded to the sway by which their leader, Horace Bushnell, had inspired the distinctive individuality of each, yet so closely bound them together that unconsciously the very tones and accent of each were reproduced in the flexible speech of the others. Dr. Edwin Pond Parker for nearly fifty years won and held the following of many of Hartford's most intellectual people. Joseph H. Twitchell, a popular Yale alumnus, was the leader of the city's most influential youth, all the while being the comrade of "Mark Twain" and the personal friend of Charles W. Warner, Harriet Beecher Stowe, and many others in the brilliant coterie living within his parish and claiming him as their pastor.

Closer and freer fellowship I had with a few men who met one another in the charmed circle of two little groups. One we called the "Pentagon" because it held together five of us younger ministers in a comradeship that cheered, counseled, broadened, and deepened one another's lives. The "Twilight Club" fulfilled the hope of unity and variety by a membership of those so different from one another in occupation and outlook as to be more interesting in the confidential exchange of personal opinions from widely varying points of view. Our meetings between daylight and dark linger in memory, as the play of sunshine and shadow on a distant meadow, still bright and fragrant in the retrospect. After forty years this Club continues to scintillate.

The degree to which men rose above the commanding position they filled in the business and professional life of the city gave distinction to Hartford. At the head of the Travelers' Insurance Company, for instance, its president, James G. Batterson, and its secretary, Rodney Dennis, were men of such liberal culture as to lead their company to make a notable contribution to its literature in publishing the works of Walter Bagehot, in six volumes, with memoirs by R. H. Hutton and edited by Forest Morgan. Notable, indeed, was it for this insurance company to issue in its own name this edition of such a scholarly work, "now first published in full and from a carefully corrected text." Both of these men counseled and encouraged me in my work with the less privileged classes of their fellow-citizens. Strangely indeed, the old Fourth Church, whose congregation was then about the poorest in the city, was rebuilt on the grounds formerly owned by Mr. Batterson, then among the richest men in town, his beautiful residence serving as its parish-house.

CHAPTER XXVII

FROM EAST TO WEST AT THE CALL
TO TEACH

THE greatest surprise of my life was the call to the professorship. While in Philadelphia considering an overture from John Wanamaker, to join the staff of Bethany Church, which had grown out of the great Sunday school of which he had been the promoter and superintendent through most of his manhood's busy life, I received a telegram from a student friend, to whose confidence I had committed the information of my errand, to "make no decision until I returned to Hartford." Upon my arrival I was informed that I had been elected professor of practical theology in the Hartford Theological Seminary. Representatives of its alumni urged my acceptance, giving me reason which influenced me more than any other, namely, that while five years before no man who had been doing what I had done in Hartford would have been thought of for this position, now I had been chosen, not in spite of, but because of my doing it. President Hartranft offset my misgivings, based upon the lack of preparation for such a teaching position as I had never imagined I would be called upon to fill, by using the same argument, that because I had "done something" I was needed to teach other men to do so.

Ever since this greatest turn in my life was taken, I have been impressed with the fact that had I sacrificed the claims of my needy parish in academic preparation for a more alluring future, I certainly would not have done what led the Seminary to offer me this professorship, had it been my goal. But strangely indeed, what seemed to lead directly away from any such preferment, there or anywhere, became the very way which led me directly into the still greater opportunity in which my lifework unexpectedly yet naturally and gradually culminated.

My acceptance, which came with fear and trembling, was nevertheless somewhat more hopeful because conditioned upon the Seminary's permission to continue to be the pastor of the Fourth Church. This I did without salary so as to secure the assistance of an able associate, Henry H. Kelsey. Thus its hospitable congregation and its almost city-wide parish became the laboratory which welcomed the field work of my students. Thus they gained rare opportunities for first-hand observation and experience in the work of the church in religious education and pastoral evangelism.

But this ideally practical adjustment gave occasion for a startling reminder—that, while in New England, I was far from being of it. I had not been unaware of antecedent and then present differences, between the lines of which I was more or less isolated. My conservative training for the ministry made it difficult for me to understand, much more to appreciate or share, the liberalism prevalent in the other Hartford Congregational churches. It seemed to me to be destructive to the very foundations of the faith "once delivered." The ministers of these churches, for the same reason, were not drawn into close relations with me, nor did they like the evangelistic efforts I was constrained to make in order to gain any hearing either within my church or outside of it. The conservative clergy connected with the Hartford Seminary faculty, directors, and constituency, though more sympathetic, yet with few exceptions at first stood off from identifying themselves with quite such aggressive methods as those which the Fourth Church felt free to employ.

The cleavage then dividing these groups of liberals and conservatives in the Congregational ministry was so irreconcilable that most of the city pastors strenuously objected to having me maintain any pastoral relations with the Fourth Church, if I entered the service of the Seminary—aloof from which they had hitherto stood. The widow of Horace Bushnell was the first to cross this cleavage. Reflecting also her husband's patience under the theological criticism which he suffered, she offered the gift of twelve copies of his volume on *Christian Nurture*, with this very humorously generous remark: "I cannot quite feel like making a gift to the seminary that opposed my husband, yet I am glad to give you these copies of his book in token of my pleasure that you have use for them in your classroom." Later when the pastors were assured of the practical, non-controversial purpose of my teaching, and of the students' practice work upon the city fields, they organized a "Pastors' Mission" to help the Fourth Church financially in carrying on its city-wide work.

Dr. George Leon Walker, pastor of the old First Church of Christ in Hartford, stood in the clear, quite by himself. With scholarly knowledge of New England's past and keen observation of its current religious transitions, he thought and preached independently of the reactionary conservatism of the one group and the radical liberalism of the other, yet without any compromise of his own affirmative views. Thus he faced and flanked clerical and other parishioners of the two opposing doctrinaire schools, that of Bennett Tyler surviving at Hartford Seminary and that of Nathaniel W. Taylor at Yale Divinity School. Dr. Walker's adherence to the forefathers' ways in pulpit and parish and his own individualistic predilections were such as to inhibit his personal support of my evangelistic ministry at the church or of my social teaching at the Seminary. He opposed neither, however, and tacitly encouraged the co-operation of some of his parishioners with me in both.

When after the twelve years of work in the church, through four of which I also served the Seminary, I began to feel acclimated in New England, and when opportunities for wider service in Hartford were opening, Chicago and the West began to beckon me. Ten years before I had gone to gather inspiration and guidance for institutional church evangelism from Dwight L. Moody and his work in Chicago, from Josiah Strong in Cincinnati, and from several church and mission leaders in other cities. Still farther West I went this eventful year of 1892, to be thrilled by my first vision of the prairies of Illinois, the billowy rolling farmland of Iowa, the great plains of Kansas and Nebraska, the mountain ranges of Colorado, and the cattle ranges of Wyoming.

Again at Chicago I was inspired by its people's will to win. This time, however, it found greatest expression in the prep-

aration for the World's Fair. The beauty and extent of the
Columbian Exposition grounds and buildings, though far
from finished, already charmed me. I was also deeply impressed by the spirit of the citizens I met, who were buoyantly
anticipating their great opportunity and preparing to follow
it up after the exposition closed. Advantage was taken of my
presence by a few of them, who long afterward confessed to
have been considering me for work in Chicago and the West.
They therefore had me speak and listen at gatherings of various church and social groups, that I might sense the spirit of
the West as given highest expression in Chicago.

On my homeward way I find that I had written in my
pocket diary: "Christian Sociology is the door—wide and
effectual—opening to me, and to all that can make the re-
mainder of my life most effectual. Henceforth I seek that
kingdom first—but whither, East or West?" Three months
later, on July 5, 1892, Chicago Theological Seminary voted
its call to me to pioneer its Department of Christian Sociology
which its directors that day resolved to establish. I was thus
thrown into the most painful dilemma between the claims of
the past and those of the future. My comrades in the old
Fourth Church besought me not to leave them. My faculty
colleagues, with the alumni and directors, pled the Seminary's
need of my classroom and my forthgoing propaganda of the
social gospel. President Hartranft proposed the establishment of a sociological department in the Seminary, if I would
remain to lead it. Citizens, from insurance-company presidents
to city firemen, urged the claims of the city upon my civic service. Re-reading these letters thirty-eight years after, I wonder
how my heart yielded to my head in breaking away from ties
so much stronger than I had known many of them to be.

But I knew how little freedom Hartford, and the Seminary's conservative giving constituency, might allow anything suspiciously challenging to laissez faire economic orthodoxy, while Chicago guaranteed unrestricted liberty. The
business and professional men with whom I had served
on the Seminary Board of Trustees eight years before they
elected me to the professorship had offered no demurrer to
my aggressive church work, but it had pled more for char-

ity than social justice. My colleagues in the faculty had been
not only generously considerate but paternally encouraging in
my immature effort to teach what I had tried to practice. It
was another heart-wrench to leave such loyal comrades, and
hardest to part with Dr. Hartranft, the inspiring leader of my
youth and early manhood. But I had stood with him through
the stress and storm of the Seminary's transition for ten
years. His lofty ideals for its transformation had won the
faith of faculty and trustees, and had begun to appeal to the
imagination of men of wealth. The future seemed secure, and
so it proved to be, unimpeded by my withdrawal, contrary to
predictions. During the next decade the Hartford Foundation was assured, with the expansion of its schools toward
university proportions, adequately provided with building
equipment.

Fourteen years after our seer and inspirer had passed from
our sight, Hartranft Hall was dedicated to his memory,
bearing this tribute to his prophetic foresight and heroic endurance in seeing and realizing the invisible:

In Loving and Reverent Memory of
CHESTER DAVID HARTRANFT
1839–1914
Eminent as Scholar, Teacher, Leader, and Counselor
In vision a Seer   In sympathy a Father
In self-forgetfulness a Saint
A Prince in the Realm of Truth and Light

I was so long hesitant in reaching a decision that Professor
Samuel Ives Curtiss was sent from Chicago to urge my acceptance of its Seminary's call. This he did by reading to me over
one hundred pages of carefully written reasons why I should
do so. Not only by well-chosen facts, stating the needs of the
West for social development, but by remarkable predictions
of opportunities, which later proved to be available, he urged
the claims of the Seminary, the city, and the western states to
be paramount to any that Hartford and the East could offer
in the present or in the future. To ease my distracted spirit
he even penned a letter of resignation, which he ventured to
suggest as appropriate for me to write. But I had already
drafted tentatively a declinature of the call to Chicago, to see
how it would fit into my feeling and the facts of the present

situation. His final telegram, however, influenced me far more. It read: "The Kingdom is one. God knows neither East nor West. The decisive question is where can one be most useful." It took me nearly a month, however, to balance future opportunities with present obligation, until at last they merged in my acceptance of the call of the West to pioneer on its social frontier. Happily the spirit and work of the old Fourth Church proved so strong as to assure its increasing stability and progress.

My one condition was promptly accepted, and has been faithfully fulfilled through all these years by the Chicago Seminary directors and faculty, namely:

Within the limits of my own department I am to have the liberty of administration for such independent development as, on the one hand, may be consistent with all deference due to institutional interests and the rights of other departments, and, on the other hand, shall be in accordance with its own distinctive sphere and different methods.

These "distinctions" called upon both professor and students for less classroom work and more individual training; less purely scholastic methods and more of the inductive procedure; less dependence upon literary sources and more reliance upon direct contact with life and personal experience in the work on the field with men, women, and children. As a means to this end I asked the directors of the Seminary to provide a place where I could live and work among the masses of the people, which would serve me and my students with a point of view and actual contact with fellow-men, thus furnishing a clinic for my classroom and a laboratory for me.

However crude and vague may have been my own and the Seminary's conception of what sociological instruction should be, my insistence upon freedom to develop and upon the provision of a social center whence to orient the evolving situation were points well taken.

However unpremeditated my previous development had been, it proved to be somewhat preparatory to what lay before me. The urge to help and fellowship the individual man, woman, and child was so strong that I had found it to be capable of gathering to itself the ways and means of its own accomplishment. So what I could be to others and they could be to me continued to be an ever open source of information and inspiration. Although with this resource I was less dependent upon money and the facilities for service, yet I had keenly felt the lack of accessories of public worship and of equipment for the educational and social work of the parish. This lack of facilities for week-day work in the church-building threw me back upon the use of my own and others' homes for parish purposes and social fellowship. Over and over again we, in the family circle, were led to say: "Well, at least we have our home to work with and to share with others." Thus our family relationships and modest household equipment, which were at first and often afterward our only dependence, again became our main reliance.

So also the neighborly relations which in my country and city parishes I found to be strong and readily responsive to my effort to enlist good fellowship and co-operation in religious endeavor still further emphasized the interdependence of the church and the community.

As the democratic spirit of the Middle West had found something in me to respond to its appeal on my first contact with its field and forcefulness, so my eastern experience possessed me with these three prime factors of all social problems and solvents—the potentiality of personality, the family as the unit of the church and state, and the neighborhood as the medium for the expansion of the fraternal spirit into the sphere of the local community and government. Equipped with these ways and means for achieving the educational ends which I was bidden to seek, I responded more hopefully to the summons to this new adventure of faith. But I confess to have felt like the first patriarchal Pilgrim Father, who when "called to go out from country, kindred and father's house, went out, not knowing whither he went." Nevertheless, and perhaps all the more, I also felt the thrill of being outward bound again. And yet I noted that the patriarch afterward "received for an inheritance the place to which he was called," because he stayed out "when he might have had the opportunity to have returned." Perhaps the lure of the West first cast its spell upon me when I chose for the topic of my graduation address the motto of Rutgers College: *Sol justitiae et occidentem illustra.*

CHAPTER XXVIII

THE DEVELOPING SOCIOLOGICAL TEACHING

THE trail which I followed in starting my teaching at Hartford Seminary and in developing its sociological trend at Chicago closely links the experiences attained East and West. It ties together both ends of my story, interweaving its early sources and its later outlook.

I was profoundly moved when entering upon my Hartford professorship to spare my students and their future parishioners the loss of the larger gospel, and the church the lack of its broader function of ministering to the community; to save both minister and church the waste of time and effort, courage, and hope which my people and I suffered from the lack of social intelligence; to acquire and impart the information and inspiration of this knowledge.

Without any technical training to teach, I faced the memorandum of the scope of my department, tersely assigning to it "Homiletics," "Liturgics," "Pedagogy," "Polity," "Pastoral Theology," and "Sociology." Few were the sources I had then in hand except the experiences in my Hopewell parish and on the hardpan of my city-center field at Hartford. Of equal or greater importance was the consciousness of the lacking elements in my own training for life and for effective work among my fellow-men.

Partly compensating for the lacking knowledge of the academic "humanities" was the personal study of the Bible for devotional purposes. As a book of lives, it was the "Book of Life" to me. It also appealed to me as a manual for personal use in learning how to live a religious life and how to do religious work. By the typical personalities who lived, moved, and had a being in its pages it introduced me to fellow-men. It inspired me to become acquainted and to identify myself with the people of my neighborhood and parish. They in turn helped me to understand and interpret the scriptural types and standards of character.

This personal use of the Scriptures led me to emphasize in my teaching the inspiration, suggestion, and guidance which the study of the English Bible offers the minister for his work in the pulpit and the parish, his community, and his world. And this led to the study, interpretation, and application of the social teachings of the Scriptures.

My inaugural address on "The Practical Training Needed for the Ministry of Today" opened with this declaration: "The facts of the Gospel's yesterday live among men today only as they are born again of their daily experience. The everlasting and unchangeable truths of the Word keep their life among the living only as they are inductively drawn afresh from the facts and things of the present."

I had been stirred deeply by Mrs. Humphrey Ward's story of her minister hero, Robert Elsmere, whose drift away from the church into agnosticism was depicted as due to the rigidly narrowing range of thought and action imposed upon its ministry. At the crisis of his young manhood this student is described as receiving his call to the ministry in the undergraduates' gallery at St. Mary's, Oxford, where the beautiful surroundings and impressive service "possessed the boy's imagination and satisfied all the poetic and dramatic instincts of a passionate nature." I followed this quotation in my address by quoting the sequel with which the story concludes, in which, after his heroic service to fellow-men, Robert Elsmere accounts for the shrinking of his early faith as his later vision of the world's life grew, in these memorable words: "Christianity seems to be something small and local; behind it, around it, and including it, I see the great drama of the world sweeping on, led by God from change to change, from act to act. It is not that Christianity is false, but that it is only an imperfect human reflection of part of the truth." This honest confession prompted these questions, which have ever since challenged my soul: Is it any wonder that such a call was followed by a ministry in which his Christianity was not nearly as large as his life, or deep as his manhood, or broad as his humanity, and not really identified with his noble work with fellow-men? Based on such an ideal and such experience, is his sad conclusion strange or unmanly?

At the same time, the loss of the church's leadership of educational, charitable, and reformatory movements, many of which were its own offsprings, I attributed to the lack of training for social ministries. The prevalent curricula of the seminaries aimed to prepare only one kind of ministers, when the parish, the community, and the world needed more diverse and distinct kinds of ministry. The use of my Fourth Church and its city-wide work as the clinic of my classroom and the practice field for my students was thus announced in my inaugural:

Many of the largest seminaries have been situated remote from the masses of men, in villages and country towns, where not only has there been no possibility to study organized Christian life, but where contact with the corporate needs of humanity has been denied. What medical school is thus remote from the centers of suffering men, and deprived of hospital clinics? What law school is remote from courts and law offices? Our normal schools have practice schools within their walls. Yet our seminaries for the training of men for the most practical of professions have, with few exceptions, scarcely a semblance of such apparatus for practical training. How then can men be expected to lead whither they have never followed, or scarcely looked, much less wrought? Is it then impossible for us to combine the practical with the theoretical? With the manifestly superior scholastic advantages of the theological seminary, may we not somehow secure the many practical benefits of student apprenticeship?

As my apologia for the introduction of the new and little-understood study of sociology to the old, hard-and-fast theological curriculum, I ventured to emphasize the following affirmations:

Heredity and environment are newly appreciated but prime factors in the problems of personal and social salvation. Without them, neither the cause nor the cure of pauperism, intemperance and crime can be apprehended. Sanitary, social and spiritual conditions are the moulds of personal and public character. To the imperative mandate "Ye must be born again" is added the church's obligation to improve the hereditary and environing conditions of birth and life in this world. God's message to "repent ye and believe the Gospel" cannot be fully delivered until the church is ready to offer the penitent something within her fold to turn to, something that will make possible the survival, maintenance and growth of the new life in the man, who at this call has turned from all that earth was to him and had for him. The adjustment of the church's thought and agencies to these social tendencies and forces is necessary both to the winning of the soul and the coming of the kingdom.

With the following very secular-sounding sentiment, I left the chapel of the Seminary inaugurated, and went to work to fulfil its implications:

The history of the English people is said to have begun when upon the tomb of a forgotten hero might have been inscribed the words which Charles Kingsley wrote over him whom he called "Hereward": "Here lies the first of the new English who by the grace of God began to drain the fens." It was also affirmed that the imperial supremacy of the English people dates from the time the nation went home from Waterloo to attend to her own housekeeping, to look to her daily bread, to care for her women and children, to build roads, shops, schools, to clean houses and streets and care for her sick. Likewise the church and seminary that will train a ministry for this world work for the Kingdom will begin to write a new and glorious page in the history of the Commonwealth of Israel and the Covenants of Promise.

A background for the social interpretation of the Scriptures was furnished me by two books. Canon W. H. Fremantle's Bampton Lectures (1882) on *The World as the Subject of Redemption* gave me a point of view entirely new to me, which made over the outlook from Scripture upon mankind and upon the field of action for the church and its ministry. No less, but not only, is the one soul to be sought and saved, but the world itself. And the world as the divinely constituted order of human life and relationships is to be won back to what it was made and meant to be—the Kingdom of the Father. Never again was it to be misinterpreted as wholly evil, fitted for destruction. Never, not even at the call of Bunyan's *Pilgrim's Progress*, was it to be so feared as to be fled from, renounced, and left to its preordained and irrevocable fate, with all men, women, and children except the comparatively few who could be counted into the church's covenants of promise. Emancipated from that final fear, which had beclouded the horizon of hope, the shadow was lifted from my teaching, which, however, I had seldom allowed to dim the cheer and hopefulness of my preaching. Not to "leave the poor, old stranded wreck and pull for the shore" with one soul at a time, but to be world-savers, kingdom-builders, I was to teach my students. Later I was fortified in this more divinely human view of the world so new to me by L. P. Jacks' article on "Church and World" in the *Hibbert Journal* for October, 1906, in which these imperatives demand an answer:

If by "the world" we mean such things as parliamentary or municipal government, the great industries of the nation, the professions of medicine, law and arms, the fine arts, the courts of justice, the hospitals, the enterprises of education, the pursuit of physical science and its application to the arts of life, the domestic economy of millions of homes, the daily work of all toilers—if, in short, we include that huge complex of secular activities which keeps the world up from hour to hour, and society as a going concern—then the churches which stand apart and describe all this as morally bankrupt are simply advertising themselves as the occupiers of a position as mischievous as it is false. In the words of Principal Caird, "The proposition would be unintelligible unless it were false." If, on the other hand, we exclude these things from our definition, what, in reason, do we mean by "the world"? The alienation from the church life of so much that is good in modern culture and so much that is earnest in every class is the natural sequel to the traditional attitude of the church to the world. And now the world takes deadly revenge by retaining the position assigned her and standing aloof from the church.

The other pioneer volume, *Ruling Ideas in Early Ages*, by J. B. Mozley (1881), was like a new Book of Genesis, restoring to us denatured individualists some share in the ancient race consciousness, yet culminating in the sanctity and development of each personality. As forecast by the prophets and exemplified by Jesus, this race-filled personality became the keystone of the arch of religion, of democracy, and of international, interracial hope.[1]

[1] There were other authors who helped establish me in the point of view whence to discover and apply the social teachings of the Scriptures. F. Herbert Stead very helpfully classified texts waymarking the development of the messianic kingdom in the Old and New Testaments, under the title *The Kingdom of God* (T. & T. Clark). Edwin Hatch laid a historical foundation by his scholarly studies of *The Organization of Early Christian Churches* and *The Influence of Greek Ideas*, which broadened the base upon which the Christian superstructures of thought and institutions were reared. J. R. Seeley, in *Ecce Homo*, so humanized the story of the gospels as to suggest a new reason for thinking Jesus to be more than a man and yet a man among men. Paul Sabatier's *Francis of Assisi* exalted the humanity of the saint above the priest and ecclesiasticized church. On the other hand, the spiritualizing of social thought and action was emphasized by Fremantle's *Christian Ordinances and Social Progress* and *The Gospel of the Secular Life*. Richard T. Ely's *Social Aspects of*

When I began to try to trace the development of the social contents of the Scriptures, especially in the consciousness of the Hebrew people, I was startled both by what I found and failed to find. Monotheism, like the pillar of cloud by day and the pillar of fire by night, hovered over, and ever beyond, the people of Israel, guiding them and all mankind. And it guided all the way from the initial postulate "in the beginning God" to the ultimate affirmed by Paul, when, standing on Mars Hill at Athens by the altar of the Unknown God, he declared: "God who made the world hath made of one blood all nations of men." Here, then, was the fact fundamental to any and all social consciousness and practice —the unity of the human race.

Out of it came the pioneering faith of the patriarchs and the elaborate Mosaic legislation in the Pentateuch, which in one of my seminary vacations I had classified and rearranged under the Ten Commandments handed down from Sinai! But where was it all, when I could find no trace of the law and government in Joshua, in Judges, and half through the history? So to the critics was I driven to find a chronological order that could be followed, and to the higher criticism for the rearrangement of the text. Then and thus only could the dramatic development of the social Spirit be traced through the rise and apostasy of the nation under its kings to the evolution of the messianic kingdom in the Remnant, as winnowed and garnered by the prophets.

This course on "The Social Teachings of the Scriptures," a syllabus of which I printed for classroom use under the title *Biblical Sociology*, became a prerequisite to other studies. Yet whenever offered as an elective it was taken by as many as had ever been required to take it. It brought my students

---

Christianity first pointed out to me "the social significance of baptism and the Lord's Supper." Other volumes summarized the socializing influence and achievements of Christianity: H. S. Nash, *The Genesis of the Social Conscience* (Macmillan, 1897); C. Schmidt, *Social Results of Early Christianity*, invaluable for its references to a wide range of sources (London: Isbiter, 1885); Francesco S. Nitti, *Catholic Socialism*, with its summaries of, and references to, patristic literature (Macmillan); Charles Loring Brace, *Gesta Christi, The Achievements of the Christ* (Armstrong, 1883); and Richard S. Storrs, *The Divine Origin of Christianity as Seen in Its Historical Results* (Randolph, 1884).

and me together on common ground and at least to one point of view. Naturally and logically this biblical data led to the study of the family, its social significance and function, and to child welfare, as protected and promoted by the home, school, church, and state. As I had preached to my people, so I taught my students that as the source and norm of society, and as the primary unit of state and church, the family is the Ark of the Covenant of the Lord of the whole earth.

In beginning to teach sociology at the Hartford Theological Seminary in 1888, and in the far more adventurous pioneering of the sociological department which the Chicago Theological Seminary in 1892 ventured to introduce to the long-prevalent theological curriculum, I well remember how completely I was thrown back upon my own resources. For more than a decade there were no such reference texts available for sociological use in the classroom as there were in the philosophy of history, economics, and political science. That the few others who preceded me or accompanied me in my struggles shared the same embarrassment is attested by Professor Albion W. Small, who began his pioneering of the first Department of Sociology to be introduced to the university curriculum at the University of Chicago the same month in 1893 that my venture began at the Seminary, then located on the West Side of the city. He wrote: "In the late '90's there was no standard literature of any sort which could be used according to the classroom methods of the older social sciences. Each instructor was thrown upon his own resources to an extent which made his task desperate."

Indeed I found no reference even to the term "sociology" in the *American Encyclopedia*, edited by Ripley and Dana in 1873, or in the 1887 edition of Johnson's *Universal Encyclopedia*. In a later edition appeared this discrediting reference to the coiner of the term: "The conception of a comprehensive social science we owe to Auguste Comte, who invented for it the objectionable name Sociology."

What I did not find in literature came to me unbidden from contemporary life. Voices rang out from very diverse fields of social action, bearing deeply home to me their incentive to

more specialized study of social phenomena and effort. The
new and impelling notes struck by these men and women who
were working far apart from one another seemed to breathe
the same spirit. They led me to realize that long before there
was any scientific formulation of the social sciences or the
philosophy of society there was a movement in life like that
of a brooding spirit—the *Zeit Geist*. What they did or wanted
done was long afterward recognized to have assumed a
"sociological attitude" which is considered to be a "pre-
sociological approach to sociology."[1]

I had read, of course, of those now so designated—the anti
slavery leaders in Great Britain and America, the forerunners
of modern penologists, the precursors of the scientific alienists
in treating the insane, and of Dr. Thomas Chalmers' initiative, leading the way from a pauperizing administration of
charity toward a rehabilitating application of temporary
relief and toward efforts to discover and obviate the causes of
poverty. But I was still more deeply stirred by what I heard
and read of those, the echoes of whose contemporary work
sounded like voices crying in the wilderness. From abroad
Octavia Hill's single-handed effort in London's city wilderness demonstrated the necessity and possibility of providing
houses fit for homes. David Livingstone's lone voice in the
dark continent inspired courage to probe and heal the "open
sore of the world" elsewhere. Dr. Cyrus Hamlin, American
missionary in Turkey, was introducing plows and bakeries as
tributary to Christian educational work in the Near East.
Dr. Jacob Chamberlain so inspired me with his story of his
medical work in India that I yielded to his persuasion to
volunteer for educational work at the Arcot Mission, from
which I was deterred by failure of my family to pass the
physical test requisite for the appointment.

In the homeland no such city-wide or nation-wide leadership appeared, at least within the limited range of my vision.
Faint echoes came to me from two classrooms as I entered my
own in 1888. Professor Francis G. Peabody had been offering
at Harvard University since 1880 a course on "The Ethics of

[1] See Professor John Gillin's presidential address, American Sociological Society,
1926.

the Social Question," which registered students both from the arts and divinity schools. His topic was so new to the academic curriculum that it was burlesqued by the students as dealing with "Drainage, Drunkenness, and Divorce." Nevertheless, this and other courses, together with his interpretative publications, continued to win favor and set a precedent that has been followed ever since by other universities and seminaries. At Andover Seminary, Professor William J. Tucker somewhat later had lectured on social problems confronting the church and its ministry in his courses on practical theology. He also inspired Robert A. Woods, then one of his students, to prepare himself to organize and lead the first social settlement to be directly connected with any theological seminary. After he had pursued studies in this country and abroad, and had resided a year at Toynbee Hall, he founded Andover House in 1891 in South Boston, later known as South End House, which under his leadership became educationally influential. But no syllabi came from these seminary or any other classrooms to guide me in the preparation of my own initial courses. Later still, Dean George Hodges inspired the Cambridge Divinity School with the spirit of his social parish work in Pittsburgh, Pennsylvania, where he had founded the Kingsley House Settlement.

My early social thought and teaching at Hartford were influenced by the Rev. David Allen Reed, the pastor of an influential church in Springfield, Massachusetts, who undertook to provide the laity with training for Christian work. He bravely persisted in following up his initiative, against unbelievable opposition from his ministerial brethren in the churches and theological seminaries. His adventures of educational faith, entailing serious financial sacrifice and risk, achieved success that is rarely attributed to his courageously farsighted pioneering. Out of his classes for training Y.M.C.A. secretaries came the Springfield Y.M.C.A. College. His school for Christian workers eventually was removed to Hartford to become the School of Religious Education in the Hartford Seminary Foundation. His Industrial Institute for training men to promote better conditions and relations in industry was too far ahead of the times to succeed then and there. But the railway branches of the Y.M.C.A., its shopwork, evening educational and occupational classes, and its employment offices all followed that first incentive, although they were not directly traceable to its suggestion. To have lent a helping hand by an occasional lecture and in extending continuous sympathy to this valiant pioneer was a privilege for which I have always been grateful. The vision and heroism of David Allen Reed's faith in his ideals have never failed to inspire and guide adventure in my own.

From one platform and one pulpit two voices rang in clarion tones. John Graham Brooks, knight-errant of social justice, entered the lists on the industrial arena in his country-wide lectures, from which his trenchant publications grew. His ethical insight, fair judgment, and undaunted courage inspired all who dared to follow where he led, and who needed his companionship and cheer when standing against odds all alone. From Massachusetts, as afterward from Ohio, echoes of what Dr. Washington Gladden was saying in his pulpit and doing within and beyond his parish caught my ear and stirred my conscience and will. His sermons addressed to workingmen, to employers, and to the public on their relations to one another in industry extended the sphere of preaching into areas within which no other preacher known to me had entered so far. His resignation of the editorship of *The Independent* magazine, in protest against advertisements inconsistent with the religious standing of that journal and his own high-keyed editorials, profoundly impressed me. Not least impressive of all the brief and incisive books that he wrote was his prophetic dream-story of the "Christian League of Connecticut." It stressed the necessity of a federation of the churches as a prerequisite to any hope of realizing Christian ideals of life, individual and social. Through his ministry of the social gospel, not only in preaching it but also in exemplifying it in his citizenship, he became my mentor before I knew him personally. But afterward, through the endearments of his friendship and the intimacies of his conversations and correspondence, he became a father in God to me. It was a cherished privilege to pay a filial tribute to his memory before the National Council of Congregational Churches and an honor to be chosen by it to do so.

How could my heart fail to burn within me as he walked and talked with me by the way? How could I falter in trying to keep step with him as from the thick of the fight his unfaltering tones rang forth in his *Ultima Veritas?*

> In the darkest night of the year,
>   When the stars have all gone out,
> I know that courage is better than fear,
>   That faith is truer than doubt.
>
> And fierce though the fiends may fight,
>   And long though the angels hide,
> I know that truth and right
>   Have the universe on their side.

How could I refrain from joining in his wayside prayer song?

> O Master, let me walk with thee
> In lowly paths of service free.

In current publications other living voices stressed the importance of studying concrete conditions. To evaluate and use reports of original investigations I was led by the Rev. Oscar McCulloch's pioneering genealogical study of *The Tribe of Ishmael.* To the Indiana State Conference of Charities this Indianapolis pastor reported his findings regarding eighteen hundred descendants from a roving couple, whose family name appeared on the charity, poorhouse, insane asylum, police court, and prison records of that and other middle western states. Later, Dugdale traced more in detail the similar history of *The Jukes* through eastern states. Amos G. Warner's *American Charities* exemplified methods and values in original research.

Then and ever since I have found in the daily and periodical press, in the proceedings of learned societies, the publications of voluntary agencies, and in the reports of local and national government departments, invaluable sources of information and suggestion. The clipping and filing of this fragmentary and fugitive material have proved indispensable to me, in making current information available long before it got into book form.

Of the early pioneer sociological theorists Auguste Comte was at first little more than a name to me. It was enough for me then to know that he defined sociology as "social physics," from which all theological and metaphysical conceptions were rigidly excluded. But his protest against investigating religious, economic, or political phenomena apart from one another as necessarily misleading lent presumptive attraction to his positive philosophy with its "hierarchy of the sciences." Yet critics regarded his "conception immeasurably superior to his performance." Herbert Spencer's *Study of Sociology*, which appeared in 1873, I hoped would be a help toward the preparation of my introductory course. But I found in it more of a foil against which to strike for the freedom of believers in any religion to think and teach within the sociological field than a help to constructive procedure. He too had such a mechanistic idea of the will as to assert that the recognition of human or divine volition, as in any way influencing social evolution, "incapacitates the mind for the study of sociology, constituting the mental attitude for which there can be no such thing as sociology." The conclusion of this volume introductory to the study of sociology was still more inhibiting in declaring that "the process of social evolution is in its general character so far predetermined that no teaching or policy can advance it beyond a certain normal rate, yet it is quite possible to perturb, to retard, or to disorder the process."

He admits "the seemingly awkward corollary that it matters not what we believe, or what we teach, since the process of social evolution will take its own course in spite of us." But his rejoinder is:

There is a very important part to be played by a true theory of social phenomena, yet the man of higher type must be content with greatly moderated expectations, while he perseveres with undiminished efforts. Nevertheless he has to see how comparatively little can be done, and yet to find it worth while to do that little.

The bias with which Mr. Spencer in this and other volumes was so unmistakably influenced did not disqualify him from performing a very distinct initial service. Far more than to any man up to that time credit is due him for the observation, classification, and tabulation of data, leading the way to more scientific procedure from fact to theory. The laissez faire individualism of Professor William Graham Sumner's teaching at Yale deferred for several years my appreciation of his valuable folk-ways researches.

In this dilemma fortunately there appeared in 1897 the informing and suggestive volumes on *Social and Ethical Interpretation of Mental Development*, by J. Mark Baldwin, then at Johns Hopkins University. Indorsing the previous publication of Professor Josiah Royce on the development of self-consciousness in the infant child, Baldwin summarized it thus: "The essence of the theory is that the child gets his material for the personality sense from persons around him by imitation, so that his growing sense of self is constantly behind his growing sense of others." His own conclusion was:

A man is a social outcome rather than a social unit; that he is always in his greatest part someone else; that his social acts are his because they are society's first, or he could not have learned them or had any tendency to do them; that everything he learns is copied, reproduced, assimilated from his fellows.

Thus was disclosed to me the common ground from which self-consciousness and social consciousness spring and grow together. Thus were relaid the firmer and abiding postulates from which to develop the religion of human relationship as the source and goal of the science of society. William T. Harris, in one of his reports as United States commissioner of education, supplemented these conclusions in words which also became memorable to me:

Social life is the realization of ideal man in a far higher sense than the life of the mere individual realizes it. Thinking, reason, a rational moral will, a religious culture in the soul, are not of the particular man, but they are the ideal of the species and denote the ascent of the individual into the species. This is not a loss of individuality, but a deepening of individuality into personality, which is the unique phenomenon found in social science.

It followed, therefore, that education is a debt, culture an obligation, which can be honestly discharged only by turning

back into the common life the best results of what others have
made it possible for each one of us to acquire and to be. Education took on a social significance. Personality came to
mean the share of the race life which any one of us acquires.
The quality and proportion of what is common to mankind
thus constituting the personality of any one of us make distinctive the individuality which differentiates one from another.

These deeper convictions and farther-sighted visions were
somewhat foreshadowed in the different outlook taken in my
inaugural address at Chicago from that at Hartford. Then I
coveted for the church the spheres of influence and action
which I claimed other agencies occupied but could not possess. Now I realized that other groups and agencies were essentially religious and constituted along with the church the
kingdom of God on earth; and that, as the church did not
always prove to be the best executor of its own ideals, it was
dependent upon other organized groups to carry them on and
out. Therefore I now held family, neighborly, industrial,
civic, cultural, and other groupings and agencies in which
men, women, and children naturally associate as tributary to
the whole endeavor to realize the ideals of religion. Then the
building-up of the church out of the community and out of
the world seemed to be the function and aim of its ministry
and membership. Now the building of the community and
of a redeemed world out of all available religious resources
seems to be the higher ideal and greater function of the church.
Then the Scriptures and the church were accepted as superimposed from above. Now freedom to account for their
origin historically was stressed as not only a right, but as essential to the understanding of the nature and function of
both.

Adhering closely to the practical purpose of the Seminary
in introducing a sociological department, I tried to start each
course on some common ground shared by my students.
Usually it was the Christian "burden of the soul," which I
interpreted as a personal concern for the whole self of each
man, woman, and child. Gradually we worked back into the
antecedents and out into the social conditions which relate

many others to every one of us. This led us farther afield than the parish and its more or less arbitrarily organized societies and agencies. "Population, Group Life, and the Function of the Church" was the title of a course relating religious views and ministries to the great natural groupings of mankind. Into the industrial sphere we went to discover "The Function of the Church in Industry." At the close of the World War we studied the programs for social reconstruction issued by organizations of labor and capital, by radical groups and governmental bodies, and by several religious fellowships—Roman Catholic, Jewish, and Protestant. Meanwhile, the study of social control was urged upon us both by the responsibility of the community for better or worse conditions, and by experiences emphasizing the betterment of conditions to be essential to the church in applying its ideals and standards of life. All the while, however, major emphasis was laid in every course upon the study and observation of concrete conditions, situations, and relations with which every local church should be in direct contact.

Neither at Hartford nor Chicago Seminary did the time assigned the department permit more than a brief outline of the main topics within the scope of general sociology. I found it possible, however, in one course to introduce the students to the literary and academic development of the science; its distinction from and relation to other sciences; and the theories of social progress, involving the goal and forces of religion. In all this development my students and I were increasingly aided both by the better preparation offered by the colleges from which they came, and by the rapid growth of sociological literature and texts which were available for reference reading. In distinctively Christian literature, Josiah Strong did valuable pioneering statistical service, as did Walter Rauschenbusch, by laying historical and interpretative bases for it, and Lyman Abbott in the pulpit and *The Outlook* by inspiring the social spirit and application of religion. They helped create precedent and collateral reading which greatly facilitated the classroom instruction.

Previous to all this development few colleges included in their curricula any very specific references to social data.

The church neither from the pulpit nor in the Sunday school inculcated the social point of view or gave religious sanction to social ethics. Consequently the students in my earlier classes had to be introduced to studies entirely new to them. Their preconceptions of religion and of the functions of the church and ministry, as well as of the objective of Christianity, were so conventionally individualistic, if not otherworldly, that the very topics of the new courses and the relations of human life they dealt with seemed quite irrelevant both to the preparation for, and the function of, the ministry. Going afield with each class, I gradually counteracted this attitude by bringing them to face facts at first hand like those that would face them on their own fields. Continuously at Chicago Commons, and in turn at hospitals and asylums, police stations and jails, courts and their probation and parole agencies, my students met submerged classes of people, with whose individuals they should deal. Interviews with union-labor and employers' officials, strike leaders and arbitrators, managers of welfare departments and trade-union benefit features gave insight into industrial conditions and relations. Inspections of relief, preventive, and restorative agencies disclosed large-scale dealings with problems that are met in personal detail by every local church and community. Heart-to-heart talks with priests, rabbis, and ministers in charge of great parish, mission, or other church agencies demonstrated what might and should be attempted on a smaller scale.

Not only was Chicago Commons the center at which and from which my students learned what Chicago's cosmopolitan life and human conditions might teach them, but it has been to me the point of contact with these conditions through which I have kept close to the life of my fellow-men and have been enabled to understand and interpret life from its original sources. Not to the building or its equipment, but to the successive groups of my fellow-resident workers at Chicago Commons, whose contacts with the people made mine closer and wider, I owe much if not most of the understanding with which I taught. Without this household, and my own inner family circle at its center to which I owe most, my classroom would have been more academic than practical, more theoretical than exemplary, more stereotyped than original or progressive.

The Seminary faculty never once gave any intimation of being doubtful about the admission of the new department, nor were they ever hesitant in leaving me unrestrained freedom to teach and to develop the social-economic activities of Chicago Commons and to enlist in them myself, there and in the city at large and throughout the Middle West. The fact that none of my Chicago colleagues could have been expected to realize the extent to which sociological teaching and action would seem extraneous both to the conventional seminary curriculum and to the scope of their own studies and experience was offset by my deference to the prior claims of the long-established and universally accredited departments of instruction.

My previous disposition to defer to the teaching, which had always been given the right of way, was strengthened by the wise counsel which I received when about to undertake this pioneering task. It was offered by Dr. Newman Smyth, of New Haven, as I was leaving Hartford for Chicago on this adventure of social faith. "Remember," he said in bidding me farewell, "that the studies you will teach are new to the theological curriculum. Therefore never fail to recognize the priority of the claim of the older departments both to the time and attention of the students. Realizing inevitable limitations, take the opportunity offered to improve it as best you can, patiently working out the development that is sure to come in time and with success." Never have I failed to heed and be grateful for this encouraging caution. Very precious have been and are the affectionate fellowships with my colleagues all these years, to whose personal confidence and unwavering, stout-hearted support I owe so much.

The faith and the fear of both my colleagues and the members of the Seminary's Board of Directors were put to an acid test by the early and long-continued attacks of a Chicago daily newspaper, representing certain vested interests. Before I had closed my first year of teaching, the *Chicago Chronicle*, then the most accredited financial journal in the city, unexpectedly and without any alleged provocation opened its very aggressive attacks upon my department, and upon me personally. Under date of November 30, 1903, a leading editorial bore the title: "Socialism, Sociology and Crime." The far-fetched occasion for this alignment was a bold robbery and murder, committed by young bandits in a distant part of the city, who were as unknown to me or my fellow-workers at Chicago Commons as we were unknown to them. Nevertheless, after reciting the atrocities for which these criminals were executed, the *Chronicle* editorial thus proceeded:

So those who commit robbery with incidental murder are your practical socialists. These remorseless robbers and butchers are regarded in the light of "studies" by our learned sociologists. Your sociologist, being a very scientific man, and of course dispassionate, is not horror stricken in the presence of monstrous crime. He has no feeling about the protection of society against moral monsters who commit such crimes. He is not disturbed by any feeling of indignation or sentiment of justice.

These men of science are careful to exonerate those who commit the atrocious deeds, to minimize personal responsibility and culpability and to throw the burden of the blame upon ancestry, or upon society, or upon any and every person and thing except the criminal himself.

There can be no doubt that the sociologists and the socialists in their respective ways have done much to relax the moral fiber of society. Happily, there is enough left of good old fashioned moral sense to take the romance out of these villainous young butchers and exterminate them for the good of society, if to the regret of sociologists.

Five years later the *Chronicle* made a frontal attack on the Seminary itself, aimed directly to cripple its financial support. Taking advantage of a crisis in its finances and the resignation of its president for purely personal reasons, whose successor I declined to be in loyalty to the specialized work of my own department, an editorial leader on "Sociology and Theology" appeared December 26, 1908. The following excerpts speak plainly enough for themselves:

As Professor Taylor is a prominent socialist, best known from his connection with Chicago Commons, the condition of the Seminary suggests the question whether there is any connection between its socialism and its financial condition. Certainly there is no lack of money in the Congregational denomination, with which this institution is connected, and if the Seminary is stranded it is necessary to look further than the denominational finances to find the cause of it. For this result Professor Taylor and his seminary, which has always backed him, are largely responsible. He has been so successful that he has undermined the church and the pulpit to some extent, and now he does not consider the presidency of his own seminary as worth taking.

That is exactly what might have been expected from a substitute of socialism for Christianity, and politics for preaching. Socialism aims directly at the destruction of the family and the church. Christian socialism is socialism propagated by Christian ministers like Professor Taylor. The Christian socialist falls between two stools. He sacrifices Christianity without winning the socialists. That is what ails the Chicago Theological Seminary.

Christianity is not a system of sociology. It is a method of getting sin pardoned through vicarious atonement so as to escape hell and reach Heaven. The trouble with a large section of the Christian ministry is that they are trying to substitute sociology for theology, and the result is that many of them are losing their jobs and the seminaries are closing their doors.

Much as this annoying notoriety must have disturbed my colleagues' peace of mind and increased the directors' sensitiveness in soliciting funds for the Seminary from their business associates, not any of them expressed to me a doubt or fear, or suggested any caution upon my part. The venerable president, Dr. Franklin W. Fisk, however, did pray at chapel prayers for my protection and guidance, naming me as he did no other of his associates. Noteworthy is the fact that the two professors whose departments reached farthest back had the vision to look farthest ahead. It was Samuel Ives Curtiss, professor of Semitics, and Hugh MacDonald Scott, professor of ecclesiastical history, who had bidden for the admission of this newest teaching to the Seminary curriculum and who sturdily stood by me, both privately and in public. That my tentative teaching came through to any permanent status is due, I am keenly aware, to the patient forbearance and steadfast fellowship of my colleagues in the old faculty and to the stalwart citizens serving on the Board of Directors. Two other seminaries were unafraid to enlist me for temporary lectureships. For several years I served as a staff lecturer at the Western Theological Seminary of the Episcopal church, to enable it to carry on its sociological instruction after its instructor had withdrawn; and also at the Garrett Biblical Institute of the Methodist church, to aid it in establishing a professorship of sociology. Elective courses offered by Northwestern University are open to students of both seminaries.

Academic recognition of this pioneering while under fire was more cautiously and much later offered. One of the earliest of these recognitions came from a professor of economics of national repute who wrote me, referring to the unexpectedly outspoken attitude of a distinguished eastern economist at a meeting of the American Economic Association, and commenting thus facetiously upon the incident:

> You advance guards of civilization must have been brought almost to the verge of palpitation of the heart by that paper, and the discussion following it. I must say that my attention was somewhat diverted from the main discussion by my speculation of what you thought of it. I kept wondering if you realized at the time how much you had accomplished, and how rapidly the world had moved when the representatives of one of the richest and oldest universities took such views as they did without creating a ripple among the membership of the association.
>
> They were views which you and your like have preached for twenty years, and for which you have been called "socialists," "anarchists" and other vague and unmeaning hard names. However you may have rejoiced at this meeting, you must have felt that the advance of the great body of the membership had deprived you and a few others of what John Morley called "Your majestic isolation." You are no longer an orphan, exiled and outcast, unless you choose to take a long breath, gird your loins, and once more run ahead of the procession. The academic contingent of the world has overtaken you, and has swallowed at one gulp the doctrine which you have preached but which they have sneered at, lo these many years.

Thirty-six years after all this pioneering began, an event occurred which far more than anything I could have hoped for or even imagined gave academic and public recognition to the results achieved. It was the dedication of the Seminary's assembly hall, adjoining the campus of the University of Chicago, the building of which was due to the initiative and initial financial support given the project by my former students, led by my devoted comrade, Ozora S. Davis. Its completion, and that of other building units, was made possible by the bequest of Victor F. Lawson, whose earlier interest in the Seminary grew through his enlistment in the development of its sociological department and the work of Chicago Commons.

To commemorate the permanent establishment of this first sociological department in any church institution, and to express their appreciation of its value to them in their work on their widely scattered fields, the Alumni wished it to bear my name—which may serve at least to date the event. The bound file of letters from nearly two hundred of them, conveying their greetings to me, is cherished even more dearly to my heart than the beautiful building which they and many others sacrificed so much to erect.

The dedicatory occasion was memorable for the notable addresses by Jane Addams; by three of my former students who had come to distinction—Ozora S. Davis as president of the Seminary, J. W. F. Davies as a leader in the religious education movement, and James Mullenbach as the successful adjuster of industrial differences in a great manufacturing industry; and by Professor Arthur E. Holt, the most capable successor who could have been chosen to carry on and out the Department of Social Ethics, into which my single professorship has developed.

Far more significant was the opening of the Social Science Research Building at the University of Chicago on December 16, 1929. It signalized the co-operative grouping of the older Departments of Economics, Political Science, and Philosophy with the newer Department of Sociology as the "social sciences." Since this title had long been denied academic status elsewhere, this token of its acceptance tacitly recognized the claim of the sociological sciences to be of co-ordinate standing and scientific value. And this acceptance was attested not only by the dedication of this building, but also by the representatives of Social Science Research councils in seven universities, including the oldest of them, Harvard, Yale, and Columbia, who participated in the dedicatory exercises. "Looking back to the early days when we had hardly enough material to construct a course of lectures," Professor Francis Greenwood Peabody, who opened at Harvard in the early eighties the first university course on social ethics, writes of the program of this recent occasion, "it is really thrilling in its interest, and we are very grateful that we had at least a chance to show the way to greater things."

The academic and practical value of this building equipment was signalized also by the publication of a volume entitled *Chicago—An Experiment in Social Science Research*.[1] It reports the experience and achievements of a local research committee representing the Departments of Economics, Sociology, Political Science, History, Philosophy, and the Graduate School of Social Service Administration. Their five years' co-operative work anticipated and led the way to this unique laboratory workshop. The wide range of local researches summarized led these experimenters to expect to share this Social Science Research Building with representatives of the Departments of Psychology, Physiology, Bacteriology, Home Economics, Hygiene, and the professional Schools of Education, Library, Law, Medicine, and Theology, numbering perhaps two hundred scholars and workers thus equipped for co-operative research.

The appearance of the first of the fifteen volumes of the *Encyclopaedia of the Social Sciences*, just as this book goes to press, is the greatest waymark of their progress yet registered, surveying the highways, the trails to which were blazed by W. D. P. Bliss in his creditable *Encyclopedia of Social Reform* in 1897.

[1] Edited by T. V. Smith and Leonard White (University of Chicago Press, 1929), pp. 283.

CHAPTER XXIX

FORTHGOINGS ON THE PLATFORM AND
IN THE PRESS

IN ADDRESSING churches and other religious assemblies on special occasions in New England cities, where the social evangelism of the Fourth Church at Hartford had attracted attention, I always took opportunity to claim that the work I described should not be considered distinctive of any one church or community more than of all others. Yet the mere human touch of it seemed to be regarded as exceptional. Gradually at first, although rapidly later, effectively practical efforts increased, especially when and where local churches federated to serve their communities co-operatively. Social-service commissions have resulted not only in interpreting and applying religious ideals and resources to community life, but also in inspiring the church membership to recognize and realize the social aims and ends of the Christian Evangel.

The platforms of schools, colleges, universities, and seminaries have called me forth from my classrooms ever since I began teaching at Hartford and Chicago seminaries. Year by year, especially in the Middle West, and also in Canada, I have responded to the invitations of students and professors to give single or brief series of addresses on special phases of the social propaganda and industrial situations. Opportunities for personal interviews, or for life-work conferences, were generally sought on these occasions by students seeking guidance either in the choice of professional pursuits or in the exertion of social and religious influence through the occupational positions which they were preparing to fill.

Beyond these church and academic circles numerous opportunities have been continuously offered to hold interviewing conferences with men's and women's clubs, bankers' and lawyers' associations, labor unions and employers' organizations, local and state conferences of charities, summer assemblies of students and chautauquas in many states. An experience on one occasion at Montreal may give a glimpse of many others, in which appointments multiplied, while fulfilling one or two engagements calling me to the city. I wrote home that my five academic lectures and my address at the twenty-fifth anniversary of the Young Women's Christian Association had led to a public meeting at the Board of Trade Hall, called especially to hear me, which, with several other hearings, gave me fifteen public appointments to meet in six days—"experiences so strangely given me." At some industrial centers I was surprised to be invited to address trades unions or federations of labor in their own halls. On some occasions their members were especially invited to attend sessions of conferences at which I spoke on social and industrial topics of interest to them. I was especially gratified when this occurrence was the first instance in which labor organizations had ever met with these churches or conferences.

Tokens were not lacking that the information concerning conditions and relationships thus given inspired social ideals and prompted educational efforts to realize them. Visitors from many of these centers followed me back to the sources of my information on my fields of labor. Resulting social achievements in some of these towns and cities followed the return of these visitors, who brought back suggestions for improvement of local conditions.

From college and university centers students came to Chicago to see for themselves what had been told them. Summer scholarships were established, on which men and women students were sent to Chicago Commons during vacation, who reported back to their teachers and fellow-students their observation or their findings attained while enlisted in the work to which they were assigned. Whole classes, led by their professors, came to be guided to observe what could be seen during their visit of a day or so. Some of the students thus interested were led to specialize in their subsequent academic courses, or in resident work at Chicago Commons after graduation. Not a few such have risen to distinction not only along the lines they then pursued, but in the service of other fields for which this special training and experience equipped them. Several social settlements and kindred local agencies took their initiative from these recitals of experience on the Chicago field, or from the incentives received in visiting one or more of these agencies.

Whatever was the influence thus exerted upon others, very profound was that which others exerted upon me while enlisted in these forthgoing platform experiences. My close personal contacts with individuals led me to trust the capacity in every one of my fellow-men, at least to recognize a higher spiritual ideal than had been visioned. In every community I found at least a remnant of the people receptive to higher social ideals and responsive to motives that could be developed into sacrificial service. My conviction of these certainties was inspired and strengthened by the eager interest of many hearers in having their attention called for the first time to the social sources of their personality and its educational development.

Chautauqua assemblies were new sources of inspiration and encouragement to me. I had never even caught sight of any such summer assembly while in the East. My first contacts with them in the West were revelations of a willingness to sacrifice, individually and with others, to realize higher social ideals, such as I had not seen before. Such flocking of farmers' families and folks from small towns to the chautauquas held at Crete (Neb.), Ottawa (Kan.), and Bay View (Mich.) astonished me. The continuity of interest which attracted the same people, not only to return year after year to these summer centers, but also to maintain local reading circles during the winter, greatly impressed me. The spell which the few art exhibits, loaned one of these chautauquas by the Chicago Art Institute, cast over those who had never seen the like before reimpressed upon me the character value of the ministry of beauty. To what a people's university this popularizing of culture might lead I did not imagine until I first visited the mother-chautauqua on Chautauqua Lake, New York. There, where with Percy Alden, of London, and Jane Addams,

of Chicago, I participated in the first Chautauqua Conference
held on the social settlements, I caught my first sight of
Bishop John Heyl Vincent, the founder and for more than fifty
years the inspirer and leader of this great movement. More
than that, he personified it, in the Christlike democracy of
his religion and his citizenship.

All these experiences were so impressive as to banish forever from my mind the last vestiges of any class consciousness
that clung to me. It left no ground for any claim to the monopoly of either the love or possession of beauty, truth, morality, and religion by any one cast, or class, or sect. This
social consciousness, thus begotten both from above and
about, grounded an unwavering faith in the might of right
and in the ultimate triumph of love. And this confidence has
strengthened every little effort put forth in the service of the
greater cause and the larger hope.

The means of promoting these aims were also revealed to
be indirect, opportune, diverse, and concessive, as well as
direct and imperative. This revelation began to come to me
when I was first publicly challenged to prove forthwith what
I had just said. This startling and disconcerting experience in
a mission hall taught me, as it might well teach all preachers,
more than I ever could have learned in having everything my
own way in preaching from the pulpit to passively silent
hearers. The memory of it led me to weigh my words and
cultivate readiness to meet such emergencies, when I ventured to preach in the streets, and still more when addressing
workingmen in their union halls or on the "free floor" of Chicago Commons. These hearers made no exception of me, or
of anyone else, in claiming the right to interrupt, challenge,
and talk back as a condition of listening to anything a speaker
might put forth. The outcome of this clash of opinion and
conviction, of assertion and denial, of taking one's self too
seriously and suffering the reduction to absurdity, proved to
be the very best way of reaching agreements on the truth, as
well as a sure way of removing the pride of self-assertion
which obstructs the pursuit of it. All this has enhanced the
safety of free speech and free assembly, of frank discussion
and open diplomacy, between those who differ on social, in-

dustrial, political, and religious issues. Repression of thought, silencing of speech, and driving minorities into secret refuge from the persecuting intolerance of majorities harden and deepen the lines of cleavage, strengthen reactions, beget counsels of despair and acts of desperation. These in turn thwart reason and hope in finding any grounds upon which to live and work together, while seriously menacing public peace and safety.

It was the National Conference of Charities and Correction which more than any other platform occasion opened to me the fellowship with many of those who became my inspirers, guides, exemplars, and associates in the field of social thought and action. The broad platform of this great fellowship beckoned me within an ever widening horizon, just when I began teaching young people to apply the common faith to the common life, to translate creed into deed, to transform little groups into broader human fellowships.

There, at my first attendance, and ever since, and often elsewhere, I found that persons are greater sources of inspiration and help than their programs, that personal fellowships make the platforms from which they speak mean more, that what they say gains weight, significance, and momentum from what one knows of who they are, what they are doing, and whom they represent.

There I met the "elder statesmen" of the social realm, for the first and many subsequent times. Among them were a few of the most prominent founders of the Conference, all of whom were members or officials of state boards of charities and correction. Foremost in this group was Mr. Frank B. Sanborn. As chairman of the Massachusetts State Board and secretary of the American Social Science Association's Committee which initiated and convened the Conference, he, more than anyone else, was its father. In appearance, manner, public speech, and personal conversation he was the very type of the New England scholar in social politics. Distinguished alike as journalist, author, and administrator, he brought both prestige and efficiency to the new organization, which from the very start established its claim and significance as national. William P. Letchworth as truly represented the very different type of New York State institutional leaders, who then were formulating its eleemosynary policies. Timothy Nicholson, of Indiana, long the Quaker patriarch of the Conference, personified the very spirit of charity itself in the reality of his friendliness, the simplicity of his manner, and the strength and wisdom of his counsel, in his expression of which he was as silent in speech as he proved to be efficient in action. Of like quality and capacity was his colleague, Amos W. Butler, who brought from his studies and authorship in the natural sciences, the precision, thoroughness, and vision which gave authority and practical efficiency to his social investigations and institutional administration. Frederick H. Wines, author of able penological works and son of a pioneer American penologist, long led the discussions of the wardens of correctional institutions and members of their boards of control both in this Conference and in the American Prison Association.

In rallying to the Conference an ever wider constituency, and in holding together its diverse elements, Hastings Hornell Hart, perhaps more than anyone else, was the link between the public officials and the voluntary agencies represented in the Conference. Alexander Johnson, who succeeded him as secretary, brought into the well-established mechanism of the Conference a human touch, a great good fellowship, an inspiring, tolerant, progressive spirit, such as only a unique personality could give. *Who's Who* well characterizes him in the one all-inclusive word "humanitarian," for such he is par excellence. Both of these brotherly wise men volunteered to be consultants to all seeking their counsel at every Conference meeting.

The expansion of the scope and constituency of the Conference was an inspiration and object lesson that broadened the spirit and vision of some of its members, but not all. For it was not achieved without opposition from institutionally self-conscious public officials who wanted to keep it within their own circle. The first to be admitted to their fellowship were representatives of the charity organization societies and other voluntary relief agencies. They had previously been welcomed as visitors, and once in a while to read papers. But it was fortunate that one of the first of them to become a member of the Conference was Robert Treat Paine, of Massachusetts. He was not only a typical Bostonian, but in appearance, courtly manner, and dignified speech he seemed to be a gentleman who had stepped out of Colonial times to steady and stabilize, if not to hold in leash, the on-coming generations. Robert W. de Forest, president, and Charles D. Kellogg, secretary of the New York Charity Organization Society, Homer Folks, of the New York State Charities Aid Society, and Joseph P. Byers, general secretary of the American Prison Association and in turn an executive of several other public welfare agencies, also commanded the deference due their public service and their personal distinction. John M. Glenn, of the Russell Sage Foundation, first interpreted the functions of the great funds. Jewish charities were represented by such able leaders as Felix Adler, N. S. Rosenau, David Blaustein, Judge Julian W. Mack, and Rabbi Emil G. Hirsch, whose names stood for administrative achievement and some of them for scholarly authorship. Cardinal Gibbons and Archbishop Ireland led the way for a long succession of spokesmen for Roman Catholic social agencies, including Professors John A. Ryan, William J. Kirby, and Frederic Siedenburg.

Nowhere more than in this national conference have women registered their leadership in social-economic work. By electing to its presidency Jane Addams, Julia C. Lathrop, Mrs. John M. Glenn, Grace Abbott, Gertrude Vaile and Miriam Van Waters, the Conference honored itself in recognizing the distinction of their public service. Strength and vision have been added to the programs and the committee work of the Conference by the distinctive part that women have taken in both.

When in 1896 the social-settlement constituency was recognized as eligible to membership in the Conference, it was not without something of the same askance attitude upon the part of the charity-workers toward them as the state officials had shown toward the representatives of the voluntary relief and charity organization agencies when they were admitted. Yet at Grand Rapids, through the hospitable broad-mindedness of the secretary, Alexander Johnson, a whole Sunday afternoon was left in charge of some of us settlement people in which to interpret the Conference to industrial workers and their employers. This first attempt of the kind has been repeated at many subsequent conferences, especially when held at the larger industrial centers. From this time on, not only did the other two constituencies of the Conference fraternize more freely with the settlement newcomers, but the latter got over their fear of being classified with either.

The settlements were the advance guard of a long procession of allied groups and agencies, which greatly enlarged the constituency and broadened the scope and spirit of the Conference. Through the interorbiting of their memberships and by holding their annual meetings at the same place and at or near the same time as the Conference, such a community of interests was recognized and shared that a broader name than the National Conference of Charities and Correction was sought to express the greater significance of the Conference. It was found in the title National Conference of Social Work.

A world-view of the Christian religion and its practical recognition of the unity of the race under the fatherhood of God had been given me at the meetings of the American Board of Commissioners for Foreign Missions. Josiah Strong's stirring books, *Our Country, The New Era, The Challenge of the City*, broadened the home-missionary fields and enterprise. These great outlooks were supplemented by this greater insight into the needs of human kind which was taken from the still broader platform of this Conference. Behind these spokesmen or silent doers of good deeds it did not require much imagination to see the multitude of the illy born and bred, of the neglected and self-neglectful, of the isolated and lonely, of those in helpless infancy and dependent old age, and of the still greater multitude of toilers bearing the burdens and carrying forward the hope of the world. Going on before and following after appeared the prophets and seers, the legislators and leaders, of a better civilization, in which more justice will make charity less necessary and brotherhood more real. It seemed more possible that even the divided faiths of Christendom might unite to be the ministering body of the Son of Man, when on this platform Roman Catholic, Protestant, Jew, and agnostic opened their hearts and spoke their minds to one another, inspired by their allied ministry to fellow-men.

In commemorating its first half-century at Washington in 1923, the Conference called upon its former presidents to express in a few words what it had meant to them personally. My response came from grateful memories of the past and from an appreciation never keener than at that impressive present. I wrote:

The National Conference did much to broaden the horizon of my early manhood, and has kept the field of vision and action extending ever since. At first it seemed like a great ecumenical council, such as used to represent all Christendom. At length it impressed me as greater, because it included and transcended all faiths in uniting all loving hearts and willing hands in the service of all who suffer.

As it became still more inclusive in associating many more groups devoted to the protection and promotion of social and industrial justice, equality of opportunity and legal rights, rising standards of living and public welfare, and more human ideals of national and international relations, the Conference grew to be the finest expression of the old aspiration which it inspires every member to claim that "nothing which is common to man is foreign to me."

Its greatest inspirations and most permanent values have come to me more through the fine fellowships and lifelong friendships formed upon the floor of the house and between sessions than from the best utterances upon the platform, or the finest contributions to its printed proceedings. And I have urged my students and fellow-workers for many a year to seek the same great advantages open to them at the cost of any personal sacrifice or interruption in their public work.

CORRESPONDENCE

Correspondence with those writing to me about the work of the church for the community grew widely with the years at Hartford. It assumed larger proportions as Chicago Commons, even more than the Seminary, became a clearing house for the exchange of information and suggestions by mail. Correspondence with six hundred contributing associates of Chicago Commons, and as many more former residents, has been reciprocally valuable to them and to us. It was so much in the direct line of our purpose to keep in vital touch with those on the field that it had to be given the right of way. To do so I was predisposed by the example of my father in writing so many personal letters to those who sought his counsel and to many others whose sorrows or joys prompted the expression of his sincere sympathy.

The increasingly large and continuous exactions laid upon me in thus giving and getting information and counsel required expert secretarial service. To Carrie Clawson (Mrs. Vance Rawson), Mabel A. Hawkins, and my daughters, Helen D. Taylor (Mrs. George Wallace Carr) and Lea D. Taylor, I owe more than I can express for invaluable aid which they rendered me at much personal sacrifice. Indispensable has been their help in the gathering, classification, and filing, not only of official reports, articles, and periodicals, findings of investigations, and surveys in great variety, but also the clipping of fugitive material from the daily and weekly press, for quite as necessary, if temporary, use. It has kept open and up to date the sources upon which I relied for information and suggestion which had not yet gotten into books. Thus especially in my work through the press, and somewhat in the preparation of my lectures and addresses, I was enabled the better to keep pace with current developments.

By this correspondence, however, I was put and kept in touch with observant and very considerate friendly people, who from widely scattered and divergent points of view contributed their letters and much printed matter to my file. To the good fellowship of many of them I owe dear friendships and much help.

THE PRESS

I was first constrained to write for the press when in my Senior year at Rutgers College I was elected by my fellow-students one of the editors of their monthly paper, the *Targum*, so called as a byplay upon President William H. Campbell's frequent reference to the old Jewish rabbinical literature collected under that name. However it may have served its student and alumni readers' interest in their college athletics, politics, and personalia, I remember nothing appearing from my own or other pens of sufficient public interest to have "set the Hudson River on fire," or even the Raritan, on the banks of which our college song forever located us.

My first real venture in print was written as early as 1898 from my country parish five years after I had entered the ministry. It appeared in *The Christian Intelligencer*, the denominational weekly of the Reformed church. Excerpts from it are here quoted as reflections of the light then dawning upon me in the consciousness that life is greater than logic, and that spirit transcends the letter. The article, which was widely quoted in the religious press, bore the title "The Heresy of Life," and struck keynotes to which my preaching, teaching, writing, and personal and public work have ever since been keyed.

More heresy is lived than is written or believed. Although less talked of and condemned, the heresy of life is more culpable and disastrous than that of opinion. The Gospel has suffered more from the underestimate of the one than from the overrated influence of the other.

When orthodoxy of profession is opposed by heresy of life, the latter term rather more than the former should designate the character in which they meet. For the principles upon which one habitually acts ever dominate, and should dominate those we profess. Whatever, therefore, we may call our theoretical belief, inconsistency between faith and life is practical skepticism.

While at Hartford only two of my contributions to the press took more permanent form than brief articles published in the religious papers. One of those was a series of eight studies entitled "Suggestions about Methods of Christian Work." They were printed with *Studies in the English Bible* by my colleague, Professor C. S. Beardslee, as the first seven numbers in the Hartford Seminary publications. In studying scriptural suggestions of what Christian work is and how it is to be done, I recorded my first impressions of some of the fundamental social concepts to be found in the Scriptures. Among them were Jesus' clear consciousness of his mission to carry on and out the messianic kingdom proclaimed by the Hebrew prophets; Paul's assertion of the solidarity of the race, in such expressions as "All have sinned," "All shall be made alive," "All baptized into one body." Forecasts of the modern conception of the social organism and the social consciousness were discerned in such declarations as, "Ye are the body of Christ and members each in his part," "the Church which is his body." The social goal found sublime expression in Isaiah's inclusion of all Israel or the whole "Remnant," as constituting the "Servant of Jehovah" commissioned to bring in the "Golden Age," which is still more gloriously revealed in the "City of God," culminating in the New Testament Scriptures.

The development of this social consciousness, however, could be traced in Scripture only through its historical interpretation based upon the readjusted chronology of the Higher Criticism. This discovery marked the first cleavage I experienced between the more or less literalistic training of my seminary course and the more modern and scientific method of interpreting the Scriptures, to which I thus found myself committed.

The second of these more permanent contributions to the press was *A Religious Census of the City of Hartford*. With the help of Seminary students I undertook a canvass of the entire city and edited its findings. It was issued by the Connecticut Bible Society, under whose auspices the work was undertaken, and was reprinted by the Hartford Seminary Press, to emphasize and illustrate the original and individual work done by the students of the seminary in its Practical Department. The facts found included under a summary of population the nationalities constituting it, the boarders in private families, the denominational and local-church preferences of individuals, ranging over thirteen sects and forty churches, the number of families in each denomination, those not attending religious service and those not possessing Bibles, and the Sunday-school statistics of all faiths. Under destructive forces were listed the saloons, their licenses and locations; the houses of prostitution with an estimate of their inmates, and the statistics of the jail and town-farm population. The pamphlet of forty pages included also descriptive summaries of the work of preventive, relief, industrial, and social agencies, more or less closely related to church and mission work.

As this survey was issued in 1890, it may claim to be one of the earliest taken in this country, since no reference to any prior city-wide canvass is found in the Russell Sage Foundation's department of surveys and exhibits. Its significance lies less in its findings than in the stress it laid upon the im-

portance of having a factual basis for the intelligent undertaking of any religious or social work.   The widespread movement to this end which has since developed has resulted in so
many more thorough and permanently valuable investigations of local, country-wide, and world-wide conditions and
situations that reference to this one is justified only by the
precedent it set.

Opportunities to contribute to religious weeklies, articles,
singly or in consecutive series along specified lines, came to me
unsought. I also conducted in the publications of the Young
Men's Christian Association and the Young People's Society
of Christian Endeavor continuous departments entitled
"Christian Citizenship," "Social Aspects of Life and Labor,"
and "Industrial Conditions and Relations." Scope was thus
afforded for a wide range of special topics, as well as for comment on current events, interpreting their social, civic, and
religious significance.

After two years of pioneering at Chicago Commons, we felt
the need of some medium of communication with our co-
operating constituencies additional ·to correspondence. We
had oriented our situation between the lines sufficiently to
venture a publication of our own. It was indeed adventurous
to undertake it not only without special funds, but when our
income was so irregular and insufficient to support the settlement work that deficits had to be covered or carried on personal accounts almost every month.

But we had working capital enough to warrant our adventure in the journalistic experience, the versatile ability, and
the socially motivated, loyal spirit of John Palmer Gavit.
These qualities fitted him for his subsequent career as chief
representative of the Associated Press at Albany and at
Washington, D.C., for several years, as managing editor of
the *New York Evening Post* subsequently, and later as the
author of several volumes. I had known him in Hartford as a
bright, young journalist, to whom our church work for the
neglected and self-neglectful made a first appeal for membership to which he had ever responded. So strongly did the
opportunity for service at Chicago Commons appeal to him
that he forsook his promising professional opening, sacrificing

also his salary, to join our settlement staff at the barest subsistence support for himself and his wife, who was of like spirit. To him belongs the credit of founding and editing for four years *The Commons*, a monthly quarto publication which was issued by Chicago Commons for nine years, 1896–1905, when it was merged with *Charities*, to be published in New York City. *Charities and the Commons* in 1909 became *The Survey*.

"Without promise for the future," Mr. Gavit announced the appearance of the first number of *The Commons*. And well he might, had he then forecast fully the uncertainties with which the continuance of any publication was beset. So great were they that he was obliged to delay issuing a next number, as far after it was due as postal regulations allowed, until we could make some payments long overdue to our patient printer. But the delay was made as inconspicuous as possible by shifting the date of the publication from where it belonged under the title on the first page to the end of an inner column, where it served the double purpose of a filler! When printed, we resident workers at Chicago Commons all rallied for nearly an all-night "bee" to wrap, paste, and address the whole edition, which grew from a few hundred to over four thousand copies.

Despite this and other economies, and because of its cost increasing with its growth, the financial burden became more burdensome, while publishing our monthly at the nominal rate of twenty-five cents for a year's subscription. It was no less so after the rate was raised to fifty cents, "with a good deal of regret and not a little embarrassment." This was due to the fact that within its first year *The Commons* had to be enlarged from eight to twelve and then to sixteen pages, in order to represent many other settlements and allied agencies seeking its publicity and advocacy. It thus attained a circulation widely scattered through many states and abroad, but nowhere locally sufficient to attract or warrant commercial advertisements.

Above these depressing and diverting embarrassments, its editor buoyantly rose, possessed by his passion to fulfil his promise to promote "the humanizing of social conditions in the river wards and other industrial districts in Chicago and elsewhere"; "to help men, women and children to be their best selves"; "to avoid controversy and yet reserve the right of comment and criticism upon those things obstructive of or hostile to the principles for which we stand."

Right valiantly did he hew to the line of this high standard, yet with a good humor as human as his aim was undeviatingly true and direct. To my caution against shedding more heat than light he replied: "If you only knew what I kept in, you would never be surprised at what I let out." The files of *The Commons* attest at a glance the range and rare quality of his editorials, his realistic accuracy in reporting events, speeches, conditions, and achievements, alike from neighborhood life, academic sociological classrooms, labor unions and legislative halls, personal interviews, and also from pulpit, parish, and foreign-mission fields. Fair and lifelike were his character sketches of persons outstanding in current life or literature. Keen was his criticism and appreciation of books. The originality and ideality of his realism appeared in the memorable quotations he gleaned from his wide reading, as well as in his own inspirational verse. Especially telling were his visions across all class distinctions separating the one or the few from the many, such as his lines on "An Unknown Workman against the Sky," "They Two," and "Love in Hell."

The withdrawal of Mr. Gavit from residence at Chicago Commons, "for personal and domestic reasons admitting of no choice," deprived me of his ever enlivening companionship for the keenly felt loss of which he has ever since partly compensated by his irresistibly characteristic correspondence. In turning over his editorial responsibility for *The Commons* to me "as the only one in position to assume it," he reaffirmed his "unabated loyalty to the free speech, fair play and the unreserving espousal of the cause of social justice and human unification" to which he and I had committed our paper and ourselves. The only other journals then circulating from Chicago, but within limited constituencies, were *The Public*, the Single Tax weekly, ably edited by Louis F. Post; and *Unity*, aggressively conducted by Jenkin Lloyd Jones in the interest of liberal religion.

In justifying my assumption of this overburdening care and responsibility, I claimed the service of *The Commons* to be so distinctive, in its interpretation and promotion of the social movement from the settlement point of view, as to warrant the struggle for its existence and development at whatever cost. Personal experiences in vital contact with actual conditions and with the lives of men, women, and children, families, industrial and other groups affected thereby afforded insight and outlook upon current situations which prompted the effort to understand and interpret them. Industrial conflicts through which we passed, for instance, moved me to report facts and impressions indicating the public to be the third and greatest party to every such issue, having rights which both belligerents were bound to respect. To help lift these issues above mere personal animosities and class antagonisms, I tried to portray the historic and economic background out of which they arose in a consecutive series of studies of the labor movement, which also formed the basis of a course of classroom lectures on "The Ethics of Industry."

The struggle to rescue our ward from the neglect and demoralization due to the political corruption then prevalent and powerful in the city drew us to the firing line, whence we could more vividly impress upon our readers and hearers both the local and larger issues at stake. The part played in this corruption by public-utility corporations drew fire from us and to us. It disclosed the trail of the serpent to be over so many sources of hitherto-unsuspected income that I was led to offset Dr. Washington Gladden's protest against the acceptance of "tainted money" by religious agencies in an article raising the inquiry, "Shall the pedigree of the dollar destroy its destiny?" Answering my own question, I urged that without condoning the offense of its acquisition or recognizing any obligation to its donor, it might be better to divert even the tainted dollar to a good purpose than to ignore the fact that it surely had some destiny to fulfil. I was sharply taken to task, however, by a leading socialist workingman on the ground that "the very worst diversion of such a dollar is that which gives its donor any claim to the gratitude of just men for beneficence."

found them to be tributary to each other. So my *apologia* ran thus:

Both the course of thought and the conclusions that follow are the out-growth of experience. They grew from the ground up. They bear the earth flavors of each field of endeavor—rural, pastoral and professorial, civic. Wherein the conclusions differ from whatever prompted the course of ac-tion which led to them, the difference is due to the trend of the times. Con-servative antecedents and training laid upon heart and conscience the burden of the soul. The soul grew into the whole self. The self took on whatever shaped it in the push from behind and the thrust from about. Then, to apply the simple Gospel to saving the soul was to extend and apply the common faith to the social conditions of the common life. This was a reordination to ministry, a rededication of the church. Evangelism became no less personal for being more social. Conditions needed to be evangelized, so as to become at least compatible with, and not destructive of, the Christian ideals and standards of life. Thus the community became both field and force for the Church. The city became the laboratory for the classroom. Civics came to share with pastoral sociology, and laymen and women with students for the ministry, efforts to teach and train. Social settlement residence seemed naturally the next step to the further-ance of this purpose, the best viewpoint and vantage when to fulfill it.

To fraternize the conditions of life and labor, to Christianize the frame-work and spirit of the community, and to humanize religion for the pro-motion of these ends, became the Holy Grail.

From this Foreword I hewed to the line of my then-present convictions along such lines of cleavage as these—life and religion, personality a social product and force, changing con-ditions of a working faith, the religion of human relation-ships, industry and religion—their common ground and in-terdependence, organized industry and organized religion, church and community—their interrelation and common aim.

Quite as significant as anything I wrote of my own attitude was Jane Addams' disclosure of hers in what she approvingly wrote of mine. Her following references to my point of view in her generous Introduction to the volume reflect her own all the more clearly for being descriptive of another:

In the light of daily living we may perhaps claim for the ideas set forth in this book that they are "true," in the definition of Professor James, in that they have been "assimilated, validated, corroborated, and verified in experience."

Throughout these chapters it is as though the author saw the arid wastes of modern life being slowly flooded by an incoming tide of religion, which will in time irresistibly bear away many impediments now blocking the path of social progress. The reader shares the consciousness that these beneficent waters are rising in response to one of those world forces which inevitably draw men's wills into one effective current.

He knows that the religious synthesis, or rather that the competing religious syntheses, are constantly changing and differentiating themselves in response to special needs; that such adaptations in organized religion are evolved, not only because new needs confront the church from without, but also because there is a vigorous minority within the church whom the existing forms of expression no longer satisfy.

A group within the church is now demanding that a new form of social action shall express their yearning sense of justice and compassion; quite as the schoolmen once insisted that creeds and dogmas should embody their philosophy or the artists that their absorbing desire for beauty should be built into cathedrals and painted upon the walls of shrines. This thirst for beauty and order in human relationships may seize upon the religious spirits of our time, as the desire for personal holiness and for unbroken communion with God in another period of history drove thousands of men to spend their lives in hermitage or monastery.

The church, with its chance of miracle, as it were, its divine help, its faith so invincible and so incalculable, offers itself as a refuge against unaided human effort and against the scientific estimate of the slow pace of social amelioration. Religion has always provided for deep-seated wants which mortals themselves cannot satisfy, and has ever comforted man for his own insufficiencies.

Religious expression in social action would be the one thing able to unite the extreme individualism taught by the evangelical churches with that concerted action which is only possible when a central authority is acknowledged. Such expression would be a veritable social growth, based upon the agreements of experience and verified by the current events in which all participate. Without it, at this moment it is difficult to see how religion can adequately perform its traditional function in the world.

Among the reviews called forth by the volume three are distinctive for laying the same imperative emphasis upon the social sphere and function of religion from very different points of view. Over his signature Dr. Emil G. Hirsch devoted an editorial review of the volume in the *Reform Advocate*, published in the interest of reformed Judaism. Noting that the book "recognizes in Judaism a religious force richly endowed with elements making for social justice" and that "nowhere are we confronted with distortions of old Jewish thought intercalated for the purpose of exacting Christianity at the expense of the mother-religion," he credited the author with having found among his fellow-Jewish workers "men and women who drew from their religion the inspiration which has been his because drawn from his Christian faith." Referring at length to the fact that believers and unbelievers alike deny religion the right and the voice to speak about social action as though an intruder upon this field, Dr. Hirsch ventured to assert that such skeptics as do not refuse to be instructed "will not lay this volume aside without realizing that without religion social action is foredoomed to failure and the social worker to disheartenment." He concluded his generous review by hoping that this exposition "will lead Jewish and Christian students alike to the endeavor each to make his own particular religion effective as the dominating force of social action."

Won by Jane Addams' introductory essay as "fruitful with vital suggestions, as well as cordially sympathetic with the author's trend of thought," and also by Rabbi Hirsch's "unhesitating and unqualified indorsement of the book," Dr. Edwin Pond Parker in the *Hartford Courant* conceded that "it has come to pass that the social conditions of human life are now such that religion, Jewish or Christian, conservative or progressive, must, in order to be effective, manifest itself in social action." While emphasizing his opinion that not all the positions taken would escape unchallenged, yet he affirmed the thesis of the volume to be maintained that "personal religion is deepened and vitalized, as well as broadened and humanized, by the application of it to social needs and civic evils and that it requires just this culture no less than that of private means of grace." Significant are these concessions because elicited by the appeal of the social spirit of religion from one of the most noted exponents of New England individualism, both in its ecclesiastical and civic expression. The breadth of his literary culture and his theological opinion gave charm to a sturdy independence in speech and action, thus markedly illustrating a liberalism that fails to broaden the outlook for social justice through political action.

Walter Rauschenbusch, still more widely known for his uncompromisingly radical ideal of the social order and his scholarly interpretation of Christianity in accordance there-

with, graciously contented himself with emphasizing the
points on which I agreed with him, without chiding me for
stopping short of the conclusions upon which we disagreed.
Yet he indorsed my advocacy of "the more wholesome methods of salvation that make less of the artificial church distinctions of saint and sinner, and deal with the fundamental
human relationships set for us by God in human nature and
human society." What struck him most, however, was that
in telling the unfolding of my experience which he had watched
so long, Miss Addams was "sketching a little history of the
growth of social feeling and activity in our own time," unconsciously using my experience "as a symbol and epitome
of the great spiritual movement."

Thus from diametrically opposite points of view these
three reviewers are found to be at one in both the ideals and
spirit of their differing views of religion—an experience all
too rare at that time, but happily quite commonly shared
now.

After ten years' residence at Chicago Commons I found
myself established in a point of view from which observations
were taken that others sought to share. Reports of platform
addresses which I made in and out of town led to newspaper
interviews and articles in weekly periodicals. What I saw and
learned of local conditions was thus sought because the information upon which it was based was credited with being
acquired at first hand from primary sources. Of the conditions
immediately surrounding our settlement residence I had eye-
and-ear testimony of my own ever ready at hand. With
other situations I came into contact by personal inspection,
or through others personally acquainted with them. Prime
sources of this understanding I found in the more or less
friendly confidence of the policeman on the beat, the judge
on the municipal-court bench, the ward superintendent of
street-cleaning, the fireman at his station, the county-relief
agent, the district charity visitor and visiting nurse, the
officials of the trade union and the employers' association,
the strike leader and the factory superintendent, the party
boss and the city and county official, the saloonkeeper, the
dance-hall proprietor, and the local movie-theater manager.

Most of these men were found to be wide open to frank personal intercourse, square dealing between man and man, with no fear of any breach of confidence when confidential interviews were held. I also came to rely upon some very bad men who could and would do good things better than some good men who did not know how to do them so well.

From the beginning of my Chicago residence I had found the *Chicago Daily News* to be the most reliable, fair and open-minded, independent and progressive, of all the city newspapers, with few rivals in these respects elsewhere. I was still further attracted to it by its leadership of forward movements. It was the first journal of the West to venture to be the people's paper at one cent a copy to serve its local fellow-citizens. It not only popularized educational material in its own columns, but conducted winter courses of free public lectures in public-school buildings at its own expense. It assumed responsibility for financing and managing the fresh-air sanitarium for children on the lake shore.

It initiated the movement for postal savings and led the way to its adoption by Congress. The parcel-post service was also established the earlier because of the influence of the *Daily News* advocacy upon the press of the country as well as upon Congress. When the American press was dependent upon foreign news agencies for what it published of events abroad, and the western papers depended also upon an eastern news monopoly for what it chose to relay to them, then Victor F. Lawson and Melville E. Stone founded the Associated Press, the world-wide agency through which the American people have so long been guaranteed the freedom and authenticity of much of the news furnished by their papers.

Most of all was I impressed with the uncompromising and aggressive opposition of the *Daily News* to social and political evils, however strongly they were intrenched. With equal independence, through its world-wide, able foreign service it has influentially promoted the cause of international understanding and world-peace. Attracted by the spirit of the paper, in these and in many other ways expressed, I have been welcomed to friendly association with its reportorial and editorial staff.

With Victor F. Lawson, the owner, editor, and publisher of the *Daily News*, what was to me at first a casual acquaintanceship ripened into a close friendship. Indeed, he veiled from me the extent of his personal interest in my coming to Chicago and in the work I had come to do. Not until after his death had rounded out the thirty-three years of our comradeship did I know that he had made it possible for the Seminary to call me here. By that silence he considerately safeguarded the freedom of our intercourse and the independence of my action.

So again when he invited me to be a contributor to the editorial page of his paper he did so explicitly as a journalistic "commercial proposition" at space rates. Although he thus intended to protect both of us from embarrassing personal presumptions, yet his agreement to my stipulation that my copy should not be changed without my consent, if printed at all, was far more friendly than it was in accordance with journalistic practice. But it left me free to build up for the column that carried my own thought under my own name a reputation for the independent expression of personal opinion. To the extent to which differences with the adjoining editorial columns occasionally appeared, the *Daily News'* own claim of independence was thereby further demonstrated. This agreement, which never failed to be kept during Mr. Lawson's control of the paper, was renewed by his successor as having "shared in the establishment of the independence secured for the *Daily News* by Mr. Lawson." And for twenty eight years I have never failed to submit copy every week, by cable when abroad, and by radio, from ship to ship, when in the Philippines.

Very frank and friendly were our efforts either to agree to concessions without compromise of conviction, or to agree to differ by Mr. Lawson's refusal to print or mine to change copy. Only three irreconcilable differences occurred, however, in all these years. Two of them were over political candidacies, and one concerned the turn of an industrial crisis. Upon his part he fairly contended that he would be "open to the criticism of inconsistency of editorial policy were he to publish contrary views on the editorial page, even under my signature, unless he distinctly disclaimed them editorially in the same issue." To this I did not object, nor did he to printing my differing opinions in another column. On my part I urged that "as I have never dodged an issue on which my readers might reasonably expect me to write, I do not want to appear to do so now, if we can see how to avoid it." He took in good part a little reminder which I had occasion to send him at a later disagreement when I wrote:

Once upon a time you referred to me as a part of "the conscience of the *Daily News*." Well, if you have such a thing around, you must expect to be pricked by it sometimes at least, or else it will belie itself. But it is either to your credit or my discredit that this pricking became intolerable only three times in seventeen years. Those questions for last Saturday, however, are pricking very many besides myself. We must get together about them.

Mr. Lawson's liberal editorial tolerance in publishing opinions from which he personally differed decidedly seems the more noteworthy in remembrance of his very conservative religious and politico-economic views. The reputation for fair and full reports of industrial conflicts, by which the *Chicago Daily News* earned its first great increase in circulation in reporting the serious railway strike of 1877, has been well sustained through all these many subsequent years. The first instance of this attitude, which I personally had occasion to appreciate, occurred prior to my enlistment as a contributor to the editorial page and may have led to that engagement. It was during the great building-trade lockout of 1899–1900, when, as narrated elsewhere, Mr. Lawson agreed to print the pleas for arbitration which I intended to make before the building-trades' unions, if assured of the publicity which the *Daily News* could best give it. Upon reading what I had written he promptly promised to print it in full, expressing his entire agreement with it.

On other occasions when I feared that both sides of such issues were not played up in the *Daily News* with equal fairness and fulness, I found Mr. Lawson ready to welcome interviews with strike leaders, to whose side of the issue he gave respectful hearing and heed. When convinced of the right, however, he withstood what he deemed to be wrong with all the urgency of his keen sense of justice. When stirred by my own sense of the injustice inflicted by certain misdirected and misled strikes, I offered to join in the attack upon them. In doing so on the occasion of the worst teamsters' strike, I wrote a short, sharp, signed comment which appeared daily at the head of the strike-news column. On another occasion, during a deadlock in an unjust strike, in which the *Daily News* was unfairly involved, not having been a party to the original issue, I expressed the opinion that nothing could be done except to let it wear itself out. With this conclusion Mr. Lawson agreed, replying: "I think you are right in your impression that there is nothing to be done under present circumstances except to put down the hoodlumism and keep on sawing wood, which we are doing. The situation is steadily improving."

The outcome of two of our differences illustrates his openmindedness. On one campaign there were three candidates running for the office of state's attorney—one who had a very bad record during a previous term, a second-best who was not very good, and a third whose personal reputation was excellent, but who was professionally little known and politically without organized support. I urged Mr. Lawson to give his support to the second-best candidate in order to defeat the very worst, as the best man had no chance to be elected. While admitting that the campaign might end as predicted, yet he decided that editorially the *Daily News* would stand by the only really good candidate of the three. But he immediately permitted me to advocate the election of the second-best man, which I did, while in the adjoining columns of the same editorial page the contrary policy was advocated. The candidate I preferred was elected and proved far from satisfactory in office. Yet he had to his credit the suppression of the segregated vice districts, reinforcing the Vice Commission's appeal to the mayor to abandon the policy of segregation, which he did contrary to the precedent which had always prevailed

The other article over which we differed was one in which I maintained the right of the church to participate in the settlement of great industrial and social issues, for which it had many historic precedents even from New Testament times. Because this interposition was just then challenged as an impertinent innovation, Mr. Lawson read the proof of my article the more critically. Upon re-reading it to me over the lunch table, however, he passed each incident as the statement of a historical fact, until we came to the last one. Without quotation, the birth hour of the church was referred to as one in which the new brotherhood of man was proclaimed and exemplified by having their possessions in common and parting them as everyone had need. This he challenged as too radical to be published. But when I assured him that not I, but St. Luke, was responsible for stating that fact in the fourth chapter of the Acts of the Apostles, he laughed merrily, threw up his hands and said, "Let it all go in."

Under the most outrageously false accusations and vicious attacks by corrupt politicians, for which he was the shining mark during his whole journalistic career, he suffered in silence. His silence was only once broken by publishing the assessors' denial that he had failed to pay the tax they had levied upon his residence, as maliciously charged by those who knew the facts to the contrary. On another occasion he published accusations against himself as an item of news, although he strictly forbade any mention of his name, except when it was part of a news item.

But he had a reason of his own for this policy as he had for every other decision, which he sometimes delayed too long while awaiting more light to make a better one. His sense of civic responsibility imposed upon him the duty of publishing truthfully all the news that his fellow-citizens had a right to know.

In personal touch with such a friend and exemplar, and in sympathetic accord with most of the policies of the *Daily News,* I never failed to find both free scope and definite direction for what I contributed to its editorial page from week to week. Through reportorial comment I have sought to share with the average reader among my fellow-citizens what I observed and thought of our human conditions and relations. Seeking to carry some news value, my contributions have been very contemporaneous with the issues outstanding for the most part in Chicago. They have ranged as widely as have the interests of the cosmopolitan industrial population, in the midst of which I lived, and as broadly as have ranged the quests of the academic circles in which I taught.

From as nearly underneath and inside as I could get, political policies, candidacies, and conspiracies; industrial strikes and lockouts; public-school and library controversies; relief and correctional administrations; and social, moral, and religious movements have been frankly and fairly discussed in a constructively critical manner, and always in the interest of the public, that third and greatest party to all these issues.

Mr. Lawson died suddenly in August, 1925, although the end came not without warning to his associates and intimate friends. For several years ominous heart action had occasionally interrupted the steady pursuit of his work, with which he allowed nothing to interfere except sheer disablement. While convalescing from a prolonged illness he wrote me restively this warning to rest:

I assure you that it seems tremendously important to a man who has been laid aside for seven months, and is now just beginning to see the prospect of coming back into the common conditions of every day life. Perhaps I should more accurately say, the uncommon conditions of present day life—for certainly things are happening at a tremendous rate these days. With a keen realization of the penalties of overwork, please pardon me if I take the liberty of again urging you to be good to yourself and the rest of us, by not overtaxing your strength under the many responsibilities you are carrying.

The suddenness of Mr. Lawson's death startled the city-wide constituency of the *Daily News* with alarm over what effect it might have upon the independence and public spirit with which the paper had so long served the city. The suspense was increased and prolonged when no reference was found to the journal in his last will and testament. His sole ownership of the *Daily News*, although by far the greatest asset in his estate, went with all his other property into the hands of the bank which he chose as his executor.

That he did not mean to leave what he considered to be his great public trust without some indication of what should be done with it had been evident from his occasional references to the future of the paper. When they were made in my hearing I urged him to provide for it in some way himself, as so much the product of his own life-work that it seemed to be too personal and public a possession to offer for sale. In reply he always referred to the almost paralyzing perplexity of planning so far into the future, and to his feeling that the dead hand of the past should not control the living present. Not long before his death, however, he intimated to others that he was approaching a conclusion in the matter, but what it was he confided to no one. Therefore it was left to others to provide for the ownership and management of the great trust.

After numerous bids had been offered by parties in the East and West who were eager to acquire the property and influence of the *Chicago Daily News*, a transaction took place that was highly creditable to all concerned as well as a great boon to Chicago and to American journalism. The three institutions to which three-quarters of the large residuary estate were bequeathed—the Chicago Congregational Missionary and Extension Society, the Chicago Theological Seminary, and the Young Men's Christian Association of Chicago—assured the bank executor that they preferred the disposal of the paper to the best bidders rather than to others who might offer a higher bid but who might be less inclined or capable to carry out Mr. Lawson's ideals and standards of public service. They were assured by John J. Mitchell, president of the executor bank, that he regarded it to be his "moral obligation" to do so, thanking them for their support in so doing.

Meanwhile, through a long suspense, the staff at headquarters and their associates all over the land and the world stood loyally by, hoping almost against hope that the new management of the paper would represent the ideals and standards which they had helped to build up. Fortunately there were enough citizens of Chicago sharing this hope who were able and willing to stand in the breach with financial resources sufficient to carry over the *Daily News* from what it had been to what Chicago needed it to continue to be. They were just, as well as generous enough, to offer to pay all that a legitimate enterprise warranted. In so doing they were credited editorially by the chief competitor of the *Daily News* with having done "a public-spirited act to insure the survival of a community asset."

Thus these loyal citizens enabled the executor to transfer the ownership of the paper to Walter A. Strong, formerly the business manager, who with Charles H. Dennis, managing editor for many years, represented the able and experienced professional newspaper men whom Mr. Lawson had gathered and trained to share with him the public service of the paper. The recognition of the city's claim to it and of the moral obligation to control and manage it as a public trust is the outstanding significance of its transfer to its present possessors. Although it had been owned by Mr. Lawson through almost all of its years, yet it had always been Chicago's *Daily News*.

The citizenship of Victor F. Lawson set high standards of civic patriotism. Back of it all there was the man within the citizen—and a manly man withal. His manliness never had to be assumed or asserted. It was there. And from first to last it held in unique combination many traits which singly distinguish other men. He was a man of his own mind, yet so open to other minds that he needed no intermediary. He stood on his own feet, yet always granted the ground upon which others stood. He was the captain of his own soul, and though loyal to deep convictions yet respected those that differed. He was so self-respecting as to let character defend reputation from attacks upon integrity, which he bore in silence as part of the day's work. So innate and invincible was his modesty that not until he died could those who shared his personal friendship tell others what they knew of him, because they felt the restraint which he imposed upon his newspaper associates by forbidding any mention of his name except when public interests required.

Journalism was his profession. He mastered it, but it never so mastered him as to obscure the greater ends of which it was one of the greatest means. He took pains, pride, and pleasure in mastering its every detail—material and mechanical, reportorial and editorial, news-gathering and advertising, and the understanding of its local, national, and foreign spheres of action.

So high over all were the ethics of journalism that, above his professional interests as publisher and editor, he always held himself responsible for being a trustee for the truth of the news he gathered and distributed and for the rectitude of the policies he advocated. He carried his conscience so far toward this great end as personally to safeguard the advertising columns of the *Daily News*, not only from business advertisements that he regarded with suspicion, but also from those that were veiled allurements to vicious practices or to trap unwary victims by offering employment to girls "of prepossessing appearance." In hewing to this line of rectitude he assured me that never in all his long experience had advertisers made any attempt either to threaten him with loss or to offer increased gain. Never had they attempted to influence his management of the news columns or his editorial policies.

In administering this great trust he was always the citizen. The obligations of his citizenship were as exacting as its rights were priceless. From his country seat in Wisconsin, where he had gone for sadly needed rest, he wrote me: "I must of course be back to vote. I had to run down to register." Both locally and nationally he felt obligated to serve the whole body-politic, never one class or party. This editorial independence he safeguarded by refusing to accept any political or public office and by declining to serve on boards of institutional directors the interests of which might influence his policies or prevent him from criticizing their management. Citizenship was his higher calling as truly as journalism was his lifelong profession. His high ideals and standards in each lifted the level of his practice in both.

His allegiance to the supremacy of character made character-building his highest purpose, not only in developing the *Daily News*, but in personal support of other agencies, preference being given to those having educational value to the masses of the people. He was not presumptuous in regarding the *Daily News* as a great educational institution. For is it not as universal in its sphere as a University? Has it not many times more readers than the largest registration of students anywhere? Does it not influence thought and prompt research, as well as guide public opinion, in initiating and helping formulate religious enactments? Does it not inspire individual and corporate action? Is not its distinctively able and independent foreign correspondence influential in promoting an international understanding basic to the peace of the world? When Lord Burnham, of the *London Daily Telegraph*, referred to Edward Price Bell, the veteran correspondent of the *Daily News*, as a minister of understanding between England and America, Mr. Lawson wrote me of his purpose to promote this understanding in hope of furthering "the working unity of the English-speaking peoples of the world, as in the last analysis the basis upon which modern civilization surely depends."

Different as they were from one another, the numerous agencies which Mr. Lawson supported may be grouped about the appeal which their educational value made to him. The fresh-air sanitarium on the lake shore taught the care of children, as well as the free lecture courses in public-school buildings broadened the intelligence of the people surrounding them. The clubs and classes at Chicago Commons educated its foreign-born neighbors for American citizenship, as did the Young Men's and Women's Christian Associations their young people for city life and work. While one of the most farsighted providers for the training of the Christian ministry, as his munificent gift to Chicago Theological Seminary proves, yet he saw far enough in another direction to make it possible for me to pioneer to its permanent establishment the Chicago School of Civics and Philanthropy by underwriting its initial budgets. In so doing he gave the following noteworthy expression of what he foresaw:

> An enlightened public sentiment is more and more demanding intelligent, skilled and faithful civic service from those who seek public employment. At the same time the larger industrial enterprises are coming to realize, not merely the duty but the business need of enlisting the best possible effort in behalf of the moral and physical betterment of their employees. All this points to the imperative need of a systematic plan of instruction by which men and women may be taught how adequately to meet these growing demands by our better civic and industrial life. I am sure your successful efforts to accomplish this great public service must meet recognition and support as they become known to, and understood by, those who have the public at heart.

Mr. Lawson knew when and how to put principles into action, ideals into practice. Of his willingness and capacity to do so, just as one citizen with others, the Municipal Voters League, the City Club of Chicago, and the Bureau of Public

Efficiency are outstanding instances of his supporting co-operation. His great influence never tempted him to accept, much less claim, leadership, nor did it prevent him from heartily participating in the teamwork through agencies Chicago has made its greatest civic achievement. His faith in the ultimate triumph of truth and right enabled him to be a good loser and a generous winner.

"I charge myself with a measure of responsibility for the support of every cause that appeals for social justice," he wrote me on one occasion when he "lacked confidence in the sanity of some good people, who once they had attained a measure of success in some good line of social work apparently lose their heads." He stood by this high resolve in accepting Governor Frank O. Lowden's appointment to the Chicago Commission on Race Relations. His fellow Commissioners were as greatly impressed with the self-exactions he assumed in attending and largely sharing in the work of its protracted sessions as they were with his fairness and broad-mindedness in helping them frame those sections of their report which dealt with the newspaper handling of racial matters.

In Mr. Lawson's religious life spirit was supreme. He revered the letter of the Word, yet knew that "the letter killeth" unless made alive by its spirit. He confessed and adhered to the historic faith and practice of the Congregational church, upon the services of which he regularly attended and in the work of which he personally joined, as a member of the New England church near his home. Yet he was more than toler-ant, even liberal, in his respect for other faiths. He firmly held definite Christian ideals and ways, yet appreciated the value of other aims and means. He loved to associate with good men and true, yet was not blind to the faults of the better, or to the good traits of the worse. From within the veil of isolating bereavement he wrote: "Our common Christian hope and faith are the only real solace and sup-port. Without my living hope, my eternal faith, I could not live."

Victor Lawson's civic enterprise is fittingly symbolized by the great building of the *Chicago Daily News* at the city center, as is his religious spirit by the Lawson Tower rising above the Chicago Seminary's school of religion.

CHAPTER XXX

FORECAST FROM THE RETROSPECT

FAITH in a democratic social order, trust in education to equip and guide it, and reliance upon a religious motive and hope for the outcome have interwoven the experiences narrated in this retrospect.

The democratic social order is that which relies more upon the experience of the race than upon that of any period or part of it; more upon the common conscience of the many than upon the virtues claimed by or for any one class; more upon the sentiment of the whole people than upon the policies of rulers. For its gains, as well as for recovery from its losses, democracy depends upon the educational promotion of social intelligence and upon the aspirations, restraints, and motive power of a religious hope. Yet both education and religion depend quite as much upon their democratic resources and results for fulfilling their functions and reaching their goals.

However unrecognized or discarded the masses may be politically by monarchs and dictators, industrially by autocratic employers, culturally by pedants and castes, or religiously by ecclesiastical hierarchies, sooner or later the people share more largely in government and legislation, in the products and management of labor, in the purposes and fruits of education, and in the formulation of their faith and the control of religious institutions. Slowly but surely "the stars in their courses" wrest the rights of the common man from the very classes that exploit him in all these spheres. What though forces now and then surge up as from primeval chaos; what though chaotic passions or stupidities make the very earth seem to be "without form and void." Even so, the spirit of God proves to be brooding within the darkness upon the face of the deep to bring forth a new and better order of life.

Backed by this attestation of age-long experience, the retrospect of my own nearly fourscore years gives no occasion for my trust to falter in the forecast of the future. No class consciousness of either class in conflict, no aristocracy of any claimants, no cowardice or excesses of the masses, has caused me to waver from my trust in the triumph of the democratic order of government and social justice. My faith stands undaunted and undimmed by present reversions to dictatorships. Now as in the past, a dictatorship is little more than a pausing-point at which the democratic movement catches fresh breath, and poises to gain a new sense of direction for further advances. Even a Napoleon made way for the Republic of France to realize many of the rights of man wildly asserted in the Revolution. The dictatorship of the proletariat in Russia and of the bourgeoisie in Italy cannot fail to be "widened with the process of the suns."

Contemptibly negative and weak are the cynical disavowals of our American democratic ideals by those whose faith in them was so self-centered as to be disillusionized. While abandoning ideals which have guided the American people to what we have become, these cynics have no others to propose. What alternative have we than the choice between constitutional democracy and chaos? Far better our democracy might be and will become, but nothing in the past proves to have been better or so good.

Education defined by its source and aim is the rise of the individual into the experience and achievements of the race. The educated individual, therefore, is the product of the race. Back to fellow-men he owes some return for what they have enabled him to be and do. The most uneducated individual comes nearest to being self-made. Having shared least in the knowledge gained by others, he is shut up to the sphere of his own little observation and limited experience, regardless of what others have learned—

> The emptiness of ages in his face
> And on his back the burden of the world.

Culture more and more recognizes the claims of life upon it. Leisure to learn is seen to incur indebtedness to labor. Institutions of learning become ever more eager and likely to make ample returns for the support and confidence which the community and age bestow upon them. Their sciences serve life. Their researches prevent waste and produce gain. Public schools and state universities receive the largest part of the taxes which the people of many communities levy upon themselves. Other educational institutions are the recipients of the largest share of private beneficence. There is no possibility of civilization stultifying itself by restricting the reach and range of its own knowledge. There is every prospect of having ever more effectively trained and equipped educational resources for the guidance of life and the safeguarding of society from self-destruction. For now we know what old George Herbert dreamed:

> Man is all symmetrie,
> Full of proportions, one limbe to another,
> And all to all the world besides;
> Each part may call the farthest, brother:
> For head with foot hath private amitie,
> And both with moons and tides.

The religious hope that has inspired confidence in the future and patience in the present is that of all the prophets and apostles, singers and seers. It is the hope that right is might and must prevail, that truth will outlive error, that love abides and cannot fail. And this hope is strengthened by knowledge of the inherent weakness in the strongest evils and the instability of the most persistent wrongs. Two aims appeal to me as the most inspiring incentive—to overarch social ideals and action with the spirit of this religious hope, and to undergird religious teaching and practice with a social consciousness and intelligence such as might give the soul of faith more of a body in which to live and work on this earth.

In striving to do so I have found it necessary to seek the most simplified term to express the ideal which differing faiths seek to realize, in order to get those unable or unwilling to believe and worship alike to live and work together for the common good. In trying to interpret this to be the function of religion, I have found "relationship" to be the one term interpretatively interchangeable with "religion." I sought and first used this term to interpret religion to men who claimed to be hostile to it. I told them that every one of them had a religion of his own, whatever he might call it; that it consisted of his own ideals of his relationship to God and fellow-men; that the Christian religion is essentially the ideal which Jesus had of relationship to God as father and to men as brothers; that only in so far as any of his followers actually practice those relationships and strive to realize them more completely are they really Christian; and that however rites and ceremonies, sacraments and creeds, may express and impress religious experiences and aspiration, religion itself is relationship to God and man.

To this reasonably humanized idea of religion these men made no objection, but insisted that it never had been the religion of the churches, which they thought consisted of what was imposed upon the many by the authority and for the profit of the few. That life and religion are alike as consisting of the same relationships, they could not deny. It was as obvious to them that the sanctity with which religion invests every human life and the sanctions with which it imposes upon each one of us the service of others are as essential to any democratic social order as they are to the practice of religion itself. Attributing these sanctions to Jesus, they claimed to be more loyal to his way of life than the churches are.

Hope for both the church and humanity gathers strength and cheer as the churches seek for their creeds and service the attestation of practically fulfilling these relationships. To whatever extent "the letter" of religious forms may be charged with killing the spirit of religion, yet the spirit not only survives but asserts its supremacy by superseding what is substituted for it. Orthodoxy of the spirit, therefore, is the supreme test of loyalty to religion itself. As the spirit of almost every faith is broader and more tolerant than its creed, we may hope for a religious fellowship more cordial than merely tolerant, for a religious unity more co-operative than organic, and, through this unity of spirit, for mankind to be united in the bonds of peace.

Hopeful and zestful has been the experience in living life over again in the fellowship of the dear comrades whose lives and labor live so long after many of them have disappeared from sight and hearing. What they were and did continues so really to be and to do in every outcome made possible by them that to think they cease to exist is incredible. Not only in the retrospect but in this present they seem too vital to have died. In the marvels of memory their faces look into mine, their voices speak in familiar tones, their hands grasp mine again. They reappear also in the history which repeats their achievements. They move with the movements to which they gave initiative and continue to give impulse. And those whom I have loved long since and lost awhile are more than ever so much of what they made me to be that the very consciousness of being alive myself banishes any fear that they may not live.

Intimations of immortality are they, one and all, confirming faith that "life is ever lord of death" and justifying hope that "love can never lose its own." Inspired by such comradeships, hope for all the future here and across the frontier of the great Hereafter, cannot fail to share their courage—the courage of

> One who never turned his back, but marched
>   breast forward;
> Never doubted clouds would break,
> Never dreamed though right were worsted,
>   wrong would triumph;
> Held we fall to rise, are baffled to fight better,
> Sleep to wake.

INDEX

INDEX

447

[PRINTED
IN U·S·A·]